FOURTH EDITION

The Humanistic Tradition

Book 1

The First Civilizations and the
Classical Legacy

FOURTH EDITION

The Humanistic Tradition

Book 1

The First Civilizations and the
Classical Legacy

Gloria K. Fiero

Boston   Burr Ridge, IL   Dubuque, IA   Madison, WI   New York
San Francisco   St. Louis   Bangkok   Bogotá   Caracas   Kuala Lumpur
Lisbon   London   Madrid   Mexico City   Milan   Montreal   New Delhi
Santiago   Seoul   Singapore   Sydney   Taipei   Toronto

McGraw-Hill Higher Education

A Division of The **McGraw-Hill** *Companies*

THE HUMANISTIC TRADITION, BOOK 1
THE FIRST CIVILIZATIONS AND THE CLASSICAL LEGACY
Published by McGraw-Hill, an imprint of the McGraw-Hill Companies, Inc.
1221 Avenue of the Americas, New York, NY, 10020.
Copyright © 2002, 1998, 1995, 1992 by The McGraw-Hill Companies, Inc.
All rights reserved. No part of this publication may be reproduced or distributed in
any form or by any means, or stored in a database or retrieval system, without the
prior written consent of The McGraw-Hill Companies, Inc., including, but not
limited to, in any network or other electronic storage or transmission, or broadcast
for distance learning.
Some ancillaries, including electronic and print components, may not be available to
customers outside the United States.

This book is printed on acid-free paper.

6 7 8 9 0 WCK/WCK 0 9 8 7 6 5

Library of Congress Control Number: 2001095307

ISBN 0-07-231730-2

Permissions Acknowledgments appear on page 173,
and on this page by reference.

Editorial director: *Phillip A. Butcher*
Executive sponsoring editor: *Christopher Freitag*
Marketing manager: *David S. Patterson*
Senior project manager: *Pat Frederickson*
Production supervisor: *Susanne Riedell*
Senior designer: *Jennifer McQueen*
Manager, publication services: *Ira Roberts*
Supplement producer: *Rose Range*
Media technology producer: *Sean Crowley*
Cover designer: *Kiera Cunningham*
Typeface: *10/12 Goudy*
Printer: *Quebecor World Versailles, Inc.*

http://www.mhhe.com

This book was designed and produced by
CALMANN & KING LTD
71 Great Russell Street, London WC1B 3BP
www.calmann-king.com

Senior editor: *Jon Haynes*
Picture researcher: *Peter Kent*
Designer: *Ian Hunt*
Cartographer: *Andrea Fairbrass*
Typesetter: *Fakenham Photosetting, Norfolk*

Front cover
Main image: Detail of pair statue of Mycerinus and Queen Kha-merer-nebty II,
Gizeh, Mycerinus, Fourth Dynasty, 2599–1571 B.C.E. Slate schist, height 4 ft. 6½ in.
(complete statue). Courtesy, Museum of Fine Arts, Boston. Harvard MFA
Expedition.
Insets: (top) "Herr Konrad von Altretten," detail of *Medieval Lovers*, from the
Manesse Codex, Zurich, ca. 1315–1330. Universitatsbibliothek, Heidelberg,
Germany, MS Pal. germ. 848, f. 84. Rheinisches Koln Bildarchiv, Cologne, Germany
(center) Detail of terra-cotta soldier, tomb of the First Emperor of the Qin Dynasty,
221–207 B.C.E. Photo: Daghi Orti, Paris.
(bottom) Lorenzo Costa, detail of *The Concert*, a. 1485–95. Oil on poplar,
95.3 × 75.6 cm. National Gallery, London.

Frontispiece: Detail of Krater with "Geometric" decoration, ca. 750 B.C.E. Terra-cotta,
height 3 ft. 4½ in. The Metropolitan Museum of Art, New York.

Series Contents

Book 1 Contents

"It's the most curious thing I ever saw in all my life!" exclaimed Lewis Carroll's Alice in Wonderland, as she watched the Cheshire Cat slowly disappear, leaving only the outline of a broad smile. "I've often seen a cat without a grin, but a grin without a cat!" A student who encounters an ancient Greek epic, a Yoruba mask, or a Mozart opera—lacking any context for these works—might be equally baffled. It may be helpful, therefore, to begin by explaining how the artifacts (the "grin") of the humanistic tradition relate to the larger and more elusive phenomenon (the "cat") of human culture.

The Humanistic Tradition and the Humanities

In its broadest sense, the term *humanistic tradition* refers to humankind's cultural legacy—the sum total of the significant ideas and achievements handed down from generation to generation. This tradition is the product of responses to conditions that have confronted all people throughout history. Since the beginnings of life on earth, human beings have tried to ensure their own survival by achieving harmony with nature. They have attempted to come to terms with the inevitable realities of disease and death. They have endeavored to establish ways of living collectively and communally. And they have persisted in the desire to understand themselves and their place in the universe. In response to these ever-present and universal challenges—*survival, communality,* and *self-knowledge*—human beings have created and transmitted the tools of science and technology, social and cultural institutions, religious and philosophic systems, and various forms of personal expression, the sum total of which we call culture.

Even the most ambitious survey cannot assess all manifestations of the humanistic tradition. This book therefore focuses on the creative legacy referred to collectively as *the humanities*: literature, philosophy, history (in its literary dimension), architecture, the visual arts (including photography and film), music, and dance. Selected examples from each of these disciplines constitute our *primary sources*. Primary sources (that is, works original to the age that produced them) provide first-hand evidence of human inventiveness and ingenuity. The primary sources in this text have been chosen on the basis of their authority, their beauty, and their enduring value. They are, simply stated, the great works of their time and, in some cases, of all time. Universal in their appeal, they have been transmitted from generation to generation. Such works are, as well, the landmark examples of a specific time and place: They offer insight into the ideas and values of the society in which they were produced. The drawings of

Leonardo da Vinci, for example, reveal a passionate determination to understand the operations and functions of nature. And while Leonardo's talents far exceeded those of the average individual of his time, his achievements may be viewed as a mirror of the robust curiosity that characterized his time and place—the age of the Renaissance in Italy. *The Humanistic Tradition* surveys such landmark works, but joins "the grin" to "the cat" by examining them within their political, economic, and social contexts.

The Humanistic Tradition explores a living legacy. History confirms that the humanities are integral forms of a given culture's values, ambitions, and beliefs. Poetry, painting, philosophy, and music are not, generally speaking, products of unstructured leisure or indulgent individuality; rather, they are tangible expressions of the human quest for the good (one might even say the "complete") life. Throughout history, these forms of expression have served the domains of the sacred, the ceremonial, and the communal. And even in the early days of the twenty-first century, as many time-honored traditions come under assault, the arts retain their power to awaken our imagination in the quest for survival, communality, and self-knowledge.

The Scope of the Humanistic Tradition

The humanistic tradition is not the exclusive achievement of any one geographic region, race, or class of human beings. For that reason, this text assumes a global and multicultural rather than exclusively Western perspective. At the same time, Western contributions are emphasized, first, because the audience for these books is predominantly Western, but also because in recent centuries the West has exercised a dominant influence on the course and substance of global history. Clearly, the humanistic tradition belongs to all of humankind, and the best way to understand the Western contribution to that tradition is to examine it in the arena of world culture.

As a survey, *The Humanistic Tradition* cannot provide an exhaustive analysis of our creative legacy. The critical reader will discover many gaps. Some aspects of culture that receive extended examination in traditional Western humanities surveys have been pared down to make room for the too often neglected contributions of Islam, Africa, and Asia. This book is necessarily selective—it omits many major figures and treats others only briefly. Primary sources are arranged, for the most part, chronologically, but they are presented as manifestations of the informing ideas of the age in which they were produced. The intent is to examine the evidence of the humanistic tradition thematically and topically, rather than to compile a series of mini-histories of the individual arts.

Studying the Humanistic Tradition

To study the creative record is to engage in a dialogue with the past, one that brings us face to face with the values of our ancestors, and, ultimately, with our own. This dialogue is (or should be) a source of personal revelation and delight; like Alice in Wonderland, our strange, new encounters will be enriched according to the degree of curiosity and patience we bring to them. Just as lasting friendships with special people are cultivated by extended familiarity, so our appreciation of a painting, a play, or a symphony depends on close attention and repeated contact. There are no short-cuts to the study of the humanistic tradition, but there are some techniques that may be helpful. It should be useful, for instance, to approach each primary source from the triple perspective of its text, its context, and its subtext.

The Text: The *text* of any primary source refers to its *medium* (that is, what it is made of), its *form* (its outward shape), and its *content* (the subject it describes). All literature, for example, whether intended to be spoken or read, depends on the medium of words—the American poet Robert Frost once defined literature as "performance in words." Literary form varies according to the manner in which words are arranged. So poetry, which shares with music and dance rhythmic organization, may be distinguished from prose, which normally lacks regular rhythmic pattern. The main purpose of prose is to convey information, to narrate, and to describe; poetry, by its freedom from conventional patterns of grammar, provides unique opportunities for the expression of intense emotions. Philosophy (the search for truth through reasoned analysis) and history (the record of the past) make use of prose to analyze and communicate ideas and information. In literature, as in most kinds of expression, content and form are usually interrelated. The subject matter or the form of a literary work determines its *genre*. For instance, a long narrative poem recounting the adventures of a hero constitutes an *epic*, while a formal, dignified speech in praise of a person or thing constitutes a *eulogy*.

The visual arts—painting, sculpture, architecture, and photography—employ a wide variety of media, such as wood, clay, colored pigments, marble, granite, steel, and (more recently) plastic, neon, film, and computers. The form or outward shape of a work of art depends on the manner in which the artist manipulates the formal elements of color, line, texture, and space. Unlike words, these formal elements lack denotative meaning. The artist may manipulate form to describe and interpret the visible world (as in such genres as portraiture and landscape painting); to generate fantastic and imaginative kinds of imagery; or to create imagery that is nonrepresentational—without identifiable subject matter. In general, however, the visual arts are spatial, that is, they operate and are apprehended in space.

The medium of music is sound. Like literature, music is durational: It unfolds over the period of time in which it occurs. The formal elements of music are melody, rhythm,

harmony, and tone color—elements that also characterize the oral life of literature. As with the visual arts, the formal elements of music are without symbolic content, but while literature, painting, and sculpture may imitate or describe nature, music is almost always nonrepresentational—it rarely has meaning beyond the sound itself. For that reason, music is the most difficult of the arts to describe in words. It is also (in the view of some) the most affective of the arts. Dance, the artform that makes the human body itself a medium of expression, resembles music in that it is temporal and performance-oriented. Like music, dance exploits rhythm as a formal tool, but, like painting and sculpture, it unfolds in space as well as time.

In analyzing the text of a work of literature, art, or music, we ask how its formal elements contribute to its meaning and affective power. We examine the ways in which the artist manipulates medium and form to achieve a characteristic manner of execution and expression that we call *style*. And we try to determine the extent to which a style reflects the personal vision of the artist and the larger vision of his or her time and place. Comparing the styles of various artworks from a single era, we may discover that they share certain defining features and characteristics. Similarities (both formal and stylistic) between, for instance, golden age Greek temples and Greek tragedies, between Chinese lyric poems and landscape paintings, and between postmodern fiction and pop sculpture, prompt us to seek the unifying moral and aesthetic values of the cultures in which they were produced.

The Context: We use the word *context* to describe the historical and cultural environment. To determine the context, we ask: In what time and place did the artifact originate? How did it function within the society in which it was created? Was the purpose of the piece decorative, didactic, magical, propagandistic? Did it serve the religious or political needs of the community? Sometimes our answers to these questions are mere guesses. Nevertheless, understanding the function of an artifact often serves to clarify the nature of its form (and vice versa). For instance, much of the literature produced prior to the fifteenth century was spoken or sung rather than read; for that reason, such literature tends to feature repetition and rhyme, devices that facilitate memorization. We can assume that literary works embellished with frequent repetitions, such as the *Epic of Gilgamesh* and the Hebrew Bible, were products of an oral tradition. Determining the original function of an artwork also permits us to assess its significance in its own time and place: The paintings on the walls of Paleolithic caves, which are among the most compelling animal illustrations in the history of world art, are not "artworks" in the modern sense of the term but, rather, magical signs that accompanied hunting rituals, the performance of which was essential to the survival of the community. Understanding the relationship between text and context is one of the principal concerns of any inquiry into the humanistic tradition.

The Subtext: The *subtext* of the literary or artistic object refers to its secondary and implied meanings. The subtext embraces the emotional or intellectual messages embedded in, or implied by, a work of art. The epic poems of the ancient Greeks, for instance, which glorify prowess and physical courage in battle, suggest that such virtues are exclusively male. The state portraits of the seventeenth-century French ruler Louis XIV carry the subtext of unassailable and absolute power. In our own century, Andy Warhol's serial adaptations of soup cans and Coca-Cola bottles offer wry commentary on the supermarket mentality of postmodern American culture. Identifying the implicit message of an artwork helps us to determine the values and customs of the age in which it was produced and to assess those values against others.

Beyond *The Humanistic Tradition*

This book offers only small, enticing samples from an enormous cultural buffet. To dine more fully, students are encouraged to go beyond the sampling presented at this table; and for the most sumptuous feasting, nothing can substitute for first-hand experience. Students, therefore, should make every effort to supplement this book with visits to art museums and galleries, concert halls, theaters, and libraries. *The Humanistic Tradition* is designed for students who may or may not be able to read music, but who surely are able to cultivate an appreciation of music in performance. The music logos that appear in the text refer to the Music Listening Selections found on two accompanying compact discs, available from the publishers. Lists of suggestions for further reading are included at the end of each chapter, while a selected general bibliography of electronic humanities resources appears in the Online Learning Center at http://www.mhhe.com/fiero.

The Fourth Edition

The fourth edition of *The Humanistic Tradition* continues to take as its main focus the topical and global themes that have informed the last three editions. Book 1, however, has been restructured: Egypt, Mesopotamia, and the East Asian civilizations now each receive separate chapters, and chapter 7, "The Bipolar Empires of Rome and China," has been divided into two separate chapters.* In Book 3, chapters 18 and 19 have been reversed, and in Book 4, chapters 21 to 23 have been reordered. There are new reading selections throughout the text. These range from the poems of Catallus to the lyrics of Derek Walcott and from Saint Francis' *Canticle of Brother Sun* to Mark Twain's *Huckleberry Finn*. Excerpts from Mary Wollstonecraft's *Vindication of the Rights of Women*, two newly translated writings by Renaissance women, the *Scivias* of Hildegard of Bingen, and the narrative of Sojourner Truth give greater dimension to the role of women in the arts. The *Analects* of Confucius appear in a 1997 translation. Greek mythology, slave songs and spirituals, and the nineteenth-century symbolist movement take their places in the appropriate chapters. Excerpts from Shakespeare's *Hamlet* and *Othello* replace the complete text of *Othello*, which is now available in the web-based resources for *The Humanistic Tradition*.

---

*In the sections in this book where ancient Greece is discussed, names and terms are transcribed according to the Greek spelling, with the exception of words that, traditionally, would have been spelt otherwise, such as 'Acropolis', 'Socrates' and 'Laocoön,' which would take a 'k' rather than a 'c' in Greek.

Keymap Indicating Areas Shown as White Highlights on the Locator Maps

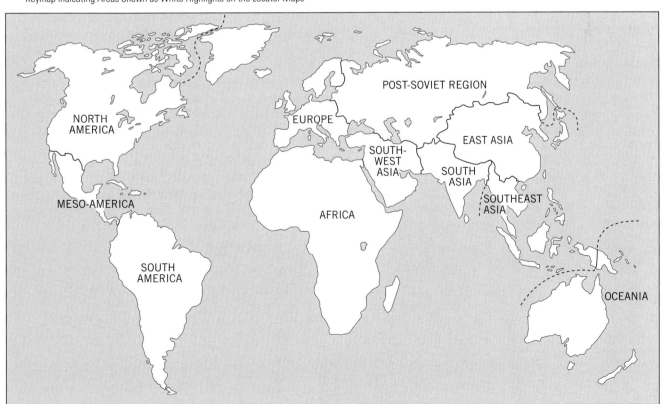

POST-SOVIET REGION

NORTH AMERICA

EUROPE

EAST ASIA

SOUTH-WEST ASIA

SOUTH ASIA

SOUTHEAST ASIA

MESO-AMERICA

AFRICA

SOUTH AMERICA

OCEANIA

Our examination of the twentieth century has been expanded to include film, and each chapter in Book 6 now brings attention to landmark developments in that medium. The contemporary chapters have been updated to include a segment on the quest for ethnic identity, focusing on the Latino voice that has made a significant mark in the arts of the past two decades. In the newly organized chapter 38, electronic and digital art receive expanded consideration.

This new edition includes more color illustrations than previous editions, as well as new diagrams that assist the reader in understanding the content, function, or construction techniques of various artworks. The Rosetta Stone, the so-called Mask of Agamemnon, the Hellenistic Altar of Zeus, and artwork by Angelica Kauffmann, Henry Ossawa Tanner, Lucca della Robbia, Piero della Francesco, Fernand Léger, and Anselm Kiefer are among the many new illustrations. The treatment of ancient China has been updated to include the information yielded by recent excavations of early dynastic graves in the People's Republic of China. Two new audio compact discs replace the older cassettes. These listening selections illustrate the musical works discussed in the text. Music by Hildegard of Bingen and Aaron Copland, African call-and-response chant, and the Muslim Call to Prayer have been added to the earlier materials, along with an excerpt from Mozart's *Marriage of Figaro*. The revised *Science and Technology Boxes*, along with *Locator Maps* and new *Timelines*, provide useful and popular study aids. The revised timelines are not exhaustive, but show selected key works. Each chapter in the fourth edition opens with a key quotation drawn from the readings and focusing on the theme of the chapter. Updated bibliographies are appended to each individual chapter.

A Note to Instructors

The key to successful classroom use of *The Humanistic Tradition* is *selectivity*. Although students may be assigned to read whole chapters that focus on a topic or theme, as well as complete works that supplement the abridged readings, the classroom should be the stage for a selective treatment of a single example or a set of examples. The organization of this textbook is designed to emphasize themes that cut across geographic boundaries—themes whose universal significance prompts students to evaluate and compare rather than simply memorize and repeat lists of names and places. To assist readers in achieving global cultural literacy, every effort has been made to resist isolating (or "ghettoizing") individual cultures and to avoid the inevitable biases we bring to our evaluation of relatively unfamiliar cultures.

Acknowledgments

Writing *The Humanistic Tradition* has been an exercise in humility. Without the assistance of learned friends and colleagues, assembling a book of this breadth would have been an impossible task. James H. Dormon read all parts of the manuscript and made extensive and substantive editorial suggestions; as his colleague, best friend, and wife, I am most deeply indebted to him.

The following readers and reviewers generously shared their insights in matters of content and style: Professors Jill Carrington (Stephen F. Austin State University), Darrell Bourque (University of Louisiana, Lafayette), Enid Housty (Hampton University), Kim Jones (Seminole Community College), Juergen Pelzer (Occidental College), Denise Rogers (University of Louisiana, Lafayette), Ralph V. Turner (Florida State University), and my colleagues, Donald Liss and Robert Butler.

In the preparation of the fourth edition, I have also benefited from the suggestions and comments generously offered by Roy Barineau (Tallahassee Community College), Carol A. Berger (St. Louis Community College), Rodney Boyd (Collin County Community College), Judith Ann Cohn (West Virginia State College), Janet L. DeCosmo (Florida A&M University), Larry Dorr (University of North Carolina), Edward M. Frame (Valencia Community College), Grant Hardy (University of North Carolina), Cynthia Ho (University of North Carolina), Connie LaMarca-Frankel (Pasco-Hernando Community College), Robert J. G. Lange (University of North Carolina), Sandra Loman (Madison Area Technical College), Susan McMichaels (University of North Carolina), Lois L. McNamara (Valencia Community College), Ann Malloy (Tulsa Community College), Sharon Rooks (Edison Community College), Charlie Schuler (Pensacola Junior College), Gerald Stacy (Central Washington University), Elisabeth Stein (Tallahassee Community College), Patricia Gailah Taylor (Southwest Texas State University), Barbara Tomlinson (Kean University), Camille Weiss (West Virginia University), and Alice Weldon (University of North Carolina).

The burden of preparing the fourth edition has been lightened by the assistance of Christopher Freitag, Executive Editor, and by the editorial vigilance of Jon Haynes, Richard Mason, and Cleia Smith at Calmann & King.

SUPPLEMENTS FOR THE INSTRUCTOR AND THE STUDENT

A number of useful supplements are available to instructors and students using *The Humanistic Tradition*. Please contact your sales representative or call 1-800-338-5371 to obtain these resources, or to ask for further details.

Online Learning Center

A complete set of web-based resources for *The Humanistic Tradition* can be found at www.mhhe.com/fiero. Material for students includes study outlines, self-tests, interactive maps and time-lines, and links to other web resources. Instructors will benefit from teaching tips, web activities and assignments, and access to material from the Instructor's Resource Manual. Instructors can also utilize PageOut, McGraw-Hill's own online course management tool. PageOut works seamlessly with the Online Learning Center resources and allows instructors to have complete control over the organization of online course content on their own course website. Instructors can register for this free service at www.pageout.net.

Compact Discs

Two audio compact discs have been designed exclusively for use with *The Humanistic Tradition*. CD One corresponds to the music listening selections discussed in books 1–3 and CD Two contains the music in books 4–6. Instructors may obtain copies of the recordings for classroom use through the local sales representative or by calling 1-800-338-5371. The recordings are also available for individual purchase by students; they can be packaged with any or all of the six texts. Consult your local sales representative for details.

Slide Sets

A set of book-specific slides is available to qualified adopters of *The Humanistic Tradition*. These slides have been especially selected to include many of the less well-known images in the books and will be a useful complement to your present slide resources. Additional slides are available for purchase directly from Universal Color Slides. For further information consult our web site at www.mhhe.com/fiero.

Instructor's Resource Manual

The Instructor's Resource Manual is designed to assist instructors as they plan and prepare for classes. Course outlines and sample syllabi for both semester and quarter systems are included. The chapter summaries emphasize key themes and topics that give focus to the primary source readings. The study questions for each chapter may be removed and copied as handouts for student discussion or written assignments. A Test Item File follows each chapter along with a correlation list that directs instructors to the appropriate supplemental resources. A list of suggested videotapes, recordings, videodiscs, and their suppliers is included.

MicroTest III

The questions in the Test Item File are available on MicroTest III, a powerful but easy-to-use test generating program. MicroTest is available for Windows, and Macintosh personal computers. With MicroTest, an instructor can easily select the questions from the Test Item File and print a test and answer key. You can customize questions, headings, and instructions and add or import questions of your own.

Student Study Guides, Volumes 1 and 2

Written by Gloria K. Fiero, two new Student Study Guides are now available to help students gain a better understanding of subjects found in *The Humanistic Tradition*. Volume 1 accompanies books 1–3 and Volume 2 accompanies books 4–6. Each chapter contains: a Chapter Objective; a Chapter Outline; Key Terms, Names (with pronunciation guides), and Dates; Vocabulary Building; Multiple Choice Questions; and Essay Questions. Many chapters also contain a Visual/Spatial Exercise and Bonus Material. At the end of each Part, Synthesis material helps students draw together ideas from a set of chapters.

Prehistory and the birth of civilization

Whether or not one believes that the beginnings of life were divinely generated, it is clear that human beings belong to a long and complex process of evolutionary development. The story of human evolution is a record of the genetic and behavioral adaptation of human beings to their natural surroundings. It is the last chapter in a long history that begins with the simplest forms of life that thrived in the primeval seas hundreds of millions of years ago and culminates in the astonishing achievements of modern human beings. Throughout their short history on this planet, human beings have faced the privations of the environment and of an often hostile geography and a threatening climate. Meeting such environmental challenges was the primary occupation of the earliest inhabitants.

Prehistory

The study of history before the appearance of written records, an enterprise that originated in France around 1860, is called **prehistory**. In the absence of written records, prehistorians depend on information about the past provided by the disciplines of geology, paleontology, anthropology, archeology, and ethnography. For instance, using instruments that measure the radioactive atoms remaining in the organic elements of the earth's strata, geologists work to determine the age of the earth. They report that our planet is approximately 4.5 billion years old. Paleontologists record the history of fossil remains and the life of the earth's earliest living creatures. Anthropologists study human biology, society, and cultural practices, while archeologists uncover, analyze, and interpret the material remains of past societies. Finally, a special group of cultural anthropologists known as ethnographers study surviving, preliterate societies. All of these specialists contribute to producing a detailed picture of humankind's earliest environment and the prehistoric past.

The earliest organic remains in the earth's strata are almost four billion years old. From one-celled organisms that inhabited the watery terrain of the ancient planet, higher forms of life very gradually evolved. Some hundred million years ago, dinosaurs stalked the earth, eventually becoming extinct—possibly because they failed to adapt to climatic change. Eighty million years ago, mammals roamed the earth's surface. Although even the most approximate dates are much disputed, it is generally agreed that between ten and five million years ago ancestral humans first appeared on the planet, probably in eastern and southern Africa. The exact genealogy of humankind is still a matter of intense debate. However, in the last fifty years, anthropologists have clarified some aspects of the relationship between human beings and earlier primates—the group of mammals that today includes monkeys, apes, and human beings. Fossil evidence reveals structural similarities between human beings and chimpanzees (and other apes). More recent research in molecular biology and genetics indicates that humans are more closely related to chimpanzees than cats are to lions.

Paleolithic ("Old Stone") Culture*
(ca. 6 million–10,000 B.C.E.**)

Early in the twentieth century, anthropologists discovered the first fossil remains of the near-human or proto-human creature known as **hominid**, who lived some five or more million years ago. Such hominids lived in packs; they gathered seeds, berries, wild fruits, and vegetables, and possibly even hunted the beasts of the African savannas. Hominid footprints found in South Africa in the mid-1990s and fossil remains uncovered in 2001 in the forest of Ethiopia suggest that hominids may have walked upright as early as 5.7 million years ago. Between two and three million years ago, a South African variety of

---

*The terms Paleolithic and Neolithic do not describe uniform time periods, but, rather, cultures that appeared at different times in different parts of the world.

**Dates are signified as B.C.E., "Before the Christian (or common) era," or C.E., "Christian (or common) era."

hominid known as *Australopithecus* was using sharp-edged pebbles for skinning animals and for chopping. Indeed, Ethiopian excavations of 1996 confirm that the fabrication of stone tools began between 2.5 and 2.6 million years ago. Yet anthropologists—who have long considered tool-making the distinguishing feature of modern humans—disagree as to the earliest dates for the emergence of the genus *Homo*, the evolutionary group that includes modern humans and their closest now-extinct relatives. Despite the continuing debate, *Homo habilis* ("tool-making human") conveniently describes those hominid descendants who met the challenge of survival by creating the earliest stone and bone tools and weapons.

Tool-making represents the beginning of **culture**, which, in its most basic sense, proceeds from the manipulation of nature. The making of tools—humankind's earliest technology—constitutes the primary act of extending control over nature and the most fundamental example of problem-solving behavior.

No matter how early this genus emerged, it is likely that more than two million years ago *Homo* drifted out of Africa, evolving into other species not once, but many times, in many places, throughout the world. In various parts of Africa and East Asia, hunter-gatherers known as *Homo erectus* ("upright human") made tools that were more varied and efficient than those used by earlier humans. These tools included hand-axes, cleavers, chisels, and a wide variety of choppers. The hand-axe became the standard tool for chopping, digging, cutting, and scraping. Fire, too, became an important part of the early culture of humankind, providing safety, warmth, and a means of cooking food. Although it is still not certain how long ago fire was first used, archeologists confirm that fire was a regular feature in the hearths of most *Homo erectus* dwellings. Some 100,000 years ago, a group of human ancestors with anatomical features and brain size similar to our own appeared in the Neander Valley near Düsseldorf, Germany. The burial of human dead (their bodies dyed with red ocher) among Neanderthals and the practice of including tools, weapons, and flowers in Neanderthal graves are evidence of the self-conscious, symbol-making human known as *Homo sapiens*. Characterized by memory and foresight, these now-extinct cousins of modern-day humans were the first to demonstrate—by their ritual preparation and disposal of the deceased—a self-conscious concern with human mortality. That concern may have involved respect for, or fear of, the dead and the anticipation of life after death.

The development of the primate brain in both size and complexity was integral to the evolution of *Homo sapiens*: Over millions of years, the average brain size of the human being grew to roughly three times the size of the gorilla's brain. Equally critical was the growth of more complex motor capacities. Gradually, verbal methods of communication complemented the nonverbal ones shared by animals and protohumans. We do not know at what point speech replaced more primitive sound codes, but, over time, our prehistoric ancestors came to use spoken language as a medium for transmitting information

and patterns of culture. Communication by means of language distinguished *Homo sapiens* from other primates. Chimpanzees have been known to bind two poles together in order to reach a bunch of bananas hanging from the top of a tree, but, short of immediate physical demonstration, they have developed no means of passing on this technique to subsequent generations of chimpanzees. *Homo sapiens*, on the other hand, have produced symbol systems that enable them to transmit their ideas and inventions. Thus, in the fullest sense, culture requires both the manipulation of nature and the formulation of a symbolic language for its transmission.

Paleolithic culture evolved during a period of climatic fluctuation called the Ice Age. Between roughly three million and 10,000 years ago, at least four large glacial advances covered the area north of the equator. As hunters and gatherers, Paleolithic people were forced either to migrate or adapt to changing climatic conditions. It is likely that more than fifteen species of humans coexisted with one another, and all but *Homo sapiens* became extinct. Ultimately, the ingenuity and imagination of *Homo sapiens* were responsible for the fact that they fared better than many other creatures.

Early modern humans devised an extensive technology of stone and bone tools and weapons that increased their comfort, safety, and almost certainly their confidence. A 7-foot stone-tipped spear enabled a hunter to attack an animal at a distance of six or more yards. Other devices increased the leverage of the arm and thus doubled that range. Spears and harpoons, and—toward the end of the Ice Age—bows and arrows, extended the efficacy and safety of Paleolithic people, just as axes and knives facilitated their food-preparing abilities.

During the last sixty years, archeologists have discovered thousands of paintings and carvings on the walls of caves and the surfaces of rocks at Paleolithic sites in Europe, Africa, Australia, and North America. Over one hundred limestone cave dwellings in southwestern France and still others discovered as recently as 1996 in southeastern France contain images of animals (bears, bison, elk, lions, and zebras, among others), birds, fish, and other signs and symbols, all of which reveal a high degree of artistic and technical sophistication. Executed between 10,000 and 30,000 years ago, these wall-paintings provide a visual record of such long-extinct animals as the hairy

−2,500,000	first stone tools are utilized in East Africa[†]
−500,000	in China, *Homo erectus* uses fire for domestic purposes
−24,000	fish hooks and line are utilized in Europe
−20,000	bows and arrows are in use in North Africa and Spain; oil lamps, fueled by animal fat, come into use
−13,000	devices to hurl harpoons and spears are in use

[†]All dates in this introduction are approximate.
Minus (−) signifies B.C.E.

mammoth and the woolly rhinoceros. Equally important, they document the culture of a hunting people. Painted with **polychrome** mineral pigments and shaded with bitumen and burnt coal, realistically depicted bison, horses, reindeer, and a host of other creatures are shown standing, running, often wounded by spears and lances (Figure **0.1**). What were the purpose and function of these vivid images? Located in the most inaccessible regions of the caves, and frequently drawn one over another, with no apparent regard for clarity of composition, it is unlikely that they were intended as decorations or even as records of the hunt. It seems possible that, much like tools and weapons, cave art functioned as part of a hunting ritual. The following episode from Pygmy life in the African Congo, recorded by the twentieth-century German ethnographer Leo Frobenius, supports this hypothesis.

READING 1.1   The Story of Rock Picture Research

In 1905 we obtained further evidence from a Congo race, hunting tribes, later famous as the "pygmies," which had been driven from the plateau to the refuge of the Congo [an area in South-central Africa bordering the Congo River]. We met in the jungle district between Kassai and Luebonn. Several of their members, three men and a woman, guided the expedition for almost a week and were soon on friendly terms with us. One afternoon, finding our larder rather depleted, I asked one of them to shoot me an antelope, surely an easy job for such an expert hunter. He and his fellows looked at me in   10

astonishment and then burst out with the answer that, yes, they'd do it gladly, but that it was naturally out of the question for that day since no preparations had been made. After a long palaver they declared themselves ready to make these at sunrise. Then they went off as though searching for a good site and finally settled on a high place on a nearby hill.

As I was eager to learn what their preparations consisted of, I left camp before dawn and crept through the bush to the open place which they had sought out the night before. The pygmies appeared in the twilight, the woman with them. The   20 men crouched on the ground, plucked a small square free of weeds and smoothed it over with their hands. One of them then drew something in the cleared space with his forefinger, while his companions murmured some kind of formula or incantation. Then a waiting silence. The sun rose on the horizon. One of the men, an arrow on his bowstring, took his place beside the square. A few minutes later the rays of the sun fell on the drawing at his feet. In that same second the woman stretched out her arms to the sun, shouting words I did not understand, the man shot the arrow and the woman cried   30 out again. Then the three men bounded off through the bush while the woman stood for a few minutes and then went slowly towards our camp. As she disappeared I came forward and, looking down at the smoothed square of sand, saw the drawing of an antelope four hands long. From the antelope's neck protruded the pygmy's arrow.

I went back for my camera intending to photograph the drawing before the men returned. But the woman, when she saw what I was up to, made such a fuss that I desisted. We broke camp and continued our march. The drawing remained   40 unphotographed. That afternoon the hunters appeared with a

Figure 0.1 Hall of Bulls, left wall, Lascaux caves, Dordogne, France, ca. 15,000–10,000 B.C.E. Paint on limestone rock, length of individual bulls 13–16 ft.

Figure 0.2 Spotted horses and negative hand imprints, Pech-Merle caves, Lot, France, ca. 15,000–10,000 B.C.E. Length 11 ft. 2 in. Photo: Jean Vertut.

fine "buschbock," an arrow in its throat. They delivered their booty and then went off to the hill we had left behind us, carrying a fistful of the antelope's hair and a gourd full of its blood. Two days passed before they caught up with us again. Then, in the evening, as we were drinking a foamy palm wine, the oldest of the three men—I had turned to him because he seemed to have more confidence in me than the others—told me that he and his companions had returned to the scene of their preparations for the hunt in order to daub the picture with the slain antelope's hair and blood, to withdraw the arrow and then to wipe the whole business away. The meaning of the formula was not clear, but I did gather that, had they not done as they did, the blood of the dead antelope would have destroyed them. The "wiping out," too, had to take place at sunrise.

50

This reading illuminates two concepts that are vital to an understanding of prehistoric art, and perhaps the art of the ancient world as well. First, the arts of the ancient world were not primarily decorative or intended as entertainment, as is the case with most modern art. Rather, drawing, painting, music, and dance held a sacred function, usually related to ritual or celebration. Among our ancient ancestors, "art" was a form of prayer, a vehicle by which humans petitioned superhuman forces. The Pygmy enactment of the hunt was a ritualized kind of *sympathetic magic*: a method by which one gains power over an object by manipulating its name or physical characteristics. Second, in the performance of such rituals, the arts were integrated: The success of the ritual depended upon the proper combination of words (chanted, sung, or spoken), visual images, and gestures (perhaps dance). If the Pygmy

episode is taken as a model, it is likely that prehistoric cave paintings belonged to rituals designed for a successful hunt.

Faith in the power to alter destiny by way of prayer and the manipulation of proper symbols has characterized religious ceremony throughout the history of humankind, but it was especially important to a culture in which control over nature was crucial to physical survival. A motif commonly found on cave walls is the image of the human hand, created in negative relief by blowing or splattering color around the actual hand of the hunter, shaman, or priest who interceded between the human realm and the spirit world (Figure **0.2**). Since the hand was the hunter's most powerful ally in making and wielding a weapon, it is fitting that it appears enshrined in the sacred precinct amid the quarry of the hunt. The precise meaning of many of the markings on prehistoric cave walls remains a matter of speculation. In that some cave paintings depict beasts and sea-creatures that humans did not hunt, it may be that these images were cult-related. Some scholars hold that certain prehistoric markings were lunar calendars—notational devices used to predict the seasonal migration of animals. The cave, symbol of the cosmic underworld and the procreative womb, served as a ceremonial chamber, a shrine, and perhaps a council room. No matter how one interprets so-called "cave-art," it is surely an expression of our early ancestors' efforts to control their environment and thus ensure their survival.

Women played important roles in Paleolithic culture. The Pygmy ritual described by Frobenius suggests a clear division of labor in the performance of ritual: As the male shoots the arrow into the image of the antelope, his female companion issues special words and pious gestures. It is

−12,000	domesticated dogs (descended from Asian wolves) appear
−10,000	goats are domesticated; herding begins in Asia and Africa
−8000	clay tokens are used in Mesopotamia to tally goods
−7000	cloth is woven in Anatolia (now Turkey)
−5000	crop irrigation is first employed in Mesopotamia

likely that similar kinds of shared responsibility characterized humankind's earliest societies. Women probably secured food by gathering fruits and berries; they acted also as healers and nurturers. Moreover, since the female (in her role as childbearer) assured the continuity of the tribe, she assumed a special importance: Perceived as life-giver and identified with the mysterious powers of procreation, she was exalted as Mother Earth. Her importance in the prehistoric community is confirmed by the great numbers of female statuettes uncovered by archeologists throughout the world. A good many of these objects show the female nude with pendulous breasts, large buttocks, and swollen abdomen, indicating pregnancy (Figure 0.3).

Figure 0.3 Venus of Willendorf, from Lower Austria, ca. 25,000–20,000 B.C.E. Limestone, height 4⅜ in. Museum of Natural History, Vienna.

Neolithic ("New Stone") Culture (ca. 8000–4000 B.C.E.)

Paleolithic people lived at the mercy of nature. However, during the transitional (or Mesolithic) phase that occurred shortly after 10,000 B.C.E., our ancient ancestors discovered that the seeds of wild grains and fruits might be planted to grow food, and wild animals might be domesticated. The rock art paintings discovered at Tassili in Africa's Sahara Desert—once fertile grasslands—tell the story of a transition from hunting to herding and the domestication of cattle and camels (Figure 0.4). Gradually, over a period of centuries, as hunters, gatherers, and herdsmen became farmers and food producers, a dynamic new culture emerged: the Neolithic. Food production freed people from a nomadic way of life. They gradually settled permanent farm communities, raising high-protein crops such as wheat and barley in Asia, rice in China, and maize in the Americas. They raised goats, pigs, cattle, and sheep that provided regular sources of food and valuable by-products such as wool and leather. The transition from the hunting-gathering phase of human subsistence to the agricultural-herding phase was a revolutionary development in human social organization, because it marked the shift from a nomadic to a sedentary way of life.

Neolithic sites excavated in Southwest Asia* (especially Israel, Jordan, Turkey, Iran, and Iraq), East Asia (China and Japan), and (as late as 1000 B.C.E.) in Meso-America, center on villages consisting of a number of mud- and limestone-faced huts, humankind's earliest architecture (Figure 0.5). At Jericho, in present-day Israel, massive defense walls surrounded the town, while tombs held the ornamented remains of local villagers. In Jarmo, in northern Iraq, a community of more than 150 people harvested wheat with stone sickles. Polished stone tools, some designed especially for farming, replaced the cruder tools of Paleolithic people. Ancient Japanese communities seem to have produced the world's oldest known pottery—handcoiled and fired clay vessels. But it was in Southwest Asia that some of the finest examples of painted pottery have come to light. Clay vessels, decorated with abstract motifs such as the long-necked birds that march around the rim of a beaker from Susa (Figure 0.6), held surplus foods for the lean months of winter, and woven rugs and textiles provided comfort against the wind, rain, and cold. Homemakers, artisans, and shepherds played significant roles in Neolithic society.

Agricultural life stimulated a new awareness of seasonal change and a profound respect for those life-giving powers, such as sun and rain, that were essential to the success of the harvest. The earth's fertility and the seasonal cycle were the principal concerns of the farming culture. A hand-modeled clay figurine from a Neolithic grave in Tlatilco in central Mexico (the region in which the Olmec—Meso-America's earliest culture—flourished)

---

*Also known as "the Near East" or "the Middle East." The geographic regions cited in this textbook are identified on the Key Map in the Preface.

Figure 0.4 Saharan rock painting, Tassili, Algeria, ca. 8000–4000 B.C.E. Photo: Sonia Halliday, Weston Turville, UK.

Figure 0.5 Isometric reconstruction of a neolithic house at Hassuna (level 4). Originally mud and limestone. The Oriental Institute, The University of Chicago.

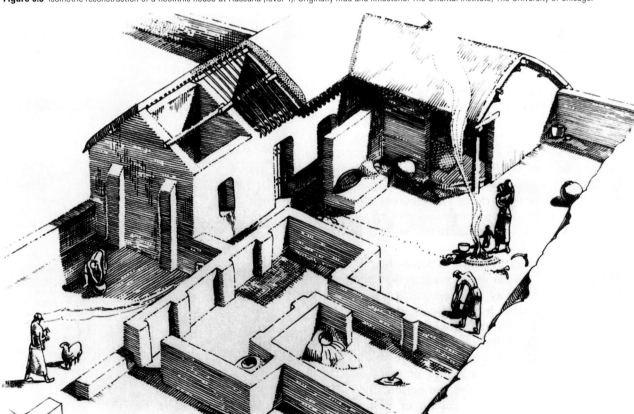

Figure 0.6 Beaker painted with goats, dogs, and long-necked birds, from Susa, southwest Iran, ca. 5000–4000 B.C.E. Baked clay, height 11¼ in. Louvre, Paris. Photo: © R.M.N.

Figure 0.7 Eternal duality of birth and death, figurine, Tlatilco, central Mexico, 1700–1300 B.C.E. Clay, height approx. 12 in. Museo Regional de Antropologia e Historia, Villahermosa, Tabasco. Richard Stirling/Photo © Ancient Art and Architecture Collection, Harrow.

illustrates the eternal duality of birth and death (Figure 0.7): One half of the man-child appears plump and vigorous, but on the other the flesh is stripped away to reveal the skeletal remains of the body. The figure, like those of infants and dwarfs common in Olmec art, may be associated with rituals celebrating regeneration and the life cycle. Its startling conjunction of infancy and degeneration reflects a profound sensitivity to the course of birth and death that governs both the crops and the people who plant them.

The overwhelming evidence of female statuettes found regularly in Neolithic graves suggests that the cult of the Earth Mother may have become even more important in the transition from food-gathering to food-production, when fertility and agricultural abundance were vital to the life of the community. Nevertheless, as with cave art, the exact meaning and function of the so-called "mother goddesses" remain a matter of speculation: They may have played a role in the performance of rites celebrating seasonal regeneration or they may have been associated with fertility cults that ensured successful childbirth. The symbolic association between the womb and "mother earth" played an important part in almost all ancient religions. In myth as well, female deities governed the earth, while male deities ruled the sky (see Reading 1.5). From culture to culture, the fertility goddess herself took many different forms. In contrast with the "Venus" of Willendorf (Figure 0.3), for instance, whose sexual characteristics are boldly exaggerated, the marble statuettes produced in great number on the Cyclades, the Greek islands of the Aegean Sea, are as streamlined and highly stylized as some modern sculptures (Figure 0.8). Though lacking the pronounced sexual characteristics of the Paleolithic Venus, the Cycladic figure probably played a similar role in rituals that sought the blessings of mother earth.

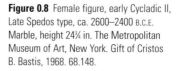

Figure 0.8 Female figure, early Cycladic II, Late Spedos type, ca. 2600–2400 B.C.E. Marble, height 24¾ in. The Metropolitan Museum of Art, New York. Gift of Cristos B. Bastis, 1968. 68.148.

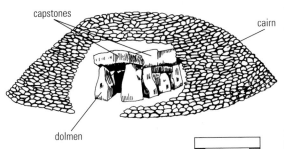

Figure 0.9 Dolmen site and post-and-lintel construction (right)

Figure 0.10 Burial site, Dolmen (upright stones supporting a horizontal slab), Crucuno, north of Carnac, France, Neolithic period. Ancient Art and Architecture Collection, Harrow.

To farming peoples, the seasonal cycle—a primary fact of subsistence—was associated with death and regeneration. The dead, whose return to the earth put them in closer touch with the forces of nature, received careful burial. Almost all early cultures regarded the dead as messengers between the world of the living and the spirit world. Neolithic folk marked graves with **megaliths** (literally, "great stones"), upright stone slabs roofed by a capstone to form a stone tomb or **dolmen** (Figure 0.9). At some sites, the tomb was covered over with dirt and rubble to form a mound (Figure 0.10), symbolic of the sacred mountain (the abode of the gods) and the procreative womb (the source of regenerative life). The shape prevails in sacred architecture that ranges from the Mesoamerican temple (see Figure 2.7) to the Buddhist shrine (see chapter 9). The dolmen tomb made use of the simplest type of architectural construction: the **post-and-lintel** principle. At ceremonial centers and burial sites, megaliths might be placed upright in circles or multiple rows and capped by horizontal slabs. One such example is the sanctuary at Stonehenge in southern England, where an elaborate group of stone circles, constructed in stages over a period of 2,000 years, forms one of the most mysterious and impressive ritual spaces of the prehistoric world (Figure 0.11). To this wind-swept site, 20-foot megaliths, some weighing 25 tons each, were dragged from a quarry some twenty miles away, then shaped and assembled without metal tools to form a huge outer circle and an inner horseshoe of post-and-lintel stones (Figure 0.12, 0.13). A special **stele** that stands apart from the complex of stone circles marks the point—visible from the exact center of the inner circle—at which the sun rises at the midsummer solstice (the longest day of the year). It is probable that Stonehenge served as a sacred calendar predicting the movements of the sun and moon, clocking the seasonal

cycle, and thus providing information that would have been essential to an agricultural society.

Other Neolithic projects offer astounding testimony to ancient ingenuity. In the coastal deserts of Peru, enormous earthwork lines form geometric figures, spirals, and bird, animal, and insect designs, the meaning and function of which are yet to be deciphered. The giant hummingbird, whose wings span some 200 feet, is one of eighteen bird images pictured on the Peruvian plains (Figure 0.14). So complex are the designs of these earthworks that some modern writers have attributed their existence to the activity of beings from outer space—much as medieval people thought Stonehenge the work of Merlin, a legendary magician. Scientific analysis of the total evidence, however, severely challenges the credibility of such theories. Indeed, recent scholarship suggests that the Peruvian earthworks may have served as starmaps or astronomical calendars designed, like Stonehenge, to help ancient farmers determine dates for planting crops, for ritual celebrations, and thus for bringing human needs into harmony with the rhythms of nature.

−4500	sailboats are used in Mesopotamia
−4200	the first known calendar (365 days) is devised in Egypt
−4000	copper ores are mined and smelted by Egyptians; bricks are fired in Mesopotamian kilns
−3600	bronze comes into use in Mesopotamia
−3500	the plow, wheeled cart, potter's wheel, tokens with pictographic impressions, fermentation processes for wine and beer are all introduced in Sumer

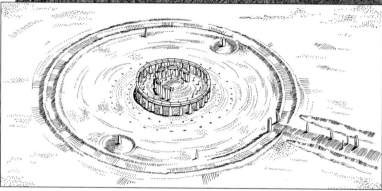

Figure 0.11 Stonehenge, Salisbury Plain, Wiltshire, England, ca. 3000–1800 B.C.E. Stone, diameter of circle 97 ft., height approx. 13 ft. 6 in. Photo: Aerofilms, Hertfordshire.

Figure 0.12 (left) Stonehenge's construction. Of the roughly eighty twenty-foot bluestones arranged in this horsehoe and circle formation, few survive. (below) Raising a sarsen stone into an upright setting. (bottom) Raising a lintel to the top of two sarsens.

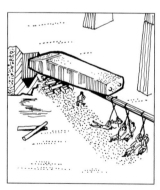
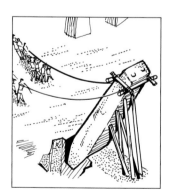

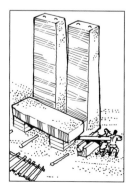
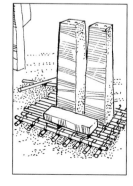
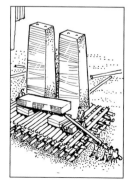

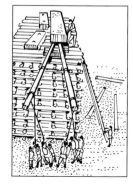

Figure 0.13 Stonehenge trilithons (lintel-topped pairs of stones at center). Height approx. 24 ft. (including lintel). © English Heritage Photographic Library.

Figure 0.14 Giant hummingbird, Nasca culture, Southwest Peru, ca. 200 B.C.E.–200 C.E. Wingspan, 900 ft. The geoglyph was created by scraping away the weathered surface of the desert and removing stones. Photo: Parabola, New York.

The Birth of Civilization

Around 4000 B.C.E., a new chapter in the history of humankind began. Neolithic villages grew in population and size. They produced surplus amounts of food and goods that might be traded with neighboring villages. The demands of increased production and trade went hand in hand with changes in division and specialization of labor. Advances in technology, such as the invention of the wheel, the plow, and the solar calendar in the earliest known civilizations of Sumer and Egypt, enhanced economic efficiency. Wheeled carts transported people, food, and goods overland, and sailboats used the natural resource of wind for travel by water. Large-scale farming required artificial systems of irrigation, which, in turn, required cooperative effort and a high degree of communal organization. Neolithic villages grew in complexity to become the bustling cities of a new era. The birth of civilization marks the shift from rural/pastoral to urban/commercial life; or more specifically, the transition from simple village life to the more complex forms of social, economic, and political organization associated with urban existence.

The first civilization of the ancient world emerged in Mesopotamia, a fertile area that lay between the Tigris and Euphrates Rivers of the Southwest Asian land mass (Map 0.1). Mesopotamia formed the eastern arc of the Fertile Crescent, which stretched westward to the Nile delta. At the southeastern perimeter of the Fertile Crescent, about a dozen cities collectively constituted Sumer, the very earliest civilization known to history. Shortly after the rise of Sumer, around 3500 B.C.E., Egyptian civilization emerged along the Nile River in Northeast Africa. In India, the earliest urban centers appeared in the valley of the Indus River that runs through the northwest portion of the Indian subcontinent. Chinese civilization was born in the northern part of China's vast central plain, watered by the Yellow River. The appearance of these four river valley civilizations was not simultaneous. Fully a thousand years separates the birth of civilization in Sumer from the rise of cities in China.

By comparison with the self-sustaining Neolithic village, the early city reached outward. Specialization and the division of labor raised productivity and encouraged trade, which, in turn, enhanced the growth of the urban economy. Activities related to the production and distribution of goods could not be committed entirely to memory, but, rather, required a system of accounting and record keeping. Writing made it possible to externalize information and transmit images by means of symbols. The newest theories of the origins of writing suggest that this form of record-keeping evolved from counting. In centuries long before the birth of civilization, tokens, that is, pieces of clay formed in the shapes of objects, were used to represent specific commodities—cattle, jars of oil, tools, and so on. Such tokens became useful in keeping track of all aspects of production, distribution, and commerce. Eventually, these tokens were placed in hollow clay balls that accompanied shipments of goods; upon arrival at their destination, the balls might be broken open and the tokens—the "record" of the shipment—counted. By the fourth millennium B.C.E., traders simplified matters by pressing an item-token into wet clay and adding symbols to indicate the number of actual goods. Around 3100 B.C.E., on clay tablets from Sumer, the **pictograph** (pictorial symbol) began to take the place of the token (Figure 0.15). In the following millennium, as scribes (using a stylus cut from a reed) found it difficult to execute the curves of pictographs on wet clay, these marks assumed a more angular and wedged

Map 0.1 Ancient River Valley Civilizations.

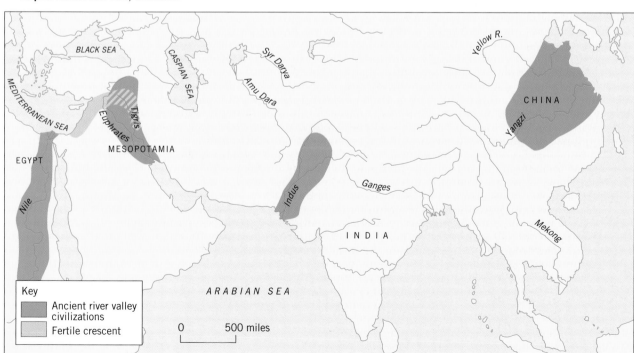

Figure 0.15 Reverse side of a pictographic tablet from Jamdat Nasr, near Kish, Iraq, ca. 3000 B.C.E., listing accounts involving animals and various commodities including bread and beer. Clay. Ashmolean Museum, Oxford.

inscription, written in two different types of Egyptian script and one Greek script, arranged in tiers, was understood only after a number of scholars, and ultimately Jean-François Champollion (1790–1832), matched the hieroglyphs for certain Egyptian rulers (such as Cleopatra) with their names in Greek.

The development of a written language is often isolated as the defining feature of a "civilized" society, but, in fact, complex urban cultures (such as those of the Pueblo and Andean peoples in the ancient Americas) have existed without writing systems. Writing in fact, was only one of many inventions mothered by necessity on the threshold of the urban revolution. For example, about the same time that systems of writing emerged in Mesopotamia, metal began to replace stone and bone tools. Metallurgy, which was first practiced around Asia Minor during the period 4000 B.C.E , afforded

shape. **Cuneiform** (from *cuneus*, the Latin word for "wedge"), a form of writing used throughout the Near East for well over 3,000 years, ushered in the world's first information age (Figure **0.16**). Of the thousands of clay tablets found in ancient Mesopotamia, the largest number are inscribed with notations concerning production and trade. In addition to inventories and business accounts, there are cuneiform texts recording historical events, religious prayers, and the names of local rulers. Essentially a practical means of record-keeping, writing was also a form of magic. As in rituals involving sympathetic magic, those who could make the marks that symbolized a thing might draw on its powers (see Reading 1.1).

In Egypt, slightly later than in Mesopotamia, a set of "sacred signs" known as **hieroglyphs**, answered similar needs. Ancient Egyptian writing remained a mystery to the world until 1822, when the Rosetta Stone (a black basalt slab discovered in 1799 in the Egyptian town of Rashid, or "Rosetta") was deciphered (Figure **0.17**). The stone's

Figure 0.16 The development of Sumerian writing from a pictographic script to cuneiform script to a phonetic system. Adapted from Samuel Noah Kramer, "The Sumerians," © 1957 by Scientific American, Inc. All rights reserved.

Earliest pictographs (3000 B.C.E.)	Denotation of pictographs	Pictographs in rotated position	Cuneiform signs ca. 1900 B.C.E.	Basic logographic values	
				Reading	Meaning
	Head and body of a man			lú	Man
	Head with mouth indicated			ka	Mouth
	Bowl of food			ninda	Food, bread
	Mouth + food			kú	To eat
	Stream of water			a	Water
	Mouth + water			nag	To drink
	Fish			kua	Fish
	Bird			mušen	Bird
	head of an ass			anše	Ass
	Ear of barley			še	Barley

−3100	cuneiform, the earliest known form of script, appears in Sumer; an early form of hieroglyphics appears in Egypt
−3000	candles are manufactured in Egypt; cotton fabric is woven in India; Sumerian math evolves based on units of 60 (60 becomes basic unit for measuring time)
−2600	Imhotep (Egyptian) produces the first known medical treatise
−2600	a lost-wax method of bronze casting is used in East Mesopotamia
−2500	the beginning of systematic standards in weights and measurement emerges in Sumer

Figure 0.17 Rosetta Stone, 196 B.C.E. Basalt, height 3 ft. 9 in. The same information is inscribed in Greek (1); demotic script, a simplified form of hieroglyphic (2); and hieroglyphic, a pictographic script (3); British Museum, London.

only to a small and well-to-do minority of the population. This minority formed a military elite who wielded power by virtue of superior arms. As the victory monument pictured in Figure 0.20 indicates, Sumerian warriors were outfitted with bronze shields, helmets, and lances.

The technology of bronze casting spread throughout the ancient world. Mesopotamians of the third millennium B.C.E. were among the first to use the **lost-wax** method of casting (Figure 0.18). Spreading eastward into the Indus valley, the lost-wax technique became popular for the manufacture of jewelry, musical instruments, horse gear, and toys (Figure 0.19). The ancient Chinese cast the separate parts of bronze vessels in sectional clay molds, and then soldered the parts together. Master metallurgists, the Chinese transformed the techniques of bronze-casting into one of the great artforms of the ancient world (see chapter 3).

People and Nature

Like their prehistoric ancestors, the inhabitants of the earliest civilizations lived in intimate association with nature. They looked upon the forces of nature—sun, wind, and rain—as vital and alive, indeed, as inhabited by living spirits—a belief known as **animism**. Just as they devised tools to manipulate the natural environment, so they devised strategies by which to understand and control that environment. *Myths*—that is, stories that explained the workings of nature—were part of the ritual fabric of everyday life. In legends and myths, the living spirits of nature assumed human (and heroic) status: They might be vengeful or beneficent, ugly or beautiful, fickle or reliable. Ultimately, they became a family of superhumans—gods and goddesses who very much resembled humans in their physical features and personalities, but whose superior strength and intelligence far exceeded that of human beings. The gods were also immortal, which made them the envy of ordinary human beings. Ritual sacrifice, prayer, and the enactment of myths honoring one or more of the gods accompanied seasonal celebrations, rites of passage, and almost every other significant communal event. In the early history of civilization, goddesses seem to have outnumbered gods, and local deities reigned supreme within their own districts. By means of specially appointed priest and priestesses, who mediated between human and divine realms, ancient people forged contractual relationships with their gods: In return for divine benefits, they lived as they believed the gods would wish.

humans a significant extension of control over nature by providing them with harder and more durable tools and weapons. At first, copper ore was extracted from surface deposits, but eventually metalsmiths devised sophisticated methods of mining and smelting ores. The result was bronze, an alloy of copper and tin that proved far superior to stone or bone in strength and durability. Since copper and tin were often located far apart, travel and trade were essential to Bronze Age cultures. (The 1995 discovery of Caucasian mummies in graves found in East Asia's Gobi desert argues for the existence of long distance trade and cross-cultural contact.) Metallurgy was a time-consuming process that required specialized training and the division of labor. Hence, bronze weapons were costly and available

Figure 0.18 The lost-wax process of bronze casting developed in Mesopotamia, third millennium B.C.E. A positive model (**1**) is used to make a negative mold (**2**) which is then coated with wax. Cool fireclay is poured into the wax shell; the mold is then removed (**3**). Metal rods are added to hold the layers in place, as are wax vents for even flow of bronze (**4**). The whole structure is immersed in sand; wax is burned out. Investment ready for molten bronze (**5**). Bronze head, ready for removal of gates and metal rods (**6**).

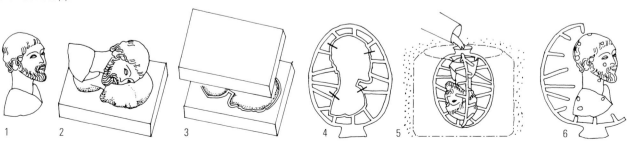

1   2   3   4   5   6

Figure 0.19 Chariot from Daimabad, Maharashtra, ca. 1500 B.C.E. Bronze, 8⅝ × 20½ × 6⅛ in. The Prince of Wales Museum of Western India, Bombay. Photo: Dirk Bakker.

Myth and the Quest for Beginnings

Today, no less than thousands of years ago, humans feel the need to explain the origins of the universe and define their place in it. While modern speculation on the origins of life takes the form of scientific theory (advanced by physicists, geologists, paleontologists, and anthropolo-

gists), the ancient quest for beginnings assumed the guise of myth. Ritually celebrated and repeated generation after generation, myths became fixed in the popular memory. As in the Pygmy ritual (Reading 1.1), words, gestures, and images formed the powerful amalgam of sacred ceremony.

In modern parlance, the word "myth" has come to suggest misconception; but, more accurately, myth describes a particular kind of speculation that, although prescientific, has enormous historical meaning. For while myth rationalizes the unknown in terms that may sound fantastic or quaint to modern ears, it constitutes the pattern of belief—the bedrock reality—of a given culture. Three further observations are noteworthy: First, the myths of ancient people are grounded in the evidence of the senses; thus, the imagery of myth is usually intensely visual. Second, the myths of a people are closely linked to that people's moral system, its rituals, and its religious beliefs, for what was taken as true was also held as sacred. Finally, the myths of humankind's earliest cultures show remarkable similarities, one of the most notable of which is the genesis of the first life forms from water.

In order to better understand these concepts, consider the following four creation myths. The first, a hymn from the *Rig Veda*—the oldest

Figure 0.20 The King of Lagash Leads His Phalanx into Battle. Detail of Eannatum's Stele of Victory, Tello, formerly Girsu, ca. 2450 B.C.E. Limestone, 70⅞ × 51⅛ in. Louvre, Paris. Photo: RMN.

religious literature of India—locates our beginnings in a watery darkness and in desire born of mind. The second is but one example drawn from the huge fund of creation stories told by African tribal people and transmitted orally for centuries. It situates the origins of life in the slender grasses that grow in wet, marshy soil. The third, an account of creation from the *Popol Vuh* ("Sacred Book") of Central America's Maya Indians, links creation to the word, that is, to language itself. Finally, from the Native American Iroquois Federation, a Mohawk tale recounts how the Good Spirit fashioned humankind in its diversity.

READING 1.2 Creation Tales

"The Song of Creation" from the *Rig Veda*

Then even nothingness was not, nor existence.   1
  There was no air then, nor the heavens beyond it
  What covered it? Where was it? In whose keeping?
  Was there then cosmic water, in depths unfathomed?
Then there were neither death nor immortality,   5
  nor was there then the torch of night and day.
  The One breathed windlessly and self-sustaining.
  There was that One then, and there was no other.
At first there was only darkness wrapped in darkness.
  All this was only unillumined water.   10
  That One which came to be, enclosed in nothing,
  arose at last, born of the power of heat.
In the beginning desire descended on it—
  that was the primal seed, born of the mind.
  The sages who have searched their hearts with wisdom   15
  know that which is, is kin to that which is not.
And they have stretched their cord across the void,
  and know what was above, and what below.
  Seminal powers made fertile mighty forces.
  Below was strength, and over it was impulse.   20
But, after all, who knows, and who can say
  whence it all came, and how creation happened?
  The gods themselves are later than creation,
  so who knows truly whence it has arisen?
Whence all creation had its origin,   25
  he, whether he fashioned it or whether he did not,
  he, who surveys it all from highest heaven,
  he knows—or maybe even he does not know.

(India)

An African Creation Tale

. . . It is said all men sprang from Unkulunkulu, who sprang   1
up first. The earth was in existence before Unkulunkulu. He had his origin from the earth in a bed of reeds.

All things as well as Unkulunkulu sprang from a bed of reeds—everything, both animals and corn, everything came into being with Unkulunkulu.

He looked at the sun when it was finished (worked into form as a potter works clay) and said: "There is a torch which will give you light, that you may see." He looked down on the cattle and said: 10
"These are cattle. Be ye broken off, and see the cattle and let them be your food; eat their flesh and their milk." He looked

on wild animals and said: "That is such an animal. That is an elephant. That is a buffalo." He looked on the fire and said: "Kindle it, and cook, and warm yourself; and eat meat when it has been dressed by the fire." He looked on all things and said: "So and so is the name of everything."

Unkulunkulu said: "Let there be marriage among men, that there may be those who can intermarry, that children may be born and men increase on earth." He said, "Let there be black   20
chiefs; and the chief be known by his people, and it be said, 'That is the chief: assemble all of you and go to your chief.'"

(Amazulu)

From the *Popol Vuh*

This is the account of how all was in suspense, all calm, in   1
silence; all motionless, still, and the expanse of the sky was empty.

This is the first account, the first narrative. There was neither man, nor animal, birds, fishes, crabs, trees, stones, caves, ravines, grasses, nor forests; there was only the sky.

The surface of the earth had not appeared. There was only the calm sea and the great expanse of the sky.

There was nothing brought together, nothing which could make a noise, nor anything which might move, or tremble, or   10
could make noise in the sky.

There was nothing standing; only the calm water, the placid sea, alone and tranquil. Nothing existed.

There was only immobility and silence in the darkness in the night. Only the Creator, the Maker, Tepeu, Gucumatz, the Forefathers, were in the water surrounded with light. They were hidden under green and blue feathers, and were therefore called Gucumatz. By nature they were great sages and great thinkers. In this manner the sky existed and also the Heart of Heaven, which is the name of God and thus He is   20
called.

Then came the word. Tepeu and Gucumatz came together in the darkness, in the night, and Tepeu and Gucumatz talked together. They talked then, discussing and deliberating; they agreed, they united their words and their thoughts.

Then while they mediated, it became clear to them that when dawn would break, man must appear. Then they planned the creation, and the growth of the trees and the thickets and the birth of life and the creation of man. Thus it was arranged in the darkness and in the night by the Heart of Heaven who   30
is called Huracán.

Then Tepeu and Gucumatz came together; then they conferred about life and light, what they would do so that there would be light and dawn, who it would be who would provide food and sustenance.

Thus let it be done! Let the emptiness be filled! Let the water recede and make a void, let the earth appear and become solid; let it be done. Thus they spoke. Let there be light, let there be dawn in the sky and on the earth! There shall be neither glory nor grandeur in our creation and formation   40
until the human being is made, man is formed. So they spoke.

Then the earth was created by them. So it was, in truth, that they created the earth. Earth! . . . they said, and instantly it was made. . . .

(Maya)

A Native American Creation Tale,
"How Man Was Created"

After Sat-kon-se-ri-io, the Good Spirit, had made the   1
animals, birds, and other creatures and had placed them to
live and multiply upon the earth, he rested. As he gazed
around at his various creations, it seemed to him that there
was something lacking. For a long time the Good Spirit
pondered over this thought. Finally he decided to make a
creature that would resemble himself.

Going to the bank of a river he took a piece of clay, and out
of it he fashioned a little clay man. After he had modeled it, he
built a fire and, setting the little clay man in the fire, waited   10
for it to bake. The day was beautiful. The songs of the birds
filled the air. The river sang a song and, as the Good Spirit
listened to this song, he became very sleepy. He soon fell
asleep beside the fire. When he finally awoke, he rushed to
the fire and removed the clay man. He had slept too long. His
little man was burnt black. According to the Mohawks, this
little man was the first Negro. His skin was black. He had
been overbaked.

The Good Spirit was not satisfied. Taking a fresh piece of
clay, he fashioned another man and, placing him in the fire,   20
waited for him to bake, determined this time to stay awake
and watch his little man to see that he would not be
overbaked. But the river sang its usual sleepy song. The Good
Spirit, in spite of all he could do, fell asleep. But this time he
slept only a little while. Awakening at last, he ran to the fire
and removed his little man. Behold, it was half baked. This,
say the Mohawks, was the first white man. He was half
baked!

The Good Spirit was still unsatisfied. Searching along the
riverbank he hunted until he found a bed of perfect red clay.   30
This time he took great care and modeled a very fine clay man.
Taking the clay man to the fire, he allowed it to bake.
Determined to stay awake, the Good Spirit stood beside the
fire, after a while Sat-kon-se-ri-io removed the clay man.
Behold, it was just right—a man the red color of the sunset sky.
It was the first Mohawk Indian.

(Mohawk)

Civilization emerged not as a fleeting moment of change, but as a slow process of urban growth. By the operation of an increasingly refined abstract intelligence, and by means of ingenuity, imagination, and cooperation, the earliest human beings took the first steps in perpetuating their own survival and the security of their communities. Technology provided the tools for manipulating nature, while mythology and the arts lent meaning and purpose to nature's hidden mysteries. By such cultural achievements, the earliest human beings laid the foundations for the humanistic tradition.

SUGGESTIONS FOR READING

Chauvet, Jean-Marie and others. *The Dawn of Art: The Chauvet Cave*. New York: Abrams, 1996.

Clottes, Jean and D. Lewis-Williams. *The Shamans of Prehistory: Trance and Magic in the Painted Caves*. New York: Abrams, 1998.

Ehrenberg, Margaret. *Women in Prehistory*. London: British Museum Press, 1992.

Hadingham, E. *Lines to the Mountain Gods: Nazca and the Mysteries of Peru*. New York: Random House, 1987.

Hawkins, G. S. *Stonehenge Decoded*. New York: Dell, 1965.

James, E. O. *The Cult of the Mother Goddess*. New York: Barnes & Noble, 1994.

Johanson, Donald, and Blake Edgar. *From Lucy to Language*. New York: Simon & Schuster, 1996.

Jolly, Alison. *Lucy's Legend: Sex and Intelligence in Human Evolution*. Cambridge, Mass.: Harvard University Press, 1999.

Leakey, Richard. *Origins Reconsidered: In Search of What Makes Us Human*. New York: Doubleday, 1992.

Ruspoli, Mario. *The Cave of Lascaux*. London: Thames and Hudson, 1987.

Sandars, N. K. *Prehistoric Art in Europe*, 2nd ed. Baltimore: Penguin, 1985.

Schmandt-Besserat, Denise. *Before Writing: From Counting to Cuneiform*. Austin, Tex.: University of Texas Press, 1992.

Schwartz, Jeffrey. *What the Bones Tell Us*. New York: Henry Holt, 1993.

GLOSSARY

animism the belief that the forces of nature are inhabited by spirits

culture the sum total of those things (including traditions, techniques, material goods, and symbol systems) that people have invented, developed, and transmitted

cuneiform ("wedge-shaped") one of humankind's earliest writing systems, consisting of wedge-shaped marks

impressed into clay by means of a reed stylus

dolmen a stone tomb formed by two posts capped by a lintel

hieroglyph (Greek, "sacred sign") the pictographic script of ancient Egypt

hominid any of a family of bipedal primate mammals, including modern humans and their ancestors, the earliest of which is *Australopithecus*

lost wax (also French, *cire-perdu*) a method of metal-

casting in which a figure is modeled in wax, then enclosed in a clay mold that is fired; the wax melts, and molten metal is poured in to replace it; finally, the clay mold is removed and the solid metal form is polished (see Figure 0.18)

megalith a large, roughly shaped stone, often used in ancient architectural construction

pictograph a pictorial symbol used in humankind's earliest

systems of writing

polychrome having many or various colors

post-and-lintel the simplest form of architectural construction, consisting of vertical members (posts) and supporting horizontals (lintels); see Figure 0.9

prehistory the study of history before written records

stele an upright stone slab or pillar

PART ONE

The first civilizations

The first chapters in the history of human life are often regarded as the most exciting. They present us with a gigantic puzzle that requires the piecing together of numerous fragments of information, most of which, like buried treasure, have been dug out of the earth. Reassembled, these fragments reveal the progress of humankind from its Bronze Age beginnings through the cultural history of ancient civilizations in Africa, South-west Asia, India, and China. In the opening chapters of this book, history's four earliest civilizations are presented geographically and chronologically. It is not, however, the detailed histories of these individual civilizations that are our major concern. Rather, each of these chapters pursues three principle *themes*: the formulation of belief systems providing bonds between the secular and spiritual realms; the establishment of rulership within the earliest urban communities; and finally, the nature and development of the social order as revealed in law and other forms of cultural expression. These three themes address concerns that are universal; inevitably, they dominate the visual and literary works of humankind's earliest civilizations.

Common to all of the civilizations of the ancient world was the belief that the forces of nature were greater and more powerful than those of mere humans. The sun that nourishes a bountiful harvest, the winds that may sweep away whole villages, the rains that cause rivers to flood the land – all of these natural forces affect daily life even in our own time. Among our early ancestors, however, those for whom survival was a day-to-day struggle, such forces, or the gods that represented them, assumed positions of primary importance. Belief systems and religious practices differed dramatically from one ancient civilization to another; but all systems and practices reflect the human effort to come to terms with the unknown: to understand the origins of life, the workings of nature, the meaning of death, and the destiny and purpose of humankind.

Throughout the ancient world, the survival of the community depended on strong leadership and communal cooperation. In Egypt, as in Mesopotamia, India, and China, rulership and the authority of law provided security and protection. The success of each civilization depended on a shared view of the earthly order as god-given or as immutably fixed in nature; as these civilizations matured, the bonds between the divine and secular realms gave shape to both social and moral life. In the arts—the astonishingly rich legacy of these four ancient civilizations—we discover a wealth of resources for an understanding of the dynamic interaction between the gods, the rulers, and the people who constituted the social order. In looking at the material evidence of the first civilizations, we come to understand not simply what happened in the ancient past, but how and why our forebears arrived at strategies and values that, in many instances, have influenced our own.

(opposite) Throne with Tutankhamen and Queen, detail of the back, late Amarna period, New Kingdom, Eighteenth Dynasty, ca. 1360 B.C.E. Wood, plated with gold and silver, inlays of glass paste, approx. 12 × 12 in. Egyptian Museum, Cairo. Photo: Andrea Jemolo, Rome.

World Events

◄ ■ PALEOLITHIC culture 5 million-10,000
Australopithecus uses stone tools and weapons

BRONZE AGE ——————— IRON AGE

■ Birth of civilization   ■ Hittites introduce iron
■ Bronze weapons developed

◄ ■ ICE AGE ca. 3 million-10,000

Mesopotamia: —— SUMER PERIOD – BABYLONIAN PERIOD – ASSYRIAN EMPIRE —— CHALDEANS ——
Nebuchadnezzar

◄ ■ NEANDERTHAL culture ca. 30,000-10,000

Egypt (Kingdoms): ├── OLD — MIDDLE ————————————— NEW ——

Aegean: ├── MINOAN ─┤   ■ Lydians invent coins ■
├─ MYCENAEAN ─┤

◄ ■ Evolution of *Homo sapiens* ca. 35,000

Canaan: ├─────────── EARLY HEBREW CIVILIZATION ──
■ Hebrews migrate to Canaan   ■ Babylonian captivity of the Jews 586-538
■ Moses ■ Solomon ■ Hebrew Prophets

■ Migrations to the Americas ca. 12,000

NEOLITHIC culture: farming communities ■

India: ├ INDUS ———— EARLY VEDIC AGE ——————— LATER VEDIC AGE
CIVILIZATION   ■ Sanskrit/caste system   Gautama Buddha ca. 563
Pottery invented ca. 5000 ■
■ Aryan invasion ca.1500

China: ├── YELLOW RIVER ——— SHANG ——— ZHOU DYNASTY ──
VALLEY CIVILIZATION   DYNASTY   ca. 1027-256
3500-1520   ca. 1520-1027
Chinese calligraphy

The Americas: ├────────────── PRE-COLUMBIAN CIVILIZATIONS ──

Literature & Philosophy

Pictographic script ■

■ *Epic of Gilgamesh*

■ *Babylonian Creation*

■ Hammurabi's Code

■ Cuneiform script

■ Phoenician alphabet

■ Hebrew Bible   Book of Job ■

■ Hieroglyphs

■ Pyramid texts

■ *Vedas* in India

■ Egyptian Book of the Dead   ■ *Hymn to the Aten*   ■ *Upanishads*

Mahabharata: *Bhagavad-Gita* ■

Oracle bones in China ■   Five Chinese Classics ■   ■ Confucian *Analects*
■ Lao-Zi/Daoism

Visual Arts, Architecture, Music, Dance

◄ ■ Cave art at Lascaux and Altamira 30,000-10,000

◄ ■ "Venus" of Willendorf

■ Neolithic beaker from Susa

■ Sumerian ziggurats

■ *Standard of Ur*

■ Statues at Tell Asmar

■ Palette of Narmer

■ Egyptian Pyramids

■ Portrait of Nefertiti

■ Coffin of Tutankhamen

■ Temple of Amon-Ra, Karnak

■ Stonehenge

■ Olmec figurines

■ Dancing Girl, Mohenjo Daro

■ Ishtar Gate, Babylon

Assyrian palaces at Nineveh and Nimrud ■

■ Chinese jade disks   ■ Chinese ritual bronzes

■ Great Wall of China

■ Han bronzes, ceramics, jade shroud 2nd/3rd cent. B.C.E. ►

◄─────────────── MUSIC AND DANCE ───────────────►
■ Harp from Royal Graves at Ur   ■ *Vedas*
■ *Hymn to the Aten*

CHAPTER ONE

Egypt: gods, rulers, and the social order

"The barges sail upstream and downstream too, for every way is open at your rising."
The Hymn to the Aten

Ancient Egyptian civilization emerged along the banks of the Nile River in northeast Africa. From the heart of Africa, the thin blue thread of the Nile flowed some 4,000 miles to its fan-shaped delta at the Mediterranean Sea. Along this river, agricultural villages thrived, coming under the rule of a sole ruler around 3150 B.C.E. Surrounded by sea and desert, Egypt was relatively invulnerable to foreign invasion (Map **1.1**), a condition that lent stability to Egyptian history. Unlike Mesopotamia, home to many different civilizations, ancient Egypt enjoyed a fairly uniform religious, political, and cultural life that lasted for almost 3,000 years. Its population shared a common language and a common world view. Although emerging slightly later than the first civilization in Mesopotamia, ancient Egypt thus provides a more accessible model for our understanding of the dynamics of the first civilizations.

The Gods of Ancient Egypt

Geography, climate, and the realities of the natural environment worked to shape the world views and religious beliefs of all ancient peoples. In the hot, arid climate of Northeast Africa, where ample sunlight made possible the cultivation of crops, the sun god held the place of honor. Variously called Amon, Re (Ra), or Aten, this god was considered greater than any other deity in the Egyptian pantheon. His cult dominated the **polytheistic** belief system of ancient Egypt for three millenia. Equally important to Egyptian life was the Nile, the world's longest river. Egypt, called by the Greek historian Herodotus "the gift of the Nile," depended on the annual overflow of Nile, which left fertile layers of rich silt along its banks. The 365-day cycle of the river's inundation became the basis of the solar calendar and the primary source of Egypt's deep sense of order. In the regularity of the sun's daily cycle and the Nile's annual deluge, ancient Egyptians found security. From the natural elements—the sun, the Nile, and the mountainless topography of North Africa—they also con-

structed their **cosmology**, that is, their theory of the origin and structure of the universe. With graphic immediacy, they described the earth as a flat platter floating on the waters of the underworld. According to Egyptian mythology, at the beginning of time, the Nile's primordial waters brought forth a mound of silt, out of which emerged the self-generating sun god; from that god, the rest of Egypt's gods were born.

Ancient Egyptians viewed the sun's daily ascent in the east as symbolic of the god's "rebirth"; his daily resurrection signified the victory of the forces of day, light, purity, goodness, and life over those of night, darkness, ignorance, evil, and death. In the cyclical regularity of nature evidenced by the daily rising and setting of the sun, the ancient Egyptians perceived both the inevitability of death and the promise of birth. "The Hymn to the Aten", a song of praise with numerous Egyptian antecedents, probably accompanied fertility rituals and celebrations honoring Egypt's pharaoh, the divinely appointed representative of the sun god (Figure **1.1**). Depictions of such rituals on the walls of Egyptian temples and tombs show the pharaoh receiving from Amon the gift of immortality in the form of the *ankh*, the hieroglyphic symbol meaning "life." In both the visual arts and in poetry, the sun is exalted as the source of light and heat, but also as the proactive life force, the "creator of seed." The optimism and sense of security that pervades this hymn typifies ancient Egyptian culture.

READING 1.3 From "The Hymn to the Aten",
(ca. 1352–1336)

You rise in perfection on the horizon of the sky   1
  living Aten,[1] who started life.
Whenever you are risen upon the eastern horizon
  you fill every land with your perfection.

---

[1] The sun disk.

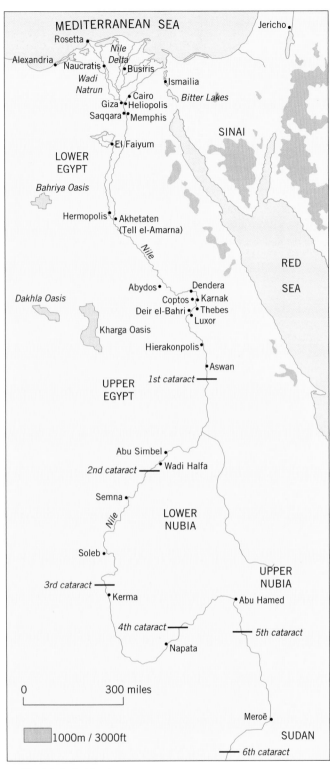

Map 1.1 Ancient Egypt.

Whenever you set on the western horizon,
  the land is in darkness in the manner of death.
They sleep in a bedroom with heads under the covers,
  and one eye does not see another.
  If all their possessions which are under their heads were
    stolen,   15
  they would not know it.
Every lion who comes out of his cave
  and all the serpents bite,
  for darkness is a blanket.
The land is silent now, because he who made them   20
  is at rest on his horizon

But when day breaks you are risen upon the horizon,
  and you shine as the Aten in the daytime.
When you dispel darkness and you give forth your rays
  the two lands[3] are in festival,   25
  alert and standing on their feet,
  now that you have raised them up.
Their bodies are clean,
  and their clothes have been put on;
  their arms are [lifted] in praise at your rising.   30
The entire land performs its work:
  all the cattle are content with their fodder,
  trees and plants grow,
  birds fly up to their nests,
  their wings [extended] in praise for your Ka.[4]   35
All the Kine[5] prance on their feet;
  everything which flies up and alights,
  they live when you
  have risen for them.
The barges sail upstream and downstream too,   40
  for every way is open at your rising.
The fishes in the river leap before your face
  when your rays are in the sea.

You who have placed seed in woman
  and have made sperm into man,   45
  who feeds the son in the womb of his mother,
  who quiets him with something to stop his crying;
  you are the nurse in the womb,
  giving breath to nourish all that has been begotten.

. . . .

Second only to the sun as the major natural force in Egyptian life was the Nile River. Ancient Egyptians identified the Nile with Osiris, ruler of the underworld and god of the dead. According to Egyptian myth, Osiris was slain by his evil brother, Set, who chopped his body into pieces

You are appealing, great, sparkling, high over every land;   5
  your rays hold together the lands as far as everything
    you have made.
Since you are Re,[2] you reach as far as they do,
  and you curb them for your beloved son.
Although you are far away, your rays are upon the land;
  you are in their faces, yet your departure is not observed.   10

------

[2]Another name for the sun god, associated with his regenerative powers.

[3]The kingdoms of Upper and Lower Egypt, so designated because the Nile flows from the heart of Africa in the south to the Mediterranean Sea in the north. Upper Egypt extended south as far as the first cataract at Syene (Aswan); Lower Egypt comprised the Nile delta north of Memphis; see Map 1.1.
[4]The governing spirit or soul of a person or god.
[5]Cow.

Figure 1.1 *Amon receives Sesostris (Senusret) I*, ca. 1925 B.C.E. Pillar relief, White Chapel, Karnak. photo: Andrea Jemolo, Rome.

Name	Role	Depicted As
Anubis	patron of embalmers, god of cemeteries	jackal
Amon	sun god, creator of heaven and earth	falcon, sun rays
Aten	god of the solar disk	solar disk
Bes	helper of women in childbirth, protector against snakes	lion-faced dwarf
Hapi	god of the Nile	bull
Hathor	mother, wife, and daughter of Ra, sky goddess	cow
Horus	son of Isis and Osiris, sky god	falcon
Isis	wife of Osiris, mother of Horus, fertility goddess	female
Maat	goddess of truth and universal order	head-feather
Osiris	god of the underworld	mummified king
Ptah	creator of humans, patron of craftspeople	mummified man
Set	brother of Osiris, god of storms and violence	pig, ass, hippopotamus
Thoth	inventor of writing, patron of scribes	ibis

Figure 1.2 Principal Egyptian gods.

and threw them into the Nile. But Osiris's loyal wife Isis, Queen of Heaven, gathered the fragments and restored Osiris to life. The union of Isis and the resurrected Osiris produced a son, Horus, who ultimately avenged his father by overthrowing Set and becoming ruler of Egypt. The Osiris myth vividly describes the idea of resurrection that was central to the ancient Egyptian belief system. Though the cult of the sun in his various aspects dominated the official religion of Egypt, local gods and goddesses—more than 2,000 of them—made up the Egyptian pantheon. These deities, most of whom held multiple powers (Figure 1.2), played protective roles in the daily lives of the ancient Egyptians. The following invocation to Isis, however, suggests her central role among the female deities of Egypt:

Praise to you, Isis, the Great One
God's Mother, Lady of Heaven,
Mistress and Queen of the Gods.

The Rulers of Ancient Egypt

Local rulers governed the Neolithic villages along the Nile until roughly 3150 B.C.E., when they were united under the authority of Egypt's first pharaoh, Narmer (also known as Menes). This important political event—the union of Upper and Lower Egypt—is commemorated on a two-foot-high slate object known as the Palette of Narmer (Figures 1.3 and 1.4). The back of the slate palette shows the triumphant Narmer seizing a fallen enemy by the hair.

Below his feet lie the bodies of the vanquished. To his left, a slave (represented smaller in size than Narmer) dutifully carries his master's sandals. At the upper right is the victorious falcon, symbol of the god Horus. Horus/Narmer holds by the leash the now-subdued lands of Lower Egypt, symbolized by a severed head and **papyrus**, the reed-like plants that grow along the Nile. On the front, the top register bears a victory procession flanked by rows of defeated soldiers, who stand with their decapitated heads between their legs. Narmer's conquest initiated Egypt's first **dynasty**. For some 2,500 years to follow, ancient Egypt was ruled by a succession of dynasties, the history of which was divided into chronological periods by an Egyptian priest of the third century B.C.E.:

Early Dynastic Period ca. 3100–2700 B.C.E.
(Dynasties I–II)
Old Kingdom ca. 2700–2150 B.C.E.
(Dynasties III–VI)
Middle Kingdom ca. 2050–1785 B.C.E.
(Dynasties XI–XII)
New Kingdom ca. 1575–1085 B.C.E.
(Dynasties XVIII–XX)

Civil dissent marked the intermediate period between the Old and Middle Kingdoms, while the era between the Middle and New Kingdoms (roughly 1785 to 1575) withstood the invasion of the Hyksos, warlike tribes who introduced the horse and chariot into Egypt. Following the expulsion of Hyksos, New Kingdom pharaohs (the word means "great house" in the sense of "first family") created Egypt's first empire, extending their authority far into Syria, Palestine, and Nubia.

Throughout their long history, ancient Egyptians viewed the land as sacred. It was owned by the gods, ruled by the pharaohs, and farmed by the peasants with the assistance of slaves. By divine decree, the fruits of each harvest were shared according to the needs of the community. This type of *theocratic socialism* provided Egypt with an abundance of food and a surplus that encouraged widespread trade. The land itself, however, passed from generation to generation not through the male but through the female line, that is, from the king's daughter to the man she married. For the pharaoh's son to come to the throne, he would have to marry his own sister or half-sister (hence the numerous brother–sister marriages in Egyptian dynastic history). This tradition, probably related to the practice of tracing parentage to the childbearer, lasted longer in Egypt than anywhere else in the ancient world. In the

–2650	Pharaoh Khufu (or Cheops) orders construction of the Great Pyramid of Gizeh†
–1500	Egyptians employ a simple form of the sundial
–1450	the water clock is devised in Egypt
–1400	glass in produced in Egypt and Mesopotamia

†All dates in this chapter are approximate;
– (minus) signifies B.C.E.

Figure 1.3 Palette of King Narmer (front and back), ca. 3100 B.C.E. Slate, height 25 in. Egyptian Museum, Cairo. © Hirmer Fotoarchiv.

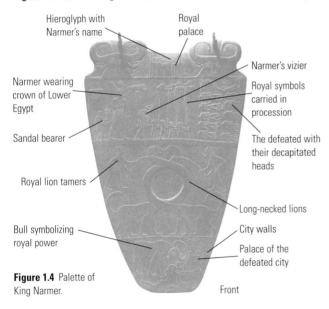

Hieroglyph with Narmer's name

Royal palace

Narmer's vizier

Narmer wearing crown of Lower Egypt

Royal symbols carried in procession

Sandal bearer

The defeated with their decapitated heads

Royal lion tamers

Long-necked lions

Bull symbolizing royal power

City walls

Palace of the defeated city

Figure 1.4 Palette of King Narmer.

Front

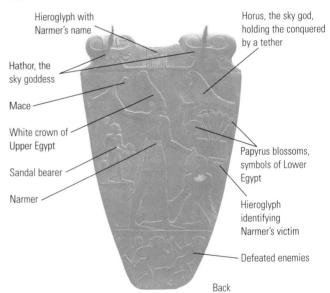

Hieroglyph with Narmer's name

Horus, the sky god, holding the conquered by a tether

Hathor, the sky goddess

Mace

White crown of Upper Egypt

Sandal bearer

Narmer

Papyrus blossoms, symbols of Lower Egypt

Hieroglyph identifying Narmer's victim

Defeated enemies

Back

freestanding sculpture of the Old Kingdom pharaoh Mycerinus, the queen stands proudly at his side, one arm around his waist and the other gently touching his arm (Figure 1.5). A sense of shared purpose is conveyed by their lifted chins and confident demeanor. While Egypt's rulers were traditionally male, women came to the throne three times. The most notable of all female pharaohs, Hatshepsut (ca. 1500–1447 B.C.E), governed Egypt for twenty-two years. She is often pictured in male attire,

wearing the royal wig and false beard, and carrying the crook and the flail—traditional symbols of rulership.

Theocracy and the Cult of the Dead

From earliest times, political power was linked with spiritual power and superhuman might. The Egyptians held that divine power flowed from the gods to their royal agents. In this **theocracy** (rule by god or god's representative), reigning **monarchs** represented heaven's will on

Figure 1.5 Pair Statue of Mycerinus and Queen Kha-merer-nebty II, Gizeh, Mycerinus, Fourth Dynasty, 2599–1571 B.C.E. Slate schist, height 4 ft. 6½ in. (complete statue). Courtesy, Museum of Fine Arts, Boston. Harvard MFA Expedition.

features of powerful animals. Such is the case with the Great Sphinx, the recumbent creature that guards the entrance to the ceremonial complex at Gizeh (Figure 1.6). This haunting figure, antiquity's largest and earliest surviving colossal statue, bears the portrait head of the Old Kingdom pharaoh Khafre and the body of a lion, king of the beasts. As such, it is a hybrid symbol of superhuman power and authority.

Ancient Egyptians venerated the pharaoh as the living representative of the sun god. They believed that on his death, the pharaoh would join with the sun to govern Egypt eternally. His body was prepared for burial by means of a special, ten-week embalming procedure that involved removing all of his internal organs (with the exception of his heart) and filling his body cavity with preservatives. His intestines, stomach, lungs, and liver were all embalmed separately—the brain was removed and discarded. The king's corpse was then wrapped in fine linen and placed in an elaborately ornamented coffin (Figure 1.7), which was floated down the Nile on a royal barge to a burial site located at Gizeh, near the southern tip of the Nile Delta (see Map 1.1). Fourth Dynasty pharaohs of the Old Kingdom built tombs in the shape of a pyramid representing the mound of silt from which the primordial sun god arose.

Constructed between 2600 and 2500 B.C.E., the pyramids are technological wonders, as well as symbols of ancient Egypt's endurance through time (Figure 1.8). A work force of some 50,000 men (divided into gangs of twenty-five) labored almost thirty years to raise the Great Pyramid of Khufu. According to recent DNA analysis of the workers found buried at Gizeh, the pyramid builders were Egyptians, not foreign slaves, as was previously assumed. This native work force quarried, transported, and assembled thousands of mammoth stone blocks, most weighing between 2 and 50 tons. These they lifted from tier to tier by means of levers—though some historians speculate they were slid into place on inclined ramps of sand and rubble (Figure 1.9). Finally, they faced the surfaces of the great tombs with finely polished limestone. All of these feats were achieved with copper saws and chisels, and without pulleys or mortar. The Great Pyramid of Khufu, which stands as part of a large walled burial complex at Gizeh (Figure 1.10), consists of more than two million stone blocks rising to a height of approximately 480 feet and covering a base area of thirteen acres. The royal burial vault, hidden within a series of chambers connected to the exterior by tunnels (Figure 1.11), was prepared as a home for eternity—a tribute to communal faith in the eternal benevolence of the pharaoh. Its chambers were fitted with his most cherished possessions: priceless treasures of jewellery, weapons, and furniture, all of which he might require in the life to come. The chamber walls were painted in **fresco** and carved in **relief** with images recreating the pharaoh's life on earth (Figure 1.13). Hieroglyphs formed an essential component of pictorial illustration, narrating the achievements of Egypt's rulers, listing the grave goods, and offering perpetual prayers for the deceased (see also Figure 1.1). Carved and painted fig-

earth. In ancient Egypt, the pharaoh ruled in the name of the immortal and generative sun god. Egypt's kings were also identified with Horus, the avenging son of Osiris and Isis, symbolized by the falcon. So close was the association between rulers and gods that Egyptian hymns to the pharaoh address him in terms identical with those used in worshiping the gods. In the visual arts, rulers and gods alike were depicted with the attributes and physical

Figure 1.6 Sphinx at Gizeh, Egypt, ca. 2540–2514 B.C.E. Limestone, length 240 ft., height 65 ft. Historical Picture Service, Inc., Chicago.

Figure 1.7 Egyptian Mummy and Coffin, ca. 1000 B.C.E. Reproduced by courtesy of the Trustees of the British Museum, London.

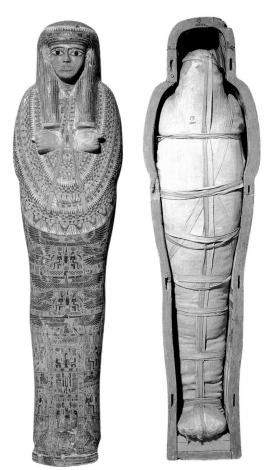

Figure 1.8 Great Pyramids of Gizeh: Menkure, ca. 2575 B.C.E., Khafre, ca. 2600 B.C.E., Khufu, ca. 2650 B.C.E. Top height approx. 480 ft. Zefa Picture Library (UK) Ltd. London.

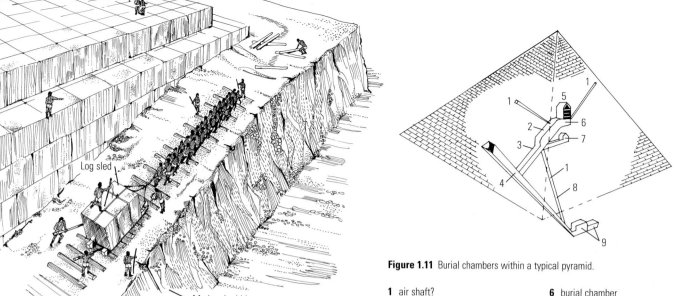

Figure 1.9 Pyramid construction. Some historians speculate that the vast stone building blocks were hauled into position using log sleds and inclined ramps made of packed sand.

Figure 1.11 Burial chambers within a typical pyramid.

1 air shaft?
2 gallery to chambers
3 ascending corridor
4 descending corridor
5 weight-relieving chamber
6 burial chamber
7 abandoned
  burial chamber
8 escape route?
9 original burial chambers

ures carrying provisions—loaves of bread, fowl, beer, and fresh linens—accompanied the pharaoh to the afterlife (Figure 1.12). And death masks or "reserve" portrait heads of the pharaoh might be placed in the tomb to provide the king's *ka* (life force or soul) with safe and familiar dwelling places.

Intended primarily as homes for the dead, the pyramids were built to assure the ruler's comfort in the afterlife.

However, in the centuries after their construction, grave robbers greedily despoiled them, and their contents were largely plundered and lost. Middle and Late Kingdom pharaohs turned to other methods of burial, including interment in the rock cliffs along the Nile and in unmarked graves in the Valley of the Kings west of Thebes. In time, these too were pillaged. One of the few royal graves to have escaped vandalism was that of a minor

Figure 1.10 Reconstruction of the Pyramids of Khufu and Khafre at Gizeh, ca. 2650–2600 B.C.E. (after Hoelscher). **1** Khafre, height approx. 470 ft. **2** Mortuary temple **3** Covered causeway **4** Valley temple **5** Great Sphinx **6** Khufu, height approx. 480 ft. **7** Pyramids of the royal family and mastabas of the nobles. From Horst de la Croix and Robert G. Tansey, *Art Through the Ages*, sixth edition, copyright © 1975 Harcourt Brace Jovanovich, Inc., reprinted by permission of the publisher.

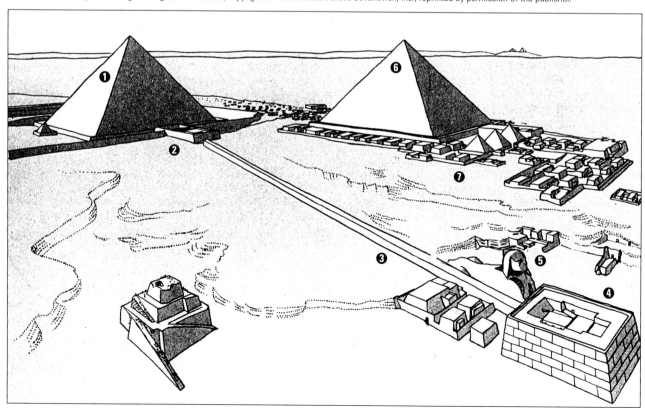

Figure 1.13 Scene of Fowling, from the Tomb of Neb-amon at Thebes, Egypt, ca. 1400 B.C.E. Fragment of a fresco secco, height 32¼ in. Reproduced by courtesy of the Trustees of the British Museum, London.

Figure 1.12 A girl carrying meat in a box and a duck, produce of an estate of Meketre, ca. 2050 B.C.E. Height 44 in. The Metropolitan Museum, New York.

fourteenth-century B.C.E. ruler named Tutankhamen (ca. 1380–1352 B.C.E.). Uncovered by the British archaeologist Howard Carter in 1922, the tomb housed riches of astonishing variety, including the pharaoh's solid gold coffin, inlaid with semi-precious carnelian and lapis lazuli (Figure **1.14**).

The promise of life after death seems to have dominated at all levels of Egyptian culture. The most elaborate homes for the dead were reserved for royalty and members of the aristocracy, but recent excavations of the lower cemetery at Gizeh reveal at least 700 graves of workmen and artisans. In the coffins of ancient Egypt's dead are found papyrus scrolls inscribed with prayers and incantations to guide the soul in the afterlife. *The Book of the Dead*, a collection of funerary prayers originating as far back as 4000 B.C.E., prepared each individual for final judgment. In the presence of the gods Osiris and Isis, the dead souls were expected to recite a lengthy confession attesting to their purity of heart, including:

I have not done iniquity.
I have not robbed with violence.
I have not done violence [to any man].
I have not committed theft.
I have not slain man or woman.
I have not made light the bushel.
I have not acted deceitfully.
I have not uttered falsehood.
I have not defiled the wife of a man.
I have not stirred up strife.
I have not cursed the god.
I have not behaved with insolence.
I have not increased my wealth, except with such things as are my own possessions.*

A painted papyrus scroll from *The Book of the Dead* depicts the last judgment itself: the enthroned Osiris, god of the underworld (far right) and his wife Isis (far left) oversee the ceremony in which the heart of the deceased Princess Entiu-ny is weighed against the figure of Truth (Figure **1.15**). Having made her testimony, the princess watches as the jackal-headed god of death, Anubis, prepares her heart for the ordeal. "Grant thou," reads the prayer to Osiris, "that I may have my being among the living, and that I may sail up and down the river among those

---

*Adapted from *The Egyptian Book of the Dead*, edited by E. Wallis Budge (Secaucus, New Jersey: University Books, Inc., 1977, pp. 576–577).

Figure 1.14 Egyptian cover of the Coffin of Tutankhamen (portion), from the Valley of the Kings, ca. 1360 B.C.E. Gold with inlay of enamel, carnelian, lapis lazuli, and turquoise. Egyptian Museum, Cairo. Photo: Wim Swann, The Getty Center, Santa Monica.

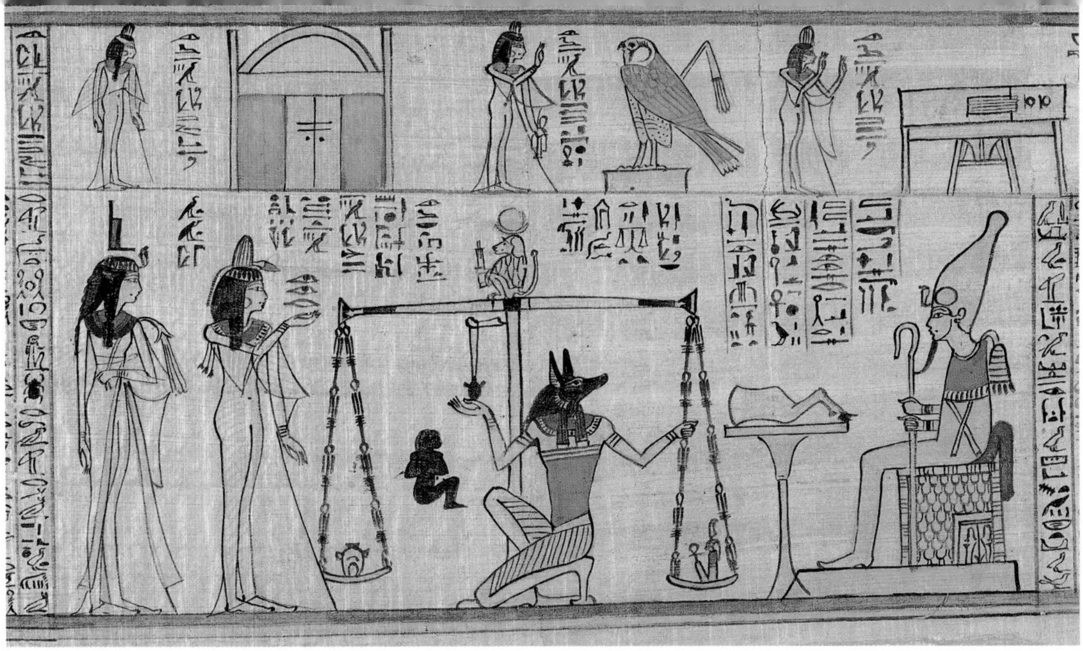

Figure 1.15 Scene from a Funerary Papyrus, Book of the Dead. Princess Entiu-ny stands to the left of a set of scales on which Anubis, the jackal-headed god, weighs her heart against the figure of Truth, while Osiris, Lord of the Dead, judges from his throne. His wife, Isis, stands behind the princess. Height 11¾ in. The Metropolitan Museum of Art, New York, Rogers Fund.

who are in thy following." If the heart is not "found true by trial of the Great Balance," it will be devoured by the monster, Ament, thus meeting a second death. If pure, it might sail with the sun "up and down the river," or flourish in a realm where wheat grows high and the living souls of the dead enjoy feasting and singing. An image of this heavenly domain is depicted on the walls of the tomb of Sennudjem: the "fields of the blessed" are bordered by beneficent gods (top) and flourishing fruit trees (bottom) (Figure 1.16). Here death is a continuation of daily life in a realm that floats eternally on the primordial waters of creation.

Figure 1.16
Illustration of Spell 110 from the Book of the Dead in the burial chamber of Sennudjem, ca. 1279 B.C.E. Photo: Abdel Gaffar Shedid, Munich.

Akhenaten's Reform

Throughout the dynastic history of Egypt, the central authority of the pharaoh was repeatedly contested by local temple priests, each of whom held religious and political authority in their own regions along the Nile. Perhaps in an effort to consolidate his authority against such encroachments, the New Kingdom pharaoh Amenhotep IV (ca. 1353–1336 B.C.E.) defied the tradition of polytheism by elevating Aten (God of the Sun Disk) to a

Figure 1.17 *The royal family under the "Aten with Rays".* Ca. 1345 B.C.E. New Kingdom, Eighteenth Dynasty. Alabaster, height 3 ft. 4 in. Egyptian Museum, Cairo. Photo: Jürgen Liepe, Berlin.

Figure 1.18 Portrait of head of Queen Nefertiti, ca. 1355 B.C.E. New Kingdom, Eighteenth Dynasty. Painted limestone, height 20 in. State Museums, Berlin.

position of supremacy over all other gods. Changing his own name to Akhenaten ("Shining Spirit of Aten"), the pharaoh abandoned the political capital at Memphis and the religious center at Thebes to build a new palace midway between the two at a site called Akhetaten ("Place of the Sun Disk's Power") (see Map 2.1). In a small stone carving from Akhenaten's palace, the pharaoh is seen with his wife Nefertiti and one of their daughters making offerings to Aten (Figure **1.17**). The sun's rays end in human hands, some of which carry the *ankh*. The elongated figures and relaxed contours suggest a conscious departure from traditional (more formal) modes of representation. Akhenaten's chief wife, Queen Nefertiti, along with her mother-in-law, assisted in organizing the affairs of state. The mother of six daughters, Nefertiti is often pictured as

Isis, the goddess from whom all Egyptian queens were said to have descended. Nefertiti's confident beauty inspired numerous sculpted likenesses, some of which are striking in their blend of realism and abstraction (Figure **1.18**). Akhenaten's monotheistic reform lasted only as long as his reign, and in the years following his death, Egypt's conservative priests and nobles returned to the polytheism of their forebears.

Nubia and Ancient Egypt

Throughout its history, ancient Egypt maintained commercial and cultural contact with other African civilizations—Libya in the north, Punt in the east, and Nubia in the south. The most significant of these, the civilization of Nubia was located between the first and sixth cataracts of the Nile (see Map 1.1). Nubia was the first literate urban society to appear in Africa south of the Sahara. Famous for its large quantities of gold, copper, iron, and cattle, it came under Egyptian rule as early as the Middle Kingdom. But during the ninth century B.C.E., the powerful state of Kush in Nubia came to rule all of southern Egypt. The history of Nubia, which dates from at least 2300 B.C.E., reflects the importation of Egyptian religion and culture, but its artifacts testify to a high level of native artistry and technical sophistication. This is especially visible in the area of metal-crafting, as reflected, for instance, in the bronze statue of the Kushan king Shabaqo (Figure **1.19**). In this small, but forceful portrait, Nubia anticipated the birth of an African tradition in portraiture that flowered in the western Sudan as early as 500 B.C.E. and continued to flourish for at least a thousand years (see chapter 18).

Figure 1.19 King Shabaqo, from the area of the ancient Kush, ca. eighth century B.C.E. Solid cast bronze, height 6 in. National Museum, Athens, no. 632. Photo: courtesy National Museum.

Law in Ancient Egypt

In ancient Egypt, long-standing customs and unwritten rules preceded the codification and transcription of civil and criminal law. Indeed, Egyptian law consisted of the unwritten decrees of the pharaoh (passed down orally until they were transcribed during the New Kingdom). An inscription on an Old Kingdom tomb wall sums up this phenomenon as follows: "the law of the land is the mouth of the pharaoh." In Egypt no written laws have been preserved from any period before the fourth century B.C.E. When one considers that toward the end of the thirteenth century B.C.E., the pharaoh Rameses II ruled approximately three million people, it is clear that the oral tradition—the verbal transmission of rules, conventions, and customs—played a vital part in establishing political continuity.

The Social Order

Like all ancient civilizations, Egypt could not have existed without a high level of cooperation among those whose individual tasks—governing, trading, farming, fighting—contributed to communal survival. Powerful families, tribes, and clans, usually those that had proved victorious in battle, established long-standing territorial claims. Such families often claimed descent from, or association with, the gods. Once royal authority was entrenched, it was almost impossible to unseat. The ruling dynasty, in conjunction with a priestly caste that supervised the religious activities of the community, formed an elite group of men and women who regulated the lives of the lower classes: merchants, farmers, herders, artisans, soldiers, and servants. Nevertheless, the class structure in ancient Egypt seems to have been quite flexible. Ambitious individuals of any class were free to rise in status, usually by way of education. The westward migration of sub-Saharan (dark-skinned)* peoples and the thriving commercial activity between Egypt and Nubia produced a multiracial and multicultural population: at all levels, light- and dark-skinned people appear to have held similar social status.

For well over 2,000 years, Egypt was administered by the pharaoh's vast bureaucracy, members of which collected taxes, regulated public works, and mobilized the army. In the social order, these individuals, along with large landowners and priests, constituted the upper classes. As in all ancient societies, power was not uniformly distributed but descended from the top rung of the hierarchy in diminishing degrees of influence. Those closest to the pharaoh participated most fully in his authority and prestige. Other individuals might advance their positions and improve their status through service to the pharaoh.

----

*Since skin pigmentation varies in accordance with the amount of melanin and keratin particles in the underskin (which regulates the permeation of sun rays), relative distance from the equator determined African skin colors, which differed from the very light brown of Mediterranean types to the very dark brown of black Nubian and sub-Saharan peoples.

At the top of the bureaucratic pyramid stood the vizier. Essential to the administration and the security of the state, the vizier was in charge of appointing members of the royal bureaucracy and dispatching the local officials. He oversaw the mobilization of troops, the irrigation of canals, the taking of inventories, and, with the assistance of official scribes, he handled all litigation for the Egyptian state. Merchants, traders, builders, and scribes made up a prosperous middle class, who ranked in status just below the aristocracy. At the base of the social pyramid, the great masses of peasants constituted the agricultural backbone of ancient Egypt. Aided by slaves, peasant men and women worked side by side to farm the land. Even in the afterlife, husbands and wives shared the tasks of reaping wheat in the fields of the blessed (see Figure 1.16). Class status seems to have extended into the afterlife: in the cemeteries recently uncovered at Gizeh, artisans received separate and more elaborate burials than common laborers.

Slaves constituted a class of unfree men and women. In the ancient world, slaves were victims of military conquest. Enslaving one's enemy captives was a humane alternative to executing them. Other people became slaves as punishment for criminal acts, and still others as a result of falling into debt. Slaves might be sold or traded like any other form of property, but in Egypt and elsewhere in the ancient world, it appears that some slaves were able to acquire sufficient wealth to buy their own or their children's freedom.

Egyptian Women

Possibly because all property was inherited through the female line, Egyptian women seem to have enjoyed a large degree of economic independence, as well as civil rights and privileges. Women who could write and calculate might go into business. Women of the pharaoh's harem oversaw textile production, while others found positions as shop-keepers, midwives, musicians, and dancers (Figure 1.20). Nevertheless, men were wary of powerful women, as is indicated in a Middle Kingdom manual of good conduct, which offers the husband this advice concerning his wife: "Make her happy while you are alive, for she is land profitable to her lord. Neither judge her nor raise her to a position of power . . . her eye is a stormwind when she sees."

The Arts in Ancient Egypt

Literature

Ancient Egypt did not produce any literary masterpieces. Nevertheless, from tomb and temple walls, and from papyrus rolls, come prayers and songs, royal decrees and letters, prose tales, and texts that served to educate the young. One school text, which reflects the fragile rela-

Figure 1.20 Painting from the tomb of Neb-aman, Dra Abu el-Naga, West Thebes, Egypt, Eighteenth Dynasty, ca. 1550–1295 B.C.E. Painted stucco, height 25 in. The upper register shows a banquet. In the lower register two young girls are dancing to the music of the double flute. Reproduced by courtesy of the Trustees of the British Museum, London.

tionship between oral and written traditions, reads, "Man decays, his corpse is dust,/All his kin have perished;/But a book makes him remembered'/Through the mouth of its reciter." The so-called "wisdom literature" of Egypt, which consists of words of advice and instruction, anticipates parts of the Hebrew Bible. From the New Kingdom, however, came a very personal type of poetry that would later be defined as **lyric** (literally, accompanied by the lyre or harp). In the following three poems, two in a male voice and one female, nature and the natural world are freely used as metaphors for sentiments of love and desire.

READING 1.4 Egyptian Poetry

Boy	I will lie down within	1
	and feign to be ill, and then	
	my neighbors will come to see.	
	My sister[1] will enter with them.	
	She'll put the physicians to shame,	5
	for she will understand	
	that I am sick for love.	

———◆———

Boy	My sister has come to me.	1
	My heart is filled with joy.	
	I open my arms wide	
	that I may embrace her.	
	My heart is as happy in	5
	my breast as a red fish	
	swimming in its pond.	
	O night, you are mine	
	forever, since my sister	
	has come in love to me.	10

———◆———

Girl	The Voice of the goose sounds forth	1
	as he's caught by the bait. Your love	
	ensnares me. I can't let it go.	
	I shall take home my nets,	
	but what shall I tell my mother,	5
	to whom I return every day	
	laden with lovely birds?	
	I set no traps today,	
	ensnared as I was by love.	

The Visual Arts

Egyptian art—at least that with which we are most familiar—comes almost exclusively from tombs and graves. Such art was not intended as decoration; rather, it was created to replicate the living world for the benefit of the dead. Stylistically, Egyptian art mirrors the deep sense of order and regularity that dominated ancient Egyptian life. Indeed, for 3,000 years, Egypt followed a set of conventions that dictated the manner in which subjects should be depicted. In representations of everyday life, figures are

[1]Meaning "mistress" or "lady."

usually sized according to a strict hierarchy, or graded order: Upper-class individuals are shown larger than lower-class ones, and males usually outsize females and servants (Figure 1.13). In monumental sculptures of royalty, however, the chief wife of the pharaoh is usually shown the same size as her husband (see Figure 1.5).

Very early in Egyptian history, artists developed a **canon** (or set of rules) by which to represent the human form. The proportions of the human body were determined according to a **module** (or standard of measurement) represented by the width of the clenched fist (Figure **1.21**). More generally, Egyptian artists adhered to a set of guidelines by which they might "capture" the most characteristic and essential aspects of the subject matter: In depicting the human figure the upper torso is shown from the front, while the lower is shown from the side; the head is depicted in profile, while the eye and eyebrow are frontal. This method of representation is *conceptual*—that is, based on ideas—rather than *perceptual*—that is, based on visual evidence. The conceptual approach represents a highly stylized record of reality.

The Egyptian approach to space was also conceptual. Spatial depth is indicated by placing one figure above (rather than behind) the next, often in horizontal registers, or rows. Cast in this timeless matrix, Egyptian figures shared the symbolic resonance of the hieroglyphs by which they are framed (see Figure 1.1). Nowhere else in the ancient world do we see such an intimate and intelligible conjunction of images and words—a union designed to immortalize ideas rather than imitate reality. This is not to say that Egyptian artists ignored the world of the senses.

Figure 1.21 The Egyptian canon of proportion.

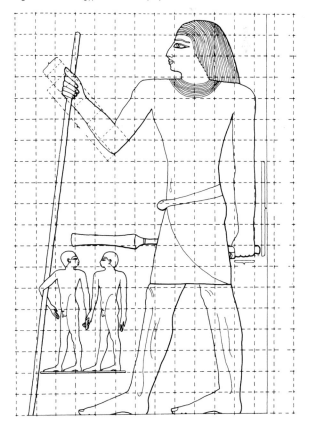

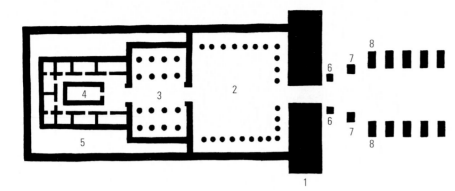

Figure 1.22 Plan of a typical pylon temple.

1 Pylon
2 Court
3 Hypostyle hall
4 Sanctuary
5 Girdle wall
6 Colossal statues of the pharaoh
7 Obelisks
8 Avenue of deities

Their love for realistic detail is evident, for example, in the hunting scene from the tomb of Neb-amon at Thebes, where fish and fowl are depicted with such extraordinary accuracy that individual species of each can be identified (see Figure 1.13). It is in the union of the particular and the general that Egyptian art achieves its defining quality.

New Kingdom Temples

Temples were built by the Egyptians from earliest times, but most of those that have survived date from the New Kingdom. The basic plan of the temple mirrored the central features of the Egyptian cosmos: the **pylons** (two truncated pyramids that made up the gateway) symbolized the mountains that rimmed the edge of the world, while the progress from the open courtyard through the **hypostyle** hall into the dark inner sanctuary housing the cult statue represented the voyage from light to darkness (and back) symbolic of the sun's cyclical journey (Figure **1.22**). Oriented on an east–west axis, the temple received the sun's morning rays, which reached through the sequence

Figure 1.23 Hypostyle Hall, Temple of Amon, Karnak, ca. 1220 B.C.E. Photo: Robert Harding Picture Library, London.

of hallways into the sanctuary. The Great Temple of Amon-Ra at Karnak was the heart of a five-acre religious complex that included a sacred lake, a sphinx-lined causeway, and numerous **obelisks** (commemorative stone pillars). The temple's hypostyle hall is adorned with painted reliefs that cover the walls and the surfaces of its 134 massive columns shaped like budding and flowering papyrus, the plants identified with the marsh of creation (Figure **1.23**). Decorated with stars and other celestial images, the ceiling of the hall symbolized the heavens. Such sacred precincts were not intended for communal assembly—in fact, commoners were forbidden to enter. Rather, Egyptian temples were sanctuaries in which priests performed daily rituals of cosmic renewal on behalf of the pharaoh and the people. Temple rituals were celebrations of the solar cycle, associated not only with the birth of the sun god but with the regeneration of the ruler upon whom cosmic order depended.

Music in Ancient Egypt

Tomb paintings reveal much about ancient Egyptian culture. They are, for example, our main source of information about ancient Egyptian music and dance. It is clear that song and poetry were interchangeable (hymns like that praising Aten were chanted, not spoken). Musical instruments, including harps, flutes, pipes, and sistrums (a type of rattle)—often found buried with the dead—accompanied song and dance. Greek sources indicate that Egyptian music was based in theory; nevertheless, we have no certain knowledge how that music actually sounded. Visual representations confirm, however, that music had a special place in religious rituals, in festive and funeral processions, and in many aspects of secular life (see Figure 1.20).

SUMMARY

Among ancient civilizations, nature and the natural environment influenced the formation of religious attitudes and beliefs. Egypt's relatively secure location, regular climate, and dependable Nile River encouraged a belief in a host of essentially benevolent nature deities, the most important of which were the gods of the sun and the Nile. The representative of the sun on earth, Egypt's theocratic monarch was accorded a burial befitting one who, after death, would work to ensure the well-being of his people. The belief in life after death, an expression of ancient Egypt's positive view of life, is evident in grave goods, tomb paintings, and hieroglyphic inscriptions, all of which manifest the artistic magnificence of ancient Egyptian civilization.

As elsewhere in the ancient world, the survival of the Egyptian community depended on cooperation among individuals with specialized responsibilities and tasks. It also depended on a shared view of the world as animated by the gods. Egypt's hierarchic social structure and its polytheistic belief system contributed to a deep sense of order. In the buoyant optimism of its poetry, the confident

imagery of its tomb paintings, and the cosmic symbolism of its temple architecture, we detect a basic trust in forces that are greater and more powerful than those of perishable humankind.

GLOSSARY

canon a set of rules or standards used to establish proportions

cosmology the theory of the origins, evolution, and structure of the universe

dynasty a sequence of rulers from the same family

fresco (Italian, "fresh") a method of painting on walls or ceilings surfaced with fresh, moist, lime plaster

hypostyle a hall whose roof is supported by columns

lyric literally "accompanied by the lyre," hence, verse that is meant to be sung rather than spoken; usually characterized by individual and personal emotion

module a unit of measurement used to determine proportion

monarch a single or sole ruler

obelisk a tall, four-sided pillar that tapers to a pyramidal apex

papyrus a reed-like plant from which the ancient Egyptians made paper

polytheism the belief in many gods

pylon a massive gateway in the form of a pair of truncated pyramids

relief a sculptural technique in which figures or forms are carved either to project from the background surface (raised relief) or cut away below the background level (sunk relief); the degree of relief is designated as high, low, or sunken

theocracy rule by god or god's representative

SUGGESTIONS FOR READING

Edwards, I. E. S. *The Pyramids of Egypt.* Baltimore: Penguin, 1986.

Frankfort, Henri, et al. *Before Philosophy.* Baltimore: Penguin, 1961.

Hodges, Peter. *How the Pyramids Were Built.* Lonmead: Element Books, 1989.

Johnson, Paul. *The Civilization of Ancient Egypt.* New York: HarperCollins, 1999.

Lehrer, Mark. *The Complete Pyramids.* London: Thames and Hudson, 1998.

Murray, M. S. *The Splendor That Was Egypt.* New York: Praeger, 1972.

Quirke, Stephen. *Ancient Egyptian Religion.* London: British Museum Press, 1992.

Robins, Gay. *Women in Ancient Egypt.* London: British Museum Press, 1993.

Taylor, John N. *Egypt and Nubia.* Cambridge, Mass.: Harvard University Press, 1991.

Tiradritti, Francesco, ed. *Egyptian Treasures from the Egyptian Museum in Cairo.* New York: Abrams, 1998.

Watterson, Barbara. *Women in Ancient Egypt.* New York: St. Martin's Press, 1992.

CHAPTER TWO

Mesopotamia: gods, rulers, and the social order

"From the days of old there is no permanence. The sleeping and the dead, how alike they are, they are like a painted death."
The Epic of Gilgamesh

Mesopotamia, literally "the land between the two rivers," describes the region in southwest Asia* that was the home of many civilizations over a period of 3,000 years. The earliest of these civilizations appeared around 3500 B.C.E. at Sumer, where the Tigris and Euphrates Rivers empty into the Persian Gulf (Map 2.1). Watered by these two rivers, the rich soil at the southeastern end of the Fertile Crescent made agricultural life possible and supported the growth of humankind's first cities—Uruk, Ur, Kish, Nippur, and Lagash. In contrast with the Nile River, which flooded its banks with comfortable regularity, the two rivers essential to food production in Mesopotamia overflowed unpredictably, often devastating whole villages and cities. Unlike Egypt, whose natural boundaries of desert and water worked to protect the civilization from

_____
Also known by Westerners as the "Near East."

foreign invasion, Mesopotamia's exposed and fertile plains invited the repeated attacks of tribal nomads, who descended from the mountainous regions north of the Fertile Crescent. And while Egypt's climate was regularly hot and dry, that of ancient Mesopotamia suffered fierce changes of weather, including drought, violent rainstorms, flood, wind, and hail. Mesopotamia's unpredictable rivers, vulnerable geographic situation, and erratic climate contributed to the mood of fear and insecurity that is reflected in all forms of Mesopotamian expression.

Mesopotamia was the stage on which many civilizations rose and fell. Some, like the Sumerian, formed small groups of city-states; others, like the Assyrian, founded great empires. And yet others, like the Hebrews, were tribal people who ultimately forged a political state. No one language or single, continuous form of government united these various Mesopotamian civilizations, yet they shared

Map 2.1 Southwest Asia (Near and Middle East)

a common world view and—with the exception of the Hebrews—a polytheistic religious outlook.

The Gods of Mesopotamia

As in ancient Egypt, Mesopotamia's gods and goddesses were associated with nature and its forces. However, like the environment of Mesopotamia, its gods were fierce and capricious (Figure 2.1), its mythology filled with physical and spiritual woe, and its cosmology based in the themes of chaos and conflict. *The Babylonian Creation*, humankind's earliest cosmological myth, illustrates all of these conditions. *The Babylonian Creation* is a Sumerian poem recorded early in the second millennium B.C.E. Recited during the festival of the New Year, it celebrates the birth of the gods and the order of creation. It describes a universe that originated by means of spontaneous generation: At a moment when there was neither heaven nor earth, the sweet and bitter waters "mingled" to produce the first family of gods. As the story unfolds, chaos and discord prevail amid the reign of Tiamat, the great goddess of the primeval waters, until Marduk, hero-god and offspring of Wisdom, takes matters in hand: He destroys the Great Mother and proceeds to establish a new order, bringing to an end the long and ancient tradition of matriarchy. Marduk founds the holy city of Babylon (literally, "home of the gods") and creates human beings, whose purpose it is to serve heaven's squabbling divinities.

READING 1.5 From *The Babylonian Creation*

When there was no heaven,	1
no earth, no height, no depth, no name,	
when Apsu[1] was alone,	
the sweet water, the first begetter; and Tiamat[2]	
the bitter water, and that	5
return to the womb, her Mummu,[3]	
when there were no gods —	
When sweet and bitter	
mingled together, no reed was plaited, no rushes	
muddied the water,	10
the gods were nameless, natureless, futureless, then	
from Apsu and Tiamat	
in the waters gods were created, in the waters	
silt precipitated,	
Lahmu and Lahamu,[4]	15
were named; they were not yet old,	
not yet grown tall	

---

[1]The primeval sweet waters.
[2]The primeval bitter waters.
[3]One of the primordial beings of the universe.
[4]Male and female primordial beings.

Name	Role
Adad	storm and rain god
Anu	father of the gods, god of heaven
Apsu	god of the primeval sweet waters
Dumuzi (Tammuz)	god of vegetation, fertility and the underworld; husband of Ishtar
Ea	god of wisdom and patron of the arts
Enlil	god of earth, wind, and air
Ishtar (Innana)	goddess of love, fertility, and war; Queen of Heaven
Ninhursag	mother goddess, creator of vegetation; wife of Enlil
Nisaba	goddess of grain
Shamash	god of the sun; judge and law-giver; god of wisdom
Sin (Nanna)	goddess of the moon

Figure 2.1 Principal Mesopotamian Gods

when Anshar and Kishar[5] overtook them both,	
the lines of sky and earth	
stretched where horizons meet to separate	20
cloud from silt.	
Days on days, years	
on years passed till Anu,[6] the empty heaven,	
heir and supplanter,	
first-born of his father, in his own nature	25
begot of Nudimmud-Ea[7]	
intellect, wisdom, wider than heaven's horizon,	
the strongest of all the kindred.	
Discord broke out among the gods although they were	
brothers, warring and jarring in the belly of Tiamat,	30
heaven shook, it reeled with the surge of the dance.	
Apsu could not silence the clamour. Their behaviour was	
bad, overbearing, and proud. . . .	

[Ea kills Apsu; Marduk is born and Tiamat spawns serpents and monsters to make war on the gods.]

When her labour of creation was ended, against her children	1
Tiamat began preparations of war. This was the evil she did to	
requite Apsu, this was the evil news that came to Ea.	

When he had learned how matters lay he was stunned, he sat in black silence till rage had worked itself out; then he remembered the gods before him. He went to Anshar, his father's father, and told him how Tiamat plotted,

'She loathes us, father, our mother Tiamat has raised up	
that Company, she rages in turbulence and all have joined her,	
all those gods whom you begot,	10

---

[5]The horizon of the sky (male) and the horizon of the earth (female).
[6]God of the sky (the offspring of Anshar and Kishar).
[7]Another name for Ea, god of wisdom (the offspring of Anu).

'Together they jostle the ranks to march with Tiamat, day and night furiously they plot, the growling roaring rout, ready for battle, while the Old Hag, the first mother, mothers a new brood. . . .'

[The gods make Marduk Supreme Commander of the wars; he leads the attack on Tiamat.]

Then Marduk made a bow and strung it to be his own weapon, **1**
he set the arrow against the bow-string, in his right hand he grasped the mace and lifted it up, bow and quiver hung at his side, lightnings played in front of him, he was altogether an incandescence.

He netted a net, a snare for Tiamat; the winds from their quarters held it, south wind, north, east wind, west, and no part of Tiamat could escape. . . .

He turned back to where Tiamat lay bound, he straddled the legs and smashed her skull (for the mace was merciless), he **10**
severed the arteries and the blood streamed down the north wind to the unknown ends of the world.

When the gods saw all this they laughed out loud, and they sent him presents. They sent him their thankful tributes.

The lord rested; he gazed at the huge body, pondering how to use it, what to create from the dead carcass. He split it apart like a cockle-shell; with the upper half he constructed the arc of sky, he pulled down the bar and set a watch on the waters, so they should never escape. . . .

[Marduk makes Babylon "the home of the gods" and proceeds **20**
to create Man.]

Now that Marduk has heard what it is the gods are saying, he is moved with desire to create a work of consummate art. He told Ea the deep thought in his heart.

> Blood to blood
> I join,
> blood to bone
> I form
> an original thing,
> its name is MAN, **30**
> aboriginal man
> is mine in making.
>
> All his occupations
> are faithful service,
> the gods that fell
> have rest,
> I will subtly alter
> their operations,
> divided companies
> equally blest. **40**

Ea answered with carefully chosen words, completing the plan for the gods' comfort. He said to Marduk,
"Let one of the kindred be taken; only one need die for the new creation. Bring the gods together in the Great Assembly; there let the guilty die, so the rest may live."

. . . .

The Search for Immortality

The theme of human vulnerability and the search for ever-lasting life are the central motifs in the *Epic of Gilgamesh*, the world's first epic. An **epic**, that is, a long narrative poem that recounts the deeds of a hero in quest of meaning and identity, embodies the ideals and values of the culture from which it comes. The *Epic of Gilgamesh* was

Figure 2.2 Gilgamesh between Two Human-Headed Bulls (top portion). Soundbox of a Harp, from Ur, Iraq, ca. 2600 B.C.E. Wood with inlaid gold, lapis lazuli, and shell, height approx. 12 in. The University Museum, University of Pennsylvania, Philadelphia (Neg. #T4–109).

recited orally for centuries before it was recorded at Sumer in the late third millennium. As literature, it precedes the Hebrew Bible and all the other major writings of antiquity. Its hero is a semi-historical figure who probably ruled the ancient Sumerian city of Uruk around 2800 B.C.E. Described as two-thirds god and one-third man, Gilgamesh is blessed by the gods with beauty and courage. But when he spurns the affections of the Queen of Heaven, Ishtar (a fertility goddess not unlike the Egyptian Isis), he is punished with the loss of his dearest companion, Enkidu. Despairing over Enkidu's death, Gilgamesh undertakes a long and hazardous quest in search of everlasting life. He meets Utnapishtim, a mortal whom the gods have rewarded with eternal life for having saved humankind from a devastating flood. Utnapishtim helps Gilgamesh locate the plant that miraculously restores lost youth. But ultimately, a serpent snatches the plant, and Gilgamesh is left with the haunting vision of death as "a house of dust" and a place of inescapable sadness. On the soundbox of a harp found in the royal graves at Ur, Gilgamesh is depicted standing between two human-headed bulls, while some of the epic's fantastic characters, such as the Man-Scorpion, appear in the registers below (Figure 2.2). The Great Harp itself (Figure 2.3) may have been used to accompany the chanting of this epic.

READING 1.6 From the Epic *of Gilgamesh*

O Gilgamesh, Lord of Kullab,[1] great is thy praise. This was   **1**
the man to whom all things were known; this was the king
who knew the countries of the world. He was wise, he saw
mysteries and knew secret things, he brought us a tale of the
days before the flood. He went on a long journey, was weary,
worn-out with labor, and returning engraved on a stone the
whole story.

When the Gods created Gilgamesh they gave him a perfect
body. Shamash the glorious sun endowed him with beauty,
Adad the god of the storm endowed him with courage, the   **10**
great gods made his beauty perfect, surpassing all others. Two
thirds they made him god and one third man.

In Uruk[2] he built walls, a great rampart, and the temple of
blessed Eanna for the god of the firmament Anu, and for Ishtar
the goddess of love.[3]

[Gilgamesh and his bosom companion, Enkidu, destroy
Humbaba, the guardian of the cedar forest, and perform other
heroic deeds. But Gilgamesh spurns the affections of Ishtar,
and in revenge, she takes Enkidu's life.]

Bitterly Gilgamesh wept for his friend Enkidu; he wandered
over the wilderness as a hunter, he roamed over the plains; in
his bitterness he cried, "How can I rest, how can I be at
peace? Despair is in my heart. What my brother is now, that

---

[1]Park of Uruk.
[2]A city located in Sumer. Gilgamesh was the fifth ruler in the Dynasty of Uruk after the flood.
[3]Also associated with fertility and war.

Figure 2.3 Lyre (reconstructed) from Ur, ca. 2600 B.C.E. Wood and inlays of gold, lapis lazuli and shell. Height 42 in. British Museum, London.

shall I be when I am dead. Because I am afraid of death I will   20
go as best I can to find Utnapishtim whom they call the
Faraway, for he has entered the assembly of the gods." So
Gilgamesh traveled over the wilderness, he wandered over the
grasslands, a long journey, in search of Utnapishtim, whom the
gods took after the deluge; and they set him to live in the land
of Dilmun,[4] in the garden of the sun; and to him alone of men
they gave everlasting life.

At night when he came to the mountain passes Gilgamesh
prayed: "In these mountain passes long ago I saw lions, I was
afraid and I lifted my eyes to the moon; I prayed and my   30
prayers went up to the gods, so now, O moon god Sin, protect
me." When he had prayed he lay down to sleep, until he was
woken from out of a dream. He saw the lions round him
glorying in life; then he took his axe in his hand, he drew his
sword from his belt, and struck and destroyed and scattered
them.

So at length Gilgamesh came to that great mountain whose
name is Mashu, the mountain which guards the rising and the
setting sun. Its twin peaks are as high as the wall of heaven
and its paps reach down to the underworld. At its gate the   40
Scorpions stand guard, half man and half dragon; their glory is
terrifying, their stare strikes death into men, their shimmering
halo sweeps the mountains that guard the rising sun. When
Gilgamesh saw them he shielded his eyes for the length of a
moment only; then he took courage and approached. When
they saw him so undismayed the Man-Scorpion called to his
mate, "This one who comes to us now is flesh of the gods."
The mate of the Man-Scorpion answered, "Two thirds is god
but one third is man."

Then he called to the man Gilgamesh, he called to the child   50
of the gods: "Why have you come so great a journey; for what
have you traveled so far, crossing the dangerous waters; tell
me the reason for your coming?" Gilgamesh answered, "For
Enkidu; I loved him dearly, together we endured all kinds of
hardships; on his account I have come, for the common lot of
man has taken him. I have wept for him day and night, I would
not give up his body for burial, I thought my friend would come
back because of my weeping. Since he went, my life is
nothing; that is why I have traveled here in search of
Utnapishtim my father; for men say he has entered the   60
assembly of the gods, and has found everlasting life. I have a
desire to question him concerning the living and the dead."
The Man-Scorpion opened his mouth and said, speaking to
Gilgamesh, "No man born of woman has done what you have
asked, no mortal man has gone into the mountain; the length
of it is twelve leagues[5] of darkness; in it there is no light, but
the heart is oppressed with darkness. From the rising of the
sun to the setting of the sun there is no light." Gilgamesh said,
"Although I should go in sorrow and in pain, with sighing and
with weeping, still I must go. Open the gate of the mountain."   70
And the Man-Scorpion said, "Go, Gilgamesh, I permit you to
pass through the mountain of Mashu and through the high
ranges; may your feet carry you safely home. The gate of the
mountain is open."

When Gilgamesh heard this he did as the Man-Scorpion had
said, he followed the sun's road to his rising, through the
mountain. When he had gone one league the darkness
became thick around him, for there was no light, he could see
nothing ahead and nothing behind him. After two leagues the
darkness was thick and there was no light, he could see   80
nothing ahead and nothing behind him. After three leagues the
darkness was thick, and there was no light, he could see
nothing ahead and nothing behind him. After four leagues the
darkness was thick and there was no light, he could see
nothing ahead and nothing behind him. At the end of five
leagues the darkness was thick and there was no light, he
could see nothing ahead and nothing behind him. At the end
of six leagues the darkness was thick and there was no light,
he could see nothing ahead and nothing behind him. When he
had gone seven leagues the darkness was thick and there was   90
no light, he could see nothing ahead and nothing behind him.
When he had gone eight leagues Gilgamesh gave a great cry,
for the darkness was thick and he could see nothing ahead
and nothing behind him. After nine leagues he felt the north
wind on his face, but the darkness was thick and there was no
light, he could see nothing ahead and nothing behind him.
After ten leagues the end was near. After eleven leagues the
dawn light appeared. At the end of twelve leagues the sun
streamed out.

There was the garden of the gods; all round him stood   100
bushes bearing gems. Seeing it he went down at once, for
there was fruit of carnelian with the vine hanging from it,
beautiful to look at; lapis lazuli leaves hung thick with fruit,
sweet to see. For thorns and thistles there were hematite and
rare stones, agate, and pearls from out of the sea. While
Gilgamesh walked in the garden by the edge of the sea
Shamash[6] saw him, and he saw that he was dressed in the
skins of animals and ate their flesh. He was distressed, and he
spoke and said, "No mortal man has gone this way before, nor
will, as long as the winds drive over the sea." And to   110
Gilgamesh he said, "You will never find the life for which you
are searching." Gilgamesh said to glorious Shamash, "Now
that I have toiled and strayed so far over the wilderness, am I
to sleep, and let the earth cover my head forever? Let my eyes
see the sun until they are dazzled with looking. Although I am
no better than a dead man, still let me see the light of the
sun."

[Gilgamesh meets Siduri, the maker of wine, who advises him
to give up his search and value more highly the good things of
the earth. Gilgamesh prepares to cross the Ocean and, with
the help of the ferryman Urshanabi, finally reaches Dilmun, the
home of Utnapishtim.]

"Oh, father Utnapishtim, you who have entered the
assembly of the gods, I wish to question you concerning the
living and the dead, how shall I find the life for which I am   120
searching?"

Utnapishtim said, "There is no permanence. Do we build a
house to stand for ever, do we seal a contract to hold for all
time? Do brothers divide an inheritance to keep for ever, does

---

[4]The Sumerian paradise, a mythical land resembling the Garden of
Eden described in the Hebrew Bible.
[5]Approximately 36 miles.

---

[6]The Semitic sun god.

the flood-time of rivers endure? It is only the nymph of the dragon-fly who sheds her larva and sees the sun in his glory. From the days of old there is no permanence. The sleeping and the dead, how alike they are, they are like a painted death. What is there between the master and the servant when both have fulfilled their doom? When the Annunaki, the judges, come together, and Mammetun the mother of destinies, together they decree the fates of men. Life and death they allot but the day of death they do not disclose."

Then Gilgamesh said to Utnapishtim the Faraway, "I look at you now, Utnapishtim, and your appearance is no different from mine; there is nothing strange in your features. I thought I should find you like a hero prepared for battle, but you lie here taking your ease on your back. Tell me truly, how was it that you came to enter the company of the gods and to possess everlasting life?" Utnapishtim said to Gilgamesh, "I will reveal to you a mystery, I will tell you a secret of the gods."

[Utnapishtim relates the story of the flood.]

In those days the world teemed, the people multiplied, the world bellowed like a wild bull, and the great god was aroused by the clamor. Enlil heard the clamor and he said to the gods in council, "The uproar of mankind is intolerable and sleep is no longer possible by reason of the babel." So the gods in their hearts were moved to let loose the deluge; but my lord Ea warned me in a dream. He whispered their words to my house of reeds. . . . "Tear down your house, I say, and build a boat. These are the measurements of the barque as you shall build her: let her beam equal her length, let her deck be roofed like the vault that covers the abyss; then take up into the boat the seed of all living creatures. . . ."

For six days and six nights the winds blew, torrent and tempest and flood overwhelmed the world, tempest and flood raged together like warring hosts. When the seventh day dawned the storm from the south subsided, the sea grew calm, the flood was stilled; I looked at the face of the world and there was silence, all mankind was turned to clay. The surface of the sea stretched as flat as a roof-top; I opened a hatch and the light fell on my face. Then I bowed low, I sat down and I wept, the tears streamed down my face, for on every side was the waste of water.

[Utnapishtim leads Gilgamesh to Urshanabi the Ferryman.]

Then Gilgamesh and Urshanabi launched the boat on to the water and boarded it, and they made ready to sail away; but the wife of Utnapishtim the Faraway said to him, "Gilgamesh came here wearied out, he is worn out; what will you give him to carry him back to his own country?" So Utnapishtim spoke, and Gilgamesh took a pole and brought the boat in to the bank. "Gilgamesh, you came here a man wearied out, you have worn yourself out; what shall I give you to carry you back to your own country? Gilgamesh, I shall reveal a secret thing, it is a mystery of the gods that I am telling you. There is a plant that grows under the water, it has a prickle like a thorn, like a rose; it will wound your hands, but if you succeed in taking it, then your hands will hold that which restores his lost youth to a man."

When Gilgamesh heard this he opened the sluices so that a sweet-water current might carry him out to the deepest channel; he tied heavy stones to his feet and they dragged him down to the water-bed. There he saw the plant growing; although it pricked him he took it in his hands; then he cut the heavy stones from his feet, and the sea carried him and threw him on the shore. Gilgamesh said to Urshanabi the ferryman, "Come here, and see this marvelous plant. By its virtue a man may win back all his former strength. I will take it to Uruk of the strong walls; there I will give it to the old to eat. Its name shall be 'the Old Men are Young Again'; and at last I shall eat it myself and have back all my lost youth." So Gilgamesh returned by the gate through which he had come, Gilgamesh and Urshanabi went together. They traveled their twenty leagues and then they broke their fast; after thirty leagues they stopped for the night.

Gilgamesh saw a well of cool water and he went down and bathed; but deep in the pool there was lying a serpent,[7] and the serpent sensed the sweetness of the flower. It rose out of the water and snatched it away, and immediately it sloughed its skin and returned to the well. Then Gilgamesh sat down and wept, the tears ran down his face, and he took the hand of Urshanabi; "O Urshanabi, was it for this that I toiled with my hands, is it for this I have wrung out my heart's blood? For myself I have gained nothing; not I, but the beast of the earth has joy of it now. Already the stream has carried it twenty leagues back to the channels where I found it. I found a sign and now I have lost it. Let us leave the boat on the bank and go."

. . . .

The *Epic of Gilgamesh* is important not only as the world's first epic poem, but also as the earliest known literary work that tries to come to terms with death, or non-being. It reflects the profound human need for an immortality ideology—a body of beliefs that anticipates the survival of some aspect of the self in a life hereafter. Typical of the mythic hero, Gilgamesh seeks to understand and control the unknown. He is driven to discover his human limits, but his quest for personal immortality is frustrated and his goals remain unfulfilled. In the uncertainty of its conclusions, the *Epic of Gilgamesh* stands in stark contrast with Egyptian writings, which confidently celebrate the promise of life after death.

The Rulers of Mesopotamia

The area collectively known as Sumer was a loosely knit group of city-states, that is, urban centers that governed the neighboring countryside. Here, men and women produced humankind's earliest Bronze Age technology and refined the cuneiform script that became the first written language. In each of the city-states of Sumer, individual priest-kings ruled as agents of one or another of the gods. The priest-king led the army, regulated the supply and

---

[7]More literally "earth lion" or "chameleon."

distribution of food, and provided political and religious leadership. From the temple at his palace, he conducted the services that were designed to win the favor of the gods.

Disunited and generally rivalrous, the city-states of Sumer were vulnerable to invasion from tribal warriors

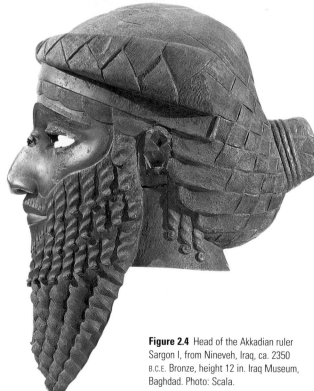

Figure 2.4 Head of the Akkadian ruler Sargon I, from Nineveh, Iraq, ca. 2350 B.C.E. Bronze, height 12 in. Iraq Museum, Baghdad. Photo: Scala.

to the north. Around 2350 B.C.E. a gifted Akkadian warlord named Sargon I (Figure **2.4**) conquered the city-states of Sumer and united them under his command. Consolidating a variety of peoples and language groups under his administration, Sargon created the world's first **empire**. By 2000 B.C.E., however, Sargon's empire fell to the attacks of nomadic tribespeople from the north. The invaders—establishing the pattern that dominated all of Mesopotamian history—built on the accomplishments of the very states they conquered. So, theocratic monarchy, religious polytheism, a socialistic economy, and established traditions of trade and barter would prevail from civilization to civilization. The myths and legends, indeed the *Epic of Gilgamesh* itself, would be transmitted from century to century to be transcribed in ever more refined versions of cuneiform script.

The Social Order

In the newly formed civilizations of the ancient world, community life demanded collective effort in matters of production and distribution, as well as in the irrigation of fields and the construction of roads, temples, palaces, and military defenses. As in Egypt, specialization of labor and the demands of urban life encouraged the development of social classes with different kinds of training, different responsibilities, and different types of authority. In early civilizations, the magician-priest who prepared the wine in the ritual vessel, the soldier who protected the city, and the farmer who cultivated the field represented fairly distinct classes of people with unique duties and responsibilities to society as a whole. The social order and division of labor that prevailed in Mesopotamia around 2700 B.C.E. are depicted in the "Standard of Ur," a wooden panel found in the royal tombs excavated at the city of Ur (Figure **2.5**). The double-sided panel, executed in shell, mother-of-pearl, and lapis lazuli, appears to commemorate a Sumerian victory. On one side, in the top and middle registers, the ruler and his soldiers are seen taking prisoners after a battle; the bottom register depicts part of the battle itself with horse-drawn chariots trampling the defeated. On the reverse side of the panel, the ruler and six high officials of the Sumerian community lift their goblets at a celebratory banquet where the entertainers include a harpist and his female companion (top register, far right). The two lower registers record the procession of bearers with cows, rams, fish, and tribute in the form of various bundles carried on the backs of foreigners, probably prisoners of war. Although the precise function of this object is unknown, the Standard of Ur provides a mirror of class divisions in Mesopotamia of the third millennium B.C.E.

Law and the Social Order in Babylon

Shortly after 2000 B.C.E., rulers of the city-state of Babylon unified the neighboring territories of Sumer to establish the first Babylonian empire. In an effort to unite these regions politically and provide them with effective leadership, Babylon's sixth ruler, Hammurabi, called for a sys-

Figure 2.5 The Standard of Ur, ca. 2700 B.C.E. Double-sided panel inlaid with shell, lapis lazuli, and red limestone, approx. 8 x 19 in. Reproduced by courtesy of the Trustees of the British Museum, London.

tematic codification of existing legal practices. He sent out envoys to collect the local statutes and had them consolidated into a single body of law. Hammurabi's Code—a collection of 282 clauses engraved on an 8-foot-high stele—is our most valuable index to life in ancient Mesopotamia (Figure 2.6). The Code is not the first example of recorded law among the Babylonian kings; it is, however, the most extensive and comprehensive set of laws to survive from ancient times. Although Hammurabi's Code addressed primarily secular matters, it bore the force of divine decree. This fact is indicated in the prologue to the Code, where Hammurabi claims descent from the gods. It is also manifested visually in the low-relief carving at the top of the stele: Here, in a scene that calls to mind the story of the biblical Moses on Mount Sinai, Hammurabi is pictured receiving the law (symbolized by a staff) from the

sun god Shamash. Wearing a conical crown topped with bull's horns, and discharging flames from his shoulders, the god sits enthroned atop a sacred mountain, symbolized by triangular markings beneath his feet.

Written law represented a significant advance in the development of human rights in that it protected the individual from the capricious decisions of monarchs. Unwritten law was subject to the hazards of memory and the eccentricities of the powerful. Written law, on the other hand, permitted a more impersonal (if more objective and impartial) kind of justice than did oral law. It replaced the flexibility of the spoken word with the rigidity of the written word. It did not usually recognize exceptions and was not easily or quickly changed. Ultimately, recorded law shifted the burden of judgment from the individual ruler to the legal establishment. Although written (clauses 162 and 168), professional obligations (clauses 218, 219, 229, and 232), and the individual's responsibilities to the community (clauses 109 and 152). It also documents the fact that under Babylonian law, individuals were not regarded as equals. Human worth was defined in terms of a person's wealth and status in society. Violence committed by one free person upon another was punished reciprocally (clause 196), but the same violence committed upon a lower-class individual drew considerably lighter punishment (clause 198), and penalties were reduced even further if the victim was a slave (clause 199). Similarly, a principle of "pay according to status" was applied in punishing thieves (clause 8): The upper-class thief was more heavily penalized or fined than the lower-class one. A thief who could not pay at all fell into slavery or was put to death. Slaves, whether captives of war or victims of debt, had no civil rights under law and enjoyed only the protection of the household to which they belonged.

In Babylonian society, women were considered intellectually and physically inferior to men and—much like slaves—were regarded as the personal property of the male head of the household. A woman went from her father's house to that of her husband, where she was expected to bear children (clause 138). Nevertheless, as indicated by the Code, women enjoyed commercial freedom (clause 109) and considerable legal protection (clause 134, 138, 209, and 210), their value as childbearers and housekeepers clearly acknowledged. Clause 142 is an astonishingly early example of no-fault divorce: Since a husband's neglect of his spouse was not punishable, neither party to the marriage was legally "at fault."

READING 1.7   From the Code of Hammurabi

(ca. 1750 B.C.E.)

. . . Hammurabi, the shepherd, named by Enlil am I, who increased plenty and abundance. The ancient seed of royalty, the powerful king, the sun of Babylon, who caused light to go forth over the lands of Sumer and Akkad . . . the favorite of Innana [Ishtar] am I. When Marduk sent me to rule the people and to bring help to the land, I established law and justice in the language of the land and promoted the welfare of the people.

Clause 8 If a man has stolen an ox, or sheep or an ass, or a pig or a goat, either from a god or a palace, he shall pay thirty-fold. If he is a plebeian,[1] he shall render ten-fold. If the thief has nothing to pay, he shall be slain.
14 If a man has stolen a man's son under age, he shall be slain.
109 If rebels meet in the house of a wine-seller and she does not seize them and take them to the palace, that wine-seller shall be slain.
129 If the wife of a man is found lying with another male, they shall be bound and thrown into the water; unless the

Figure 2.6 Stele of Hammurabi, ca. 1760 B.C.E. Babylonian. Basalt, entire stele approx. 7ft. 4 in. Louvre, Paris. Photo: RMN.

law necessarily restricted individual freedom, it safe-guarded the basic values of the community.

Hammurabi's Code covers a broad spectrum of moral, social, and commercial obligations. Its civil and criminal statutes specify penalties for murder, theft, incest, adultery, kidnapping, assault and battery, and many other crimes. More important for our understanding of ancient culture, it is a storehouse of information concerning the nature of class divisions, family relations, and human rights. The Code informs us, for instance, on matters of inheritance

---

[1]A member of the lower class, probably a peasant who worked the land for the ruling class.

husband lets his wife live, and the king lets his servant live.

134 If a man has been taken prisoner, and there is no food in his house, and his wife enters the house of another; then that woman bears no blame.

138 If a man divorces his spouse who has not borne him children, he shall give to her all the silver of the bride-price, and restore to her the dowry which she brought from the house of her father; and so he shall divorce her.

141 If a man's wife, dwelling in a man's house, has set her face to leave, has been guilty of dissipation, has wasted her house, and has neglected her husband; then she shall be prosecuted. If her husband says she is divorced, he shall let her go her way; he shall give her nothing for divorce. If her husband says she is not divorced, her husband may espouse another woman, and that woman shall remain a slave in the house of her husband.

142 If a woman hate her husband, and says "Thou shalt not possess me," the reason for her dislike shall be inquired into. If she is careful and has no fault, but her husband takes himself away and neglects her; then that woman is not to blame. She shall take her dowry and go back to her father's house.

143 If she has not been careful, but runs out, wastes her house and neglects her husband; then that woman shall be thrown into the water.

152 If, after that woman has entered the man's house, they incur debt, both of them must satisfy the trader.

154 If a man has known his daughter, that man shall be banished from his city.

157 If a man after his father has lain in the breasts of his mother, both of them shall be burned.

162 If a man has married a wife, and she has borne children, and that woman has gone to her fate; then her father has no claim upon her dowry. The dowry is her children's.

168 If a man has set his face to disown his son, and has said to the judge, "I disown my son," then the judge shall look into his reasons. If the son has not borne a heavy crime which would justify his being disowned from filiation, then the father shall not disown his son from filiation.

195 If a son has struck his father, his hand shall be cut off.

196 If a man has destroyed the eye of a free man,[2] his own eye shall be destroyed.

198 If he has destroyed the eye of a plebeian, or broken the bone of a plebeian, he shall pay one mina[3] of silver.

199 If he has destroyed the eye of a man's slave, or broken the bone of a man's slave, he shall pay half his value.

209 If a man strike the daughter of a free man, and causes her foetus to fall; he shall pay ten shekels[4] of silver for her foetus.

210 If that woman die, his daughter shall be slain.

213 If he has struck the slave of a man, and made her foetus fall; he shall pay two shekels of silver.

214 If that slave die, he shall pay a third of a mina of silver.

---

[2]Above the lower-class peasant, the free man who rented land owed only a percentage of the produce to the ruling class.

[3]A monetary unit equal to approximately one pound of silver.

[4]60 shekels = 1 mina.

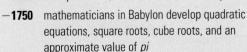

−1800	multiplication tables are devised in Babylon
−1750	mathematicians in Babylon develop quadratic equations, square roots, cube roots, and an approximate value of *pi*
−1700	windmills are employed for irrigation in Babylon

All dates in this chapter are approximate; − (minus) signifies B.C.E.

218 If a doctor has treated a man with a metal knife for a severe wound, and has caused the man to die, or has opened a man's tumor with a metal knife, and destroyed the man's eye; his hands shall be cut off.

219 If a doctor has treated a slave of a plebeian with a metal knife for a severe wound, and caused him to die he shall render slave for slave.

229 If a builder has built a house for a man, and his work is not strong, and if the house he has built falls in and kills the householder, that builder shall be slain.

232 If goods have been destroyed, he shall replace all that has been destroyed; and because the house that he built was not made strong, and it has fallen in, he shall restore the fallen house out of his own personal property.

282 If a slave shall say to his master, "Thou are not my master," he shall be prosecuted as a slave, and his owner shall cut off his ear.

The Arts in Mesopotamia

Although not as elaborate as the tombs of the Egyptians, the royal graves found at Ur and elsewhere in Mesopotamia have yielded artifacts of great beauty. Jewelry, weapons, household goods, and musical instruments testify to the wealth of Mesopotamia's princely rulers (see Figures 2.2 and 2.3). Rather than building elaborate homes for the dead, however, the inhabitants of Sumer and Babylon raised structures that might bring them closer to heaven. The **ziggurat**—a massive terraced tower made of rubble and brick—symbolized the sacred mountain linking the realms of heaven and earth (Figure 2.7). Ascended by a steep stairway, it provided a platform for sanctuaries dedicated to local deities and tended by priests and priestesses. Unlike the Egyptian pyramid, which functioned as a tomb, the ziggurat served as a shrine and temple. Hence, it formed the spiritual center of the city-state. Striking similarities exist between the ziggurats of Mesopotamia and the stepped platform pyramids of ancient Mexico, built somewhat later (Figure 2.8). Erected atop rubble mounds much like the Mesopotamian ziggurat, the temples of Meso-America functioned as solar observatories, religious sanctuaries, and gravesites. Whether or not any historical link exists between these Mesopotamian and the structurally similar Native American monuments remains among the many mysteries of ancient history.

In the shrine rooms located some 250 feet atop the ziggurat, local priests stored clay tablets inscribed with

Figure 2.7 Ziggurat at Ur (partially reconstructed), Third Dynasty of Ur, Iraq, ca. 2150–2050 B.C.E. © Hirmer Fotoarchiv.

cuneiform records of the city's economic activities, its religious customs, and its rites. The shrine room of the ziggurat at Tell Asmar in Sumer also housed a remarkable group of statues representing men and women of various sizes, with large, staring eyes and hands clasped across their chests (Figure **2.9**). Carved out of soft stone, these cult images may represent the gods, but it is more likely that they are votive (devotional) figures that represent the townspeople of Tell Asmar in the act of worshipping their local deities. The larger figures may be priests, and the smaller figures, laypersons. Rigid and attentive, they stand as if in perpetual prayer. Their enlarged eyes, inlaid with shell and black limestone convey the impression of dread and awe, visual testimony to the sense of human apprehension in the face of divine power. These images do not share the buoyant confident of the Egyptians; rather, they convey the insecurities of a people whose vulnerability was an ever-present fact of life.

The Hebrews

While the civilizations of the Fertile Crescent established the cultural roots of the ancient world, a small group of Mesopotamians known as the Hebrews formulated a lasting contribution to the humanistic tradition in the form of ethical monotheism. Almost everything we know about the Hebrew people comes from the Bible—the word derives from the Greek *biblia*, meaning "books." Nevertheless, the archeology of the Near East offers considerable information by which we may reconstruct the history of the Hebrews before the formation of their first political state around 1000 B.C.E. The tribal people called by their neighbors "Hebrews" originated in Sumer. Some time after 2000 B.C.E., under the leadership of Abraham of Ur, they migrated westward across the Fertile Crescent and settled in Canaan along the Mediterranean Sea (see Map 2.1). In Canaan, according to the Book of Genesis, Abraham received God's word that his descendants would return to that land and become a "great nation." God's promise to Abraham established the Hebrew claim to the land of Canaan (modern-day Israel). At the same time, a special bond between God and the Hebrews ("I will be your God; you will be my people," Genesis 17:7–8) marked the beginning of the Hebrew belief that they were God's Chosen (or Holy) People.

Some time after 1700 B.C.E., the Hebrews migrated into Egypt, but falling subject to pharaohic efforts to rid Egypt of the Hyksos, they were reduced to the status of state slaves. Around 1300 B.C.E., under a dynamic leader named Moses, they departed Egypt and headed back toward Canaan.

Figure 2.8 Pyramid of the Magician, Uxmal, Yucatan, late classic Maya, ca. 550–900 C.E. Photo: Werner Forman, London.

Figure 2.9 Statuettes from the Abu Temple, Tell Asmar, Iraq, ca. 2900–2600 B.C.E. Marble, tallest figure ca. 30 in. The Iraq Museum, Baghdad, and The Oriental Institute, University of Chicago.

This event became the basis for Exodus (literally, "going out"), the second book of the Hebrew Bible. Since Canaan was now occupied by local tribes with sizable military strength, the Hebrews settled briefly in an arid region near the Dead Sea. During a forty-year period—which archeologists place sometime between 1300 and 1150 B.C.E.—the Hebrews forged the fundamentals of their faith: **monotheism** (the belief in one and only one god); a set of ethical and spiritual obligations; and a **covenant** (or contract) that bound the Hebrew community to God in return for God's protection. The covenant rested in a set of ten laws (the Decalogue), which defined the proper relationship between God and the faithful, as well as between and among all members of the Hebrew community. The "Ten Commandments," like the testimonials of the Egyptian *Book of the Dead*, are framed in the negative. The consequence for the violation of each law is unspecified. The Hebrew god provides no prophecy of hell and damnation and no heavenly reward for obedience; only the terrible warning (Exodus 20:5) to those who do not "keep the commandments:" Their children will suffer "to the third and fourth generation."

Hebrew monotheism focused on devotion to a single Supreme Being, the god that came to be called Yahweh*

(in Latin, Jehovah). The idea of a single creator-god appeared as well in Egypt around 1350 B.C.E., when the pharaoh Amenhotep IV (Akhenaten) made the sun god Aten the sole deity of Egypt (see chapter 1). Like other ancient gods and goddesses, Aten was an arbitrary force associated with a specific natural phenomenon: the sun. The Hebrew deity, on the other hand, transcended nature and all natural phenomena. As Supreme Creator, the Hebrew god preceded the physical universe. Whereas in Babylonian myth the universe is spontaneously generated and initially chaotic, the Hebrew Creation describes a universe that is systematically planned and invested with a preconceived moral order; it is the miraculous feat of a single benevolent, all-knowing Being. In contrast to the Babylonian universe, where squabbling gods require human beings as their servants, the Hebrew universe is the gift given by God, its creator, to God's supreme creation: humankind. Hebrew monotheism stands apart from other ancient conceptions of divine power (including that of Akhenaten's Aten) in yet another essential dimension: its ethical charge. The veneration of Yahweh as the source of

---

*An acronym based on four Hebrew letters used to represent the Divine Name.

and guide for an ethical life was unique to the Hebrew faith. Ethical monotheism, the belief in a moral system that derives from a sole, omnipotent God, became the most lasting of the Hebrew contributions to world culture.

The excerpts below belong to the Hebrew Bible, a collection of stories and songs passed down orally for hundreds of years. The first five books of the Bible, known as the **Torah** (literally "instruction"), were assembled from four main sources some time during the tenth century B.C.E. Parts of Genesis, the first book of the Torah, belong to a common pool of traditions rooted in Mesopotamia, where the Hebrews originated; so the story of the Flood, for instance, appears in both Genesis and the *Epic of Gilgamesh* (as well as in other Mesopotamian texts). Two groups of laws are represented below: the first, whose penalties are unspecified, constitute the unconditional law of the Decalogue. The second, which belongs to a much larger body of Hebrew laws, resemble those of Hammurabi. Unlike the Ten Commandments, the latter, which deal primarily with social obligations, prescribe specific consequences for their violation. Some so closely parallel the laws of the First Babylonian Empire that scholars think both may look back to a common source. The Bible—like the *Epic of Gilgamesh*—conflates centuries of legend and fact, and its significance as great literature is unquestionable; but its value as an historical document has been hotly debated for well over a century. It is exalted by many as the revelation of divine authority, and it is regarded as sacred scripture by three world religions: Judaism, Christianity, and Islam. Even as it expounds a message of faith and moral instruction, it narrates the saga of a people who came to view all history as divinely directed.

READING 1.8a From the Hebrew Bible (Genesis 1, 2)

The Creation

Chapter 1

²⁶God said, "Let us make man in our own image, in the likeness of ourselves, and let them be masters of the fish of the sea, the birds of heaven, the cattle, all the wild animals and all the creatures that creep along the ground."

²⁷God created man in the image of himself,
in the image of God he created him,
male and female he created them.

²⁸God blessed them, saying to them, "Be fruitful, multiply, fill the earth and subdue it. Be masters of the fish of the sea, the birds of heaven and all the living creatures that move on earth." ²⁹God also said, "Look, to you I give all the seed-bearing plants everywhere on the surface of the earth, and all the trees with seed-bearing fruit; this will be your food. ³⁰And to all the wild animals, all the birds of heaven and all the living creatures that creep along the ground, I give all the foliage of the plants as their food." And so it was. ³¹God saw all he had made, and indeed it was very good. Evening came and morning came: the sixth day.

Chapter 2

¹Thus heaven and earth were completed with all their array. ²On the seventh day God had completed the work he had been doing. He rested on the seventh day after all the work he had been doing. ³God blessed the seventh day and made it holy, because on that day he rested after all his work of creating.

⁴Such was the story of heaven and earth as they were created.

Paradise, and the test of free will

At the time when Yahweh God made earth and heaven ⁵there was as yet no wild bush on the earth nor had any wild plant yet sprung up, for Yahweh God had not sent rain on the earth, nor was there any man to till the soil. ⁶Instead, water flowed out of the ground and watered all the surface of the soil. ⁷Yahweh God shaped man from the soil of the ground and blew the breath of life into his nostrils, and man became a living being.

⁸Yahweh God planted a garden in Eden, which is in the east, and there he put the man he had fashioned. ⁹From the soil, Yahweh God caused to grow every kind of tree, enticing to look at and good to eat, with the tree of life in the middle of the garden, and the tree of the knowledge of good and evil.

¹⁰A river flowed from Eden to water the garden, and from there it divided to make four streams. ¹¹The first is named the Pishon, and this winds all through the land of Havilah where there is gold. ¹²The gold of this country is pure; bdellium* and cornelian** stone are found there. ¹³The second river is named the Gihon, and this winds all through the land of Cush. ¹⁴The third river is named the Tigris, and this flows to the east of Ashur. The fourth river is the Euphrates.

¹⁵Yahweh God took the man and settled him in the garden of Eden to cultivate and take care of it. ¹⁶Then Yahweh God gave the man this command, "You are free to eat of all the trees in the garden. ¹⁷But of the tree of the knowledge of good and evil you are not to eat; for, the day you eat of that, you are doomed to die."

¹⁸Yahweh God said, "It is not right that the man should be alone. I shall make him a helper." ¹⁹So from the soil Yahweh God fashioned all the wild animals and all the birds of heaven. These he brought to the man to see what he would call them; each one was to bear the name the man would give it. ²⁰The man gave names to all the cattle, all the birds of heaven and all the wild animals. But no helper suitable for the man was found for him. ²¹Then, Yahweh God made the man fall into a deep sleep. And, while he was asleep, he took one of his ribs and closed the flesh up again forthwith. ²²Yahweh God fashioned the rib he had taken from the man into a woman, and brought her to the man. ²³And the man said:

This one at last is bone of my bones
    and flesh of my flesh!
She is to be called Woman,
    because she was taken from Man.

²⁴This is why a man leaves his father and mother and becomes attached to his wife, and they become one flesh.

²⁵Now, both of them were naked, the man and his wife, but they felt no shame before each other.

---

*Variously interpreted as a deep-red gem or a pearl.
**A semi-precious red stone (carnelian).

READING 1.8b From the Hebrew Bible

(Exodus 20:1–20; 21:1–2, 18–27, 37; 23:1–9)

The Decalogue (Ten Commandments)

¹Then God spoke all these words. He said, ²"I am Yahweh your God who brought you out of Egypt, where you lived as slaves.

³"You shall have no other gods to rival me.

⁴"You shall not make yourself a carved image or any likeness of anything in heaven above or on earth beneath or in the waters under the earth.

⁵"You shall not bow down to them or serve them. For I, Yahweh your God, am a jealous God and I punish a parent's fault in the children, the grandchildren, and the great grandchildren among those who hate me; ⁶but I act with faithful love towards thousands of those who love me and keep my commandments.

⁷"You shall not misuse the name of Yahweh your God, for Yahweh will not leave unpunished anyone who misuses his name.

⁸"Remember the Sabbath day and keep it holy. ⁹For six days you shall labour and do all your work, ¹⁰but the seventh day is a Sabbath for Yahweh your God. You shall do no work that day, neither you nor your son nor your daughter nor your servants, men or women, nor your animals nor the alien living with you. ¹¹For in six days Yahweh made the heavens, earth and sea and all that these contain, but on the seventh day he rested; that is why Yahweh has blessed the Sabbath day and made it sacred.

¹²Honour your father and your mother so that you may live long in the land that Yahweh your God is giving you.

¹³"You shall not kill.

¹⁴"You shall not commit adultery.

¹⁵"You shall not steal.

¹⁶"You shall not give false evidence against your neighbour.

¹⁷"You shall not set your heart on your neighbour's house. You shall not set your heart on your neighbour's spouse, or servant, man or woman, or ox, or donkey, or any of your neighbour's possessions."

¹⁸Seeing the thunder pealing, the lightning flashing, the trumpet blasting and the mountain smoking, the people were all terrified and kept their distance. ¹⁹"Speak to us yourself," they said to Moses, "and we will obey; but do not let God speak to us, or we shall die." ²⁰Moses said to the people, "Do not be afraid; God has come to test you, so that your fear of him, being always in your mind, may keep you from sinning." ²¹So the people kept their distance while Moses approached the dark cloud where God was.

Laws Concerning Slaves

¹"These are the laws you must give them: ²When you buy a Hebrew slave, his service will last for six years. In the seventh year he will leave a free man without paying compensation."

Blows and Wounds

¹⁸"If people quarrel and one strikes the other a blow with stone or fist so that the injured party, though not dead, is confined to bed,¹⁹ but later recovers and can go about, even with a stick, the one who struck the blow will have no liability, other than to compensate the injured party for the enforced inactivity and to take care of the injured party until the cure is complete.

²⁰"If someone beats his slave, male or female, and the slave dies at his hands, he must pay the penalty. ²¹But should the slave survive for one or two days, he will pay no penalty because the slave is his by right of purchase.

²²"If people, when brawling, hurt a pregnant woman and she suffers a miscarriage but no further harm is done, the person responsible will pay compensation as fixed by the woman's master, paying as much as the judges decide. ²³If further harm is done, however, you will award life for life, ²⁴eye for eye, tooth for tooth, hand for hand, foot for foot, ²⁵burn for burn, wound for wound, stroke for stroke.

²⁶"If anyone strikes the eye of his slave, male or female, and destroys the use of it, he will give the slave his freedom to compensate for the eye. ²⁷If he knocks out the tooth of his slave, male or female, he will give the slave his freedom to compensate for the tooth."

Theft of Animals

³⁷"If anyone steals an ox or a sheep and slaughters or sells it, he will pay back five beasts from the herd for the ox, and four animals from the flock for the sheep."

Justice. Duties towards Enemies

¹"You will not spread false rumours. You will not lend support to the wicked by giving untrue evidence. ²You will not be led into wrong-doing by the majority nor, when giving evidence in a lawsuit, side with the majority to pervert the course of justice; ³nor will you show partiality to the poor in a lawsuit.
⁴"If you come on your enemy's ox or donkey straying, you will take it back to him. ⁵If you see the donkey of someone who hates you fallen under its load, do not stand back; you must go and help him with it.
⁶"You will not cheat the poor among you of their rights at law. ⁷Keep clear of fraud. Do not cause the death of the innocent or upright, and do not acquit the guilty. ⁸You will accept no bribes, for a bribe blinds the clear-sighted and is the ruin of the cause of the upright.
⁹"You will not oppress the alien; you know how an alien feels, for you yourselves were once aliens in Egypt. . . ."

It is worth noting that there is a major difference between the laws of the Hebrews and those of Babylon: Among the Hebrews, punishment was not levied according to social class. This is not to say that class distinctions did not exist in Hebrew society, but rather that the law was meant to apply equally to all classes, with the exception of slaves. The humanitarian bias of the Hebrew laws is best reflected in God's frequent reminder to the Hebrews that since they themselves were once aliens and slaves, they must treat even the lowest members of the social order as worthy human beings. If Babylonian law prized economic prosperity and political stability, it was the unity of religious and moral life that lay at the heart of the Hebrew laws.

Figure 2.10 The Ark of the Covenant and sanctuary implements, Hammath near Tiberias, fourth century. Mosaic. Israel Antiquities Authority, Jerusalem. Photo: Zev Rodovan, Jerusalem.

The Hebrew State and the Social Order

By the beginning of the first millennium B.C.E., the Hebrews had reestablished themselves in Palestine—as ancient Canaan came to be called following its occupation by powerful tribes of Philistines in the twelfth century B.C.E. Under the rule of the Hebrew kings, Saul (ca. 1040–1000 B.C.E.), David (ca. 1000–960 B.C.E.), and Solomon (ca. 960–920 B.C.E.), Canaan became a powerful state defended by armies equipped with iron war chariots. In the city of Jerusalem (see Map 2.1), King Solomon constructed a royal palace and a magnificent temple (no longer standing) to enshrine the Ark of the Covenant. The curtained Ark that sheltered the Torah, along with the **menorah** (a seven-branched candelabrum) and other sacramental objects (Figure 2.10) took the place of pictorial representations of Yahweh in Hebrew houses of worship.

The social order of the Hebrews was shaped by biblical precepts. Between Hebrew kings and their people, there existed a covenant—protection in exchange for loyalty and obedience—similar to that which characterized the relationship between God and the Hebrews. This same patriarchal bond also prevailed between Jewish fathers and their families. Hebrew kings were considered the divinely appointed representatives of God; and Hebrew wives and children came under the direct control of the male head of the household and were listed among his possessions. In short, the covenant between God and the Hebrews, as expressed in the laws, established the model for both secular and familial authority.

In the course of his reign, Solomon divided the Hebrew state into two administrative divisions: a northern portion called Israel, and a southern portion called Judah (hence the name "Jews"). While commercial pursuits of the young Hebrew nation generated wealth and material comforts, the cults of the Canaanite fertility gods and goddesses—"carved images" of which gave them tangible presence on earth—seduced many Hebrews to stray from their rigorous and wholly abstract monotheistic faith. By the eighth century B.C.E., as signs of moral laxity increased, a group of zealous teachers worked to renew the ancient covenant: Known as *prophets* (literally "those who speak for another"), Amos, Hosea, and Isaiah voiced urgent pleas for spiritual reform. They warned that violations of the covenant and the laws would result in divine punishment. A century after the fall of Israel to the Assyrians in 722 B.C.E., the prophet Jeremiah explained the event as an expression of divine chastisement. He warned the people of Judah to shun local religious cults and urged them to reaffirm the covenant or again feel God's wrath. The Hebrew concept of destiny as divinely governed is confirmed in Jeremiah's message: God rewards and punishes not in a life hereafter, but here on earth.

Jeremiah and the Observance of the Covenant

¹The word that came to Jeremiah from Yahweh, ²"Hear the terms of this covenant; tell them to the people of Judah and to the inhabitants of Jerusalem. ³Tell them, 'Yahweh, God of Israel, says this: Cursed be anyone who will not listen to the terms of this covenant ⁴which I ordained for your ancestors when I brought them out of Egypt, out of that iron-foundry. Listen to my voice, I told them, carry out all my orders, then you will be my people and I shall be your God, ⁵so that I may fulfil the oath I swore to your ancestors, that I may give them a country flowing with milk and honey, as is the case today.'" I replied, "So be it, Yahweh!" ⁶Then Yahweh said to me, "Proclaim all these terms in the towns of Judah and in the streets of Jerusalem, saying, 'Listen to the terms of this covenant and obey them. ⁷For when I brought your ancestors out of Egypt, I solemnly warned them, and have persistently warned them until today, saying: Listen to my voice. ⁸But they did not listen, did not pay attention; instead, each followed his own stubborn and wicked inclinations. And against them, in consequence, I put into action the words of this covenant which I had ordered them to obey and which they had not obeyed.'"

⁹Yahweh said to me, "Plainly there is conspiracy among the people of Judah and the citizens of Jerusalem. ¹⁰They have reverted to the sins of their ancestors who refused to listen to my words: they too are following other gods and serving them. The House of Israel and the House of Judah have broken my covenant which I made with their ancestors. ¹¹And so, Yahweh says this, 'I shall now bring a disaster on them which they cannot escape; they will call to me for help, but I shall not listen to them. ¹²The towns of Judah and the citizens of Jerusalem will then go and call for help to the gods to whom they burn incense, but these will be no help at all to them in their time of distress!

¹³'For you have as many gods
as you have towns, Judah!
You have built as many altars to Shame,
as many incense altars to Baal,
as Jerusalem has streets!

¹⁴'You, for your part, must not intercede for this people, nor raise either plea or prayer on their behalf, for I will not listen when their distress forces them to call to me for help.'"

· · · · · · · · · ·

The Babylonian Captivity and the Book of Job

In 586 B.C.E., Judah fell to Chaldean armies led by the mighty King Nebuchadnezzar (ca. 630–562 B.C.E.). Nebuchadnezzar burned the city, raided the Temple, and took the inhabitants of Jerusalem into captivity. In the newly restored city of Babylon, with its glazed brick portals (Figure 2.11), its resplendent "hanging" gardens, its towering ziggurat—the model for the Tower of Babel described in Genesis—the Hebrews experienced almost fifty years of exile (586–538 B.C.E.). Their despair and doubt in the absolute goodness of God are voiced in the Book of Job, probably written in the years after the Babylonian Captivity. The finest example of wisdom literature in the Hebrew Bible, the Book of Job raises the question of unjustified suffering in a universe governed by a merciful god. The "blameless and upright" Job has obeyed the Commandments and has been a devoted servant of God throughout his life. Yet he is tested unmercifully by the loss of his possessions, his family, and his health. His wife begs him to renounce God, and his friends encourage him to acknowledge his sinfulness. But Job defiantly protests that he has given God no cause for anger. Job asks a universal question: "If there is no heaven (and thus no justice after death), how can a good man's suffering be justified?" or simply phrased, "Why do bad things happen to good people?"

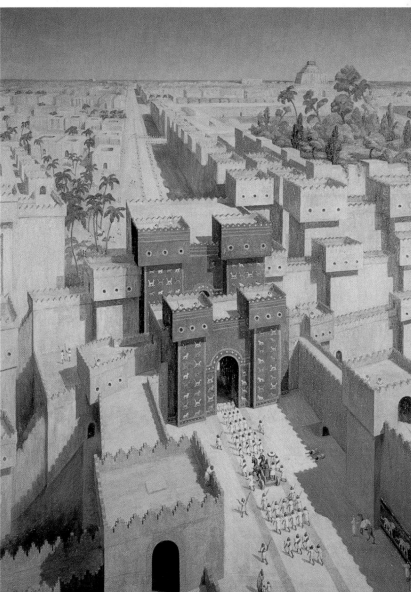

Figure 2.11 A drawing of Babylon as it might have looked in the sixth century B.C.E. The Ishtar Gate stands at the center, with the palace of Nebuchadnezzar II and the Hanging Gardens behind and to its right. On the horizon and the east bank of the Euphrates looms the Marduk Ziggurat. The Oriental Institute of the University of Chicago.

The Book of Job

Chapter 1

¹There was once a man in the land of Uz called Job: a sound and honest man who feared God and shunned evil. ²Seven sons and three daughters were born to him.. ³And he owned seven thousand sheep, three thousand camels, five hundred yoke of oxen and five hundred she-donkeys, and many servants besides. This man was the most prosperous of all the Sons of the East. ⁴It was the custom of his sons to hold banquets in one another's houses in turn, and to invite their three sisters to eat and drink with them. ⁵Once each series of banquets was over, Job would send for them to come and be purified, and at dawn on the following day he would make a burnt offering for each of them. "Perhaps," Job would say, "my sons have sinned and in their heart blasphemed." So that was what Job used to do each time.

⁶One day when the sons of God came to attend on Yahweh, among them came Satan. *⁷So Yahweh said to Satan, "Where have you been?" "Prowling about on earth," he answered, "roaming around there." ⁸So Yahweh asked him, "Did you pay any attention to my servant Job? There is no one like him on the earth: a sound and honest man who fears God and shuns evil." ⁹"Yes," Satan said, "but Job is not God-fearing for nothing, is he? ¹⁰Have you not put a wall round him and his house and all his domain? You have blessed all he undertakes, and his flocks throng the countryside. ¹¹But stretch out your hand and lay a finger on his possessions: then, I warrant you, he will curse you to your face." ¹²"Very well," Yahweh said to Satan, "all he has is in your power. But keep your hands off his person." So Satan left the presence of Yahweh.

¹³On the day when Job's sons and daughters were eating and drinking in their eldest brother's house, ¹⁴a messenger came to Job. "Your oxen," he said, "were at the plough, with the donkeys grazing at their side, ¹⁵when the Sabaeans swept down on them and carried them off, and put the servants to the sword: I alone have escaped to tell you." ¹⁶He had not finished speaking when another messenger arrived. "The fire of God," he said, "has fallen from heaven and burnt the sheep and shepherds to ashes: I alone have escaped to tell you." ¹⁷He had not finished speaking when another messenger arrived. "The Chaldeans," he said, "three bands of them, have raided the camels and made off with them, and put the servants to the sword: I alone have escaped to tell you." ¹⁸He had not finished speaking when another messenger arrived. "Your sons and daughters," he said, "were eating and drinking at their eldest brother's house, ¹⁹ when suddenly from the desert a gale sprang up, and it battered all four corners of the house which fell in on the young people. They are dead: I alone have escaped to tell you."

²⁰Then Job stood up, tore his robe and shaved his head. Then, falling to the ground, he prostrated himself ²¹ and said:

Naked I came from my mother's womb,
naked I shall return again.

---

*Literally, "adversary."

Yahweh gave, Yahweh has taken back.
Blessed be the name of Yahweh!

²²In all this misfortune Job committed no sin, and he did not reproach God. . . .

Chapter 2

¹Another day, the sons of God came to attend on Yahweh and Satan came with them too. ²So Yahweh said to Satan, "Where have you been?" "Prowling about on earth," he answered, "roaming around there." ³So Yahweh asked him, "Did you pay any attention to my servant Job? There is no one like him on the earth: a sound and honest man who fears God and shuns evil. He persists in his integrity still; you achieved nothing by provoking me to ruin him." ⁴"Skin after skin!" Satan replied. "Someone will give away all he has to save his life. ⁵But stretch out your hand and lay a finger on his bone and flesh; I warrant you, he will curse you to your face." ⁶"Very well," Yahweh said to Satan, "he is in your power. But spare his life." ⁷So Satan left the presence of Yahweh.

He struck Job down with malignant ulcers from the sole of his foot to the top of his head. ⁸Job took a piece of pot to scrape himself, and went and sat among the ashes. ⁹Then his wife said to him, "Why persist in this integrity of yours? Curse God and die." ¹⁰"That is how a fool of a woman talks," Job replied. "If we take happiness from God's hand, must we not take sorrow too?" And in all this misfortune Job uttered no sinful word.

¹¹The news of all the disasters that had fallen on Job came to the ears of three of his friends. Each of them set out from home—Eliphaz of Teman, Bildad of Shuah and Zophar of Naamath—and by common consent they decided to go and offer him sympathy and consolation. ¹²Looking at him from a distance, they could not recognise him; they wept aloud and tore their robes and threw dust over their heads. ¹³They sat there on the ground beside him for seven days and seven nights. To Job they spoke never a word, for they saw how much he was suffering.

Chapter 3: Job Curses the Day of his Birth

¹In the end it was Job who broke his silence and cursed the day of his birth. ²This is what he said:

³Perish the day on which I was born
and the night that told of a boy conceived.
⁴May that day be darkness,
may God on high have no thought for it,
may no light shine on it.
⁵May murk and shadow dark as death claim it for their own,
clouds hang over it,
eclipse swoop down on it.

. . . .

¹⁷What are human beings that you should take them so seriously,
subjecting them to your scrutiny,
¹⁸that morning after morning you should examine them
and at every instant test them?
¹⁹Will you never take your eyes off me
long enough for me to swallow my spittle?
²⁰Suppose I have sinned, what have I done to you,

you tireless watcher of humanity?
Why do you choose me as your target?
　　Why should I be a burden to you?
²¹Can you not tolerate my sin,
　　not overlook my fault?
For soon I shall be lying in the dust,
　　you will look for me and I shall be no more.

Chapter 14

¹A human being, born of woman,
　　[his] life is short but full of trouble.
²Like a flower, such a one blossoms and withers,
　　fleeting as a shadow, transient.
³And this is the creature on whom you fix your gaze,
　　and bring to judgement before you!
⁴But will anyone produce the pure from what is impure?
　　No one can!
⁵Since his days are measured out,
　　since his tale of months depends on you,
　　since you assign him bounds he cannot pass,
⁶turn your eyes from him, leave him alone,
　　like a hired labourer, to finish his day in peace.
⁷There is always hope for a tree:
　　when felled, it can start its life again;
　　its shoots continue to sprout.
⁸Its roots may have grown old in the earth,
　　its stump rotting in the ground,
⁹but let it scent the water, and it buds,
　　and puts out branches like a plant newly set.
¹⁰But a human being? He dies, and dead he remains,
　　breathes his last, and then where is he?
¹¹The waters of the sea will vanish,
　　the rivers stop flowing and run dry:
¹²a human being, once laid to rest, will never rise again,
　　the heavens will wear out before he wakes up,
　　or before he is roused from his sleep.
¹³Will no one hide me in Sheol,
　　and shelter me there till your anger is past,
　　fixing a certain day for calling me to mind—
¹⁴can the dead come back to life?—
　　　day after day of my service, I should be waiting
　　　for my relief to come.
¹⁵Then you would call, and I should answer,
　　you would want to see once more what you have made.
¹⁶Whereas now you count every step I take,
　　you would then stop spying on my sin;
¹⁷you would seal up my crime in a bag,
　　and put a cover over my fault.
¹⁸Alas! Just as, eventually, the mountain falls down,
　　the rock moves from its place,
¹⁹water wears away the stones,
　　the cloudburst erodes the soil;
　　so you destroy whatever hope a person has.
²⁰You crush him once for all, and he is gone;
　　first you disfigure him, then you dismiss him.
²¹His children may rise to honours—he does not know it;
　　they may come down in the world—he does not care.
²²He feels no pangs, except for his own body,
　　makes no lament, except for his own self.

Chapter 38: Job Must Bow to the Creator's Wisdom

¹Then from the heart of the tempest Yahweh gave Job his answer. He said:

²Who is this, obscuring my intentions
　　with his ignorant words?
³Brace yourself like a fighter;
　　I am going to ask the questions, and you are to inform me!
⁴Where were you when I laid the earth's foundations?
　　Tell me, since you are so well-informed!
⁵Who decided its dimensions, do you know?
　　Or who stretched the measuring line across it?
⁶What supports its pillars at their bases?
　　Who laid its cornerstone
⁷to the joyful concert of the morning stars
　　and the unanimous acclaim of the sons of God?
⁸Who pent up the sea behind closed doors
　　when it leapt tumultuous from the womb,
⁹when I wrapped it in a robe of mist
　　and made black clouds its swaddling bands;
¹⁰when I cut out the place I had decreed for it
　　and imposed gates and a bolt?
¹¹"Come so far," I said, "and no further;
　　here your proud waves must break!"
¹²Have you ever in your life given orders to the morning
　　or sent the dawn to its post,
¹³to grasp the earth by its edges
　　and shake the wicked out of it?
¹⁴She turns it as red as a clay seal,
　　she tints it as though it were a dress,
¹⁵stealing the light from evil-doers
　　and breaking the arm raised to strike.
¹⁶Have you been right down to the sources of the sea
　　and walked about at the bottom of the Abyss?
¹⁷Have you been shown the gates of Death,
　　have you seen the janitors of the Shadow dark as death?
¹⁸Have you an inkling of the extent of the earth?
　　Tell me all about it if you have!

Chapter 42: Job's Final Answer

¹This was the answer Job gave to Yahweh:

²I know that you are all-powerful:
　　what you conceive, you can perform.
³I was the man who misrepresented your intentions
　　with my ignorant words.
You have told me about great works that I cannot understand,
about marvels which are beyond me, of which I know
　　nothing.
⁴(Listen, please, and let me speak:
I am going to ask the questions, and you are to inform me.)
⁵Before, I knew you only by hearsay
　　but now, having seen you with my own eyes,
⁶I retract what I have said,
　　and repent in dust and ashes.

God's answer to Job is an eloquent vindication of unquestioned faith: God's power is immense and human beings cannot expect rational explanations of the divine will;

indeed, they have no business demanding such. Proclaiming the magnitude of divine power and the fragility of humankind, the Book of Job confirms the pivotal role of human faith (the belief and trust in God) that sustains the Hebrew covenant. The anxious sense of human vulnerability that pervades the Book of Job recalls the *Epic of Gilgamesh*. Indeed, the two works bear comparison. Both heroes, Job and Gilgamesh, are tested by superhuman forces, and both come to realize that misfortune and suffering are typical of the human condition. Gilgamesh seeks but fails to secure personal immortality; Job solicits God's promise of heavenly reward but fails to secure assurance that once dead, he might return to life. Just as Utnapishtim tells Gilgamesh, "There is no permanence," so Job laments that man born of woman "Like a flower, such a one blossoms and withers, . . . He dies and dead he remains." Such pessimism was not uncommon in Mesopotamia, the area in which both the *Epic of Gilgamesh* and the Hebrew Bible originated. The notion of life after death (so prominent in Egyptian religious thought) is as elusive a concept in Hebraic literature as it is in Mesopotamian myth. Nevertheless, following the Babylonian Captivity, Jews speculated on the idea of an afterlife. Job anticipates a final departure to an underworld, an abode of the dead known among the Hebrews as *Sheol* or Shadowland. Yet, even without the promise of reward, Job remains stubbornly faithful to the covenant. His tragic vision involves the gradual but dignified acceptance of his place in a divinely governed universe.

The Hebrew Bible played a major role in shaping the humanistic tradition in the West. It provided the religious and ethical foundations for Judaism, and, almost 2,000 years after the death of Abraham, for Christianity and Islam. Biblical teachings, including the belief in a single, personal, caring god who intervenes on behalf of a faithful people, have become fundamental to Western thought. And Bible stories—from Genesis to Job—have inspired some of humankind's greatest works of art, music, and literature.

The Iron Age

While the first kings of Israel administered the laws of the young Hebrew nation, all of Mesopotamia felt the effects of a new technology: Iron was introduced into Asia Minor by the Hittites, a nomadic tribe that entered the area before 2000 B.C.E. Cheaper to produce and more durable than bronze, iron represented new, superior technology. In addition to their iron weapons, the Hittites made active use of horse-drawn war chariots, which provided increased speed and mobility in battle. The combination of war chariots and iron weapons gave the Hittites clear military superiority over all of Mesopotamia.

As iron technology spread slowly throughout the Near East, it transformed the ancient world. Iron tools contributed to increased agricultural production, which in turn supported an increased population. In the wake of the Iron Age, numerous small states came to flower, bringing with them major cultural innovations. By 1500 B.C.E., for instance, the Phoenicians, an energetic, seafaring people

—1800	Hittites introduce iron into Mesopotamia
—850	first known arched bridge is constructed in Asia Minor
—700	the Assyrians are the first to construct aqueducts
—650	the Lydians introduce standard coinage

located on the Mediterranean Sea (see Map 2.1), had developed an alphabet of twenty-two signs. These signs eventually replaced earlier forms of script and became the basis of all Western alphabets. In Asia Minor, the Lydians, successors to the Hittites, began the practice of minting coins. Cheaper and stronger weapons also meant larger, more efficient armies. By the first millennium B.C.E., war was no longer the monopoly of the elite. Iron technology encouraged the rapid rise of large and powerful empires: Equipped with iron weapons, the Assyrians (ca. 750–600 B.C.E.), the Chaldeans (ca. 600–540 B.C.E.), and the Persians (ca. 550–330 B.C.E.) followed one another in conquering vast portions of Mesopotamia. Each of these empires grew in size and authority by imposing military control over territories outside their own natural boundaries—a practice known as *imperialism*.

The Assyrian Empire

The first of the great empire-builders, the Assyrians earned a reputation as the most militant civilization of ancient Mesopotamia. Held together by a powerful army that systematically combined engineering and fighting techniques, the Assyrians turned their iron weapons against most of Mesopotamia. In 721 B.C.E., they conquered Israel and dispersed its population. By the middle of the seventh century B.C.E. they had swallowed up most of the land between the Persian Gulf and the Nile valley. Assyrian power is reflected in the imposing walled citadel of Khorsabad, located some 10 miles from Nineveh (see Map 2.1). Covering 25 acres, this walled complex featured a ziggurat and an elaborate palace with more than 200 rooms: a maze of courtyards, harem quarters, treasuries, and state apartments (Figure 2.12). The palace walls were adorned with low-relief scenes of war and pillage and with cuneiform inscriptions that celebrate Assyrian military victories. One seventh-century B.C.E. relief shows the imperial armies of King Ashurbanipal (668–627 B.C.E.) storming the battlements of an African city (Figure 2.13). In the lower left, male captives (their chieftains still wearing the feathers of authority) are led away, followed in procession by women, children, and the spoils of war.

Flanking the scenes of military conquest on the palace walls at Nineveh and Nimrud are depictions of the royal lion hunt. Hunting and war, two closely related enterprises, were ideal vehicles by which to display the ruler's courage and physical might. In Assyrian reliefs, the lion, a traditional symbol of power throughout the ancient world (see Figure 1.6) is depicted as the adversary of the king. Ceremonial lion hunts celebrated the invincibility of the monarch, who, in earlier times, might have proved his prowess by combating wild animals in the field—in the

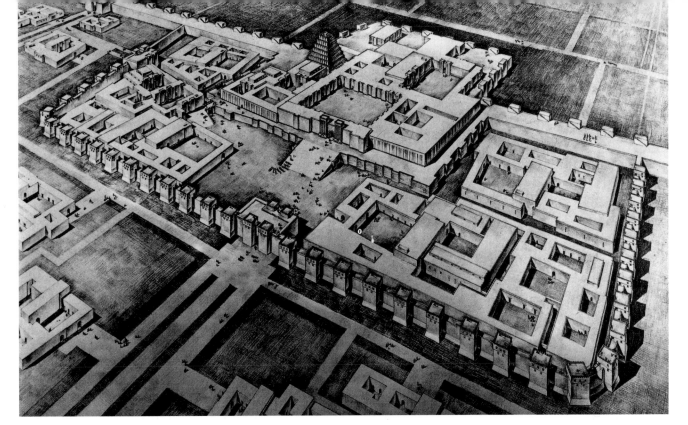

Figure 2.12 The citadel of Sargon II, Khorsabad, Iraq, ca. 720 B.C.E., reconstruction drawing. Artist: Charles Altman. Institute of Archeology Library, University of London.

Figure 2.13 Ashurbanipal besieging an Egyptian city, 667 B.C.E. Alabaster relief. Reproduced by courtesy of the Trustees of the British Museum, London.

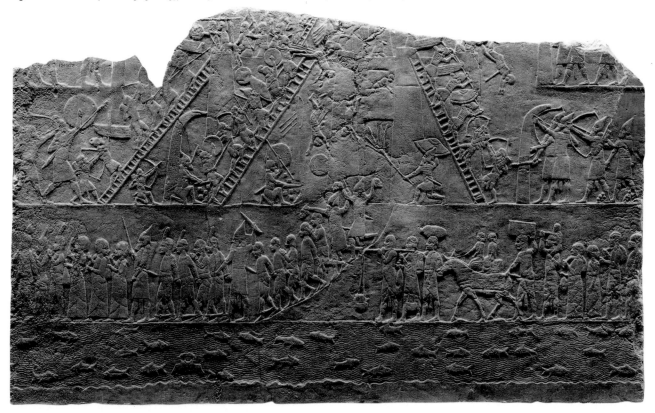

manner of the legendary Gilgamesh (see Figure 2.2). One dramatic scene from Nimrud depicts a wounded lion fiercely pursuing the royal chariot as it speeds away, while another beast lies dying before the wheels of the king's chariot (Figure 2.14). Spatial depth is indicated by super-imposing the chariot wheels over the rear lion's legs. Yet the heads and legs of the horses are shown on a single plane, and clarity of design dictates that the second wounded lion, crouching in pain, fit precisely within the space between the front and rear legs of the prancing steeds. The balance between figures (positive shapes) and ground (negative or "empty" space) results in a brilliant formal

Figure 2.14 King Ashurnarsipal II Killing Lions, from Palace of King Ashurnarsipal II, Nimrud, ca. 883–859 B.C.E. Alabaster relief, 3 ft. 3 in. X 8 ft. 4 in. Reproduced by courtesy of the Trustees of the British Museum, London.

design. The Assyrian reliefs—housed in large numbers at the British Museum in London—are superb examples of the artist's ability to infuse violent subject matter with narrative grandeur. If the lion hunt reliefs made implicit reference to the ruler's invincibility, colossal sculpture clearly manifested his superhuman status. Ten-foot-tall hybrid beasts guarded the gateways of Assyrian palaces (Figure 2.15), much in the way the sphinx guarded the royal tombs of Egypt. Bearing the facial features of the monarch, these colossi united the physical attributes of the bull (virility), the lion (physical strength), and the eagle (predatory agility). The winged, human-headed bulls from the citadel at Khorsabad were power-symbols designed to inspire awe and fear among those who passed beneath their impassive gaze. The art of Assyria was a form of visual propaganda, designed not simply to celebrate Assyrian rulership, but to intimidate its enemies.

The Persian Empire

The Persian Empire, the last and the largest of the empires of Mesopotamia, was brought to its peak by Cyrus II (ca. 585–ca. 529 B.C.E.), called "the Great" for his conquests over territories ranging from the frontiers of India to the Mediterranean Sea. Persia's monarchs, aided by efficient administrators, oversaw a network of roads connecting the major cities of the Near East. Persian message-bearers traveled swiftly throughout the empire. Described by the Greek historian Herodotus as men unhindered "by snow, or rain, or heat, or by the darkness of night," they provided a model and a motto for the United States Postal Service.

The Persians devised a monotheistic religion based on the teachings of the prophet Zoroaster (ca. 628–ca. 551 B.C.E.). Denying the nature gods of earlier times, Zoroaster exalted the sole god Ahura-Mazda ("Wise Lord"), who demanded good thoughts, good works, and good deeds from his followers. Zoroaster taught that life was a battlefield on which the opposing forces of light and darkness contended for supremacy. Human beings took part in this cosmic struggle by way of their freedom to choose between good and evil, the consequences of which would determine their fate at the end of time. According to Zoroaster, a Last Judgment would consign the wicked to everlasting

darkness, while the good would live eternally in an abode of luxury and light—the Persian *pairidaeza*, from which the English word "paradise" derives. Zoroastrianism came to influence the moral teachings of three great world religions: Judaism, Christianity, and Islam (see chapters 8 and 10).

At the Persian capital of Persepolis (in modern-day Iran), artists perpetuated the architectural and sculptural traditions of Assyria. The Persians also brought to perfection the art of metalworking that had flourished in Mesopotamia since the beginning of the Bronze Age. Utensils, vessels, and jewellery produced by Persian craftspeople, display some of the most intricate and sophisticat-

Figure 2.15 Winged human-headed bull from Khorsabad, Iraq, ca. 720 B.C.E. Limestone, approx. height 13 ft. 10 in. Louvre, Paris.

Figure 2.16 Achaemenid (Persian) gold vessel, fifth to third century B.C.E. Archaeological Museum, Teheran.

ed techniques of gold-working known to the history of that medium (Figure **2.16**). Many of these techniques would be practiced for centuries to come (see chapter 11).

SUMMARY

Mesopotamia's vulnerable geographic location contributed to the rise and fall of many different civilizations. Despite the differences in languages and ethnicity, the civilizations of this region, beginning with Sumer and ending with the Persian Empire, shared elements of a common culture. Unstable climate and the irregular overflow of the Tigris and Euphrates Rivers contributed to the formulation of a pantheon of fierce and capricious Mesopotamian deities and the evolution of a generally pessimistic world view. The world's first major literary work, the *Epic of Gilgamesh*, describes the futility of the human search for immortal life. Neither the Sumerians nor the Hebrews inhabiting the region developed the deep sense of order that characterized ancient Egyptian culture; nor did any of the civilizations of the Near East (with the exception of Persia) produce a clearly defined picture of life after death comparable to that of the Egyptians. Among the Hebrews, the covenant with a single, personal and transcendent god formed the basis for a religion that emphasized unswerving faith and high moral conduct. The Hebraic emphasis on ethical monotheism strongly influenced Western religious thought.

Mesopotamian rulers acted as agents of the gods. Within the civilizations of the Fertile Crescent, "divine-right monarchs" from Sargon to Cyrus the Great brought law and order to their societies. The close association between secular authority and spiritual power fostered the concept of law as a form of divine justice. From Mesopotamia came the world's first system of recorded law: Under the Babylonian ruler Hammurabi, laws were recorded and codified. Unlike the Hebrews, whose laws

applied equally to all classes, the Babylonians punished violators according to their status in society. Iron technology made possible the establishment of large armies and ushered in centuries of imperialism. Yet the empires of the Near East perpetuated cultural traditions that reached back to Sumer: Civilization after civilization honored the gods with ziggurats, copied and recopied the *Epic of Gilgamesh*, and passed on the technology of metalworking. Yet it may be on Assyria's palace walls, inscribed with violent scenes of warfare, that the turbulent history of Mesopotamia is most vividly recorded. The arts of Mesopotamia reflect the lives of people for whom survival was a day-to-day struggle. These artworks proclaim the power of the ruler, the omnipotence of the gods, and the frailties of human beings as they try to understand the workings of nature, the meaning of death, and the destiny and purpose of humankind.

GLOSSARY

covenant contract; the bond between the Hebrew people and their God

epic a long narrative poem that recounts the deeds of a legendary or historical hero in his quest for meaning or identity

empire a state achieved militarily by the unification of territories under a single sovereign power

menorah a seven-branched candelabrum

monotheism the belief in one and only one god

Torah (Hebrew, "instruction," "law," or "teaching") the first five books of the Hebrew Bible: Genesis, Exodus, Leviticus, Numbers, and Deuteronomy

ziggurat a terraced tower of rubble and brick that served ancient Mesopotamians as a temple-shrine

SUGGESTIONS FOR READING

Anderson, Bernhard. *Understanding the Old Testament*, 4th ed. Englewood Cliffs, N.J.: Prentice-Hall, 1986.

Collon, Dominique. *Ancient Near Eastern Art*. Berkeley: University of California Press, 1993.

Cotterell, Arthur, ed. *The Penguin Book of Ancient Civilization*. London: Penguin, 1980.

Gabel, John B., and C. B. Wheeler. *The Bible as Literature: An Introduction*, 2nd ed. New York: Oxford University Press, 1990.

Gorden, Cyrus H. And Gary Rendsburg. *The Bible and the Ancient Near East.*, 4th edition. New York: Norton, 1997.

Holbrook, Clyde A. *The Iconoclastic Deity: Biblical Images of God*. Lewisburg, Pa.: Bucknell University Press, 1984.

Kramer, S. N. *History Begins at Sumer*, 3rd ed. Philadelphia: University of Pennsylvania Press, 1981.

Mellaart, Henry. *The Earliest Civilizations of the Near East*. London: Thames and Hudson, 1965.

Saggs, H. W. F. *The Babylonians*. Norman: University of Oklahoma, 1995.

——— *The Might That Was Assyria*. Salem, N.H.: Merrimack, 1984.

CHAPTER THREE

India and China: gods, rulers, and the social order

*"He knows peace who has forgotten desire.
He lives without craving:
Free from ego, free from pride."*
The *Bhagavad-Gita*

India and China, two of the oldest continuous civilizations in world history, emerged somewhat later than the civilizations of Egypt and Mesopotamia. These ancient Asian cultures nevertheless contributed significantly to the humanistic tradition, producing literature, philosophy, art, and music that ranks with that of the other great civilizations. But the Asian world view differs somewhat from that of the Western cultures we have examined. In India, for example, the fundamentals of spirituality were grounded in **pantheism**, the belief that all things in the universe are pervaded by an ineffable divine spirit. For the ancient Chinese, the natural order of the universe was central to all aspects of material and spiritual existence. In both of these cultures, all aspects of reality, whether human or divine, were thought to belong to the larger organic whole. This holistic outlook contributed to the evolution of rulership and the formation of the social order.

Ancient India

Indus Valley Civilization (ca. 2700–1500 B.C.E.)

India's earliest known civilization was located in the lower Indus valley, in an area called Sind—from which the words "India" and "Hindu" derive (Map **3.1**). At Mohenjo-daro (part of modern-day Pakistan) and other urban centers, a sophisticated Bronze Age culture flourished before 2500 B.C.E. India's first cities were planned communities: their streets, lined with fired-brick houses were laid out in a grid pattern, and their covered sewage systems were unmatched in other parts of the civilized world. Bronze Age India also claimed a form of written language, although the 400 pictographic signs that constitute their earliest script is still undeciphered. There is little evidence of temple or tomb architecture, but a vigorous sculptural tradition is evident in both bronze and stone. The lively female dancer pictured in Figure **3.2** is one of many objects (see also Figure 0.19)

that reflect India's mastery of the lost-wax method of working bronze. In the medium of stone, the powerful portrait of a bearded man (possibly a priest or ruler) distinguished by an introspective expression, anticipates the meditative images of India's later religious art (Figure **3.1**).

Figure 3.1 *Bearded Man*, Mohenjo-daro, Indus valley, ca. 2000 B.C.E. Limestone, height 7 in. Karachi Museum. Photo: Robert Harding, London.

Figure 3.2
Dancing Girl, Mohenjo-daro, Indus valley, ca. 2300–1750 B.C.E. Bronze, height 4¼ in. National Museum, New Delhi.

The Vedic Era (ca. 1500–322 B.C.E.)

Some time after 1500 B.C.E., warring, semi-nomadic tribes known as Aryans ("lords" or "nobles") invaded the Indus valley. These light-skinned peoples enslaved or removed the dark-skinned populations of Sind and established a set of societal divisions that anticipated the **caste system**. While a hierarchical order marked the social systems of all ancient civilizations, India developed the most rigid kind of class stratification, which prevailed until modern times. By 1000 B.C.E., four principal castes existed: priests and scholars, rulers and warriors, artisans and merchants, and unskilled workers. Slowly, these castes began to subdivide according to occupation. At the very bottom of the social order, or, more accurately, outside it, lay those who held the most menial and degrading occupations. They became known as Untouchables.

It was the Aryans who introduced Sanskrit, which would become the classic language of India. The bards of India recounted stories of the bitter tribal wars between competing Aryan families. These stories were the basis for India's two great epics—the *Mahabharata* (*Great Deeds of the Bharata Clan*) and the *Ramayana* (*Song of Prince Rama*), transmitted orally for generations but not recorded until the eighth century B.C.E. The *Mahabharata*—the world's longest folk epic—recreates the ten-year-long struggle for control of the Ganges valley occurring around the year 1000 B.C.E. Along with the *Ramayana*, this epic assumed a role in the cultural history of India not unlike that of the *Iliad* and the *Odyssey* in Hellenic history. Indeed, the two epics have been treasured resources for

much of the poetry, drama, and art produced throughout India's long history.

India's oldest devotional tests, the *Vedas* (literally, "sacred knowledge"), also originate in (and give their name to) the thousand-year period after 1500 B.C.E. The *Vedas* are a collection of prayers, sacrificial formulae, and hymns, one example of which appears in Reading 1.2 in the Introduction. Transmitted orally for centuries, the *Vedas* reflect the blending of the native folk traditions of the Indus valley and that of the invading Aryans. Among the chief Vedic deities were the sky gods Indra and Rudra (later known as Shiva), the fire god Agni, and the sun god Vishnu. The *Vedas* provide a wealth of information concerning astronomical phenomena. The study of the stars, along with the practice of surgery and dissection, mark the beginnings of scientific inquiry in India.

Hindu Pantheism

From the Indus valley civilization came the most ancient of today's world religions: Hinduism. Hinduism is markedly different from the religions of the West. It identifies the sacred not as a superhuman personality, but as an objective, all-pervading cosmic Spirit. Pantheism, the belief that divinity inheres in all things, is basic to the Hindu view that the universe itself is sacred. While neither polytheistic nor monotheistic in the traditional sense, Hinduism venerates all forms and manifestations of the

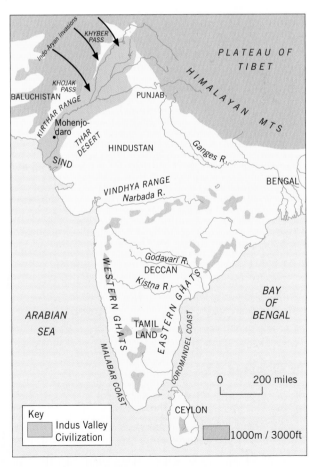

Map 3.1 Ancient India.

all-pervasive Spirit. Hence, Hinduism embraces all of the Vedic gods, who themselves take countless forms. Hindus believe in the oneness of Spirit, but worship that Spirit by way of a multitude of deities, who are perceived as emanations of the divine. In the words of the *Rig Veda*, "Truth is one, but the wise call it by many names."

Hinduism is best understood by way of the religious texts known as the *Upanishads*, some 250 prose commentaries on the *Vedas*. Like the *Vedas* themselves, the *Upanishads* were orally transmitted and recorded in Sanskrit between the eighth and sixth centuries B.C.E. While the *Vedas* teach worship through prayer and sacrifice, the *Upanishads* teach enlightenment through meditation. They predicate the concept of the single, all-pervading cosmic force called **Brahman**. Unlike the nature deities of Egypt and Mesopotamia, Brahman is infinite, formless, and ultimately unknowable. Unlike the Hebrew Yahweh, Brahman assumes no personal and contractual relationship with humankind. Brahman is the Uncaused Cause and the Ultimate Reality. In every human being, there resides the individual manifestation of Brahman: the Self, or **Atman**, which, according to the *Upanishads*, is "soundless, formless, intangible, undying, tasteless, odorless, without beginning, without end, eternal, immutable, [and] beyond nature." Although housed in the material prison of the human body, the Self (Atman) seeks to be one with the Absolute Spirit (Brahman). The (re)union of Brahman and Atman—a condition known as **nirvana**—is the goal of the Hindu. This blissful reabsorption of the Self into Absolute Spirit must be preceded by one's gradual rejection of the material world, that is, the world of illusion and ignorance, and by the mastery of the techniques of meditation. On reaching nirvana, however, the Hindu is released from the endless cycle of death and rebirth.

Essentially a literature of humility, the *Upanishads* offer no guidelines for worship, no moral laws, and no religious dogma. They neither exalt divine power, nor do they interpret it. They do, however, instruct the individual Hindu on the subject of death and rebirth. The Hindu anticipates a succession of lives: that is, the successive return of the Atman in various physical forms. The physical form, whether animal or human and of whatever species or class, is determined by the level of spiritual purity that Hindu has achieved by the time of his or her death. The Law of **Karma** holds that the collective spiritual energy gained from accumulated deeds determines one's physical state in the next life. Reincarnation, or the Wheel of Rebirth, is the fate of Hindus until they achieve nirvana. In this ultimate state, the enlightened Atman is both liberated and absorbed—a process that may be likened to the dissolution of a grain of salt in the vast waters of the ocean.

The *Bhagavad-Gita*

The fundamental teachings of Hinduism are lyrically expressed in one of India's most popular religious poems: the *Bhagavad-Gita* (Song of God), which constitutes one episode from the *Mahabharata*. In this most famous part of the poem, a dialogue takes place between Arjuna, the warrior-hero, and Krishna, the incarnation of the god Vishnu and a divine manifestation of Brahman. Facing the prospect of shedding the blood of his own kinsmen in the battle to come, Arjuna seeks to reconcile his material obligations with his spiritual quest for selflessness. Krishna's answer to Arjuna—a classic statement of resignation—represents the essence of Hindu thought as distilled from the *Upanishads*. Although probably in existence earlier, the *Bhagavad-Gita* was not recorded until sometime between the fifth and second centuries B.C.E.

READING 1.9 From the *Bhagavad-Gita*

He [who] knows bliss in the Atman	1
And wants nothing else.	
Cravings torment the heart:	
He renounces cravings.	
I call him illumined.	5
Not shaken by adversity,	
Not hankering after happiness:	
Free from fear, free from anger,	
Free from the things of desire,	
I call him a seer, and illumined.	10
The bonds of his flesh are broken.	
He is lucky, and does not rejoice:	
He is unlucky, and does not weep.	
I call him illumined.	

. . . .

Thinking about sense-objects	15
Will attach you to sense-objects;	
Grow attached, and you become addicted;	
Thwart your addiction, it turns to anger;	
Be angry, and you confuse your mind;	
Confuse your mind, you forget the lesson of experience;	20
Forget experience, you lose discrimination;	
Lose discrimination, and you miss life's only purpose.	
When he has no lust, no hatred,	
A man walks safely among the things of lust and hatred.	
To obey the Atman	25
Is his peaceful joy:	
Sorrow melts	
Into that clear peace;	
His quiet mind	
Is soon established in peace.	30

The uncontrolled mind	
Does not guess that the Atman is present:	
How can it meditate?	
Without meditation, where is peace?	
Without peace, where is happiness?	35

The wind turns a ship	
From its course upon the waters:	
The wandering winds of the senses	
Cast man's mind adrift	
And turn his better judgment from its course.	40
When a man can still the senses	

I call him illumined.
The recollected mind is awake
In the knowledge of the Atman
Which is dark night to the ignorant: 45
The ignorant are awake in their sense-life
Which they think is daylight:
To the seer it is darkness.
Water flows continually into the ocean
But the ocean is never disturbed: 50
Desire flows into the mind of the seer
But he is never disturbed.
The seer knows peace:
The man who stirs up his own lusts
Can never know peace.   55
He knows peace who has forgotten desire.
He lives without craving:
Free from ego, free from pride.

This is the state of enlightenment in Brahman:
A man who does not fall back from it   60
Into delusion.
Even at the moment of death
He is alive in that enlightenment:
Brahman and he are one. . . .

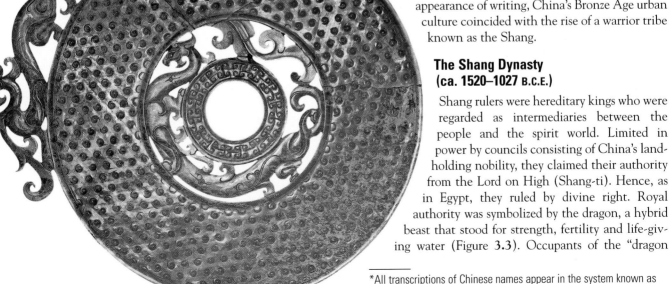

Figure 3.3 Ritual disc, Zhou Dynasty, fifth to third century B.C.E. Jade, diameter 6½ in. Nelson Atluns Museum, Kansas City, Missouri. 33–81.

The Hindu view of the relationship between people and gods differs significantly from the religious views of ancient Egyptians and Mesopotamians. While the latter held human beings as separate from the gods, Hindus, guided by the *Upanishads* and the *Bhagavad-Gita*, asserted the oneness of matter and spirit. Where Western religions emphasized the imperishability of individual consciousness, Hinduism aspired to its sublimation, or rather, its reabsorption into the spiritual infinite. Although Hinduism still embraces the vast pantheon of Vedic gods and goddesses, it has remained relatively unaffected by the religious precepts of Western Judaism and Christianity. Unlike the latter, Hinduism has no institutional forms of worship and no doctrinal laws. On the other hand, since the nineteenth century, Hinduism's holistic view of nature has increasingly influenced Western thought and belief. And since the last decades of the twentieth century, Hindu techniques of deep meditation have made a notable impact on the disciplines of religion, philosophy, and medical science.

Ancient China

Ancient Chinese civilization emerged in the fertile valleys of two great waterways: the Yellow and the Yangzi* Rivers (Map **3.2**). As early as 3500 B.C.E., the Neolithic villages of China were producing silk, a commodity that would bring wealth and fame to Chinese culture, but the hallmarks of civilization—urban centers, metallurgy, and writing—did not appear until the second millennium B.C.E. By 1750 B.C.E., the Chinese had developed a script that employed some 4,500 characters (each character representing an individual word), some of which are still used today. A combination of pictographic and phonetic elements, Chinese characters became the basis for writing throughout East Asia. Although it is likely that China's first dynasties flourished for some three centuries before the appearance of writing, China's Bronze Age urban culture coincided with the rise of a warrior tribe known as the Shang.

The Shang Dynasty (ca. 1520–1027 B.C.E.)

Shang rulers were hereditary kings who were regarded as intermediaries between the people and the spirit world. Limited in power by councils consisting of China's landholding nobility, they claimed their authority from the Lord on High (Shang-ti). Hence, as in Egypt, they ruled by divine right. Royal authority was symbolized by the dragon, a hybrid beast that stood for strength, fertility and life-giving water (Figure **3.3**). Occupants of the "dragon

*All transcriptions of Chinese names appear in the system known as Hanyu Pinyin.

Map 3.2 Ancient China.

Figure 3.4 Ceremonial vessel with a cover, late Shang Dynasty, China, ca. 1000 B.C.E. Bronze, height 20⁹⁄₁₆ in. Freer Gallery of Art, Smithsonian Institution, Washington, D.C. Accession No. 30.26 AB.

Figure 3.5 Standing figure, Late Shang, ca. 1300–1100 B.C.E., from Pit 2 at Sanxingdui, Guanghan, Sichuan Province. Bronze, height 8 ft. 7 in.

throne," China's early kings defended their position by way of a powerful bureaucracy and huge armies of archer-warriors recruited from the provinces. The king's soldiers consisted of peasants, who, in peacetime, farmed the land with the assistance of slaves captured in war. The Chinese social order is clearly articulated in Shang royal tombs, where the king is surrounded by the men and women who served him. Royal graves also include several hundred headless bodies, probably those of the slaves who built the tomb. As in Egypt and Mesopotamia, China's royal tombs were filled with treasures, most of which took the form of carved jade (see Figure 3.3) and magnificently worked bronze objects. Bronze bells used in rituals and bronze vessels designed to hold food and drink for the deceased appear in great number (Figure **3.4**). In their linear vitality, the surfaces of these ritual objects, adorned with a complex of dragons, birds, and maze-like motifs, express the ancient Chinese view of the cosmos as animated by natural spirits. In 1986, archeologists working in Sichuan province (an area beyond the rule of the Shang) uncovered graves that contained gold and silver objects, along with more than 200 bronze objects, including the earliest life-size human figures in Chinese art (Figure **3.5**). This and even more recent finds suggest that the early history of China is still largely hidden from us.

Beginning in Neolithic times and throughout ancient Chinese history, large numbers of jade objects, including and especially jade discs (see Figure 3.3) are found in royal graves. The meaning and function of these ubiquitous objects is the matter of some speculation. The Chinese used jade for tools, but also for carved insignias and talismans probably related to ceremonial ritual. Apart from its durability, jade was prized by the Chinese for its musical qualities, its subtle, translucent colors, and its alleged protective powers—it was thought to prevent fatigue and delay the decomposition of the body. In the tombs of later rulers, the deceased were encased with

Figure 3.6 Shroud, Han Dynasty, 206 B.C.E.–24 C.E. Jade and gold wire, length 74 in. From the tomb of Liu Sheng at Lingshan, Mancheng, Hebei Province.

shrouds made up of thousands of carved jade plaques sewn with gold wire (Figure **3.6**).

The Zhou Dynasty (1027–256 B.C.E.)

The sacred right to rule was known in China as the Mandate of Heaven. Although the notion of divine-right kingship began in the earliest centuries of China's dynasties, the concept of a divine mandate was not fixed until early in the Zhou era, when the rebel Zhou tribe justified their assault on the Shang by claiming that Shang kings had failed to rule virtuously; hence, Heaven had withdrawn its mandate. Charged with maintaining the will of heaven on earth, the king's political authority required obedience to pre-established moral law, which, in turn reflected the natural order.

According to the Chinese, the natural order—a holistic and primordial arrangement in nature—determined human intelligence and ability, as well as the individual's proper place in society. Within the natural hierarchy, those with greater intellectual abilities should govern, and those with lesser abilities should fulfill the physical needs of the state. Exactly how those with greater abilities were distinguished from those with lesser abilities is difficult to discern. Nevertheless, between the twelfth and eighth centuries B.C.E., when the Zhou kings controlled most of civilized China, the principle of the natural hierarchy already provided the basis for China's political and social hierarchy. Since the Zhou rulers delegated local authority to aristocrats of their choosing, it is probable that the assumptions of superiority and inferiority among people came after the fact of a division of labor among the members of society. Nevertheless, well before the second century B.C.E., the Chinese put into practice

the world's first system whereby individuals were selected for government service on the basis of merit and education. Written examinations tested the competence and skill of those who sought government office. Such a system persisted for centuries and became the basis for an aristocracy of merit that has characterized Chinese culture well into modern times.

Spirits, Gods, and the Natural Order

The agricultural communities of ancient China venerated an assortment of local spirits associated with the natural forces, and with rivers, mountains, and crops. But the most powerful of the personalized spirits of ancient China were those of deceased ancestors, the members of an extended familial community (Figure **3.7**). According to the Chinese, the spirits of deceased ancestors continued to exist in Heaven, where they assumed their role as mediators between Heaven and Earth. Since the ancestors exerted a direct influence upon human affairs, their welfare was of deep concern to ancient Chinese families. They buried the dead in elaborate tombs, regularly made sacrifices to them, and brought offerings of food and wine to their graves. One of the earliest odes in China's classic *Book of Songs (Shi jing)* celebrates the veneration of ancestors of both sexes:

Rich is the year with much millet and rice;
And we have tall granaries
With hundreds and thousands and millions of sheaves.
We make wind and sweet spirits
And offer them to our ancestors, male and female;
Thus to fulfill all the rites
And bring down blessings in full.*

Figure 3.7 Mask, Shang Dynasty, ca. 1500–1050 B.C.E. Bronze, lifesize. Academia Sinica, Taipei.

*From William Theodore de Bry, and others, eds. *Sources of Chinese Tradition* (New York: Colombia University Press, 1960), 15.

–2,700 first experiments in acupuncture and herbal medicine are made in China
–2,600 silk manufacture begins in China
–2,296 first reported sighting of a comet occurs in China
–1,350 decimal numerals are introduced in China
–1,000 the Chinese introduce an early version of the abacus

The dead and the living shared a cosmos animated by nature and regulated by the natural order. In the regularity of the seasonal cycle, the growth of trees and plants, and the everyday workings of nature, the Chinese found harmony and order. The natural order might be symbolized by way of abstract symbols, such as the circle, but it was also worshipped in the form of nature spirits and celestial deities. The creative principle, for instance, was known interchangeably as the Lord on High (Shang-ti) and, more abstractly, as Heaven (Qian). Although not an anthropomorphic deity of the kind found in ancient Egypt and Mesopotamia, Shang-ti/Qian regulated the workings of the universe and impartially guided the destinies of all people. For the Chinese, the cosmic and human order was a single sacred system. This holistic viewpoint identified ***qi*** (pronounced "key") as the substance of the universe and, thus, the vital energy that pervades the human body. An understanding of nature's order was deemed essential to the well-being of both the individual and the ancient Chinese community; hence, it became the job of a special group of priests to examine that order and to divine (or foretell) the future. Shang diviners inscribed questions—whether the harvest would be bountiful, whether to make war, and so on—on tortoise shells and animal bones. The bones were heated to produce cracks that the diviners might read and interpret. For modern-day scholars, the bones offer information about the ceremonies, wars, and administrative life of Shang rulers; they also reveal fascinating details about weather, disease, and many other routine topics. Inscriptions on oracle bones dating from between ca. 1500 and 1000 B.C.E. constitute some of the earliest examples of Chinese writing (Figure **3.8**).

Figure 3.8 Inscribed oracle bone, China, ca. 1500–1000 B.C.E. C. V. Starr. East Asian Library, Columbian University.

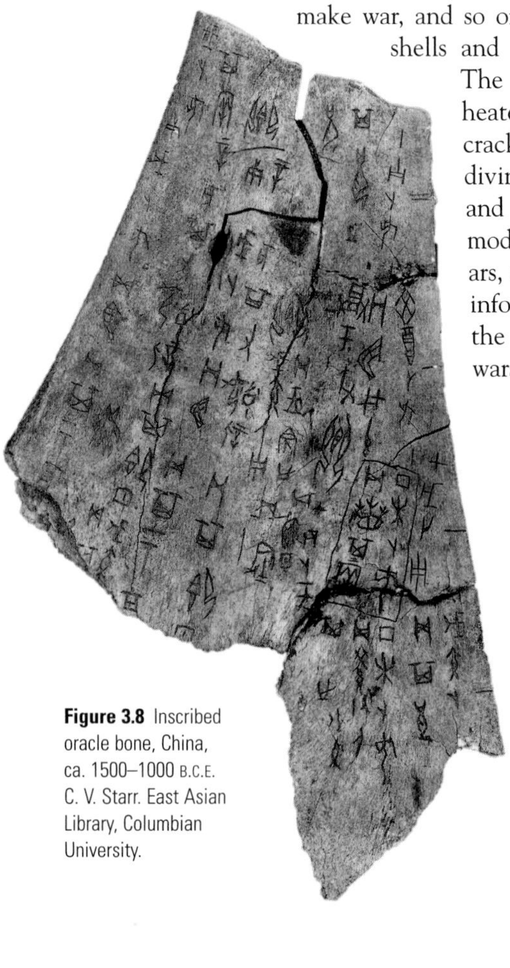

The ancient Chinese perception of an inviolable natural order dominated all aspects of China's long and productive history. Unlike the civilizations of Egypt and Mesopotamia, China left no mythological tales or heroic epics. Rather, China's oldest text, *The Book of Changes (I jing)*, is a directory for interpreting the operations of the universe. *The Book of Changes*, which originated in the Shang era but was not recorded until the sixth century B.C.E., consists of cryptic symbols and commentaries on which diviners drew to predict the future. Order derived from the balance between the four seasons, the five elements (wood, fire, earth, metal, water), and the five powers of creation (cold, heat, dryness, moisture, and wind). And Chinese mythology described cosmic unity in terms of the marriage of Qian (the creative principle, or Heaven) and Kun (the receptive principle, or Earth). Signifying the order of nature most graphically is the cosmological metaphor of the *yin/yang*. This principle, which ancient Chinese emperors called "the foundation of the entire universe," interprets all nature as the dynamic product of two interacting cosmic forces, or modes of energy, commonly configured as twin interpenetrating shapes enclosed within a circle (Figure **3.9**). The interaction of yang, the male principle (associated with lightness, hardness, brightness, warmth, and the sun) and yin, the female principle (associated with darkness, softness, moisture, coolness, the earth, and the moon) describes the creative energy of the universe and the natural order itself. For the Chinese, this order inheres in the balance between the forces of hot and cold, day and night, heaven and earth, male and female, and so on. In the circle, a figure with no beginning or end, and the ring or disc, which unifies positive form and negative space, the complementary polarities of *yin/yang* are implicit. Perhaps, then, the jade discs found in such great numbers in Chinese graves served as cosmic talismans.

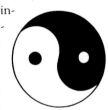

Figure 3.9 The Yin and the Yang as interpenetrating shapes in a circle.

Daoism

The most eloquent expression of the natural order as it relates to humankind is preserved in the ancient Chinese belief system known as Daoism. As much a philosophy as a religion, Daoism embraces a universal and natural principle—the Dao, or "Way." While the Dao is ineffable—indeed, it resists all intellectual analysis—it manifests itself in the harmony of things. It may be thought of as the unity underlying nature's multiplicity; and it is understood only by those who live in total simplicity and in harmony with nature. Daoists seek to cultivate tranquillity, spontaneity, compassion, and spiritual insight. Like the Hindu, the Daoist practices meditation and breath control, along with dietary and other physical means of prolonging and enriching life.

Daoism existed in China as early as 1000 B.C.E., but its basic text, the *Dao de jing* (*The Way and Its Power*), did not appear until the sixth century B.C.E. This modest "scripture" of some 5,000 words is associated with the name Lao Zi ("the Old One"), who may or may not have ever actually existed. The following poem, one of the eighty-one chapters of the *Dao de jing*, conveys the Daoist idea of nature's unity. It uses a series of simple images to illustrate the complementary and harmonious function of positive and negative elements in ordinary things, as in nature. Like all Daoist teaching, it relies on subtle wit and paradox as springboards to enlightenment.

READING 1.10 From the *Dao de jing* (ca. 550 B.C.E.)

Thirty spokes will converge	1
In the hub of a wheel;	
But the use of the cart	
Will depend on the part	
Of the hub that is void.	5
With a wall all around	
A clay bowl is molded;	
But the use of the bowl	
Will depend on the part	
Of the bowl that is void.	10
Cut out windows and doors	
In the house as you build;	
But the use of the house	
Will depend on the space	
In the walls that is void.	15
So advantage is had	
From whatever is there;	
But usefulness rises	
From whatever is not.	

SUMMARY

India's first civilization, the Bronze Age culture at Mohenjo-daro, was overturned by the Aryans, who introduced the principal features of ancient Indian society: the caste system, epic poetry, India's earliest religious texts, and the religion known as Hinduism. Hinduism is a pantheistic faith that perceives all nature as an expression of the Absolute One or Brahman. Ancient Hindus viewed the life of the individual as one with, rather than subject to, an impersonal divine force. They sought the sublimation of the Self by means of meditation and a stilling of the senses. Achieving nirvana permitted the Hindu to escape the Wheel of Rebirth. To this day, Hinduism retains its holistic character and has remained relatively unaffected by Western religious precepts.

In ancient China, concepts of social and spiritual harmony were deeply rooted in the idea of an order governed by nature, rather than by individual and personal gods. The leaders of China's earliest dynasties ruled by the Mandate of Heaven, which enforced the order of heaven on earth. As in Egypt, China's kings were buried in elaborately furnished graves whose contents reflect a high level of artistic achievement. A holistic world view linked the realm of the dead with all living descendants. For the Chinese, the natural order was inseparable from the moral and social order; it governed China's doctrines of natural equality and justified its system of advancement based on merit. It also generated the school of thought known as Daoism, the way of nature. China's earliest dynasties established the foundations for a unified culture whose fundamental ideas and values endure well into our own time.

GLOSSARY

Atman the Hindu name for the Self; the personal part of Brahman

Brahman the Hindu name for the Absolute Spirit; an impersonal World Soul that pervades all things

caste system a rigid social stratification in India based on differences in wealth, rank, or occupation

karma (Sanskrit, "deed") the law that holds that one's deeds determine one's future life in the Wheel of Rebirth

nirvana (Sanskrit, "extinction") the blissful reabsorption of the Self into the Absolute Spirit (Brahman): release from the endless cycle of rebirth (see also Buddhism, chapters 8, 9)

pantheism the belief that a divine spirit pervades all things in the universe

qi (Chinese, "substance" or "breath") the material substance or vital force of the universe

SUGGESTIONS FOR READING

Basham, A. L. *The Wonder That Was India: A Survey of the Culture of the Indian Subcontinent before the Coming of the Muslims.* 3rd edition. London: Sidgwick and Jackson, 1985.

Creel, H. G. *What is Daoism?* Chicago: University of Chicago Press, 1970.

Jian, Li, ed. *External China: Splendors from the First Dynasties.* Dayton, Ohio: The Dayton Art Institute, 1998.

Loewe, Michael. *Everyday Life in Early Imperial China.* New York: Dorset Press, 1988.

Schwartz, Benjamin J. *The World of Thought in Ancient China.* Cambridge, Mass.: Harvard University Press, 1985.

Sommer, Deborah. *Chinese Religion: An Anthology of Sources.* New York: Oxford University Press, 1995.

Yang, Xiaoneng, ed. *The Golden Age of Chinese Archeology: Celebrated Discoveries from the People's Republic of China.* New Haven, Conn.: Yale University Press, 1999.

Zimmer, Heinrich. *Myths and Symbols in Indian Art and Civilization.* Reprint. Princeton: Princeton/Bollington, 1992.

PART TWO

The classical legacy

Between 500 B.C.E. and 500 C.E., the civilizations of ancient Greece and Rome came to flower in the Mediterranean world. Their influence on the humanistic tradition was both prefound and long lasting, far exceeding that of any culture preceeding them. To the civilizations of Greece and Rome the West owes the refinement of almost all of the basic forms of literary expression (including drama, the epistle, lyric poetry, satire, and historical narrative), the fundamentals of philosophic and scientific inquiry, the development of civil and judicial law, and the formulation of aesthetic norms in art and music that have persisted for well over a thousand years.

The word "classical" may be used in several ways. Most generally, "classic" or "classical" means "first-ranking," "enduring," or "the best of its kind." So, "classic" cars refer to vintage automobiles, and "classic" films are those that attract generation after generation of viewers. In this usage, "classic" implies superiority: What is classic is "first rate." The term "classical" is also used to designate the characteristic phase of a culture or civilization, especially if that phase has had an enduring influence on subsequent cultures. Because the civilizations of Greece and Rome have provided authoritative models for the arts and ideas of the West, they are called "classical," and the age in which they flourished is known as the Classical Age. A similar situation holds for ancient China: In a period approximately contemporaneous with the Greco-Roman era, China developed a body of learning and a legacy in the arts that not only endured for thousands of years, but became the cultural model for much of East Asia. The era of the Han (ca. 200 B.C.E. to 200 C.E.) is regarded as China's classical age.

Finally, the word "classical" may be used stylistically. As a style, "classical" describes a mode of expression that came to its peak in the "Golden Age" of Greece, the fifth

century B.C.E. That style is characterized by the principles of clarity, harmony, balance, simplicity (or moderation), and refinement. Its focus is this-worldly and humanistic. These features marked Greco-Roman cultural expression, and, to a great extent, that of Han China as well.

The Greek and Roman civilizations emerged at the western end of the Asian landmass, north and west of the ancient civilizations of Egypt and Mesopotamia. Between 1200 and 750 B.C.E., the first Greek city-states appeared on the islands and peninsulas in the Aegean Sea, the coast of Asia Minor, at the southern tip of Italy, and in Sicily. This ancient civilization called itself "Hellas" and its people "Hellenes" (the name "Greece" derives from the Latin *Graecus*). During and just after the Golden Age, the Hellenic city-states produced some of the most engaging works of art, literature, and philosophy in the history of culture. Hellenic culture would not die with the fall of Greece in 338 B.C.E.; rather, by way of the imperial ambitions of Alexander the Great, it would permeate all of Asia, generating a Greek-like, or Hellenistic, era. And well into the period of Roman dominance in the Mediterranean, the legacy of Greece would continue to influence the history of culture.

While Greek culture was savoring its Golden Age, Rome was establishing itself as the leading city-state of the Italian peninsula. Rome's history is usually divided into two phases: the Republic (509–31 B.C.E.) and the Empire (31 B.C.E.–476 C.E.). The Romans created the largest and most powerful empire in the ancient world. Their achievements in engineering, architecture, literature, and law would be imitated in the West long after the collapse of Rome itself. Moreover, Roman civilization would transmit westward the legacy of classical Greek culture as well as the fundamentals of a young religious faith called Christianity.

(opposite) Apollo Belvedere. Roman marble copy of a Greek original, late fourth century B.C.E. Height 7 ft. 4 in. Vatican Museums, Rome.

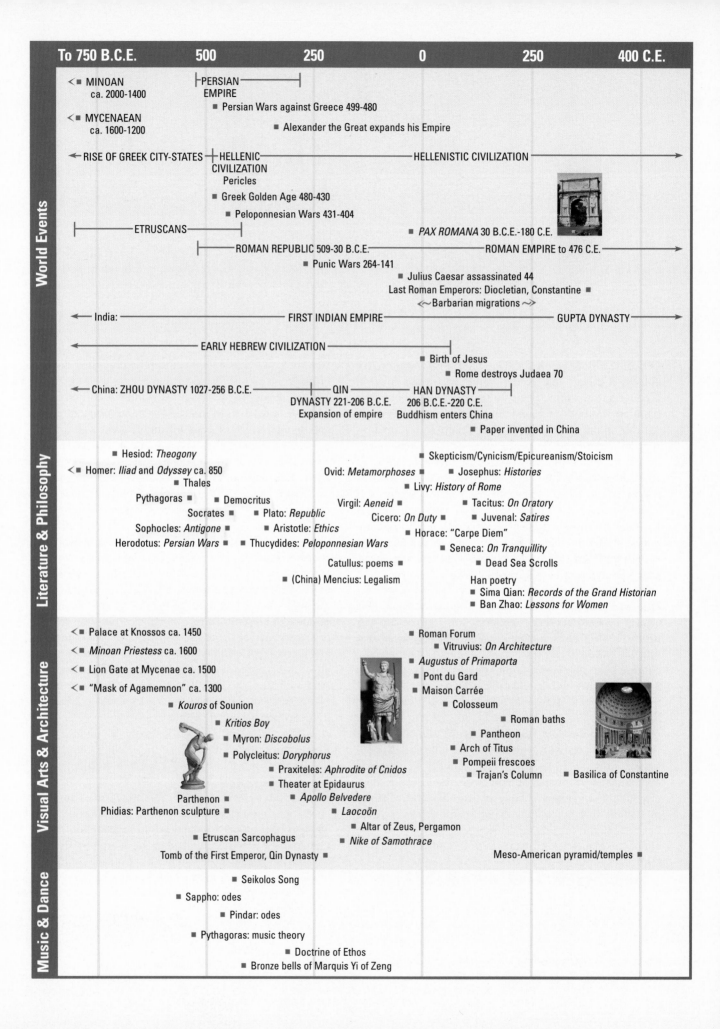

To 750 B.C.E.	500	250	0	250	400 C.E.

World Events

< ■ MINOAN ca. 2000–1400

├ PERSIAN EMPIRE ┤

■ Persian Wars against Greece 499–480

< ■ MYCENAEAN ca. 1600–1200

■ Alexander the Great expands his Empire

← RISE OF GREEK CITY-STATES → ┤ HELLENIC CIVILIZATION — Pericles — HELLENISTIC CIVILIZATION →

■ Greek Golden Age 480–430

■ Peloponnesian Wars 431–404

├ ETRUSCANS ┤

■ *PAX ROMANA* 30 B.C.E.–180 C.E.

├ ROMAN REPUBLIC 509–30 B.C.E. ┤ ROMAN EMPIRE to 476 C.E. →

■ Punic Wars 264–141

■ Julius Caesar assassinated 44

Last Roman Emperors: Diocletian, Constantine ■

←~ Barbarian migrations ~→

← India: ── FIRST INDIAN EMPIRE ── GUPTA DYNASTY →

← EARLY HEBREW CIVILIZATION ┤

■ Birth of Jesus

■ Rome destroys Judaea 70

← China: ZHOU DYNASTY 1027–256 B.C.E. ┤ QIN HAN DYNASTY ┤
DYNASTY 221–206 B.C.E.   206 B.C.E.–220 C.E.
Expansion of empire   Buddhism enters China

■ Paper invented in China

Literature & Philosophy

■ Hesiod: *Theogony*

< ■ Homer: *Iliad* and *Odyssey* ca. 850

■ Thales

Pythagoras ■   ■ Democritus

Socrates ■   ■ Plato: *Republic*

Sophocles: *Antigone* ■   ■ Aristotle: *Ethics*

Herodotus: *Persian Wars* ■   ■ Thucydides: *Peloponnesian Wars*

■ Skepticism/Cynicism/Epicureanism/Stoicism

Ovid: *Metamorphoses* ■   ■ Josephus: *Histories*

■ Livy: *History of Rome*

Virgil: *Aeneid* ■   ■ Tacitus: *On Oratory*

Cicero: *On Duty* ■   ■ Juvenal: *Satires*

■ Horace: "Carpe Diem"

■ Seneca: *On Tranquillity*

Catullus: poems ■   ■ Dead Sea Scrolls

■ (China) Mencius: Legalism

Han poetry
■ Sima Qian: *Records of the Grand Historian*
■ Ban Zhao: *Lessons for Women*

Visual Arts & Architecture

< ■ Palace at Knossos ca. 1450

< ■ *Minoan Priestess* ca. 1600

< ■ Lion Gate at Mycenae ca. 1500

< ■ "Mask of Agamemnon" ca. 1300

■ *Kouros* of Sounion

■ *Kritios Boy*

■ Myron: *Discobolus*

■ Polycleitus: *Doryphorus*

■ Praxiteles: *Aphrodite of Cnidos*

■ Theater at Epidaurus

■ *Apollo Belvedere*

Parthenon ■

Phidias: Parthenon sculpture ■

■ *Laocoön*

■ Altar of Zeus, Pergamon

■ Etruscan Sarcophagus

■ *Nike of Samothrace*

Tomb of the First Emperor, Qin Dynasty ■

■ Roman Forum
■ Vitruvius: *On Architecture*
■ *Augustus of Primaporta*
■ Pont du Gard
■ Maison Carrée
■ Colosseum
■ Roman baths
■ Pantheon
■ Arch of Titus
■ Pompeii frescoes
■ Trajan's Column
■ Basilica of Constantine

Meso-American pyramid/temples ■

Music & Dance

■ Seikolos Song

■ Sappho: odes

■ Pindar: odes

■ Pythagoras: music theory

■ Doctrine of Ethos

■ Bronze bells of Marquis Yi of Zeng

CHAPTER FOUR

Greece: humanism and the speculative leap

"I say that Athens is the school of Hellas, and that the individual Athenian in his own person seems to have the power of adapting himself to the most varied forms of action with the utmost versatility and grace."
Thucydides

The nineteenth-century British poet Percy Bysshe Shelley once proclaimed, "We are all Greeks." He meant by this that modern humankind—profoundly influenced by Hellenic notions of reason, beauty, and the good life—bears the stamp of ancient Greece. Few civilizations have been so deeply concerned with the quality of human life as that of the ancient Greeks. And few have been so committed to the role of the individual intellect in shaping the destiny of the community. Because their art, their literature, and their religious beliefs celebrate human interests and concerns, the Greeks have been called the humanists of the ancient world. The worldliness and robust optimism that marks Hellenic culture is apparent even in the formative stages of Greek civilization.

Bronze Age Civilizations of the Aegean (ca. 3000–1200 B.C.E.)

The Bronze Age culture of Mycenae was not known to the world until the late nineteenth century, when an amateur German archeologist named Heinrich Schliemann uncovered the first artifacts of ancient Troy (Map **4.1**). Schliemann's excavations brought to light the civilization of an adventuresome tribal people, the Mycenaeans, who had established themselves on the Greek mainland around 1600 B.C.E. Subsequent discoveries by other archeologists disclosed an even earlier pre-Greek civilization located on the island of Crete in the Aegean Sea. Named Minoan after the legendary King Minos, this maritime civilization

Map 4.1 Ancient Greece.

flourished between 2000 and 1400 B.C.E., when it seems to have been absorbed or destroyed by the Mycenaeans.

Minoan Civilization (ca. 2000–1400 B.C.E.)

Centered in the Palace of Minos at Knossos on the island of Crete (Figure 4.1), Minoan culture was prosperous and seafaring. The absence of protective walls around the palace complex suggests that the Minoans enjoyed a sense of security. The three-story palace at Knossos was a labyrinthine masonry structure with dozens of rooms and corridors built around a central courtyard. The interior walls of the palace bear magnificent frescoes illustrating natural and marine motifs (Figure 4.2), ceremonial processions, and other aspects of Cretan life. The most famous of the palace frescoes, the so-called "bull-leaping" fresco, shows two women and a man, the latter vigorously somersaulting over the back of a bull (Figure 4.3). Probably associated with the cult of the bull—ancient symbol of virility (see Figures 1.3 and 2.15)—the ritual game prefigures the modern bullfight, the "rules" of which were codified in Roman times by Julius Caesar. Since 1979, when modern archeologists uncovered the evidence of human sacrifice in Minoan Crete, historians have speculated on the meaning of ancient bull-vaulting (a sport still practiced in Portugal), and its possible relationship to rituals of blood sacrifice. Nevertheless, the significance of the representation lies in the authority it bestows upon the players: Human beings are pictured here not as pawns in a divine game, but, rather, as challengers in a contest of wit and physical agility. Other Minoan artifacts suggest the persistence of ancient fertility cults honoring gods traditionally associated with procreation: The small statue of a bare-breasted female brandishing snakes may represent a popular fertility goddess; or it may depict a priestess performing specific cult rites, such as those accompanying ancient Greek dances that featured live snakes (Figure 4.4). Minoan writing (known as "Linear A") has not yet been deciphered, but a later version of the script ("Linear B") found on mainland Greece appears to be an early form of Greek. Modern archeologists were not the first to prize Minoan culture; the Greeks immortalized the Minoans in myth and legend. The most famous of these legends describes a Minotaur—a monstrous half-man, half-bull hybrid born of the union of Minos' queen and a sacred white bull. According to the story, the clever Athenian hero Theseus, aided by the king's daughter Ariadne, threaded his way through the Minotaur's labyrinthine lair to kill the monster, thus freeing Athens from its ancient bondage to the Minoans. Around 1700 B.C.E., some three centuries before mainland Greece absorbed Crete, an earthquake brought devastation to Minoan civilization.

Figure 4.1 Palace of Minos, Knossos, Crete, ca. 1500 B.C.E. Photo: Gloria K. Fiero.

Figure 4.2 The Queen's Quarters, Palace of Minos, Knossos, Crete, ca. 1450 B.C.E. Ancient Art and Architecture Collection, Middlesex.

Figure 4.3 Bull-leaping fresco from the Palace of Minos, Knossos, Crete, ca. 1500 B.C.E. Height 32 in. Archeological Museum, Heraklion, Crete. Scala, Florence.

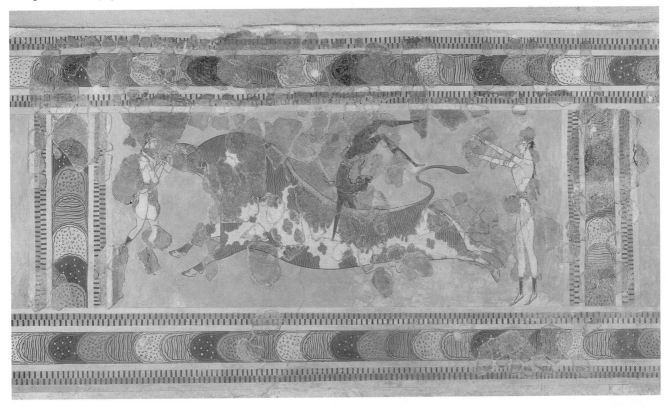

Figure 4.4 Priestess with Snakes, Minoan, ca. 1600 B.C.E. Faience, height 13½ in. Archeological Museum, Heraklion, Crete. Photo: Craigo Marie Mauzy, Athens.

Figure 4.5 Lion Gate, Citadel at Mycenae, ca. 1500–1300 B.C.E. Limestone, height of relief 9 ft. 6 in. Photo: Craigo Marie Mauzy, Athens.

Figure 4.6 Funerary mask, possibly of Agamemnon, ca. 1500 B.C.E. Gold, height 12 in. National Archeological Museum, Athens. Photo: Craigo Marie Mauzy, Athens.

Mycenaean Civilization (ca. 1600–1200 B.C.E.)

By 1600 B.C.E., the Mycenaeans had established themselves in the Aegean. By contrast with the Minoans, the Mycenaeans were a militant and aggressive people: Their warships challenged other traders for control of the eastern Mediterranean. On mainland Greece at Tiryns and Mycenae (see Map 4.1), the Mycenaeans constructed heavily fortified citadels and walls so massive that later generations thought they had been built by a mythical race of giants known as the Cyclops. These "cyclopean" walls were guarded by symbols of royal power: in the triangular arch above the entrance gate to the citadel, two 9-foot high stone lions flank a column that rests on a stone altar (Figure 4.5). Master stonemasons, the Mycenaeans buried their rulers in beehive-shaped tombs. The royal graves, uncovered by Schliemann in 1876, are filled with weapons and jewelry fit for an Egyptian pharaoh. These items, and in particular the gold death mask that once covered the face of the deceased, Schliemann identified as belonging to Agamemnon (Figure 4.6), the legendary king who led the ancient Greeks against the city of Troy. This tale is immortalized in the first of the Greek epic poems, the *Iliad*. Although later archeologists have proved Schliemann wrong—the tombs are actually earlier than he thought—the legends and the myths of the Greek world would flower in Mycenaean soil.

Around 1200 B.C.E., the Mycenaeans attacked Troy ("Ilion" in Greek), a commercial stronghold on the northwest coast of Asia Minor. The ten-year-long war between Mycenae and Troy would provide the historical context for the two great epic poems of the ancient Greeks: the *Iliad* and the *Odyssey*.

The Heroic Age (ca. 1200–750 B.C.E.)

Soon after 1200 B.C.E., more powerful, iron-bearing tribes of Dorians, a Greek-speaking people from the north, destroyed Mycenaean civilization. During the long period of darkness that followed, storytellers kept alive the history of early Greece, the adventures of the Mycenaeans, and the tales of the Trojan War, passing them orally from generation to generation. It was not until at least the ninth century B.C.E that these stories, in the form of two epic poems, were transcribed; and it was yet another three hundred years before they reached their present form. The *Iliad* and the *Odyssey* became the "national" poems of ancient Greece, uniting Greek-speaking people by giving literary authority to their common heritage. Although much of what is known about the early history of the Greeks comes from these two poems, little is known about the blind poet Homer, to whom they are traditionally attributed. Scholars are not sure when or where he lived, or, indeed, if he existed at all. It is unlikely that he composed the poems, though legend has it that he actually memorized the whole of each poem. The only fact of which we can be fairly certain is that Homer represents the culmination of a long and vigorous tradition in which oral recitation—possibly to instrumental accompaniment—was a popular kind of entertainment.

The *Iliad* takes place in the last days of the Trojan War. It is the story of the Achaean hero Achilles (or Achilleus), who, moved to anger by an affront to his honor, refuses to join the battle against Troy alongside his Achaean comrades. However, when his dearest friend Patroclus is killed by Hector (leader of the Trojan forces), Achilles finally and vengefully goes to war. The *Odyssey*, the second of the two epics, recounts the long, adventure-packed sea journey undertaken by Odysseus, a resourceful hero of the Trojan War, in his effort to return to his home and family in Ithaca. Like the *Epic of Gilgamesh*, the *Iliad* and the *Odyssey* belong to the oral tradition of an heroic age, but whereas the *Epic of Gilgamesh* takes as its theme the pursuit of everlasting life, the Greek epics give voice to the quest for individual honor and glory.

The *Iliad* is a robust tale of war, but its true subject is the personality of Achilles as he attempts to reconcile selfhood and communal responsibility. Achilles is the offspring of Peleus, King of Thessaly, and the sea nymph Thetis, who had dipped her infant son in the river Styx, thus making him invulnerable except for the heel by which she held him. Like Gilgamesh, Achilles is part-god and part-man: But the Greek superhero is a more psychologically complex character than Gilgamesh; the emotions he exhibits—anger, love, rage, and grief—are wholly human. The plot of the *Iliad* turns on Achilles' decision to take action that will bring glory to his tribe and to himself. The importance of heroic action in proving virtue, or excellence (the Greek word *arete* connotes both), is central to the *Iliad* and to the male-dominated culture of the Heroic Age. To the ancient Greeks, moral value lay in proper action, even if the consequence of that action meant death (Figure **4.7**).

Figure 4.7 Attr. The "Botkin Class" painter, Contest of Two Warriors. Attic black figure amphora. Terra-cotta, 11½ × 9½ in. Courtesy, Henry Lillie Pierce Fund, Museum of Fine Arts, Boston.

The language of the *Iliad*, no less than its theme, is charged with heroic vigor. It makes use of vivid **similes** (anger "blinds like smoke"), graphic **epithets** ("the bronze-armed Achaeans"), and lengthy **catalogs** of particulars. Both in its almost 16,000 lines of majestic poetry and for its heroic personalities, the *Iliad* has inspired generations of Western writers, including Virgil and Milton (to be discussed in later chapters). The following excerpts from the *Iliad*, rendered in a 1990 translation by Robert Fagles, illustrate the qualities that have made the work a classic.

READING 1.11 From the *Iliad* (ca. 850 B.C.E.)

(Book 18, ll. 1–42, 82–150; Book 19, ll. 423–477; Book 24, ll. 471–707)

So the men fought on like a mass of whirling fire   **1**
as swift Antilochus raced the message toward Achilles.
Sheltered under his curving, beaked ships he found him,
foreboding, deep down, all that had come to pass.
Agonizing now he probed his own great heart: **5**
"Why, why? Our long-haired Achaeans[1] routed again,
driven in terror off the plain to crowd the ships, but why?
Dear gods, don't bring to pass the grief that haunts my
    heart—
the prophecy that mother revealed to me one time . . .
she said the best of the Myrmidons[2]—while I lived—   **10**
would fall at Trojan hands and leave the light of day.
And now he's dead, I know it: Menoetius' gallant son,[3]
my headstrong friend! And I told Patroclus clearly,
'Once you have beaten off the lethal fire, quick,
come back to the ships—you must not battle Hector!'"   **15**

As such fears went churning through his mind
the warlord Nestor's son drew near him now,
streaming warm tears, to give the dreaded message:
"Ah son of royal Peleus, what you must hear from me!
What painful news—would to god it had never happened!   **20**
Patroclus has fallen. They're fighting over his corpse.
He's stripped, naked—Hector with that flashing helmet,
Hector has your arms!"
    So the captain reported.
A black cloud of grief came shrouding over Achilles.
Both hands clawing the ground for soot and filth,   **25**
he poured it over his head, fouled his handsome face
and black ashes settled onto his fresh clean war-shirt.
Overpowered in all his power, he sprawled in the dust.
Achilles lay there, fallen . . .
tearing his hair, defiling it with his own hands.   **30**
And the women he and Patroclus carried off as captives
caught the grief in their hearts and keened and wailed,
out of the tents they ran to ring the great Achilles,

---

[1]The Mycenaeans, who inhabited the kingdom near Thessaly, and, more broadly, the Greek army that besieged Troy.
[2]The name by which the subject warriors of Peleus and Achilles are known in Homer. It derives from the Greek word for ants, the creatures out of which Zeus was said to have created the inhabitants of the island of Aegina, ruled by Peleus.
[3]Patroclus, Achilles' favorite companion and friend.

all of them beat their breasts with clenched fists,
sank to the ground, each woman's knees gave way.   **35**
Antilochus kneeling near, weeping uncontrollably,
clutched Achilles' hands as he wept his proud heart out—
for fear he would slash his throat with an iron blade.
Achilles suddenly loosed a terrible, wrenching cry
and his noble mother heard him, seated near her father,   **40**
the Old Man of the Sea[4] in the salt green depths,
and she cried out in turn.

   . . . .

As he groaned from the depths his mother rose before him
and sobbing a sharp cry, cradled her son's head in her hands
and her words were all compassion, winging pity: "My child—   **45**
why in tears? What sorrow has touched your heart?
Tell me, please. Don't harbor it deep inside you.
Zeus has accomplished everything you wanted,
just as you raised your hands and prayed that day.
All the sons of Achaea are pinned against the ships   **50**
and all for want of you—they suffer shattering losses."

And groaning deeply the matchless runner answered,
"O dear mother, true! All those burning desires
Olympian Zeus has brought to pass for me—
but what joy to me now? My dear comrade's dead—   **55**
Patroclus—the man I loved beyond all other comrades,
loved as my own life—I've lost him—Hector's killed him,
stripped the gigantic armor off his back, a marvel to behold—
my burnished gear! Radiant gifts the gods presented Peleus
that day they drove you into a mortal's marriage bed . . .   **60**
I wish you'd lingered deep with the deathless sea-nymphs,
lived at ease, and Peleus carried home a mortal bride.
But now, as it is, sorrows, unending sorrows must surge
within your heart as well—for your own son's death.
Never again will you embrace him striding home.   **65**
My spirits rebel—I've lost the will to live,
to take my stand in the world of men—unless,
before all else, Hector's battered down by my spear
and gasps away his life, the blood-price for Patroclus,
Menoetius' gallant son he's killed and stripped!"   **70**

But Thetis answered, warning through her tears,
"You're doomed to a short life, my son, from all you say!
For hard on the heels of Hector's death your death
must come at once—"
    "Then let me die at once"—
Achilles burst out, despairing—"since it was not my fate   **75**
to save my dearest comrade from his death! Look,
a world away from his fatherland he's perished,
lacking me, my fighting strength, to defend him.
But now, since I shall not return to my fatherland . . .
nor did I bring one ray of hope to my Patroclus,   **80**
nor to the rest of all my steadfast comrades,
countless ranks struck down by mighty Hector—
No, no, here I sit by the ships . . .
a useless, dead weight on the good green earth—

---

[4]A sea god, the "Old Man" of the sea and father of some fifty to one hundred daughters, including Thetis, mother of Achilles.

I, no man my equal among the bronze-armed Achaeans,
not in battle, only in wars of words that others win.
If only strife could die from the lives of gods and men
and anger that drives the sanest man to flare in outrage—
bitter gall, sweeter than dripping streams of honey,
that swarms in people's chests and blinds like smoke—
just like the anger Agamemnon[5] king of men
has roused within me now . . .
                                    Enough.
Let bygones be bygones. Done is done.
Despite my anguish I will beat it down,
the fury mounting inside me, down by force.
But now I'll go and meet that murderer head-on,
that Hector who destroyed the dearest life I know.
For my own death, I'll meet it freely—whenever Zeus
and the other deathless gods would like to bring it on!
Not even Heracles fled his death, for all his power,
favorite son as he was to father Zeus the King.
Fate crushed him, and Hera's savage anger.
And I too, if the same fate waits for me . . .
I'll lie in peace, once I've gone down to death.
But now, for the moment, let me seize great glory!—
and drive some woman of Troy or deep-breasted Dardan
to claw with both hands at her tender cheeks and wipe away
her burning tears as the sobs come choking from her throat—
they'll learn that I refrained from war a good long time!
Don't try to hold me back from the fighting, mother,
love me as you do. You can't persuade me now."

. . . .

[Hephaestus (Hephaistos), god of fire and of metalworking,
has forged a special set of arms for Achilles. In the following
lines from Book 19, Achilles prepares to lead the Achaeans
into battle.]

Thick-and-fast as the snow comes swirling down from Zeus,
frozen sharp when the North Wind born in heaven blasts it
        on—
so massed, so dense the glistening burnished helmets shone,
streaming out of the ships, and shields with jutting bosses,
breastplates welded front and back and the long ashen spears.
The glory of armor lit the skies and the whole earth laughed,
rippling under the glitter of bronze, thunder resounding
under trampling feet of armies. And in their midst
the brilliant Achilles began to arm for battle . . .
A sound of grinding came from the fighter's teeth,
his eyes blazed forth in searing points of fire,
unbearable grief came surging through his heart
and now, bursting with rage against the men of Troy,
he donned Hephaestus' gifts—magnificent armor
the god of fire forged with all his labor.
First he wrapped his legs with well-made greaves,
fastened behind his heels with silver ankle-clasps,
next he strapped the breastplate round his chest
then over his shoulder Achilles slung his sword,
the fine bronze blade with its silver-studded hilt,

85

90

95

100

105

110

115

120

125

130

then hoisted the massive shield flashing far and wide
like a full round moon—and gleaming bright as the light
that reaches sailors out at sea, the flare of a watchfire
burning strong in a lonely sheepfold up some mountain slope
when the gale-winds hurl the crew that fights against them
far over the fish-swarming sea, far from loved ones—
so the gleam from Achilles' well-wrought blazoned shield
shot up and hit the skies. Then lifting his rugged helmet
he set it down on his brows, and the horsehair crest
shone like a star and the waving golden plumes shook
that Hephaestus drove in bristling thick along its ridge.
And brilliant Achilles tested himself in all his gear,
Achilles spun on his heels to see if it fit tightly,
see if his shining limbs ran free within it, yes,
and it felt like buoyant wings lifting the great captain.
And then, last, Achilles drew his father's spear
from its socket-stand—weighted, heavy, tough.
No other Achaean fighter could heft that shaft,
only Achilles had the skill to wield it well;
Pelian ash it was, a gift to his father Peleus
presented by Chiron[6] once, hewn on Pelion's crest
to be the death of heroes.
                                    Now the war-team—
Alcimus and Automedon worked to yoke them quickly.
They clinched the supple breast-straps round their chests
and driving the bridle irons home between their jaws,
pulled the reins back taut to the bolted chariot.
Seizing a glinting whip, his fist on the handgrip,
Automedon leapt aboard behind the team and behind him
Achilles struck his stance, helmed for battle now,
glittering in his armor like the sun astride the skies,
his ringing, daunting voice commanding his father's horses:
"Roan Beauty and Charger, illustrious foals of Lightfoot!
Try hard, do better this time—bring your charioteer
back home alive to his waiting Argive comrades
once we're through with fighting. Don't leave Achilles
there on the battlefield as you left Patroclus—dead!"

. . . .

[After Achilles defeats Hector, Priam, Hector's father and king
of Troy, comes to the Achaean camp. In the following lines
from Book 24, Priam begs for the return of his son's body.]

. . . the old king went straight up to the lodge
where Achilles dear to Zeus would always sit.
Priam found the warrior there inside . . .
many captains sitting some way off, but two,
veteran Automedon and the fine fighter Alcimus
were busy serving him. He had just finished dinner,
eating, drinking, and the table still stood near.
The majestic king of Troy slipped past the rest
and kneeling down beside Achilles, clasped his knees
and kissed his hands, those terrible, man-killing hands
that had slaughtered Priam's many sons in battle.
Awesome—as when the grip of madness seizes one
who murders a man in his own fatherland and flees

135

140

145

150

155

160

165

170

175

180

---
[5]King of Mycenae, who led the Greek forces in the Trojan War.

[6]A centaur (half-man, half-horse), one of the creatures driven from
Mount Pelion by the Lapiths (see Figure 5.22).

abroad to foreign shores, to a wealthy, noble host,
and a sense of marvel runs through all who see him—
so Achilles marveled, beholding majestic Priam.
His men marveled too, trading startled glances.
But Priam prayed his heart out to Achilles: 185
"Remember your own father, great godlike Achilles—
as old as I am, past the threshold of deadly old age!
No doubt the countrymen round about him plague him now,
with no one there to defend him, beat away disaster.
No one—but at least he hears you're still alive   190
and his old heart rejoices, hopes rising, day by day,
to see his beloved son come sailing home from Troy.
But I—dear god, my life so cursed by fate . . .
I fathered hero sons in the wide realm of Troy
and now not a single one is left, I tell you.   195
Fifty sons I had when the sons of Achaea came,
nineteen born to me from a single mother's womb
and the rest by other women in the palace. Many,
most of them violent Ares cut the knees from under.
But one, one was left me, to guard my walls, my people—   200
the one you killed the other day, defending his fatherland,
my Hector! It's all for him I've come to the ships now,
to win him back from you—I bring a priceless ransom.
Revere the gods, Achilles! Pity me in my own right,
remember your own father! I deserve more pity . . .   205
I have endured what no one on earth has ever done before—
I put to my lips the hands of the man who killed my son."

    Those words stirred within Achilles a deep desire
to grieve for his own father. Taking the old man's hand
he gently moved him back. And overpowered by memory   210
both men gave way to grief. Priam wept freely
for man-killing Hector, throbbing, crouching
before Achilles' feet as Achilles wept himself,
now for his father, now for Patroclus once again,
and their sobbing rose and fell throughout the house.   215
Then, when brilliant Achilles had his fill of tears
and the longing for it had left his mind and body,
he rose from his seat, raised the old man by the hand
and filled with pity now for his gray head and gray beard,
he spoke out winging words, flying straight to the heart: 220
"Poor man, how much you've borne—pain to break the spirit!
What daring brought you down to the ships, all alone,
to face the glance of the man who killed your sons,
so many fine brave boys? You have a heart of iron.
Come, please, sit down on this chair here . . .   225
Let us put our griefs to rest in our own hearts,
rake them up no more, raw as we are with mourning.
What good's to be won from tears that chill the spirit?
So the immortals spun our lives that we, we wretched men
live on to bear such torments—the gods live free of sorrows. 230
There are two great jars that stand on the floor of Zeus's halls
and hold his gifts, our miseries one, the other blessings.
When Zeus who loves the lightning mixes gifts for a man,
now he meets with misfortune, now good times in turn.
When Zeus dispenses gifts from the jar of sorrows only,   235
he makes a man an outcast—brutal, ravenous hunger
drives him down the face of the shining earth,
stalking far and wide, cursed by gods and men.

So with my father, Peleus. What glittering gifts
the gods rained down from the day that he was born!   240
He excelled all men in wealth and pride of place,
he lorded the Myrmidons, and mortal that he was,
they gave the man an immortal goddess for a wife.
Yes, but even on him the Father piled hardships,
no powerful race of princes born in his royal halls,   245
only a single son he fathered, doomed at birth,
cut off in the spring of life—
and I, I give the man no care as he grows old
since here I sit in Troy, far from my fatherland,
a grief to you, a grief to all your children.   250
And you too, old man, we hear you prospered once:
as far as Lesbos, Macar's kingdom, bounds to seaward,
Phrygia east and upland, the Hellespont vast and north—
that entire realm, they say, you lorded over once,
you excelled all men, old king, in sons and wealth.   255
But then the gods of heaven brought this agony on you—
ceaseless battles round your walls, your armies slaughtered.
You must bear up now. Enough of endless tears,
the pain that breaks the spirit.
Grief for your son will do no good at all.   260
You will never bring him back to life—
sooner you must suffer something worse."

    But the old and noble Priam protested strongly:
"Don't make me sit on a chair, Achilles, Prince,
not while Hector lies uncared-for in your camp!   265
Give him back to me, now, no more delay—
I must see my son with my own eyes.
Accept the ransom I bring you, a king's ransom!
Enjoy it, all of it—return to your own native land,
safe and sound . . . since now you've spared my life."   270
    A dark glance—and the headstrong runner answered,
"No more, old man, don't tempt my wrath, not now!
My own mind's made up to give you back your son.
A messenger brought me word from Zeus—my mother,
Thetis who bore me, the Old Man of the Sea's daughter.   275
And what's more, I can see through you, Priam—
no hiding the fact from me: one of the gods
has led you down to Achaea's fast ships.
No man alive, not even a rugged young fighter,
would dare to venture into our camp. Never—   280
how could he slip past the sentries unchallenged?
Or shoot back the bolt of my gates with so much ease?
So don't anger me now. Don't stir my raging heart still more.
Or under my own roof I may not spare your life, old man—
suppliant that you are—may break the laws of Zeus!"   285

    The old man was terrified. He obeyed the order.
But Achilles bounded out of doors like a lion—
not alone but flanked by his two aides-in-arms,
veteran Automedon and Alcimus, steady comrades,
Achilles' favorites next to the dead Patroclus.   290
They loosed from harness the horses and the mules,
they led the herald in, the old king's crier,
and sat him down on a bench. From the polished wagon
they lifted the priceless ransom brought for Hector's corpse
but they left behind two capes and a finely-woven shirt   295

to shroud the body well when Priam bore him home.
Then Achilles called the serving-women out:
"Bathe and anoint the body—
bear it aside first. Priam must not see his son."
He feared that, overwhelmed by the sight of Hector,   300
wild with grief, Priam might let his anger flare
and Achilles might fly into fresh rage himself,
cut the old man down and break the laws of Zeus.
So when the maids had bathed and anointed the body
sleek with olive oil and wrapped it round and round   305
in a braided battle-shirt and handsome battle-cape,
then Achilles lifted Hector up in his own arms
and laid him down on a bier, and comrades helped him
raise the bier and body onto the sturdy wagon . . .
Then with a groan he called his dear friend by name: 310
"Feel no anger at me, Patroclus, if you learn—
even there in the House of Death—I let his father
have Prince Hector back. He gave me worthy ransom
and you shall have your share from me, as always,
your fitting, lordly share."
                              So he vowed   315
and brilliant Achilles strode back to his shelter,
sat down on the well-carved chair that he had left,
at the far wall of the room, leaned toward Priam
and firmly spoke the words the king had come to hear:
"Your son is now set free, old man, as you requested.   320
Hector lies in state. With the first light of day
you will see for yourself as you convey him home.
Now, at last, let us turn our thoughts to supper."

. . . .

The Greek Gods

The ancient Greeks envisioned their gods as a family of immortals who intervened in the lives of human beings. Originating in the cultures of Crete and Mycenae, the Greek pantheon exalted Zeus, the powerful sky god, and his wife, Hera, as the ruling deities. Among the lesser gods were Poseidon, god of the sea; Apollo, god of light, medicine, and music; Dionysus, god of wine and vegetation; Athena, goddess of wisdom and war; and Aphrodite, goddess of love and procreation. Around these and other deities (Figure 4.8) there emerged an elaborate mythology.

Many Greek myths look back to the common pool of legends and tales that traveled throughout the Mediterranean and the Near East. In the *Theogony (The Birth of the Gods)*, a poem recounting the history and genealogy of the gods, Homer's contemporary Hesiod (fl. 700 B.C.E.) describes the origins of the universe in a manner reminiscent of *The Babylonian Creation*:

> First of all, the Void came into being, next broad-bosomed Earth, the solid and eternal home of all, and Eros [Desire], the most beautiful of the immortal gods, who in every man and every god softens the sinews and overpowers the prudent purpose of the mind. Out of Void came Darkness and black Night, and out of Night came Light and day, her children conceived after union in love with Darkness. Earth

first produced starry Sky, equal in size with herself . . .*

The Greeks also had their own version of the Isis/Osiris myth. When Hades, god of the underworld, abducts the beautiful Persephone, her mother, Demeter, rescues her; tricked by Hades, however, this goddess of vegetation is forced to return annually to the underworld, leaving the earth above barren and desolate. Cults based in myths of death and rebirth offered their devotees the hope for personal regeneration.

The Greeks traced their origins to events related to the fury of Zeus: Angered by human evil, Zeus decided to destroy humankind by sending a flood. Deucalion, the Greek Noah, built a boat for himself and his wife and obeyed an oracle that commanded them to throw the "bones" of Mother Earth overboard. From these stones sprang up human beings, the first of whom was Hellen, the legendary ancestor of the Greeks, or "Hellenes."

Although immortal, the Greek gods were much like the human beings who worshipped them: They were amorous, capricious, and quarrelsome. They lived not in some remote heaven, but (conveniently enough) atop a mountain in northern Greece—that is, among the Greeks themselves. From their home on Mount Olympus, the gods might take sides in human combat (as they regularly do in the *Iliad*), seduce mortal women, and meddle in the lives of ordinary people. The Greek gods were not always benevolent or just. Unlike the Hebrew God, they set forth

---

*Hesiod, *Theogony*, translated by Norman O. Brown (New York: Bobbs-Merrill, 1953), 56.

Figure 4.8 The Principal Greek Gods.

Greek Name	Roman Name	Represents
Aphrodite	Venus	Love, beauty
Apollo	Phoebus	Solar light, medicine, music
Artemis	Diana	Hunting, wildlife, the moon
Athena	Minerva	War, wisdom
Demeter	Ceres	Agriculture, grain
Dionysus	Bacchus	Wine, vegetation
Eros	Amor/Cupid	Erotic love, desire
Hades	Pluto	Underworld
Helios	Phoebus	Sun
Hephaestus	Vulcan	Fire, metallurgy
Hera	Juno	Queen of the gods
Heracles	Hercules	Strength, courage
Hestia	Vesta	Hearth, domestic life
Hermes	Mercury	Male messenger of the gods
Nike		Victory
Persephone	Prosperina	Underworld
Poseidon	Neptune	Sea
Selene	Diana	Moon
Zeus	Jupiter	King of the gods, sky

no clear principles of moral conduct and no guidelines for religious worship. Priests and priestesses tended the temples and shrines and oversaw rituals, including human and animal sacrifices performed to win the favor of the gods. Popular Greek religion produced no sacred scripture and no doctrines—circumstances that may have contributed to the freedom of intellectual inquiry for which the Greeks became famous. Equally famous, at least in ancient times, was the ancient oracle at Delphi, the shrine of Apollo and the site that marked for the Greeks the center of the universe and the "navel" of the earth. Here the priestess of Apollo sat on a tripod over a fissure in the rock, and, in a state of ecstasy (which recent archeologists attribute to hallucinogenic fumes from narcotic gases in two geologic faults below), uttered inscrutable replies to the questions of suppliants from near and far. The oracle at Delphi remained the supreme source of prophecy and mystical wisdom until the temple-shrine was destroyed in late Roman times.

The Greek City-State and the Persian Wars (ca. 750–480 B.C.E.)

Toward the end of the Homeric Age, the Greeks formed small rural colonies that gradually grew into urban communities, mainly through maritime trade. Geographic conditions—a rocky terrain interrupted by mountains, valleys, and narrow rivers—made overland travel and trade difficult. At the same time, Greek geography (see Map 4.1) encouraged the evolution of the independent city-state (in Greek, *polis*). Ancient Greece consisted of a constellation of some 200 city-states, a few as large as 400 square miles and others as tiny as 2 square miles. Many of these (Athens, for instance) were small enough that a person might walk around their walls in only a few hours. Although all of the Greek city-states shared the same language, traditions, and religion, each *polis* governed itself, issued its own coinage, and provided its own military defenses. The autonomy of the Greek city-states—so unlike the monolithic Egyptian state—fostered fierce competition and commercial rivalry. However, like the squabbling members of a family who are suddenly menaced by aggressive neighbors, the Greek city-states, confronted by the rising power of Persia, united in self-defense.

By the sixth century B.C.E., the Persian Empire had conquered most of the territories between the western frontier of India and Asia Minor. Advancing westward, Persia annexed Ionia, the Greek region on the coast of Asia Minor (see Map 4.1), a move that clearly threatened mainland Greece. Thus, when in 499 B.C.E. the Ionian cities revolted against Persian rule, their Greek neighbors came to their aid. In retaliation, the Persians sent military expeditions to punish the rebel cities of the Greek mainland. In 490 B.C.E., on the plain of Marathon, 25 miles from Athens, a Greek force of 11,000 men met a Persian army with twice its numbers and defeated them, losing only 192 men. Persian casualties exceeded 6,000. The Greek warrior who brought news of the victory at Marathon to Athens died upon completing the 26-mile run. (Hence the word "marathon" has come to designate a long-distance endurance contest.) But the Greeks soon realized that without a strong navy even the combined land forces of all the city-states could not hope to oust the Persians. They thus proceeded to build a fleet of warships, which, in 480 B.C.E., ultimately defeated the Persian armada at Salamis in one of the final battles of the Persian Wars.

The story of the Persian Wars intrigued the world's first known historian, Herodotus (ca. 485–425 B.C.E), "the father of history." Writing not as an eye-witness to the wars, but a half-century later, Herodotus nevertheless brought keen critical judgment to sources that included hearsay as well as record. His sprawling narrative is filled with fascinating anecdotes and colorful digressions, including a "travelogue" of his visits to Egypt and Asia—accounts that remain among our most detailed sources of information about ancient African and West Asian life. The chapters on Africa, filled with numerous comparisons between Greek and Egyptian social practices and religious beliefs, show Herodotus as an early investigator of what would today be called "comparative culture." By presenting various (and often contradictory) pieces of evidence and weighing them before arriving at a conclusion, Herodotus laid the basis for the historical method. His procedures and his writings established a boundary between myth and history. *The Persian Wars*, which followed the Homeric poems by some 300 years, remains significant as the Western world's first major work in prose.

Athens and the Greek Golden Age (ca. 480–430 B.C.E.)

Although all of the city-states had contributed to expelling the Persians, it was Athens that claimed the crown of victory. Indeed, in the wake of the Persian Wars, Athens assumed political dominion among the city-states, as well as commercial supremacy in the Aegean Sea. The defeat of Persia inspired a mood of confidence and a spirit of vigorous chauvinism. This spirit ushered in a Golden Age of drama, philosophy, music, art, and architecture. In fact, the period between 480 and 430 B.C.E., often called a Golden Age, was one of the most creative in the history of the world. In Athens, it was as if the heroic idealism of the *Iliad* had bloomed into civic patriotism.

Athens, the most cosmopolitan of the city-states, was unique among the Greek communities, for the democratic government that came to prevail there was the exception rather than the rule in ancient Greece. In its early history, Athens—like most of the other Greek city-states—was an **oligarchy**, that is, a government controlled by an elite minority. But a series of enlightened rulers who governed Athens between roughly 600 and 500 B.C.E. introduced reforms that placed increasing authority in the hands of its citizens. The Athenian statesman, poet, and legislator Solon (ca. 638–558 B.C.E) fixed the democratic course of Athenian history by abolishing the custom of debt slavery and encouraging members of the lower classes to serve in public office. By broadening the civic responsibilities of Athenians, Solon educated citizens of all classes in the activities of government. By 550 B.C.E., the Popular Assembly of Citizens (made up of all citizens) was operating alongside the Council of Five Hundred (made up of aristocrats who handled routine state business) and the Board of Ten Generals (an annually elected executive body). When, at last, in the year 508 B.C.E., the Popular Assembly acquired the right to make laws, Athens became the first direct democracy in world history.

The word **"democracy"** derives from Greek words describing a government in which the people (*demos*) hold power (*kratos*). In the democracy of ancient Athens, Athenian citizens exercised political power directly, thus—unlike the United States, where power rests in the hands of representatives of the people—the citizens of Athens themselves held the authority to make the laws and approve state policy. Athenian democracy was, however, highly exclusive. Its citizenry included only landowning males over the age of eighteen. Of an estimated population of 250,000, this probably constituted some 40,000 people. Women, children, resident aliens, and slaves—approximately 150,000 individuals—did not qualify as citizens. (Slaves, as in earlier civilizations, arrived at their unfree condition as a result of warfare or debt, not race or skin color.) Clearly, in the mind of the Athenian, Hellenes were superior to non-Greeks (or outsiders, whom the Greeks called *barbaros*, from which comes the English word "barbarians"), Athenians were superior to non-Athenians, Athenian males were superior to Athenian females, and all classes of free men and women were superior to slaves.

Fundamental to Athenian democracy was a commitment to the legal equality of its participants: One citizen's vote weighed as heavily as the next. Equally important to Athenian (as to any) democracy was the hypothesis that individuals who had the right to vote would do so, and, moreover, were willing to take responsible action in the interest of the common good. (Such ideals are still highly valued in many parts of the modern world.) The small size of Athens probably contributed to the success of its unique form of government. Although probably no more than 5,000 Athenians attended the Assembly that met four times a month to make laws in the open-air marketplace (the Agora) located at the foot of the Acropolis, these men were the proponents of a brave new enterprise in governing.

Golden Age Athens stands in vivid contrast to those ancient civilizations whose rulers—the incarnate representatives of the gods—held absolute power while its citizens held none. Athens also stands in contrast to its rival, Sparta, the largest *polis* on the Peloponnesus (see Map 4.1). In Sparta, an oligarchy of five officials, elected annually, held tight reins on a society whose male citizens (from the age of seven on) were trained as soldiers. All physical labor fell to a class of unfree workers called *helots*, the captives of Sparta's frequent local wars. Spartan soldiers were renowned for their bravery; their women, expected to live up to the ideas of a warrior culture, enjoyed a measure of freedom that was unknown in Athens. Yet, the history of Sparta would be one in which a strict social order left little room for creativity, in government or in the arts.

Pericles' Glorification of Athens

The leading proponent of Athenian democracy was the statesman Pericles (ca. 495–429 B.C.E.) (Figure **4.9**), who dominated the Board of Ten Generals for more than thirty years until his death. An aristocrat by birth, Pericles was a democrat at heart. In the interest of broadening the democratic system, he initiated some of Athens' most sweeping domestic reforms, such as payment for holding public office and a system of public audit in which the finances of outgoing magistrates were subject to critical scrutiny. In Pericles' time many public offices were filled by lottery—a procedure that invited all citizens to seek governmental office, and one so egalitarian as to be unthinkable today. Pericles' foreign policy was even more ambitious than his domestic policies. In the wake of the Persian Wars, he encouraged the Greek city-states to form a defensive alliance against future invaders. At the outset, the league's collective funds were kept in a treasury on the sacred island of Delos (hence the name "Delian League"). But, in a bold display of chauvinism, Pericles moved the fund to Athens and expropriated its monies to rebuild the Athenian temples that had been burned by the Persians.

Figure 4.9 Marble bust from Tivoli inscribed with the name of Pericles. Roman copy after a bronze original of 450–425 B.C.E. Reproduced by courtesy of the Trustees of the British Museum, London.

Pericles' high-handed actions, along with his imperialistic efforts to dominate the commercial policies of league members, led to antagonism and armed dispute between Athens and a federation of rival city-states led by Sparta. The ensuing Peloponnesian Wars (431–404 B.C.E.), which culminated in the defeat of Athens, brought an end to the Greek Golden Age. Our knowledge of the Peloponnesian Wars is based mainly on the account written by the great historian Thucydides (ca. 460–400 B.C.E.), himself a general in the combat. Thucydides went beyond merely recording the events of the war to provide insights into its causes and a first-hand assessment of its political and moral consequences. Thucydides' terse, graphic descriptions and his detached analyses of events distinguish his style from that of Herodotus.

The following speech by Pericles, excerpted from Thucydides' *History of the Peloponnesian Wars*, was presented on the occasion of a mass funeral held outside the walls of Athens to honor those who had died in the first battles of the war. Nowhere are the concepts of humanism and individualism more closely linked to civic patriotism than in this speech. Pericles reviews the "principles of action" by which Athens rose to power. He describes Athens as "the school of Hellas," that is, as the ultimate model for other Greek communities in matters of political, social, and cultural significance. The greatness of Athens, according to Pericles, lies not merely in its military might and in the superiority of its political institutions, but in the quality of its citizens, their nobility of spirit, and their love of beauty and wisdom. Pericles' views, which were shared by most Athenians as primary articles of faith, reflect the spirit of civic pride that characterized Hellenic culture at its peak.

READING 1.12 From Thucydides' *Peloponnesian Wars* (ca. 410 B.C.E.)

Pericles' Funeral Speech

"I will speak first of our ancestors, for it is right and becoming that now, when we are lamenting the dead, a tribute should be paid to their memory. There has never been a time when they did not inhabit this land, which by their valor they have handed down from generation to generation, and we have received from them a free state. But if they were worthy of praise, still more were our fathers, who added to their inheritance, and after many a struggle transmitted to us their sons this great empire. And we ourselves assembled here to-day, who are still most of us in the vigor of life, have   10
chiefly done the work of improvement, and have richly endowed our city with all things, so that she is sufficient for herself both in peace and war. Of the military exploits by which our various possessions were acquired, or of the energy with which we or our fathers drove back the tide of war, Hellenic or barbarian, I will not speak; for the tale would be long and is familiar to you. But before I praise the dead, I should like to point out by what principles of action we rose to power, and under what institutions and through what manner of life our empire became great. For I conceive that such   20

thoughts are not unsuited to the occasion, and that this numerous assembly of citizens and strangers may profitably listen to them.

"Our form of government does not enter into rivalry with the institutions of others. We do not copy our neighbors, but are an example to them. It is true that we are called a democracy, for the administration is in the hands of the many and not of the few. But while the law secures equal justice to all alike in their private disputes, the claim of excellence is also recognized; and when a citizen is in any way distinguished,   30
he is preferred to the public service, not as a matter of privilege, but as the reward of merit. Neither is poverty a bar, but a man may benefit his country whatever be the obscurity of his condition. There is no exclusiveness in our public life, and in our private intercourse we are not suspicious of one another, nor angry with our neighbor if he does what he likes; we do not put on sour looks at him which, though harmless, are not pleasant. While we are thus unconstrained in our private intercourse, a spirit of reverence pervades our public acts; we are prevented from doing wrong by respect for   40
authority and for the laws, having an especial regard to those which are ordained for the protection of the injured as well as to those unwritten laws which bring upon the transgressor of them the reprobation of the general sentiment.

"And we have not forgotten to provide for our weary spirits many relaxations from toil; we have regular games[1] and sacrifices throughout the year; at home the style of our life is refined; and the delight which we daily feel in all these things helps to banish melancholy. Because of the greatness of our city the fruits of the whole earth flow in upon us; so that we   50
enjoy the goods of other countries as freely as of our own. "Then, again, our military training is in many respects superior to that of our adversaries. Our city is thrown open to the world, and we never expel a foreigner or prevent him from seeing or learning anything of which the secret if revealed to an enemy might profit him. We rely not upon management or trickery, but upon our own hearts and hands. And in the matter of education, whereas they from early youth are always undergoing laborious exercises which are to make them brave, we live at ease, and yet are equally ready to face the perils   60
which they face. And here is the proof. The Lacedaemonians[2] come into Attica not by themselves, but with their whole confederacy following; we go alone into a neighbor's country; and although our opponents are fighting for their homes and we on a foreign soil, we have seldom any difficulty in overcoming them. Our enemies have never yet felt our united strength; the care of a navy divides our attention, and on land we are obliged to send our own citizens everywhere. But they, if they meet and defeat a part of our army, are as proud as if they had routed us all, and when defeated they pretend to   70
have been vanquished by us all.

"If then we prefer to meet danger with a light heart but without laborious training, and with a courage which is gained by habit and not enforced by law, are we not greatly the

---

[1]Athletic games were part of many Greek festivals, the most famous of which was the Panhellenic festival (see below).
[2]Citizens of the city-state of Sparta, ideologically opposed to Athens.

gainers? Since we do not anticipate the pain, although, when the hour comes, we can be as brave as those who never allow themselves to rest; and thus too our city is equally admirable in peace and in war.

"For we are lovers of the beautiful, yet with economy, and we cultivate the mind without loss of manliness. Wealth we employ, not for talk and ostentation, but when there is a real use for it. To avow poverty with us is no disgrace; the true disgrace is in doing nothing to avoid it. An Athenian citizen does not neglect the state because he takes care of his own household; and even those of us who are engaged in business have a very fair idea of politics. We alone regard a man who takes no interest in public affairs, not as a harmless, but as a useless character; and if few of us are originators, we are all sound judges of a policy. The great impediment to action is, in our opinion, not discussion, but the want of that knowledge which is gained by discussion preparatory to action. For we have a peculiar power of thinking before we act and of acting too, whereas other men are courageous from ignorance but hesitate upon reflection. And they are surely to be esteemed the bravest spirits who, having the clearest sense both of the pains and pleasures of life, do not on that account shrink from danger. In doing good, again, we are unlike others; we make our friends by conferring, not by receiving favors. . . . We alone do good to our neighbors not upon a calculation of interest, but in the confidence of freedom and in a frank and fearless spirit.

"To sum up: I say that Athens is the school of Hellas, and that the individual Athenian in his own person seems to have the power of adapting himself to the most varied forms of action with the utmost versatility and grace. This is no passing and idle word, but truth and fact; and the assertion is verified by the position to which these qualities have raised the state. For in the hour of trial Athens alone among her contemporaries is superior to the report of her. No enemy who comes against her is indignant at the reverses which he sustains at the hands of such a city; no subject complains that his masters are unworthy of him. And we shall assuredly not

be without witnesses; there are mighty monuments of our power which will make us the wonder of this and of succeeding ages; we shall not need the praises of Homer or of any other panegyrist whose poetry may please for the moment, although his representation of the facts will not bear the light of day. For we have compelled every land and every sea to open a path for our valor, and have everywhere planted eternal memorials of our friendship and of our enmity. Such is the city for whose sake these men nobly fought and died; they could not bear the thought that she might be taken from them; and every one of us who survive should gladly toil on her behalf.

"I have dwelt upon the greatness of Athens because I want to show you that we are contending for a higher prize than those who enjoy none of these privileges, and to establish by manifest proof the merit of these men whom I am now commemorating. Their loftiest praise has been already spoken. For in magnifying the city I have magnified them, and men like them whose virtues made her glorious."

The Olympic Games

Pericles makes proud reference to the "regular games" that provide Athenians with "relaxations from toil." But, in fact, the most famous of the "games" were those athletic contests in which all the city-states of Greece participated. These games were the chief feature of the Panhellenic ("all-Greek") Festival, instituted in 776 B.C.E. in honor of the Greek gods. Located in Olympia, one of the great religious centers of Greece, the festival took place at midsummer every four years, even during wartime: A sacred truce guaranteed safe-conduct to all visitors. So significant were the games that they became the basis for the reckoning of time. While Egypt and Mesopotamia calculated time according to the rule of dynasties and kings, the ancient Greeks marked time in "Olympiads," four-year periods beginning with the first games in 776 B.C.E. The central event of the games was a 200-yard sprint (Figure **4.10**)

Figure 4.10 Attr. The Euphiletos painter, detail from Greek black-figured Panathenaic amphora showing foot race, ca. 530 B.C.E. Terra-cotta, height 24½ in. The Metropolitan Museum of Art, New York. Rogers Fund, 1914 (14.130.12).

Figure 4.11 Theater at Epidaurus, Greece, ca. 350 B.C.E. Designed by Polycleitus the Younger. This view shows the great size (13,000 capacity) typical of Greek theaters. Nevertheless, actors and chorus could be heard even from the top row.

called the *stadion* (hence our word "stadium"). But there were also many other contests: a footrace of one and a half miles, the discus-throw, the long-jump, wrestling, boxing, and other games that probably looked back to Minoan tradition (see Figure 4.3). Greek athletes competed in the nude—from the Greek word *gymnos* ("naked") we get "gymnasium." Winners received garlands consisting of wild olive or laurel leaves and the acclaim of Greek painters and poets (see chapter 5), but no financial reward.

Although women were not permitted to compete in the Olympics, they could hold games of their own. Prowess rather than cunning was valued in the games: In wrestling, hair-pulling and finger-bending were permitted, but biting and finger-breaking were forbidden. A match terminated when either wrestler gave up, lost consciousness, or fell dead. True "sport" was that which gave athletes an opportunity to rival the divinity of the gods. Nevertheless, the Olympics were a national event that, typically, promoted both individual excellence and communal pride.

Greek Drama

While the Olympic games were held only once in four years, theatrical performances in the city of Athens occurred twice annually. Like the games, Greek drama was a form of play that addressed the dynamic relationship between the individual, the community, and the gods. The ancient Greeks were the first masters in the art of drama, the literary genre that tells a story through the imitation of

action. Drama originated in religious rituals: Recitation and chant, music, dance, and mime animated the enactment of myths that celebrated rites of passage or marked seasonal change. In a manner similar to the Pygmy hunting ceremony discussed in the Introduction (Reading 1.1), ceremonial drama was designed to bring about favorable results in hunting, farming, and in ensuring the survival of the community.

Greek drama grew out of a complex of imitative actions associated with the worship of Dionysus, god of wine, vegetation, and seasonal regeneration. In early Homeric times, religious rites performed in honor of Dionysus featured a dialogue between two choruses or between a leader (originally perhaps the shaman or priest) and a chorus (the worshipers or ritual participants). With the advent of the poet Thespis (fl. 534 B.C.E.), actor and chorus (the performers) seem to have become separate from those who witnessed the action (the audience). At the same time, dramatic action assumed two principal forms: *tragedy* and *comedy*. Although the origins of each are still the subject of speculation among scholars, tragedy probably evolved from fertility rituals surrounding the death and decay of the crops, while comedy seems to have developed out of village revels celebrating seasonal rebirth. It is possible, as well, that such performances had something to do with the healing cults of ancient Greece: The great Theater at Epidaurus (Figure **4.11**) was dedicated to Aesclepius, the god of medicine. Like the more ancient theater of

Dionysus in Athens, it stood adjacent to a chief sanctuary for the worship of the god of healing.

The two annual festivals dedicated to Dionysus were the occasion for the performances of tragedies and comedies, and on each occasion (lasting several days) the author of the best play in its category received a prize. By the fifth century B.C.E. Greece had become a mecca for theater, and while hundreds of plays were performed during the century in which Athenian theater flourished, only forty-four have survived.* They are the products of but four playwrights: Aeschylus (ca. 525–456 B.C.E.), Sophocles (496–406 B.C.E.), Euripides (480–406 B.C.E.) and Aristophanes (ca. 450–ca. 388 B.C.E.). Their plays were staged in the open-air theaters built into the hillsides at sacred sites throughout Greece. These acoustically superb structures, which seated between 13,000 and 27,000 people, featured a *proscenium* (the ancient "stage"), an *orchestra* (the semi-circular "dancing space" in front of the stage), and an *altar* dedicated to the god Dionysus (Figure **4.12**). Music, dance, and song were essential to dramatic performance; scenery and props were few; and actors (all of whom were male) wore elaborate costumes, along with masks that served to amplify their voices.

The tragedies of Aeschylus, Sophocles, and Euripides deal with human conflicts as revealed in Greek history, myth, and legend. Since such stories would have been generally familiar to the average Greek who attended the Dionysian theater, the way in which the playwright intrigued the theatergoer would depend upon his treatment of the story or the manner in which the story was enacted. The tragic drama concentrated on issues involving a specific moment of friction between the individual and fate, the gods, or the community. The events of the play unfolded by way of dialogue spoken by individual characters but also through the commentary of the chorus. Aeschylus, the author of the oldest surviving Western tragedy, introduced a second actor and gave the chorus a principal role in the drama. He brought deep religious feel-

*All of the Greek plays in English translation may be found at the following website: http://classics.mit.edu.

Figure 4.12 Plan of the theater at Epidaurus. **1** gangway **2** aisles **3** tiered seating for audience **4** ramp **5** *parodos* **6** *orchestra* **7** *skene* **8** *proscenium*

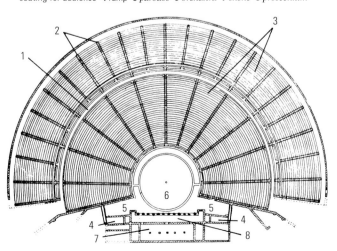

ing to his tragedies, the most famous of which is the series of three plays, or trilogy, known as the *Oresteia* (Orestes plays). These plays deal with the history of the family of Agamemnon, who led the Greeks to Troy, and whose murder at the hands of his wife upon his return from Troy is avenged by their son, Orestes.

While Aeschylus advanced the story of the play by way of sonorous language, Sophocles, the second of the great tragedians, developed his plots through the actions of the characters. He modified the ceremonial formality of earlier Greek tragedies by individualizing the characters and introducing moments of great psychological intimacy. Euripides, the last of the great tragedians, brought even greater realism to his characters; his striking psychological portraits explore the human soul in its experience of grief.

Tragedy, which gave formal expression to the most awful kinds of human experience—disaster and death—invited the spectator to participate vicariously in the dramatic action, thus undergoing a kind of emotional liberation. Comedy, on the other hand, drew its ability to provoke laughter from incongruity and the unexpected. Probably originating in revels celebrating agricultural fertility, comedy involved satires and parodies of sexual union and erotic play of the kind found to this day in seasonal festivals and carnivals such as Mardi Gras. Obscene jokes, grotesque masks, fantastic costumes, and provocative dance and song were common to ancient comedy, as they are in various forms of modern slapstick and burlesque. In the history of ancient Greek drama, the only comic plays to survive are those of Aristophanes, whose inventive wit, sharply directed against Athenian politics and current affairs, is best revealed in the comedy *Lysistrata*, the oldest of his eleven surviving works. In *Lysistrata*, written in the wake of the bitter military conflict between Athens and Sparta, the playwright has the leading character—the wife of an Athenian soldier—launch a "strike" that will deprive all husbands of sexual satisfaction until they agree to refrain from war. As timely today as it was in ancient Athens, *Lysistrata* is a hilarious attack on the idealized, heroic image of armed combat.

The Individual and the Community

The Case of Antigone

The drama that is most relevant to the theme of this chapter is Sophocles' *Antigone*, the third of a group of plays that includes *Oedipus the King* and *Oedipus at Colonus*. The story of *Antigone* proceeds from the last phase of the history of Thebes, a history with which most Athenians would have been familiar, since it recalled the ancient ascendancy of Athens over Thebes: Following the death of Oedipus, King of Thebes, his sons Polynices and Eteocles kill each other in a dispute over the throne, thus leaving the crown to Creon, the brother-in-law of Oedipus and the only surviving male member of the ill-fated royal family. Upon becoming king, Creon forbids the burial of Polynices, contending that Eteocles had been the rightful ruler of Thebes. Driven by familial duty and the wish to fulfill the divine laws requiring burial of the dead, Oedipus' daughter Antigone violates Creon's decree and buries her brother Polynices. These circumstances provoke further violence and tragic death.

   Antigone is a play that deals with many issues: It explores the conflict between the rights of the individual and the laws of the state; between dedication to family and loyalty to community; between personal and political obligations; between female willpower and male authority, and, finally, between human and divine law. It reflects Sophocles' effort to reconcile human passions, the will of the gods, and the sovereignty of the *polis*. Heroic idealism is a major motif in *Antigone*. It drives the action of the play, which weighs the grandeur of human beings against their frailties.

READING 1.13 From Sophocles' *Antigone*

(ca. 440 B.C.E.)

Characters

Antigone and Ismene, daughters of Oedipus
Creon, king of Thebes, brother of Jocasta
Haemon, son of Creon
Teiresias, a blind prophet
A Sentry
A Messenger
Eurydice, wife of Creon
Chorus of Theban elders
Attendants of the king and queen
Soldiers
A Boy who leads Teiresias

Scene

An open space before the house of Creon. The house is at the back, with gates opening from it. On the right, the city is to be supposed; to the left and in the distance, the Theban plain and the hills rising beyond it. Antigone and Ismene come from the middle door of three in the King's house.

   Antigone: Ismene, O my dear, my little sister, of all the   1
griefs bequeathed us by our father Oedipus, is there any that Zeus will share with us while we live? There is no sorrow and no shame we have not known. And now what is this new edict they tell about, that our Captain has published all through Thebes? Do you know? Have you heard? Or is it kept from you that our friends are threatened with the punishment due to foes?

   Ismene: I have heard no news, Antigone, glad or sad, about our friends, since we two sisters lost two brothers at a single   10
blow; and since the Argive army fled last night, I do not know whether my fortune is better or worse.

   Antigone: I know, I know it well. That is why I sent for you to come outside the gates, to speak to you alone.

   Ismene: What is it? I can see that you are troubled.

   Antigone: Should I not be?—when Creon gives honors to one of our brothers, but condemns the other to shame?

Eteocles, they say, he has laid in the earth with due observance of right and custom, that all may be well with him among the shades below. But the poor corpse of Polynices—   20
it has been published to the city that none shall bury him, none shall mourn him; but he shall be left unwept and unsepulchred, and the birds are welcome to feast upon him!

   Such, they say, are the orders the good Creon has given for you and me—yes, for me! He is coming now to make his wishes clear; and it is no light matter, for whoever disobeys him is condemned to death by stoning before all the people. Now you know!—and now you will show whether you are nobly bred, or the unworthy daughter of a noble line.

   Ismene: Sister, sister!—if we are caught in this web,   30
what could I do to loose or tighten the knot?

   Antigone: Decide if you will share the work and the danger.

   Ismene: What are you planning?—what are you thinking of?

   Antigone: Will you help this hand to lift the dead?

   Ismene: Oh, you would bury him!—when it is forbidden to anyone in Thebes?

   Antigone: He is still my brother, if he is not yours. No one shall say I failed in my duty to him.

   Ismene: But how can you dare, when Creon has forbidden   40
it?

   Antigone: He has no right to keep me from my own.

   Ismene: Alas, sister, remember how our father perished hated and scorned, when he had struck out his eyes in horror of the sins his own persistency had brought to light. Remember how she who was both his mother and his wife hung herself with a twisted cord. And only yesterday our two brothers came to their terrible end, each by the other's hand. Now only we two are left, and we are all alone. Think how we shall perish, more miserably than all the rest, if in defiance of   50
the law we brave the King's decree and the King's power. No, no, we must remember we were born women, not meant to strive with men. We are in the grip of those stronger than ourselves, and must obey them in this and in things still more cruel. Therefore I will ask forgiveness of the gods and spirits who dwell below, for they will see that I yield to force, and I will hearken to our rulers. It is foolish to be too zealous even in a good cause.

   Antigone: I will not urge you. No, if you wished to join me now I would not let you. Do as you think best. As for me, I   60
will bury him; and if I die for that, I am content. I shall rest like a loved one with him whom I have loved, innocent in my guilt. For I owe a longer allegiance to the dead than to the living; I must dwell with them forever. You, if you wish, may dishonor the laws which the gods have established.

   Ismene: I would not dishonor them, but to defy the State—I am not strong enough for that!

   Antigone: Well, make your excuses—I am going now to heap the earth above the brother whom I love.

   Ismene: Oh, I fear something terrible will happen to you!   70

   Antigone: Fear not for me; but look to your own fate.

   Ismene: At least, then, tell no one what you intend, but hide it closely—and so too will I.

   Antigone: No, but cry it aloud! I will condemn you more if you are silent than if you proclaim my deed to all.

Ismene: You have so hot a heart for deeds that make the blood run cold!

Antigone: My deeds will please those they are meant to please.

Ismene: Ah yes, if you can do what you plan—but you cannot. 80

Antigone: When my strength fails, I shall confess my failure.

Ismene: The impossible should not be tried at all.

Antigone: If you say such things I will hate you, and the dead will haunt you!—But leave me, and the folly that is mine alone, to suffer what I must; for I shall not suffer anything so dreadful as an ignoble death.

Ismene: Go then, if you must, though your errand is mad; and be sure of this, my love goes with you! 90

(Antigone goes toward the plain. Ismene retires into the King's house. The Chorus, being the elders of Thebes, comes into the place before the house.)

Chorus: Over the waters, see!—over the stream of Dirke, the golden eye of the dawn opens on the seven gates;
Terror crouched in the night, how welcome to Thebes is the morning, when the warriors of the white shields flee from the spears of the sun.

From Argos mailed they came, swords drawn for Polynices; like eagles that scream in the air these plumed ones fell on our land.
They ravened around our towers, and burst the doors of our dwellings; their spears sniffed at our blood—but they fled without quenching that thirst. 100

They heaped the eager pine-boughs, flaming, against our bastions, calling upon Hephaestos; but he the fire-god failed them.
The clash of battle was loud, the clamor beloved of the war-god; but a thing they found too hard was to conquer the dragon's brood.

And a thing abhorred by Zeus is the boastful tongue of the haughty: one proud chief, armored in gold, with triumph in his throat, 110
The stormy wave of the foe flung to the crest of our rampart—the god, with a crooked bolt, smites him crashing to earth.

At the seven gates of the city, seven of the host's grim captains yielded to Zeus who turns the tide of battle, their arms of bronze;
And woe to those two sons of the same father and mother, they crossed their angry spears, and brought each other low.

But now since Victory, most desired of all men, to 120
Thebes of the many chariots has come scattering joy,
Let us forget the wars, and dance before the temples; and Bacchus be our leader, loved by the land of Thebes!

But see, the King of this land comes yonder—Creon, son of Menoekeus, our new ruler by virtue of the new turn the gods have given things. What counsel is he pondering, that he has called by special summons this gathering of the elders?

Creon: Sirs, our State has been like a ship tossed by 130 stormy waves; but thanks to the gods, it sails once more upon a steady keel. You I have summoned here apart from all the people because I remember that of old you had great reverence for the royal power of Laius; and I know how you upheld Oedipus when he ruled this land, and, when he died, you loyally supported his two sons. Those sons have fallen, both in one moment, each smitten by the other, each stained with a brother's blood; now I possess the throne and all its powers, since I am nearest kindred of the dead.

No man's worthiness to rule can be known until his mind 140 and soul have been tested by the duties of government and lawgiving. For my part, I have always held that any man who is the supreme guardian of the State, and who fails in his duty through fear, remaining silent when evil is done, is base and contemptible; nor have I any regard for him who puts friendship above the common welfare. Zeus, who sees all things, be my witness that I will not be silent when danger threatens the people; nor will I ever call my country's foe my friend. For our country is the ship that bears us all, and he only 150 is our friend who helps us sail a prosperous course.

Such are the rules by which I will guard this city's greatness; and in keeping with them is the edict I have published touching the sons of Oedipus. For Eteocles, who fell like a true soldier defending his native land, there shall be such funeral as we give the noblest dead. But as to his brother Polynices—he who came out of exile and sought to destroy with fire the city of his fathers and the shrines of his fathers' gods—he who thirsted for the blood of his kin, and would have led into slavery all who escaped death—as to this man, it has been proclaimed that none shall honor him, none shall 160 lament over him, but he shall lie unburied, a corpse mangled by birds and dogs, a gruesome thing to see. Such is my way with traitors.

Chorus: Such is your way, Creon, son of Menoekeus, with the false and with the faithful; and you have power, I know, to give such orders as you please, both for the dead and for all of us who live.

Creon: Then look to it that my mandate is observed.

Chorus: Call on some younger man for this hard task.

Creon: No, watchers of the corpse have been appointed. 170

Chorus: What is this duty, then, you lay on us?

Creon: To side with no one breaking this command.

Chorus: No man is foolish enough to go courting death.

Creon: That indeed shall be the penalty; but men have been lured even to death by the hope of gain.

(A Guard, coming from the direction of the plain, approaches Creon.)

Guard: Sire, I will not say that I am out of breath from hurrying, nor that I have come here on the run; for in fact my thoughts made me pause more than once, and even turn in my path, to go back. My mind was telling me two different things. "Fool," it said to me, "why do you go where you are sure to 180 be condemned?" And then on the other hand, "Wretch, tarrying again? If Creon hears of this from another, you'll smart for it." Torn between these fears, I came on slowly and unwillingly, making a short road long. But at last I got up courage to come to you, and though there is little to my story, I will tell it; for I have got a good grip on one thought—that I can suffer nothing but what is my fate.

Creon: Well, and what is it that makes you so upset?

Guard: First let me tell you that I did not do the deed and I did not see it done, so it would not be just to make me suffer for it. 190

Creon: You have a good care for your own skin, and armor yourself well against blame. I take it that you have news to tell?

Guard: Yes, that I have, but bad news is nothing to be in a hurry about.

Creon: Tell it, man, will you?—tell it and be off.

Guard: Well, this is it. The corpse—someone has done it funeral honors—sprinkled dust upon it, and other pious rites.

Creon: What—what do you say? What man has dared 200 this deed?

Guard: That I cannot tell you. There was no sign of a pick being used, no earth torn up the way it is by a mattock. The ground was hard and dry, there was no track of wheels. Whoever did it left no trace; when the first day-watchman showed it to us, we were struck dumb. You couldn't see the dead man at all; not that he was in any grave, but dry dust was strewn that thick all over him. It was the hand of someone warding off a curse did that. There was no sign that any dog or wild beast had been at the body. 210

Then there were loud words, and hard words, among us of the guard, everyone accusing someone else, 'til we nearly came to blows, and it's a wonder we didn't. Everyone was accused and no one was convicted, and each man stuck to it that he knew nothing about it. We were ready to take red-hot iron in our hands—to walk through fire—to swear by the gods that we did not do the deed and were not in the secret of whoever did it.

At last, when all our disputing got us nowhere, one of the men spoke up in a way that made us look down at the ground 220 in silence and fear; for we could not see how to gainsay him, nor how to escape trouble if we heeded him. What he said was, that this must be reported to you, it was no use hiding it. There was no doubt of it, he was right; so we cast lots, and it was my bad luck to win the prize. Here I am, then, as unwelcome as unwilling, I know; for no man likes the bearer of bad news.

Chorus: O King, my thoughts have been whispering, could this deed perhaps have been the work of gods?

Creon: Silence, before your words fill me with anger, and 230 you prove yourself as foolish as you are old! You say what is not to be borne, that the gods would concern themselves with this corpse. What!—did they cover his nakedness to reward the reverence he paid them, coming to burn their pillared shrines and sacred treasures, to harry their land, to put scorn upon their laws? Do you think it is the way of the gods to honor the wicked? No! From the first there were some in this city who muttered against me, chafing at this edict, wagging their heads in secret; they would not bow to the yoke, not they, like men contented with my rule. 240

I know well enough, it is such malcontents who have bribed and beguiled these guards to do this deed or let it be done.

Nothing so evil as money ever arose among men. It lays cities low, drives peoples from their homes, warps honest souls 'til they give themselves to works of shame; it teaches men to practice villainies and grow familiar with impious deeds.

But the men who did this thing for hire, sooner or later they shall pay the price. Now, as Zeus still has my reverence, know this—I tell you on my oath: Unless you find the very man whose hand strewed dust upon that body, and bring him here 250 before mine eyes, death alone shall not be enough for you, but you shall first be hung up alive until you reveal the truth about this outrage; that henceforth you may have a better idea about how to get money, and learn that it is not wise to grasp at it from any source. I will teach you that ill-gotten gains bring more men to ruin than to prosperity.

Guard: May I speak? Or shall I turn and go?

Creon: Can you not see that your voice offends me?

Guard: Are your ears troubled, or your soul?

Creon: And why should you try to fix the seat of my pain? 260

Guard: The doer of the deed inflames your mind, but I, only your ears.

Creon: Bah, you are a babbler born!

Guard: I may be that, but I never did this deed.

Creon: You did, for silver; but you shall pay with your life.

Guard: It is bad when a judge misjudges.

Creon: Prate about "judgment" all you like; but unless you show me the culprit in this crime, you will admit before long that guilty wages were better never earned.

(Creon goes into his house.)

Guard: Well, may the guilty man be found, that's all I ask. 270 But whether he's found or not—fate will decide that—you will not see me here again. I have escaped better than I ever hoped or thought—I owe the gods much thanks.

(The Guard departs, going toward the plain.)

Chorus: Wonders are many in the world, and the
    wonder of all is man.
With his bit in the teeth of the storm and his faith in a
    fragile prow,
Far he sails, where the waves leap white-fanged, wroth at
    his plan.
And he has his will of the earth by the strength of his
    hand on the plough.

The birds, the clan of the light heart, he snares with his
    woven cord,
And the beasts with wary eyes, and the stealthy fish in
    the sea;
That shaggy freedom-lover, the horse, obeys his word, 280
And the sullen bull must serve him, for cunning of wit is
    he.

Against all ills providing, he tempers the dark and the
    light,
The creeping siege of the frost and the arrows of sleet
    and rain,
The grievous wounds of the daytime and the fever that
    steals in the night;
Only against Death man arms himself in vain.

With speech and wind-swift thought he builds the State
   to his mood,
Prospering while he honors the gods and the laws of the
   land.
Yet in his rashness often he scorns the ways that are
   good—
May such as walk with evil be far from my hearth and
   hand!

(The Guard reappears leading Antigone.)

Chorus: But what is this?—what portent from the gods is 290
this? I am bewildered, for surely this maiden is Antigone; I
know her well. O luckless daughter of a luckless father, child
of Oedipus, what does this mean? Why have they made you
prisoner? Surely they did not take you in the folly of breaking
the King's laws?

Guard: Here she is, the doer of the deed! We caught this
girl burying him. But where is Creon?

Chorus: Look, he is coming from the house now.

(Creon comes from the house.)

Creon: What is it? What has happened that makes my
coming timely? 300

Guard: Sire, a man should never say positively "I will do
this" or "I won't do that," for things happen to change the
mind. I vowed I would not soon come here again, after the
way you scared me, lashing me with your threats. But there's
nothing so pleasant as a happy turn when we've given up
hope, so I have broken my sworn oath to hurry back here with
this girl, who was taken showing grace to the dead. This time
there was no casting of lots; no, this is my good luck, no one
else's. And now, Sire, take her yourself, question her, examine
her, all you please; but I have a right to free and final 310
quittance of this trouble.

Creon: Stay!—this prisoner—how and where did you take
her?

Guard: She was burying the man; that's all there is to tell
you.

Creon: Do you mean what you say? Are you telling the
truth?

Guard: I saw her burying the corpse that you had forbidden
to bury. Is that plain and clear?

Creon: What did you see? Did you take her in the act? 320

Guard: It happened this way. When we came to the place
where he lay, worrying over your threats, we swept away all
the dirt, leaving the rotting corpse bare. Then we sat us down
on the brow of the hill to windward, so that the smell from
him would not strike us. We kept wide awake frightening
each other with what you would do to us if we didn't carry out
your command. So it went until the sun was bright in the top
of the sky, and the heat began to burn. Then suddenly a
whirlwind came roaring down, making the sky all black, hiding
the plain under clouds of choking dust and leaves torn from 330
the trees. We closed our eyes and bore this plague from the
gods.

And when, after a long while, the storm had passed, we
saw this girl, and she crying aloud with the sharp cry of a bird
in its grief; the way a bird will cry when it sees the nest bare
and the nestlings gone, it was that way she lifted up her voice

when she saw the corpse uncovered; and she called down
dreadful curses on those that did it. Then straightway she
scooped up dust in her hands, and she had a shapely ewer of
bronze, and she held that high while she honored the dead 340
with three drink-offerings.

We rushed forward at this and closed on our quarry, who
was not at all frightened at us. Then we charged her with the
past and present offences, and she denied nothing—I was
both happy and sorry for that. It is good to escape danger
one's self, but hard to bring trouble to one's friends. However,
nothing counts with me so much as my own safety.

Creon: You, then—you whose face is bent to the earth—
do you confess or do you deny the deed?

Antigone: I did it; I make no denial. 350

Creon (*to Guard*); You may go your way, wherever you will,
free and clear of a grave charge. (*To Antigone*); Now tell me—
not in many words, but briefly—did you know of the edict that
forbade what you did?

Antigone: I knew it. How could I help knowing?—it was
public.

Creon: And you had the boldness to transgress that law?

Antigone: Yes, for it was not Zeus made such a law; such
is not the Justice of the gods. Nor did I think that your decrees
had so much force, that a mortal could override the unwritten 360
and unchanging statutes of heaven. For their authority is not
of today nor yesterday, but from all time, and no man knows
when they were first put forth.

Not through dread or any human power could I answer to
the gods for breaking these. That I must die I knew without
your edict. But if I am to die before my time, I count that a
gain; for who, living as I do in the midst of many woes, would
not call death a friend?

It saddens me little, therefore, to come to my end. If I had
let my mother's son lie in death an unburied corpse, that 370
would have saddened me, but for myself I do not grieve. And if
my acts are foolish in your eyes, it may be that a foolish judge
condemns my folly.

Chorus: The maiden shows herself the passionate daughter
of a passionate father, she does not know how to bend the
neck.

Creon: Let me remind you that those who are too stiff and
stubborn are most often humbled; it is the iron baked too hard
in the furnace you will oftenest see snapped and splintered.
But I have seen horses that show temper brought to order by 380
a little curb. Too much pride is out of place in one who lives
subject to another. This girl was already versed in insolence
when she transgressed the law that had been published; and
now, behold, a second insult—to boast about it, to exult in her
misdeed!

But I am no man, she is the man, if she can carry this off
unpunished. No! She is my sister's child, but if she were
nearer to me in blood than any who worships Zeus at the altar
of my house, she should not escape a dreadful doom—nor her
sister either, for indeed I charge her too with plotting this 390
burial.

And summon that sister—for I saw her just now within,
raving and out of her wits. That is the way minds plotting evil
in the dark give away their secret and convict themselves even
before they are found out. But the most intolerable thing is

that one who has been caught in wickedness should glory in the crime.

Antigone: Would you do more than slay me?

Creon: No more than that—no, and nothing less.

Antigone: Then why do you delay? Your speeches give me no pleasure, and never will; and my words, I suppose, buzz hatefully in your ear. I am ready; for there is no better way I could prepare for death than by giving burial to my brother. Everyone would say so if their lips were not sealed by fear. But a king has many advantages, he can do and say what he pleases.

Creon: You slander the race of Cadmus;[1] not one of them shares your view of this deed.

Antigone: They see it as I do, but their tails are between their legs.

Creon: They are loyal to their king; are you not ashamed to be otherwise?

Antigone: No; there is nothing shameful in piety to a brother.

Creon: Was it not a brother also who died in the good cause?

Antigone: Born of the same mother and sired by the same father.

Creon: Why then do you dishonor him by honoring that other?

Antigone: The dead will not look upon it that way.

Creon: Yes, if you honor the wicked equally with the virtuous.

Antigone: It was his brother, not his slave, that died.

Creon: One perished ravaging his fatherland, the other defending it.

Antigone: Nevertheless, Hades desires these rites.

Creon: Surely the good are not pleased to be made equal with the evil!

Antigone: Who knows how the gods see good and evil?

Creon: A foe is never a friend—even in death.

Antigone: It is not my nature to join in hating, but in loving.

Creon: Your place, then, is with the dead. If you must love, love them. While I live, no woman shall overbear me.

(Ismene is led from the King's house by two attendants.)

Chorus: See, Ismene come through the gate shedding such tears as loving sisters weep. It seems as if a cloud gathers about her brow and breaks in rain upon her cheek.

Creon: And you, who lurked like a viper in my house, sucking the blood of my honor, while I knew not that I was nursing two reptiles ready to strike at my throne—come, tell me now, will you confess your part in this guilty burial, or will you swear you knew nothing of it?

Ismene: I am guilty if she is, and share the blame.

Antigone: No, no! Justice will not permit this. You did not consent to the deed, nor would I let you have part in it.

Ismene: But now that danger threatens you, I am not ashamed to come to your side.

Antigone: Who did the deed, the gods and the dead know; a friend in words is not the friend I love.

---

[1]The ancestor of the noble families of Thebes.

Ismene: Sister, do not reject me, but let me die with you, and duly honor the dead.

Antigone: Do not court death, nor claim a deed to which you did not put your hand. My death will suffice.

Ismene: How could life be dear to me without you?

Antigone: Ask Creon, you think highly of his word.

Ismene: Why taunt me so, when it does you no good?

Antigone: Ah, if I mock you, it is with pain I do it.

Ismene: Oh tell me, how can I serve you, even now?

Antigone: Save yourself; I do not grudge your escape.

Ismene: Oh, my grief! Can I not share your fate?

Antigone: You chose to live, and I to die.

Ismene: At least I begged you not to make that choice.

Antigone: This world approved your caution, but the gods my courage.

Ismene: But now I approve, and so I am guilty too.

Antigone: Ah little sister, be of good cheer, and live. My life has long been given to death, that I might serve the dead.

Creon: Behold, one of these girls turns to folly now, as the other one has ever since she was born.

Ismene: Yes, Sire, such reason as nature gives us may break under misfortune, and go astray.

Creon: Yours did, when you chose to share evil deeds with the evil.

Ismene: But I cannot live without her.

Creon: You mistake; she lives no more.

Ismene: Surely you will not slay your own son's betrothed?

Creon: He can plough other fields.

Ismene: But he cannot find such love again.

Creon: I will not have an evil wife for my son.

Antigone: Ah, Haemon, my beloved! Dishonored by your father!

Creon: Enough! I'll hear no more of you and your marriage!

Chorus: Will you indeed rob your son of his bride?

Creon: Death will do that for me.

Chorus: It seems determined then, that she shall die.

Creon: Determined, yes—for me and for you. No more delay—servants, take them within. Let them know that they are women, not meant to roam abroad. For even the boldest seek to fly when they see Death stretching his hand their way.

(Attendants lead Antigone and Ismene into the house.)

Chorus: Blest are they whose days have not tasted of sorrow:
For if a house has dared the anger of heaven,
Evil strikes at it down the generations,
Wave after wave, like seas that batter a headland.

I see how fate has harried the seed of Labdakos;
Son cannot fly the curse that was laid on the sire,
The doom incurred by the dead must fall on the living:
When gods pursue, no race can find deliverance.

And even these, the last of the children of Oedipus—
Because of the frenzy that rose in a passionate heart,
Because of a handful of blood-stained dust that was sprinkled—
The last of the roots is cut, and the light extinguished.

O Zeus, how vain is the mortal will that opposes
The Will Immortal that neither sleeps nor ages,

The Imperturbable Power that on Olympus
Dwells in unclouded glory, the All-Beholding!
Wise was he who said that ancient saying:
Whom the gods bewilder, at last takes evil for virtue;
And let no man lament if his lot is humble—
No great things come to mortals without a curse.

But look, Sire: Haemon, the last of your sons, approaches. I 510
wonder if he comes grieving over the doom of his promised
bride, Antigone, and bitter that his marriage-hopes are
baffled?

(*Haemon comes before his father.*)

Creon: We shall know soon, better than seers could tell us.
My son, you have heard the irrevocable doom decreed for your
betrothed. Do you come to rage against your father, or do you
remember the duty of filial love, no matter what I do.

Haemon: Father, I am yours; and knowing you are wise, I
follow the paths you trace for me. No marriage could be more
to me than your good guidance. 520

Creon: Yes, my son, this should be your heart's first law, in
all things to obey your father's will. Men pray for dutiful
children growing up about them in their homes, that such may
pay their father's foe with evil, and honor as their father does,
his friend. But if a man begets undutiful children, what shall
we say that he has sown, only sorrow for himself and triumph
for his enemies? Do not then, my son, thinking of pleasures,
put aside reason for a woman's sake. If you brought an evil
woman to your bed and home, you would find that such
embraces soon grow hateful; and nothing can wound so 530
deeply as to find a loved one false. No, but with loathing, and
as if she were your enemy, let this girl go to find a husband
in the house of Hades. For she alone in all the city defied and
disobeyed me; I have taken her in the act, and I will not be a
liar to my people—I will slay her.

Let her appeal all she pleases to the claims of kindred
blood. If I am to rear my own kin to evil deeds, certainly I must
expect evil among the people. Only a man who rules his own
household justly can do justice in the State. If anyone
transgresses, and does violence to the laws, or thinks to 540
dictate to the ruler, I will not tolerate it. No!—whoever the
city shall appoint to rule, that man must be obeyed, in little
things and great things, in just things and unjust; for the man
who is a good subject is the one who would be a good ruler,
and it is he who in time of war will stand his ground where he
is placed, loyal to his comrades and without fear, though the
spears fall around him like rain in a storm.

But disobedience is the worst of evils. It desolates
households; it ruins cities; it throws the ranks of allies into
confusion and rout. On the other hand, note those whose 550
lives are prosperous: they owe it, you will generally find, to
obedience. Therefore we must uphold the cause of order; and
certainly we must not let a woman defy us. It would be better
to fall from power by a man's hand, than to be called weaker
than a woman.

Chorus: Unless the years have stolen our wits, all that you
say seems wise.

Haemon: Father, the gods implant reason in men, the
highest of all things that we call our own. I have no skill to

prove, and I would not wish to show, that you speak 560
unwisely; and yet another man, too, might have some useful
thought. I count it a duty to keep my ears alert for what men
say about you, noting especially when they find fault. The
people dare not say to your face what would displease you;
but I can hear the things murmured in the dark, and the whole
city weeps for this maiden. "No woman ever," they say, "so
little merited a cruel fate. None was ever doomed to a
shameful death for deeds so noble as hers; who, when her
brother lay dead from bloody wounds, would not leave him
unburied for the birds and dogs to mangle. Does not so pious 570
an act deserve golden praise?"

Such is the way the people speak in secret. To me, father,
nothing is so precious as your welfare. What is there father or
son can so rejoice in as the other's fair repute? I pray you
therefore do not wear one mood too stubbornly, as if no one
else could possibly be right. For the man who thinks he is the
only wise man always proves hollow when we sound him. No,
though a man be wise, it is no shame for him to learn many
things, and to yield at the right time. When the streams rage
and overflow in Winter, you know how those trees that yield 580
come safely through the flood; but the stubborn are torn up
and perish, root and branch. Consider too, the sailor who
keeps his sheet always taut, and never slackens it; presently
his boat overturns and his keel floats uppermost. So, though
you are angry, permit reason to move you. If I, young as I am,
may offer a thought, I would say it were best if men were by
nature always wise; but that being seldom so, it is prudent to
listen to those who offer honest counsel.

Chorus: Sire, it is fitting that you should weigh his words,
if he speaks in season; and you, Haemon, should mark your 590
father's words; for on both parts there has been wise speech.

Creon: What! Shall men of our age be schooled by youths
like this?

Haemon: In nothing that does not go with reason; but as to
my youth, you should weigh my merits, not my years.

Creon: Is it your merit that you honor the lawless?

Haemon: I could wish no one to respect evil-doers.

Creon: This girl—is she not tainted with that plague?

Haemon: Our Theban folk deny it, with one voice.

Creon: Shall Thebes, then, tell me how to rule? 600

Haemon: Now who speaks like a boy?

Creon: Tell me—am I to rule by my own judgment or the
views of others?

Haemon: That is no city which belongs to one man.

Creon: Is not the city held to be the ruler's?

Haemon: That kind of monarchy would do well in a desert.

Creon: Ho, this boy, it seems, is the woman's champion!

Haemon: Yes, if you are a woman, for my concern is for
you.

Creon: Shameless, to bandy arguments with your father! 610

Haemon: Only because I see you flouting justice.

Creon: Is it wrong for me to respect my royal position?

Haemon: It is a poor way to respect it, trampling on the
laws of the gods.

Creon: This is depravity, putting a woman foremost!

Haemon: At least you will not find me so depraved that I
fear to plead for justice.

Creon: Every word you speak is a plea for that girl.

Haemon: And for you, and for me, and for the gods below.

Creon: Marry her you shall not, this side the grave. 620

Haemon: She must die then, and in dying destroy others?

Creon: Ha, you go so far as open threats?

Haemon: I speak no threats, but grieve for your fatal stubbornness.

Creon: You shall rue your unwise teaching of wisdom.

Haemon: If you were not my father, I would call you unwise.

Creon: Slave of a woman, do not think you can cajole me.

Haemon: Then no one but yourself may speak, you will hear no reason? 630

Creon: Enough of this—now, by Olympus, you shall smart for baiting me this way! Bring her here, that hateful rebel, that she may die forthwith before his eyes—yes, at her bridegroom's side!

Haemon: No, no, never think it, I shall not witness her death; but my face your eyes shall never see again. Give your passion its way before those who can endure you!

(*Haemon rushes away.*)

Chorus: He has gone, O King, in angry haste; a youthful mind, when stung, is impetuous.

Creon: Let him do what he will, let him dream himself 640 more than a common man, but he shall not save those girls from their doom.

Chorus: Are you indeed determined to slay them both?

Creon: Not the one whose hands are clean of the crime—you do well to remind me of that.

Chorus: But how will you put the other one to death?

Creon: I will take her where the path is loneliest, and hide her, living, in a rocky vault, with only so much food as the pious laws require, that the city may avoid reproach. There she can pray to Hades, whose gods alone she worships; 650 perhaps they will bargain with death for her escape. And if they do not, she will learn, too late, that it is lost labor to revere the dead.

[*Antigone engages in an impassioned lament over her destiny. Creon will not relent, and the guards lead Antigone to the tomb.*]

Teiresias: Princes of Thebes, it is a hard journey for me to come here, for the blind must walk by another's steps and see with another's eyes; yet I have come.

Creon: And what, Teiresias, are your tidings?

Teiresias: I shall tell you; and listen well to the seer.

Creon: I have never slighted your counsel.

Teiresias: It is that way you have steered the city well. 660

Creon: I know, and bear witness, to the worth of your words.

Teiresias: Then mark them now: for I tell you, you stand on fate's thin edge.

Creon: What do you mean? I shudder at your message.

Teiresias: You will know, when you hear the signs my art has disclosed. For lately, as I took my place in my ancient seat of augury, where all the birds of the air gather about me, I heard strange things. They were screaming with feverish rage, their usual clear notes were a frightful jargon; and I knew 670

they were rending each other murderously with their talons: the whir of their wings told an angry tale.

Straightway, these things filling me with fear, I kindled fire upon an altar, with due ceremony, and laid a sacrifice among the faggots; but Hephaestus would not consume my offering with flame. A moisture oozing out from the bones and flesh trickled upon the embers, making them smoke and sputter. Then the gall burst and scattered on the air, and the steaming thighs lay bared of the fat that had wrapped them.

Such was the failure of the rites by which I vainly asked a 680 sign, as this boy reported them; for his eyes serve me, as I serve others. And I tell you, it is your deeds that have brought a sickness on the State. For the altars of our city and the altars of our hearths have been polluted, one and all, by birds and dogs who have fed on that outraged corpse that was the son of Oedipus. It is for this reason the gods refuse prayer and sacrifice at our hands, and will not consume the meat-offering with flame; nor does any bird give a clear sign by its shrill cry, for they have tasted the fatness of a slain man's blood.

Think then on these things, my son. All men are liable to 690 err; but he shows wisdom and earns blessings who heals the ills his errors caused, being not too stubborn; too stiff a will is folly. Yield to the dead, I counsel you, and do not stab the fallen; what prowess is it to slay the slain anew? I have sought your welfare, it is for your good I speak; and it should be a pleasant thing to hear a good counselor when he counsels for your own gain.

Creon: Old man, you all shoot your shafts at me, like archers at a butt—you must practice your prophecies on me! Indeed, the tribe of augurs has long trafficked in me and 700 made me their merchandise! Go, seek your price, drive your trade, if you will, in the precious ore of Sardis and the gold of India; but you shall not buy that corpse a grave! No, though the eagles of Zeus should bear their carrion dainties to their Master's throne—no, not even for dread of that will I permit this burial!—for I know that no mortal can pollute the gods. So, hoary prophet, the wisest come to a shameful fall when they clothe shameful counsels in fair words to earn a bribe.

Teiresias: Alas! Does no man know, does none consider . . .

Creon: What pompous precept now? 710

Teiresias: . . . that honest counsel is the most priceless gift?

Creon: Yes, and folly the most worthless.

Teiresias: True, and you are infected with that disease.

Creon: This wise man's taunts I shall not answer in kind.

Teiresias: Yet you slander me, saying I augur falsely.

Creon: Well, the tribe of seers always liked money.

Teiresias: And the race of tyrants was ever proud and covetous.

Creon: Do you know you are speaking to your king? 720

Teiresias: I know it: you saved the city when you followed my advice.

Creon: You have your gifts, but you love evil deeds.

Teiresias: Ah, you will sting me to utter the dread secret I have kept hidden in my soul.

Creon: Out with it!—but if you hope to earn a fee by shaking my purpose, you babble in vain.

Teiresias: Indeed I think I shall earn no reward from you.

Creon: Be sure you shall not trade on my resolve.

Teiresias: Know then—aye, know it well!—you will not 730 live through many days, seeing the sun's swift chariot coursing heaven, 'til one whose blood comes from your own heart shall be a corpse, matching two other corpses; because you have given to the shadows one who belongs to the sun, you have lodged a living soul in the grave; yet in this world you detain one who belongs to the world below, a corpse unburied, unhonored and unblest. These things outrage the gods; therefore those dread Airiness, who serve the fury of the gods, lie now in wait for you, preparing a vengeance equal to your guilt. 740

And mark well if I speak these things as a hireling. A time not long delayed will waken the wailing of men and women in your house. But after these cries I hear a more dreadful tumult. For wrath and hatred will stir to arms against you every city whose mangled sons had the burial-rite from dogs and wild beasts, or from birds that will bear the taint of this crime even to the startled hearths of the unburied dead.

Such arrows I do indeed aim at your heart, since you provoke me—they will find their mark, and you shall not escape the sting.—Boy, lead me home, that he may spend 750 his rage on younger men, or learn to curb his bitter tongue and temper his violent mind.

(*Teiresias is led away.*)

Chorus: The seer has gone, O King, predicting terrible things. And since the days when my white hair was dark, I know that he has never spoken false auguries for our city.

Creon: I know that too, I know it well, and I am troubled in soul. It is hard to yield; but if by stubbornness I bring my pride to ruin—that too would be hard.

Chorus: Son of Menoekeus, it is time to heed good counsel. 760

Creon: What shall I do, then? Speak, and I will obey.

Chorus: Go free the living maiden from her grave, and make a grave for the unburied dead.

Creon: Is this indeed your counsel? Do you bid me yield?

Chorus: Yes, and without delay; for the swift judgments of the gods cut short the folly of men.

Creon: It is hard to do—to retreat from a firm stand— but I yield, I will obey you. We must not wage a vain war with Fate.

Chorus: Go then, let your own hand do these things; do not leave them to others. 770

Creon: Even as I am I will go: come, servants, all of you, bring tools to raise one grave and open another. Since our judgment has taken this turn, I who buried the girl will free her myself.—My heart misgive me, it is best to keep the established laws, even to life's end.

(*Creon and his servants go toward the plain.*)

[*The Chorus sings a hymn in praise of Dionysus.*]

(*A Messenger appears, from the direction of the plain.*)

Messenger: Neighbors of the house of Cadmus, dwellers within Amphion's[2] walls, there is no state of mortal life that I would praise or pity, for none is beyond swift change. Fortune raises men up and fortune casts them down from day to day, and no man can foretell the fate of things established. For 780

Creon was blest in all that I count happiness; he had honor as our savior; power as our king; pride as the father of princely children. Now all is ended. For when a man is stripped of happiness, I count him not with the living—he is but a breathing corpse. Let a man have riches heaped in his house, and live in royal splendor; yet I would not give the shadow of a breath for all, if they bring no gladness.

Chorus: What fearful news have you about our princes?

Messenger: Death; and the living are guilty of the dead.

Chorus: Who is the slayer—who is slain? 790

Messenger: Haemon has perished, and it was no stranger shed his blood.

Chorus: His father's hand, or his own?

Messenger: His own, maddened by his father's crime.

Chorus: O prophet, how true your word has proved!

Messenger: This is the way things are: consider then, how to act.

Chorus: Look!—the unhappy Eurydice, Creon's consort, comes from the house; is it by chance, or has she heard these tidings of her son? 800

(*Eurydice comes from the house.*)

Eurydice: I heard your words, citizens, as I was going to the shrine of Pallas with my prayers. As I loosed the bolts of the gate, the message of woe to my household smote my ear. I sank back, stricken with horror, into the arms of my handmaids, and my senses left me. Yet say again these tidings. I shall hear them as one who is no stranger to grief.

Messenger: Dear lady, I will tell you what I saw, I will hide nothing of the truth. I would gladly tell you a happier tale, but it would soon be found out false. Truth is the only way.—I 810 guided your lord the King to the furthest part of the plain, where the body of Polynices, torn by dogs, still lay unpitied. There we prayed to the goddess of the roads, and to Pluto,[3] in mercy to restrain their wrath. We washed the dead with holy rites, and all that was left of the mortal man we burned with fresh-plucked branches; and over the ashes at last we raised a mound of his native earth.

That done, we turned our steps toward those fearsome caves where in a cold nuptial chamber, with couch of stone, that maiden had been given as a bride of Death. But from 820 afar off, one of us heard a voice wailing aloud, and turned to tell our master Creon.

And as the King drew nearer, the sharp anguish of broken cries came to his ears. Then he groaned and said like one in pain, "Can my sudden fear be true? Am I on the saddest road I ever went? That voice is my son's! Hurry, my servants, to the tomb, and through the gap where the stones have been torn out, look into the cell— tell me if it is Haemon's voice I hear, or if my wits are tortured by the gods."

At these words from our stricken master, we went to make that search; and in the dim furthest part of the tomb we saw 830 Antigone hanging by the neck, her scarf of fine linen twisted into a cruel noose. And there too we saw Haemon—his arms about her waist, while he cried out upon the loss of his bride, and his father's deed, and his ill-starred love.

But now the King approached, and saw him, and cried out with horror, and went in and called with piteous voice, "Unhappy boy, what a deed have you done, breaking into this tomb! What purpose have you? Has grief stolen your reason? Come forth, my son! I pray you—I implore!" The boy answered no word, but glared at him with fierce eyes, spat in his face, and drew his cross-hilted sword. His father turned and fled, and the blow missed its mark. Then that maddened boy, torn between grief and rage and penitence, straightway leaned upon his sword, and drove it half its length into his side; and in the little moment before death, he clasped the maiden in his arms, and her pale cheek was red where his blood gushed forth. **840**

Corpse enfolding corpse they lie; he has won his bride, poor lad, not here but in the halls of Death; to all of us he has left a terrible witness that man's worst error is to reject good counsel. **850**

(*Eurydice goes into the house.*)

Chorus: What does this mean? The lady turns and goes without a word.

Messenger: I too am startled; but I think it means she is too proud to cry out before the people. Within the house, with her hand-maids about her, the tears will flow. Life has taught her prudence.

Chorus: It may be; yet I fear. To me such silence seems more ominous than many lamentations.

Messenger: Then I will go into the house, and learn if some tragic purpose has formed in her tortured heart. Yes, you speak wisely; too much silence may hide terrible meanings. **860**

(*The Messenger enters the house. As he goes, Creon comes into the open place before the house with attendants carrying the shrouded body of Haemon on a bier.*)

Chorus: See, the King himself draws near, with the sad proof of his folly; this tells a tale of no violence by strangers, but—if I may say it—of his own misdeeds.

Creon: Woe for the sins of a darkened soul, the sins of a stubborn pride that played with death! Behold me, the father who has slain, behold the son who has perished! I am punished for the blindness of my counsels. Alas my son, cut down in youth untimely, woe is me!—your spirit fled—not yours the fault and folly, but my own! **870**

Chorus: Too late, too late your eyes are opened!

Creon: I have learned that bitter lesson. But it was some god, I think, darkened my mind and turned me into ways of cruelty. Now my days are overthrown and my joys trampled. Alas, man's labors come but to foolish ends!

(*The Messenger comes from the house.*)

Messenger: Sire, one sees your hands are not empty, but there is more laid up in store for you. Woeful is the burden you bear, and you must look on further woes within your house. **880**

Creon: Why, how can there be more?

Messenger: Your queen is dead, the mother of that lad—

unhappy lady! This is Fate's latest blow.

Creon: Death, Death, how many deaths will stay your hunger? For me is there no mercy? O messenger of evil, bearer of bitter tidings, what is this you tell me? I was already dead, but you smite me anew. What do you say?—what is this news you bring of slaughter heaped on slaughter?

(*The doors of the King's house are opened, and the corpse of Eurydice is disclosed.*)

Chorus: Behold with your own eyes!

Creon: Oh, horror!—woe upon woe! Can any further dreadful thing await me? I have but now raised my son in these arms—and here again I see a corpse before me. Alas, unhappy mother—alas, alas my child! **890**

Messenger: At the altar of your house, self-stabbed with a keen knife, she suffered her darkening eyes to close, while she lamented that other son, Megareus, who died so nobly but a while ago, and then this boy whose corpse is here beside you. But with her last breath and with a bitter cry she invoked evil upon you, the slayer of your sons.

Creon: Will no one strike me to the heart with the two-edged sword?—miserable that I am, and plunged in misery! **900**

Messenger: Yes, both this son's death and that other son's were charged to you by her whose corpse you see.

Creon: But how did she do this violence upon herself?

Messenger: Her own hand struck her to the heart, when she had heard how this boy died.

Creon: I cannot escape the guilt of these things, it rests on no other of mortal kind. I, only I, am the slayer, wretched that I am—I own the truth. Lead me away, my servants, lead me quickly hence, for my life is but death. **910**

Chorus: You speak well, if any speech is good amid so much evil. When all is trouble, the briefest way is best.

Creon: Oh let it come now, the fate most merciful for me, my last day—that will be the best fate of all. Oh let it come swiftly, that I may not look upon tomorrow's light!

Chorus: That is hidden in the future. Present tasks claim our care. The ordering of the future does not rest with mortals.

Creon: Yet all my desire is summed up in that prayer.

Chorus: Pray no more: no man evades his destiny.

Creon: Lead me away, I pray you; a rash, foolish man, who has slain you, O my son, unwittingly, and you too my wife—unhappy that I am! Where can I find comfort, where can I turn my gaze?—for where I have turned my hand, all has gone wrong; and this last blow breaks me and bows my head. **920**

(*Creon is led into his house as the Chorus speaks.*)

Chorus: If any man would be happy, and not broken by Fate, Wisdom is the thing he should seek, for happiness hides there. Let him revere the gods and keep their words inviolate, for proud men who speak great words come in the end to despair. And learn wisdom in sorrow, when it is too late.

The tragic action in *Antigone* springs from the irreconcil-ability of Antigone's personal idealism and Creon's hard-headed political realism. Creon means well by the state; he is committed to the exercise of justice under the law. As a king newly come to power, he perceives his duty in terms

---

[2] Son of Zeus and Antiope; with his twin brother Zethus, be built the walls of Thebes.

[3] Another name for Hades, the Greek god of the netherworld, the shadowy realm where the souls of the dead were thought to rest.

of his authority: "whoever the city shall appoint to rule," says Creon, "that man must be obeyed, in little things and in great things, in just things and unjust; for the man who is a good subject is the one who would be a good ruler . . ." But Creon ignores the ancient imperatives of divine law and familial duty. His blind devotion to the state and his unwillingness to compromise trap him into making a decision whose consequences are disastrous.

In the Greek tragedy, the weakness or "tragic flaw" of the **protagonist** (the leading character) brings that character into conflict with fate or with the **antagonist** (one who opposes the protagonist), and ultimately to his or her fall. Creon's excessive pride (in Greek, *hubris*) results in the loss of those who are dearest to him. But Antigone is also a victim of self-righteous inflexibility. In an age that confined women to the domestic household and expected them to conform to male opinion, Antigone was unique. In ancient Greece, a girl in her early teens might marry a man considerably older than she. Along with the other female members of the household, she oversaw the daily chores associated with child-rearing, food preparation, and the production of clothing—spinning, weaving, and sewing. She could not inherit or own property and could not choose to divorce her husband (though he could divorce her); hence she was subordinate to her husband, as she had been to her father. While there were exceptions to this pattern (usually among the courtesans of male aristocrats), it seems clear that by challenging male authority, Antigone threatened the status quo: "*She* is the man," Creon angrily objects, "if she can carry this off unpunished." Antigone's sister, Ismene, argues, "We must remember we were born women, not meant to strive with men." But Antigone persists: Her heroism derives from her unswerving dedication to the ideals of divine justice and to the duty of the individual to honor family, even if it challenges the laws of the state.

Sophocles perceived the difficulties involved in reconciling public good and private conscience, and in achieving harmony between the individual and the community. In *Antigone*, he offers a moving plea for sound judgment and rational action, a plea that rings with the unbounded optimism of the choral chant: "Wonders are many in the world, and the wonder of all is man. . . . With speech and wind-swift thought he builds the State to his mood / Prospering while he honors the gods and the laws of the land" (lines 284, 296–297).

Aristotle on Tragedy

In modern parlance, the word "tragedy" is often used to describe a terrible act of fate that befalls an unwitting individual. With regard to drama, however, the word (and the form it describes) has a very different meaning. As a literary genre, tragedy deals not so much with catastrophic events as with *how* these events work to affect individuals in shaping their character and in determining their fate. The protagonist becomes a tragic hero not because of what befalls him, but rather as a result of the manner in which he confronts his destiny. In the *Poetics*, the world's first treatise on literary criticism, the Greek philosopher

Aristotle (384–322 B.C.E.) describes tragedy as an imitation of an action involving incidents that arouse pity and fear. Tragic action, he argues, should involve an error in judgment made by an individual who is "better than the ordinary man" but with whom the audience may sympathize.

The *Poetics* further clarifies the importance of "proper construction": the play must have a balanced arrangement of parts, and the action of the story should be limited to the events of a single day. The plot should consist of a single action made up of several closely connected incidents (without irrelevant additions). If we apply Aristotle's aesthetic principles of tragedy to Sophocles' *Antigone*, we arrive at an understanding of the so-called "unities" of action and time that characterize classic Greek tragedy. (Seventeenth-century playwrights added "unity of place" to neoclassical drama.) In *Antigone*, the action rests on a single incident: the rash decision of Creon. The events of the play occur within a single place and are acted out within a time span comparable to their occurrence in real life. Every episode in the play is relevant to the central action. Proportion and order apply to the writing of drama, suggests Aristotle, even as they must apply to the conduct and the fate of the tragic hero.

READING 1.14 From Aristotle's *Poetics* (ca. 340 B.C.E.)

. . . let us now consider the proper construction of the Fable   1
or Plot, as that is at once the first and the most important
thing in Tragedy. We have laid it down that a tragedy is an
imitation of an action that is complete in itself, as a whole of
some magnitude; for a whole may be of no magnitude to
speak of. Now a whole is that which has beginning, middle,
and end. A beginning is that which is not itself necessarily
after anything else, and which has naturally something else
after it; an end is that which is naturally after something itself,
either as its necessary or usual consequent, and with nothing   10
else after it; and a middle, that which is by nature after one
thing and has also another after it. A well-constructed Plot,
therefore, cannot either begin or end at any point one likes;
beginning and end in it must be of the forms just described.
Again: to be beautiful, a living creature, and every whole
made up of parts, must not only present a certain order in its
arrangement of parts, but also be of certain definite
magnitude. Beauty is a matter of size and order, and therefore
impossible either (1) in a very minute creature, since our
perception becomes indistinct as it approaches instantaneity;   20
or (2) in a creature of vast size—one, say, 1000 miles long—
as in that case, instead of the object being seen all at once,
the unity and wholeness of it is lost to the beholder. Just in
the same way, then, as a beautiful whole made up of parts, or
a beautiful living creature, must be of some size, but a size to
be taken in by the eye, so a story or Plot must be of some
length, but of a length to be taken in by the eye, so a story or
Plot must be of some length, but of a length to be taken in by
the memory. . . . The truth is that, just as in the other imitative
arts one imitation is always of one thing, so in poetry the   30
story, as an imitation of action, must represent one action, a

complete whole, with its several incidents so closely connected that the transposal or withdrawal of any one of them will disjoin and dislocate the whole. For that which makes no perceptible difference by its presence or absence is no real part of the whole. . . . The perfect Plot, accordingly, must have a single, and not (as some tell us) a double issue; the change in the hero's fortunes must be not from misery to happiness, but on the contrary from happiness to misery; and the cause of it must lie not in any depravity, but in some great error on his part; . . . As Tragedy is an imitation of personages better than the ordinary man, we in our way should follow the example of good portrait-painters, who reproduce the distinctive features of a man, and at the same time, without losing the likeness, make him handsomer than he is. . . .

40

Greek Philosophy: The Speculative Leap

In the ancient world, where most people saw themselves at the mercy of forces they could not comprehend, shamans and priestesses explored the unknown by means of sympathetic magic, myth, and ritual. During the sixth century B.C.E., a small group of Greek thinkers offered an intellectual alternative that combined careful observation, systematic analysis, and the exercise of pure reason. These individuals, whom we call philosophers (literally, "lovers of wisdom"), laid the foundations for Western scientific and philosophic inquiry. Instead of making nature the object of worship, they made it the object of study. To those who interpreted disasters such as earthquakes and lightning as expressions of divine anger, they submitted that such events might have natural, not supernatural, causes. Challenging all prevailing myths, the Greek philosophers made the speculative leap from supernatural to natural explanations of the unknown.

The Greeks were not the first to argue that the universe was governed by a natural order. The ancient Chinese, for instance, described the cosmos in terms of complimentary and interacting polarities, the *yin* and the *yang* (see chapter 3). In India, Hindu culture had stressed the oneness of all things in the universe. But while Asians might hypothesize on the wholeness of nature, the Greeks subjected it to rigorous analysis, a process that required the separation of the whole into its component parts. The ancient Greeks defended rationalism and objectivity as alternatives to intuition, holism, and supernaturalism. Their claims to intellectual detachment and objectivity—the fundamentals of the scientific method—put them at odds with East Asian claims to intuitively grasped truths. They also stand in clear contrast to the Hebrew call for unswerving faith. Indeed, the Greek glorification of reason provides a sharp contrast to the Hebrew exaltation of faith, as exemplified, for instance, in the Book of Job. These two modes of experience—reason (rooted in the Greco-Roman tradition) and faith (rooted in the Judeo-Christian tradition)—have competed for primacy in shaping Western culture from earliest times to the present.

Naturalist Philosophy: The Pre-Socratics

The earliest of the Greek philosopher-scientists lived just prior to the time of Socrates in the city of Miletus on the Ionian coast of Asia Minor. Although their senses reported a world of constant change, they reasoned that there must be a single, unifying substance that formed the basic "stuff" of nature. They asked, "What is everything made of?" "How do things come into existence?" and "What permanent substance lies behind the world of appearance?" Thales (ca. 625–ca. 547 B.C.E.), the "father of philosophy," held that water was the fundamental substance and source from which all things proceeded. Water's potential for change (from solid to liquid to gas) and its pervasiveness on earth convinced him that water formed the primary matter of the universe. While Thales argued that water formed the basic stuff of nature, his followers challenged this view: "Air," said one, "fire," countered another, and still others identified the basic substance as a mixture of the primordial elements. The concept that a single, unifying substance underlay reality drew opposition from some of the pre-Socratics. The universe, argued Heraclitus of Ephesus (ca. 540–ca. 480 B.C.E.), has no permanence, but, rather, is in constant process or flux. Heraclitus defended the idea that change itself was the basis of reality. "You cannot step twice into the same river," he wrote, "for fresh waters are ever flowing in upon you." Yet, Heraclitus believed that an underlying Form or Guiding Force (in Greek, *logos*) permeates nature, an idea that resembles Hindu pantheism and anticipated the Christian concept (found in the Gospel of John) of a Great Intelligence governing the beginning of time. For Heraclitus the Force was impersonal, universal, and eternal.

Around 500 B.C.E., Leucippus of Miletus theorized that physical reality consisted of minute, invisible particles that moved ceaselessly in the void. These he called *atoms*, the Greek word meaning "indivisible." Democritus (ca. 460–370 B.C.E.), a follower of Leucippus and the best known of the naturalist philosophers, developed the atomic theory of matter. For Democritus, the mind consisted of the same indivisible physical substances as everything else in nature. According to this materialist view, atoms moved constantly and eternally according to chance in infinite time and space. The atomic theory survived into Roman times, and although forgotten for two thousand years thereafter, it was validated by physicists of the early twentieth century.

Yet another pre-Socratic thinker named Pythagoras (ca. 580–ca. 500 B.C.E.) advanced an idea that departed from both the material and nonmaterial views of the universe. Pythagoras believed that proportion, discovered through number, was the true basis of reality. According to Pythagoras, all universal relationships may be expressed through numbers, the truths of which are eternal and unchanging. The formula in plane geometry that equates the square of the hypotenuse in right angle triangles to the sum of the square of the other two sides—a theorem traditionally associated with Pythagoras—is an example of such an unchanging and eternal truth, as is the simplest of mathematical equations: $2 + 2 = 4$. Pythagoras was the

−600 Thales of Miletus produces an accurate theory of the solar eclipse; he also advances the study of deductive geometry†

−540 Anaximander claims that life evolved from beginnings in the sea and that man evolved from a more primitive species

−530 Pythagoras argues for a spherical earth around which five planets revolve; he also develops the "Pythagorean Theorem"

−500 Leucippus theorizes that all matter is composed of "atoms"

−480 Anaxagoras postulates that the sun is a large, glowing rock; he explains solar eclipses

†All dates in this chapter are approximate. Minus (−) signifies B.C.E.

founding father of pure mathematics. He was also the first to demonstrate the relationship between musical harmonics and numbers. His view that number gives order and harmony to the universe is basic to the principles of balance and proportion that dominate classical art and music (see chapter 5).

In contrast with the Egyptians and the Mesopotamians, who deified the sun, the rivers, and other natural elements, the pre-Socratics stripped nature of all supernatural associations. They made accurate predictions of solar and lunar eclipses, plotted astronomical charts, and hypothesized on the processes of regeneration in plants and animals. Yet, in the areas of geometry, astronomy, and mathematics, it is likely that they inherited a large body of practical and theoretical data from the pyramid builders and calendar keepers of Egypt, and from the astrologists and palace engineers of Babylon, who knew how to solve linear and quadratic equations. It is also likely that the philosophic and religious theories originating in China and India influenced the speculative systems of Heraclitus, Pythagoras, and other pre-Socratics. Ideas, along with goods like silk, ivory, and cotton, moved back and forth along the overland trade routes that linked East Asia to the Mediterranean. For example, the Pythagorean proscription against eating animal flesh and certain plants suggests Greek familiarity with the Hindu

belief in reincarnation and the transmigration of souls (see chapter 1). And the Chinese association between illness and an imbalance of vital body energy seems to have made its way westwards into the purview of Hippocrates. Hippocrates (ca. 460–377 B.C.E.), the most famous of the Greek physicians and so-called "father of medicine," investigated the influence of diet and environment on general health and initiated the idea that an imbalance among bodily "humours"—blood, phlegm, black bile, and yellow bile—was the cause of disease. He insisted on the necessary relationship of cause and effect in matters of physical illness, and he raised questions concerning the influence of the mind on the body. He may also be deemed the "father of medical ethics": To this day, graduating physicians are encouraged to practice medicine according to the precepts of the Hippocratic Oath (probably not written by Hippocrates himself), which binds them to heal the sick and abstain from unprofessional medical practices.

The separation of the natural from the supernatural was as essential to the birth of medical science as it was to speculative philosophy. And although no agreement as to the nature of reality was ever reached among the pre-Socratics, these intellectuals laid the groundwork and the methodology for the rational investigation of the universe. Their efforts represent the beginnings of Western science and philosophy as formal disciplines.

Humanist Philosophy

The Sophists

The naturalist philosophers were concerned with describing physical reality in terms of the unity that lay behind the chaos of human perceptions. The philosophers who followed them pursued a different course: They turned their attention from the world of nature to the world of the mind, from physical matters to moral concerns, and from the gathering of information to the cultivation of wisdom. Significantly, these thinkers fathered the field of inquiry known as metaphysics (literally, "beyond physics"), that branch of philosophy concerned with abstract

Figure 4.13 Interior of a red-figured *kylix* (a Greek drinking cup), Douris, ca. 480 B.C.E. Terra-cotta, height 4⅞ in, diameter 11¾ in. The Metropolitan Museum of Art, New York. Rogers Fund, 1952 (52.11.4).

Figure 4.14 Portrait bust of Socrates. Roman marble copy of an original bronze supposedly created by Lysippos, ca. 350 B.C.E. © Hirmer Fotoarchiv.

thought. They asked not simply "*What* do we know (about nature)?" but "*How* do we know what we know?" The transition from the examination of matter to the exploration of mind established the humanistic direction of Greek philosophy for at least two centuries (Figure **4.13**).

The first humanist philosophers were a group of traveling scholar-teachers called Sophists. Masters of formal debate, the Sophists were concerned with defining the limits of human knowledge. The Thracian Sophist Protagoras (ca. 485–410 B.C.E.) believed that knowledge could not exceed human opinion, a position summed up in his memorable dictum: "Man is the measure of all things." His contemporary Gorgias (ca. 483–ca. 376 B.C.E.) tried to prove that reality is incomprehensible and that even if one could comprehend it, one could not describe the real to others. Such skepticism was common to the Sophists, who argued that truth and justice were relative: What might be considered just and true for one individual or situation might not be just and true for another.

Socrates and the Quest for Virtue

Athens' foremost philosopher, Socrates (ca. 470–399 B.C.E.), vigorously opposed the views of the Sophists. Insisting on the absolute nature of truth and justice, he described the ethical life as belonging to a larger set of universal truths and an unchanging moral order. For Socrates, virtue was not discovered by means of clever but misleading argumentation—a kind of reasoning that would come to be called (after the Sophists) *sophistry*, nor was it relative to individual circumstances. Rather, virtue was a condition of the *psyche**, the seat of both the moral and intellectual faculties of the individual. Hence, understanding the true meaning of virtue was preliminary to acting virtuously: To know good was to do good.

The question of right conduct was central to Socrates' life and teachings. A stonemason by profession, Socrates preferred to roam the streets of Athens and engage his fellow-citizens in conversation and debate (Figure **4.14**). Insisting that the unexamined life was not worth living, he challenged his peers on matters of public and private virtue, constantly posing the question, "What is the great-

est good?" In this pursuit, Socrates employed a rigorous question-and-answer technique known as the **dialectical method**. Unlike the Sophists, he refused to charge fees for teaching: he argued that wealth did not produce excellence; rather, wealth derived *from* excellence. Socrates described himself as a large horsefly, alighting upon and pestering the well-bred but rather sluggish horse—that is, Athens. So Socrates "alighted" on the citizens of Athens, arousing, persuading, and reproaching them and—most important—demanding that they give rational justification for their actions. His style of intellectual cross-examination, the question-and-answer method, proceeded from his first principle of inquiry, "Know thyself," while the progress of his analysis moved from specific examples to general principles, and from particular to universal truths, a type of reasoning known as *inductive*. The inductive method demands a process of abstraction: a shift of focus from the individual thing (the city) to all things (cities) and from the individual action (just or unjust) to the idea of justice. Central to Socratic inquiry was discourse. The notion that talk itself humanizes the individual is typically Greek and even more typically Socratic. Indeed, the art of conversation—the dialectical exchange of ideas—united the citizens of the *polis* (Figure 4.14).

As gadfly, Socrates won as many enemies as he won friends. The great masses of Greek citizens found comfort in the traditional Greek gods and goddesses. They had little use for Socrates' religious skepticism and stringent

---

*Often translated as "soul," but more accurately understood as representing one's individual personality.

methods of self-examination. Outspoken in his commitment to free inquiry, Socrates fell into disfavor with the reactionary regime that governed Athens after its defeat in the Peloponnesian Wars. Although he had fought bravely in the wars, he vigorously opposed the new regime and the moral chaos of post-war Athens. In the year 399 B.C.E., when he was over seventy years old, he was brought to trial for subversive behavior, impiety, and atheism. The Athenian jury found him guilty by a narrow margin of votes and sentenced him to death by drinking hemlock, a poisonous herb.

In his lifetime, Socrates wrote no books or letters: What we know of him comes mainly from the writings of his students. The dialogue called *Crito* (written by Plato) narrates the last events of Socrates' life: Crito, Socrates' friend and pupil, urges him to escape from prison, but the old philosopher refuses. He explains that to run away would be to subvert the laws by which he has lived. His escape would represent an implicit criticism of the democratic system and the city-state that he had defended throughout his life. For Socrates, the loyalty of the citizen to the *polis*, like that of the child to its parents, is a primary obligation. To violate the will of the community to which he belongs would constitute dishonor. Like Antigone, Socrates prefers death to dishonor. In the excerpt from *Crito*, Socrates explains why right action is crucial to the destiny of both the individual and the community. These words reaffirm the Hellenic view that immortality is achieved through human deeds, which outlast human lives.

READING 1.15 From Plato's *Crito* (ca. 390 B.C.E.)

Crito: . . . O my good Socrates, I beg you for the last time   1
to listen to me and save yourself. For to me your death will be more than a single disaster: not only shall I lose a friend the like of whom I shall never find again, but many persons who do not know you and me well will think that I might have saved you if I had been willing to spend money, but that I neglected to do so. And what reputation could be more disgraceful than the reputation of caring more for money than for one's friends? The public will never believe that we were anxious to save you, but that you yourself refused to escape.   10

Socrates: But, my dear Crito, why should we care so much about public opinion? Reasonable men, of whose opinion it is worth our while to think, will believe that we acted as we really did.

Crito: But you see, Socrates, that it is necessary to care about public opinion, too. This very thing that has happened to you proves that the multitude can do a man not the least, but almost the greatest harm, if he is falsely accused to them.

Socrates: I wish that the multitude were able to do a man the greatest harm, Crito, for then they would be able to do   20
him the greatest good, too. That would have been fine. But, as it is, they can do neither. They cannot make a man either wise or foolish: they act wholly at random . . . . Consider it in this way. Suppose the laws and the commonwealth were to come and appear to me as I was preparing to run away (if that is the

right phrase to describe my escape) and were to ask, "Tell us, Socrates, what have you in your mind to do? What do you mean by trying to escape but to destroy us, the laws, and the whole state, so far as you are able? Do you think that a state can exist and not be overthrown, in which the decisions of   30
law are of no force, and are disregarded and undermined by private individuals?" How shall we answer questions like that, Crito? Much might be said, especially by an orator, in defense of the law which makes judicial decisions supreme. Shall I reply, "But the state has injured me by judging my case unjustly." Shall we say that?

Crito: Certainly we will, Socrates.

Socrates: And suppose the laws were to reply, "Was that our agreement? Or was it that you would abide by whatever judgments the state should pronounce?" And if we were   40
surprised by their words, perhaps they would say, "Socrates, don't be surprised by our words, but answer us; you yourself are accustomed to ask questions and to answer them. What complaint have you against us and the state, that you are trying to destroy us? Are we not, first of all, your parents? Through us your father took your mother and brought you into the world. Tell us, have you any fault to find with those of us that are the laws of marriage?" "I have none," I should reply. "Or have you any fault to find with those of us that regulate the raising of the child and the education which you, like   50
others, received? Did we not do well in telling your father to educate you in music and athletics?" "You did," I should say. "Well, then, since you were brought into the world and raised and educated by us, how, in the first place, can you deny that you are our child and our slave, as your fathers were before you? And if this be so, do you think that your rights are on a level with ours? Do you think that you have a right to retaliate if we should try to do anything to you? You had not the same rights that your father had, or that your master would have had if you had been a slave. You had no right to retaliate if   60
they ill-treated you, or to answer them if they scolded you, or to strike them back if they struck you, or to repay them evil with evil in any way. And do you think that you may retaliate in the case of your country and its laws? If we try to destroy you, because we think it just, will you in return do all that you can to destroy us, the laws, and your country, and say that in so doing you are acting justly—you, the man who really thinks so much of excellence? Or are you too wise to see that your country is worthier, more to be revered, more sacred, and held in higher honor both by the gods and by all men of   70
understanding, than your father and your mother and all your ancestors; and that you ought to reverence it, and to submit to it, and to approach it more humbly when it is angry with you than you would approach your father; and either to do whatever it tells you to do or to persuade it to excuse you; and to obey in silence if it orders you to endure flogging or imprisonment, or if it sends you to battle to be wounded or die? That is just. You must not give way, nor retreat, nor desert your station. In war, and in the court of justice, and everywhere, you must do whatever your state and your   80
country tell you to do, or you must persuade them that their commands are unjust. But it is impious to use violence against your father or your mother; and much more impious to use violence against your country." What answer shall we make,

Crito? Shall we say that the laws speak the truth, or not?

Crito: I think that they do.

Socrates: "Then consider, Socrates," perhaps they would say, "if we are right in saying that by attempting to escape you are attempting an injustice. We brought you into the world, we raised you, we educated you, we gave you and every other citizen a share of all the good things we could. Yet we proclaim that if any man of the Athenians is dissatisfied with us, he may take his goods and go away wherever he pleases; we give that privilege to every man who chooses to avail himself of it, so soon as he has reached manhood, and sees us, the laws, and the administration of our state. No one of us stands in his way or forbids him to take his goods and go wherever he likes, whether it be to an Athenian colony, or to any foreign country, if he is dissatisfied with us and with the state. But we say that every man of you who remains here, seeing how we administer justice, and how we govern the state in other matters, has agreed, by the very fact of remaining here, to do whatsoever we tell him. And, we say, he who disobeys us acts unjustly on three counts: he disobeys us who are his parents, and he disobeys us who reared him, and he disobeys us after he has agreed to obey us, without persuading us that we are wrong. Yet we did not tell him sternly to do whatever we told him. We offered him an alternative; we gave him his choice either to obey us or to convince us that we were wrong; but he does neither. "These are the charges, Socrates, to which we say that you will expose yourself if you do what you intend; and you are more exposed to these charges than other Athenians." And if I were to ask, "Why?" they might retort with justice that I have bound myself by the agreement with them more than other Athenians. They would say, "Socrates, we have very strong evidence that you were satisfied with us and with the state. You would not have been content to stay at home in it more than other Athenians unless you had been satisfied with it more than they. You never went away from Athens to the festivals, nor elsewhere except on military service; you never made other journeys like other men; you had no desire to see other states or other laws; you were contented with us and our state; so strongly did you prefer us, and agree to be governed by us. And what is more, you had children in this city, you found it so satisfactory. Besides, if you had wished, you might at your trial have offered to go into exile. At that time you could have done with the state's consent what you are trying now to do without it. But then you gloried in being willing to die. You said that you preferred death to exile. And now you do not honor those words: you do not respect us, the laws, for you are trying to destroy us; and you are acting just as a miserable slave would act, trying to run away, and breaking the contracts and agreement which you made to live as our citizen. First, therefore, answer this question. Are we right, or are we wrong, in saying that you have agreed not in mere words, but in your actions, to live under our government?" What are we to say, Crito? Must we not admit that it is true?

Crito: We must, Socrates. . . .

. . . .

Plato and the Theory of Forms

Socrates' teachings were an inspiration to his pupil Plato (ca. 428–ca. 347 B.C.E.). Born in Athens during the Peloponnesian Wars, Plato reaped the benefits of Golden Age culture along with the insecurities of the post-war era. In 387 B.C.E, more than a decade after the death of his master, he founded the world's first school of philosophy, the Academy. Plato wrote some two dozen treatises, most of which were cast in the dialogue or dialectical format that Socrates had made famous. Some of the dialogues may be precise transcriptions of actual conversations, whereas others are clearly fictional, but the major philosophical arguments in almost all of Plato's treatises are put into the mouth of Socrates. Since Socrates himself wrote nothing, it is almost impossible to distinguish between the ideas of Plato and those of his teacher Socrates.

Plato's most famous treatise, the *Republic*, asks two central questions: "What is the meaning of justice?" and "What is the nature of a just society?" In trying to answer these questions, Plato introduces a theory of knowledge that is both visionary and dogmatic. It asserts the existence of a two-level reality, one consisting of constantly changing particulars available to our senses, the other consisting of unchanging eternal truths understood by way of the intellect. According to Plato, the higher reality of eternal truths, which he calls Forms, is distinct from the imperfect and transient objects of sensory experience, which are mere copies of Forms. Plato's Theory of Forms proposes that all sensory objects are imitations of the Forms, which, like the simplest mathematical equations, are imperishable and forever true. For example, the circle and its three-dimensional counterpart, the sphere, exist independent of any *particular* circle and sphere. They have always existed and will always exist. But the beach ball I toss in the air, an imperfect copy of the sphere, is transitory. Indeed, if all of the particular beach balls in the world were destroyed, the Universal Form—Sphere—would still exist. Similarly, suggests Plato, Justice, Love, and Beauty (along with other Forms) stand as unchanging and eternal models for the many individual and particular instances of each in the sensory world.

According to Plato, Forms descend from an ultimate Form, the Form of the Good. Plato never located or defined the Ultimate Good, except by analogy with the sun. Like the sun, the Form of the Good illuminates all that is intelligible and makes possible the mind's perception of Forms as objects of thought. The Ultimate Good, knowledge of which is the goal of dialectical inquiry, is the most difficult to reach.

In the *Republic*, Plato uses a literary device known as **allegory** to illustrate the dilemma facing the *psyche* in its ascent to knowledge of the imperishable and unchanging Forms. By way of allegory, the device by which the literal meaning of the text implies a figurative or "hidden" meaning, Plato describes a group of ordinary mortals chained within an underground chamber (the *psyche* imprisoned within the human body); their woeful position permits them to see only the shadows on the walls of the cave (the imperfect and perishable imitations of the

Figure 4.15 "Allegory of the Cave" from *The Great Dialogues of Plato*, translated by W.H.D. Rouse, translation copyright © 1956, renewed 1984 by J.C.G. Rouse. Used by permission of Dutton Signet, a division of Penguin Books USA Inc.

The Cave

The roadway

The fire

Diffused daylight

The rough ascent to sunlight

Forms that occupy the world of the senses), which the prisoners, in their ignorance, believe to be real (Figure **4.15**). Only when one of the prisoners (the philosopher-hero) ascends to the domain of light (true knowledge, or knowledge of the Forms) does it become clear that what the cave-dwellers perceive as truth is nothing more than shadows of Reality. This intriguing parable is presented as a dialogue between Socrates and Plato's older brother, Glaucon.

READING 1.16 The "Allegory of the Cave" from Plato's *Republic* (ca. 375 B.C.E.)

Next, said [Socrates], here is a parable to illustrate the degrees in which our nature may be enlightened or unenlightened. Imagine the condition of men living in a sort of cavernous chamber underground, with an entrance open to the light and a long passage all down the cave. Here they have been from childhood, chained by the leg and also by the neck, so that they cannot move and can see only what is in front of them, because the chains will not let them turn their heads. At some distance higher up is the light of a fire burning behind them; and between the prisoners and the fire is a track[1] with a parapet built along it, like the screen at a puppet-show, which hides the performers while they show their puppets over the top. **10**

I see, said he.

Now behind this parapet imagine persons carrying along various artificial objects, including figures of men and animals in wood or stone or other materials, which project above the parapet. Naturally, some of these persons will be talking, others silent.[2]

It is a strange picture, he said, and a strange sort of prisoners. **20**

Like ourselves, I replied; for in the first place prisoners so confined would have seen nothing of themselves or of one another, except the shadows thrown by the fire-light on the wall of the Cave facing them, would they?

Not if all their lives they had been prevented from moving their heads.

And they would have seen as little of the objects carried past.

Of course. **30**

Now, if they could talk to one another, would they not suppose that their words referred only to those passing shadows which they saw?

Necessarily.

And suppose their prison had an echo from the wall facing them? When one of the people crossing behind them spoke, they could only suppose that the sound came from the shadow passing before their eyes.

No doubt.

In every way, then, such prisoners would recognize as reality nothing but the shadows of those artificial objects. **40**

Inevitably.

Now consider what would happen if their release from the chains and the healing of their unwisdom should come about in this way. Suppose one of them were set free and forced suddenly to stand up, turn his head, and walk with eyes lifted to the light; all these movements would be painful, and he would be too dazzled to make out the objects whose shadows he had been used to see. What do you think he would say, if someone told him that what he had formerly seen was **50** meaningless illusion, but now, being somewhat nearer to

[1]The track crosses the passage into the cave at right angles and is above the parapet built along it.

[2]A modern Plato would compare his Cave to an underground cinema, where the audience watch the play of shadows thrown by the film passing before a light at their backs. The film itself is only an image of "real" things and events in the world outside the cinema. For the film Plato has to substitute the clumsier apparatus of a procession of artificial objects carried on their heads by persons who are merely part of the machinery, providing for the movement of the objects and the sound whose echo the prisoners hear. The parapet prevents these persons' shadows from being cast on the wall of the Cave.

reality and turned towards more real objects, he was getting a truer view? Suppose further that he were shown the various objects being carried by and were made to say, in reply to questions, what each of them was. Would he not be perplexed and believe the objects now shown him to be not so real as what he formerly saw?

Yes, not nearly so real.

And if he were forced to look at the fire-light itself, would not his eyes ache, so that he would try to escape and turn back to the things which he could see distinctly, convinced that they really were clearer than these other objects now being shown to him?

Yes.

And suppose someone were to drag him away forcibly up the steep and rugged ascent and not let him go until he had hauled him out into the sunlight, would he not suffer pain and vexation at such treatment, and, when he had come out into the light, find his eyes so full of its radiance that he could not see a single one of the things that he was now told were real?

Certainly he would not see them all at once.

He would need, then, to grow accustomed before he could see things in that upper world. At first it would be easiest to make out shadows, and then the images of men and things reflected in water, and later on the things themselves. After that, it would be easier to watch the heavenly bodies and the sky itself by night, looking at the light of the moon and stars rather than the Sun and the Sun's light in the day-time.

Yes, surely.

Last of all, he would be able to look at the Sun and contemplate its nature, not as it appears when reflected in water or any alien medium, but as it is in itself in its own domain.

No doubt.

And now he would begin to draw the conclusion that it is the Sun that produces the seasons and the course of the year and controls everything in the visible world, and moreover is in a way the cause of all that he and his companions used to see.

Clearly he would come at last to that conclusion.

Then if he called to mind his fellow prisoners and what passed for wisdom in his former dwelling-place, he would surely think himself happy in the change and be sorry for them. They may have had a practice of honoring and commending one another, with prizes for the man who had the keenest eye for the passing shadows and the best memory for the order in which they followed or accompanied one another, so that he could make a good guess as to which was going to come next. Would our released prisoner be likely to covet those prizes or to envy the men exalted to honor and power in the Cave? Would he not feel like Homer's Achilles, that he would far sooner "be on earth as a hired servant in the house of a landless man"[3] or endure anything rather than go back to his old beliefs and live in the old way?

Yes, he would prefer any fate to such a life.

Now imagine what would happen if he went down again to take his former seat in the Cave. Coming suddenly out of the sunlight, his eyes would be filled with darkness. He might be required once more to deliver his opinion on those shadows, in competition with the prisoners who had never been released, while his eyesight was still dim and unsteady; and it might take some time to become used to the darkness. They would laugh at him and say that he had gone up only to come back with his sight ruined; it was worth no one's while even to attempt the ascent. If they could lay hands on the man who was trying to set them free and lead them up, they would kill him.[4]

Yes, they would.

Every feature in this parable, my dear Glaucon, is meant to fit our earlier analysis. The prison dwelling corresponds to the region revealed to us through the sense of sight, and the fire-light within it to the power of the Sun. The ascent to see the things in the upper world you may take as standing for the upward journey of the soul into the region of the intelligible; then you will be in possession of what I surmise, since that is what you wish to be told. Heaven knows whether it is true; but this, at any rate, is how it appears to me. In the world of knowledge, the last thing to be perceived and only with great difficulty is the essential Form of Goodness. Once it is perceived, the conclusion must follow that, for all things, this is the cause of whatever is right and good; in the visible world it gives birth to light and to the lord of light, while it is itself sovereign in the intelligible world and the parent of intelligence and truth. Without having had a vision of this Form no one can act with wisdom, either in his own life or in matters of state.

So far as I can understand, I share your belief.

Then you may also agree that it is no wonder if those who have reached this height are reluctant to manage the affairs of men. Their souls long to spend all their time in that upper world—naturally enough, if here once more our parable holds true. Nor, again, is it at all strange that one who comes from the contemplation of divine things to the miseries of human life should appear awkward and ridiculous when, with eyes still dazed and not yet accustomed to the darkness, he is compelled, in a law-court or elsewhere, to dispute about the shadows of justice or the images that cast those shadows, and to wrangle over the notions of what is right in the minds of men who have never beheld Justice itself.

It is not at all strange.

No; a sensible man will remember that the eyes may be confused in two ways—by a change from light to darkness or from darkness to light; and he will recognize that the same thing happens to the soul. When he sees it troubled and unable to discern anything clearly, instead of laughing thoughtlessly, he will ask whether, coming from a brighter existence, its unaccustomed vision is obscured by the darkness, in which case he will think its condition enviable and its life a happy one; or whether, emerging from the depths of ignorance, it is dazzled by excess of light. If so, he will rather feel sorry for it; or, if he were inclined to laugh, that would be less ridiculous than to laugh at the soul which has

---

[3]This verse, spoken by the ghost of Achilles, suggests that the Cave is comparable with Hades, the Greek underworld.

---

[4]An allusion to the fate of Socrates.

come down from the light.

That is a fair statement.

If this is true, then, we must conclude that education is not what it is said to be by some, who profess to put knowledge into a soul which does not possess it, as if they could put sight into blind eyes. On the contrary, our own account signifies that the soul of every man does possess the power of learning the truth and the organ to see it with; and that, just as one might have to turn the whole body round in order that the eye should see light instead of darkness, so the entire soul must be turned away from this changing world, until its eye can bear to contemplate reality and that supreme splendor which we have called the Good. Hence there may well be an art whose aim would be to effect this very thing, the conversion of the soul, in the readiest way; not to put the power of sight into the soul's eye, which already has it, but to ensure that, instead of looking in the wrong direction, it is turned the way it ought to be.

Yes, it may well be so.

It looks, then, as though wisdom were different from those ordinary virtues, as they are called, which are not far removed from bodily qualities, in that they can be produced by habituation and exercise in a soul which has not possessed them from the first. Wisdom, it seems, is certainly the virtue of some diviner faculty, which never loses its power, though its use for good or harm depends on the direction towards which it is turned. You must have noticed in dishonest men with a reputation for sagacity the shrewd glance of a narrow intelligence piercing the objects to which it is directed. There is nothing wrong with their power of vision, but it has been forced into the service of evil, so that the keener its sight, the more harm it works.

Quite true.

And yet if the growth of a nature like this had been pruned from earliest childhood, cleared of those clinging overgrowths which come of gluttony and all luxurious pleasure and, like leaden weights charged with affinity to this mortal world, hang upon the soul, bending its vision downwards; if, freed from these, the soul were turned round towards true reality, then this same power in these very men would see the truth as keenly as the objects it is turned to now.

Yes, very likely.

Is it not also likely, or indeed certain after what has been said, that a state can never be properly governed either by the uneducated who know nothing of truth or by men who are allowed to spend all their days in the pursuit of culture? The ignorant have no single mark before their eyes at which they must aim in all the conduct of their own lives and of affairs of state; and the others will not engage in action if they can help it, dreaming that, while still alive, they have been translated to the Island of the Blest.

Quite true.

It is for us, then, as founders of a commonwealth, to bring compulsion to bear on the noblest natures. They must be made to climb the ascent to the vision of Goodness, which we called the highest object of knowledge; and, when they have looked upon it long enough, they must not be allowed, as they now are, to remain on the heights, refusing to come down again to the prisoners or to take any part in their labors

and rewards, however much or little these may be worth.

Shall we not be doing them an injustice, if we force on them a worse life than they might have?

You have forgotten again, my friend, that the law is not concerned to make any one class specially happy, but to ensure the welfare of the commonwealth as a whole. By persuasion or constraint it will unite the citizens in harmony, making them share whatever benefits each class can contribute to the common good; and its purpose in forming men of that spirit was not that each should be left to go his own way, but that they should be instrumental in binding the community into one.

True, I had forgotten.

You will see, then, Glaucon, that there will be no real injustice in compelling our philosophers to watch over and care for the other citizens. We can fairly tell them that their compeers in other states may quite reasonably refuse to collaborate: there they have sprung up, like a self-sown plant, in despite of their country's institutions; no one has fostered their growth, and they cannot be expected to show gratitude for a care they have never received. "But," we shall say, "it is not so with you. We have brought you into existence for your country's sake as well as for your own, to be like leaders and king-bees in a hive; you have been better and more thoroughly educated than those others and hence you are more capable of playing your part both as men of thought and as men of action. You must go down, then, each in his turn, to live with the rest and let your eyes grow accustomed to the darkness. You will then see a thousand times better than those who live there always; you will recognize every image for what it is and know what it represents, because you have seen justice, beauty, and goodness in their reality; and so you and we shall find life in our commonwealth no mere dream, as it is in most existing states, where men live fighting one another about shadows and quarreling for power, as if that were a great prize; whereas in truth government can be at its best and free from dissension only where the destined rulers are least desirous of holding office."

Quite true.

Then will our pupils refuse to listen and to take their turns at sharing in the work of the community, though they may live together for most of their time in a purer air?

No; it is a fair demand, and they are fair-minded men. No doubt, unlike any ruler of the present day, they will think of holding power as an unavoidable necessity.

Yes, my friend; for the truth is that you can have a well-governed society only if you can discover for your future rulers a better way of life than being in office; then only will power be in the hands of men who are rich, not in gold, but in the wealth that brings happiness, a good and wise life. All goes wrong when, starved for lack of anything good in their own lives, men turn to public affairs hoping to snatch from thence the happiness they hunger for. They set about fighting for power, and this internecine conflict ruins them and their country. The life of true philosophy is the only one that looks down upon offices of state; and access to power must be confined to men who are not in love with it; otherwise rivals will start fighting. So whom else can you compel to undertake the guardianship of the commonwealth, if not those who, besides understanding best the principles of government, enjoy a nobler life than the politician's and look for rewards of a different kind?

There is indeed no other choice. . . .

The "Allegory of the Cave" illustrates some key theories in the teachings of Plato. The first of these is **idealism**, the theory that holds that reality lies in the realm of unchanging, immaterial ideas, rather than in material objects. Platonic idealism implies a dualistic (spirit-and-matter or mind-and-body) model of the universe: The *psyche* belongs to the world of the eternal Forms, while the *soma* belongs to the sensory or material world. Imprisoned in the body, the mind forgets its once-perfect knowledge of the Forms. It is, nevertheless, capable of recovering its prenatal intelligence. The business of philosophy is to educate the *psyche*, to draw it out of its material prison so that it can regain perfect awareness.

Plato's concept of an unchanging force behind the flux of our perceptions looks back to the theories of Heraclitus, while his description of the Forms resembles Pythagorean assertions of the unchanging reality of number. It is not without significance that Plato's Theory of Forms has been hailed in modern physics: The celebrated twentieth-century German physicist Werner Heisenberg argued that the smallest units of matter are not physical objects in the ordinary sense; rather, he asserted, they are "forms," or ideas that can be expressed unambiguously only in mathematical language. In constructing the Theory of Forms, Plato may also have been influenced by Asian religious thought. The spiritual "spark" with which humans are born, according to Plato, and which must be kindled and cultivated, resembles the Hindu Atman (see chapter 3). And Plato's distinction between the realm of the senses and the ultimate, all-embracing Form recalls the Hindu belief that the illusory world of matter stands apart from Ultimate Being or Brahman. In contrast with Hinduism, however, Plato's teachings do not advocate enlightenment as escape from the material world. Rather, Plato perceives the mind's ascent to knowledge as a prerequisite of individual well-being and the attainment of the good life here on earth. Such enlightenment is essential to achieving a just state and a healthy society. Unlike the Hindu philosophers, whose mystical ascent to enlightenment is accomplished through withdrawal from the world, meditation, and self-denial, Plato defends a practical system of education by which individuals might arrive at knowledge of the Good. That educational system is expounded in the *Republic*.

Plato's utopian community permitted no private property and little family life, but exalted education as fundamental to society. While all people (male and female) would be educated equally, the ability of each would determine that person's place within society. Thus the roles of all citizens—laborers, soldiers, or governors—would be consistent with their mental and physical abilities. Plato had little use for democracy of the kind practiced in Athens. Governing, according to Plato, should fall to those who are the most intellectually able, that is, those who have most fully recovered a knowledge of the Forms, are obliged to act as "king-bees" in the communal hive. (Plato might have been surprised to discover that the ruling bee in a beehive is female.) The life of contemplation carried with it heavy responsibilities, for in the hands of the philosopher-kings lay "the welfare of the commonwealth as a whole." Plato's views on the ideal state were remarkably compatible with the ancient Chinese belief that a natural hierarchy determined who was intellectually fit to govern (see chapter 3).

Aristotle and the Life of Reason

Among Plato's students at the Academy was a young Macedonian named Aristotle, whose contributions to philosophy ultimately rivaled those of his teacher. After a period of travel in the eastern Mediterranean and a brief career as tutor to the young prince of Macedonia (the future Alexander the Great), Aristotle returned to Athens and founded a school known as the Lyceum. Aristotle's habit of walking up and down as he lectured gave him the nickname the "peripatetic philosopher." His teachings, which exist only in the form of lecture notes compiled by his students, cover a wider and more practical range of subjects than those of Plato. Aristotle did not accept the Theory of Forms. Insisting that mind and matter could not exist independently of each other, he rejected Plato's notion of an eternal *psyche*. Nevertheless, he theorized that a portion of the soul identified with reason (and with the impersonal force he called the Unmoved Mover) might be immortal.

Aristotle's interests spanned many fields, including those of biology, physics, politics, poetry, drama, logic, and ethics. The son of a physician, Aristotle's formative education inspired him to gather specimens of plant and animal life and classify them according to their physical similarities and differences. Over five hundred different animals, some of which Aristotle himself dissected, are mentioned in his zoological treatises. Though he did little in the way of modern scientific experimentation, Aristotle's practice of basing conclusions on very careful observation advanced the **empirical method**—a method of inquiry dependent on direct experience. Indeed, whereas Plato was the traditional rationalist, Aristotle pursued the path of the empiricist. He brought to his analysis of political life, literature, and human conduct the same principles he employed in classifying plants and animals: objectivity, clarity, and consistency. Before writing the *Politics*, he examined the constitutions of more than 150 Greek city-states. And in the *Poetics* he defined the various genres of literary expression (see chapter 5). In the fields of biology, astronomy, and physics, Aristotle's conclusions (including many that were incorrect) remained unchallenged for centuries. For instance, Aristotle theorized that in sexual union, the male was the "generator" and the female the "receptacle," since procreation involved the imposition of life-giving form (the male) on chaotic matter (the female). In short, Aristotle's views on female biology and sexuality led centuries of scholars to regard woman as an imperfect and incomplete version of man.

Aristotle's application of scientific principles to the reasoning process was the basis for the science of logic. Aristotelian logic requires the division of an argument into individual terms, followed—in Socratic fashion—by an examination of the meaning of those terms. Aristotle formulated the **syllogism**, a deductive scheme that presents two premises from which a conclusion may be drawn (Figure **4.16**). As a procedure for reasoned thought without reference to specific content, the syllogism is a system of notation that is similar to mathematics. Not the least of Aristotle's contributions was that which he made to **ethics**, that branch of philosophy that sets forth the principles of human conduct. Proceeding from an examination of human values, Aristotle hypothesizes that happiness or "the good life" (the Greek word *eudaimonia* means both) is the only human value that might be considered a final goal or end (*telos*) in itself, rather than a means to any other end. Is not happiness the one goal to which all human beings aspire? If so, then how does one achieve it? The answer, says Aristotle, lies in fulfilling one's unique function. The function of any thing is that by which it is defined: The function of the eye is to see; the function of the racehorse is to run fast; the function of a knife is to cut, and so on. How well a thing performs is synonymous with its excellence or virtue (in Greek, the word *arete* denotes both): The excellence of the eye, then, lies in seeing well; the excellence of a racehorse lies in how fast it runs; the excellence of a knife depends on how sharp it cuts, and so on. The unique function of the human being, observes Aristotle, is the ability to reason; hence, the excellence of any human creature lies in the exercise of reason.

In the *Ethics*, edited by Aristotle's son Nicomachus, Aristotle examines the Theory of the Good Life and the Nature of Happiness. He explains that action in accordance with reason is necessary for the acquisition of excellence, or virtue. Ideal conduct, suggests Aristotle, lies in the Golden Mean, the middle ground between any two extremes of behavior. Between cowardice and recklessness, for instance, one should seek the middle ground: courage. Between boastfulness and timidity, one should cultivate modesty. The Doctrine of the Mean rationalized the classical search for moderation and balance. In contrast with the divinely ordained moral texts of other ancient cultures, Aristotle's teachings required individuals to reason their way to ethical conduct.

THE SYLLOGISM
All men are mortal.
a:b
Socrates is a man.
c:a
Therefore, Socrates
is mortal.
∴ c = b

Figure 4.16 The Syllogism.

Every art and every scientific inquiry, and similarly every action and purpose, may be said to aim at some good. Hence the good has been well defined as that at which all things aim. But it is clear that there is a difference in the ends; for the ends are sometimes activities, and sometimes results beyond the mere activities. Also, where there are certain ends beyond the actions, the results are naturally superior to the activities. . . . [1]

If it is true that in the sphere of action there is an end which we wish for its own sake, and for the sake of which we wish for everything else, and that we do not desire all things for the sake of something else (for, if that is so, the process will go on *ad infinitum*, and our desire will be idle and futile) it is clear that this will be the good or the supreme good. Does it not follow then that the knowledge of this supreme good is of great importance for the conduct of life, and that, if we know it, we shall be like archers who have a mark at which to aim, we shall have a better chance of attaining what we want? But, if this is the case, we must endeavor to comprehend, at least in outline, its nature, and the science or faculty to which it belongs. . . . [10] [20]

It seems not unreasonable that people should derive their conception of the good or of happiness from men's lives. Thus ordinary or vulgar people conceive it to be pleasure, and accordingly approve a life of enjoyment. For there are practically three prominent lives, the sensual, the political, and, thirdly, the speculative. Now the mass of men present an absolutely slavish appearance, as choosing the life of brute beasts, but they meet with consideration because so many persons in authority share the tastes of Sardanapalus.[1] Cultivated and practical people, on the other hand, identify happiness with honor, as honor is the general end of political life. But this appears too superficial for our present purpose; for honor seems to depend more upon the people who pay it than upon the person to whom it is paid, and we have an intuitive feeling that the good is something which is proper to a man himself and cannot easily be taken away from him. It seems too that the reason why men seek honor is that they may be confident of their own goodness. Accordingly they seek it at the hands of the wise and of those who know them well, and they seek it on the ground of virtue; hence it is clear that in their judgment at any rate virtue is superior to honor. . . . [30] [40]

We speak of that which is sought after for its own sake as more final than that which is sought after as a means to something else; we speak of that which is never desired as a means to something else as more final than the things which are desired both in themselves and as means to something else; and we speak of a thing as absolutely final, if it is always desired in itself and never as a means to something else. [50]

It seems that happiness preeminently answers to this description, as we always desire happiness for its own sake and never as a means to something else, whereas we desire

---

[1] The legendary king of Assyria, known for his sensuality.

honor, pleasure, intellect, and every virtue, partly for their own sakes (for we should desire them independently of what might result from them) but partly also as being means to happiness, because we suppose they will prove the instruments of happiness. Happiness, on the other hand, nobody desires for the sake of these things, nor indeed as a means to anything else at all. . . .   60

Perhaps, however, it seems a truth which is generally admitted, that happiness is the supreme good; what is wanted is to define its nature a little more clearly. The best way of arriving at such a definition will probably be to ascertain the function of Man. For, as with a flute- player, a statuary, or any artisan, or in fact anybody who has a definite function and action, his goodness, or excellence seems to lie in his function, so it would seem to be with Man, if indeed he has a definite function. Can it be said then that, while a carpenter and a cobbler have definite functions and actions, Man,   70 unlike them, is naturally functionless? The reasonable view is that, as the eye, the hand, the foot, and similarly each . . . part of the body has a definite function, so Man may be regarded as having a definite function apart from all these. What then, can this function be? It is not life; for life is apparently something which man shares with the plants; and it is something peculiar to him that we are looking for. We must exclude therefore the life of nutrition and increase. There is next what may be called the life of sensation. But this too, is apparently shared by Man with horses, cattle, and all other   80 animals. There remains what I may call the practical life of the rational part of *Man's being*. But the rational part is twofold; it is rational partly in the sense of being obedient to reason, and partly in the sense of possessing reason and intelligence. The practical life too may be conceived of in two ways, viz., *either as a moral state, or as a moral activity*: but we must understand by it the life of activity, as this seems to be the truer form of the conception.

The function of Man then is an activity of soul in accordance with reason, or not independently of reason. . . .   90

Our present study is not, like other studies, purely speculative in its intention; for the object of our inquiry is not to know the nature of virtue but to become ourselves virtuous, as that is the sole benefit which it conveys. It is necessary therefore to consider the right way of performing actions, for it is actions as we have said that determine the character of the resulting moral states. . . .

The first point to be observed then is that in such matters as we are considering[,] deficiency and excess are equally fatal. It is so, as we observe, in regard to health and   100

strength; for we must judge of what we cannot see by the evidence of what we do see. Excess or deficiency of gymnastic exercise is fatal to strength. Similarly an excess or deficiency of meat and drink is fatal to health, whereas a suitable amount produces, augments and sustains it. It is the same then with temperance, courage, and the other virtues. A person who avoids and is afraid of everything and faces nothing becomes a coward; a person who is not afraid of anything but is ready to face everything becomes foolhardy. Similarly he who enjoys every pleasure and never abstains   110 from any pleasure is licentious; he who eschews all pleasures like a boor is an insensible sort of person. For temperance and courage are destroyed by excess and deficiency but preserved by the mean state. . . .

The nature of virtue has been now generically described. But it is not enough to state merely that virtue is a moral state, we must also describe the character of that moral state.

It must be laid down then that every virtue or excellence has the effect of producing a good condition of that of which it is a virtue or excellence, and of enabling it to perform its   120 function well. Thus the excellence of the eye makes the eye good and its function good, as it is by the excellence of the eye that we see well. Similarly, the excellence of the horse makes a horse excellent and good at racing, at carrying its rider and at facing the enemy. If then this is universally true, the virtue or excellence of man will be such a moral state as makes a man good and able to perform his proper function well. We have already explained how this will be the case, but another way of making it clear will be to study the nature or character of this virtue.   130

Now in everything, whether it be continuous or discrete, it is possible to take a greater, a smaller, or an equal amount, and this either absolutely or in relation to ourselves, the equal being a mean between excess and deficiency. By the mean in respect of the thing itself, or the absolute mean, I understand that which is equally distinct from both extremes; and this is one and the same thing for everybody. By the mean considered relatively to ourselves I understand that which is neither too much nor too little; but this is not one thing, nor is it the same for everybody. Thus if 10 be too much and 2 too little we take   140 6 as a mean in respect of the thing itself; for 6 is as much greater than 2 as it is less than 10, and this is a mean in arithmetical proportion. But the mean considered relatively to ourselves must not be ascertained in this way. It does not follow that if 10 pounds of *meat* be too much and 2 be too little for a man to eat, a trainer will order him 6 pounds, as this may itself be too much or too little for the person who is to take it; it will be too little [for instance] for Milo,[2] but too much for a beginner in gymnastics. It will be the same with running and wrestling; *the right amount will vary with the*   150 *individual*. This being so, everybody who understands his business avoids alike excess and deficiency; he seeks and chooses the mean, not the absolute mean, but the mean considered relatively to ourselves.

---

[2]A famous athlete from the Greek city-state of Crotona in southern Italy. As a teenager, he began lifting a calf each day, until, as both his strength and the calf grew, he could lift a full-grown bullock.

Every science then performs its function well, if it regards the mean and refers the works which it produces to the mean. This is the reason why it is usually said of successful works that it is impossible to take anything from them or to add anything to them, which implies that excess or deficiency is fatal to excellence but that the mean state ensures it. Good **160** artists too, as we say, have an eye to the mean in their works. But virtue, like Nature herself, is more accurate and better than any art; virtue therefore will aim at the mean;—I speak of moral virtue, as it is moral virtue which is concerned with emotions and actions, and it is these which admit of excess and deficiency and the mean. Thus it is possible to go too far, or not to go far enough, in respect of fear, courage, desire, anger, pity, and pleasure and pain generally, and the excess and the deficiency are alike wrong; but to experience these emotions at the right times and on the right occasions and **170** towards the right persons and for the right causes and in the right manner is the mean or the supreme good, which is characteristic of virtue. Similarly there may be excess, deficiency, or the mean, in regard to actions. But virtue is concerned with emotions and actions, and here excess is an error and deficiency a fault, whereas the mean is successful and laudable, and success and merit are both characteristics of virtue.

Virtue then is a state of deliberate moral purpose consisting in a mean that is relative to ourselves, the mean being **180** determined by reason, or as a prudent man would determine it. . . .

Aristotle and the State

While the Golden Mean gave every individual a method for determining right action, Aristotle was uncertain that citizens would put it to efficient use in governing themselves. Like Plato, he questioned the viability of the democratic state. Political privilege, argued Aristotle, was the logical consequence of the fact that some human beings were naturally superior to others: From the hour of their birth some were marked out for subjection and others for rule. Aristotle also insisted that governments must function in the interest of the state, not in the interest of any single individual or group. He criticized democracy because, at least in theory, it put power in the hands of great masses of poor people who might rule in their own interests. He also pointed out that Athenian demagogues were capable of persuading the Assembly to pass less-than-worthy laws. In his *Politics*, the first treatise on political theory produced in the West, Aristotle concluded that the best type of government was a constitutional one ruled by the middle class. Aristotle defined the human being as a *polis*-person (the term from which we derive the word "political"). Humans are, in other words, political creatures, who can reach their full potential only within the political framework of the state. Only beasts and gods, he noted, have no need for the state—he gracefully excluded women from such considerations. Aristotle resolved the relationship between the individual and the state as follows:

[The] state is by nature clearly prior to the family and to the individual, since the whole is of necessity prior to the part. . . . The proof that the state is a creation of nature and prior to the individual is that the individual, when isolated, is not self-sufficing; and therefore he is like a part in relation to the whole. But he who is unable to live in society, or who has no need because he is sufficient for himself, must be either a beast or a god: he is no part of a state. A social instinct is implanted in all men by nature, and yet he who first founded the state was the greatest of benefactors.

For man, when perfected, is the best of animals, but, when separated from law and justice, he is the worst of all; since armed injustice is the more dangerous, and he is equipped at birth with arms, meant to be used by intelligence and virtue, he is the most unholy and the most savage of animals, and the most full of lust and gluttony. But justice is the bond of men in states, for the administration of justice, which is the determination of what is just, is the principle of order in political society.

SUMMARY

The Aegean civilizations of Crete and Mycenae laid the foundations for much of Greek life and legend. Based in these pre-Greek cultures, the Homeric epics describe an aggressive and warlike people who balance vigorous individualism against a deep devotion to the tribal community. The heroes of the *Iliad*, unlike those of other ancient civilizations, do not place themselves at the mercy of the gods; rather, they determine their own destinies.

This spirit of individualism also shaped the values of the emerging Greek city-states. It contributed to the creation of Athenian democracy—the world's first and only direct democracy—and to the Golden Age in cultural productivity that followed the Persian Wars. In Pericles' Funeral Speech the heroic ideal assumes a civic context. In Sophocles' *Antigone* individual choice challenges the inflexible demands of the state. These works confirm the humanistic thrust of Greek culture. In them, we encounter the Hellenic claim that freedom was no gift of heaven, but rather, a human enterprise involving the active engagement of the individual in the life of the community. The literary achievements of the ancient Greeks in epic poetry, historical narrative, and drama are memorable for the majesty of their language and the profundity of their insights into the human condition. They convey the enduring belief that the good life is within the grasp of mortals.

The ancient Greeks made the speculative leap from belief to reason and from supernatural to natural explanations of the universe. The naturalist philosophers tried to determine the material basis of the universe: Democritus advanced the atomic theory of matter, and Pythagoras held that proportion based on number constituted the underlying cosmic order. The Sophists and the humanist philosophers Socrates, Plato, and Aristotle moved "beyond physics" to probe the limits of human knowledge and the nature of moral action. The Sophists argued that knowledge and virtue were relative, while their critic Socrates pursued absolute standards for moral conduct. Induction and the dialectical method served Socrates in his quest for virtue. Plato's Theory of Forms laid the basis for philosophical idealism and for the separation of mind and matter. In the *Republic*, Plato explained how virtue might be cultivated for the mutual benefit of the individual and the community. The more practical Aristotle investigated a wide variety of subjects ranging from logic and zoology to the art of poetry and the science of statecraft. In his *Ethics*, Aristotle asserted that the good life was identical with the life of reason, a life guided by the Golden Mean. The writings of Plato and Aristotle are the fountainhead of Western philosophic thought. They explore methods of critical thinking that lie at the heart of Western rationalism. As such, they have made an immeasurable contribution to the humanistic tradition.

SUGGESTIONS FOR READING

Blundell, Sue. *Women in Ancient Greece*. Cambridge, Mass.: Harvard University Press, 1995.

Cartledge, Paul. *The Greeks: A Portrait of Self and Others*. New York: Oxford University Press, 1993.

Dover, K. J. *Greek Popular Morality in the Time of Plato and Aristotle*. Berkeley, Calif.: University of California Press, 1980.

Finley, M. I., ed. *The Legacy of Greece: A New Appraisal*. Oxford: Oxford University Press, 1981.

Green, Richard and Eric Handley. *Images of the Greek Theater*. Austin: University of Texas Press, 1995.

Lear, Jonathan. *Aristotle: The Desire to Understand*. New York: Oxford University Press, 1993.

Loraux, Nicole. *The Children of Athena: Athenian Ideas about Citizenship and the Division Between the Sexes*, trans. by C. Levine. Princeton, N.J.: Princeton University Press, 1993.

Martin, Thomas R. *Ancient Greece: From Prehistoric to Hellenistic Times*. New Haven, Conn.: Yale University Press, 1996.

Miller, Dean A. *The Epic Hero*. Baltimore, Md.: Johns Hopkins Press, 2000.

Morgan, Michael L. *Platonic Piety: Philosophy and Ritual in Fourth-Century Athens*. New Haven, Conn.: Yale University Press, 1990.

Reeder, Ellen D., ed. *Pandora: Women in Classical Greece*. Princeton: Princeton University Press, 1996.

Sinn, Ulrich. *Olympia: Cult, Sport, and Ancient Festival*. Princeton: Markus Weiner, 2000.

Stone, I. F. *The Trial of Socrates*. New York: Doubleday, 1989.

Vlastos, Gregory. *Socrates, Ironist and Moral Philosopher*. Ithaca, N.Y.: Cornell University Press, 1991.

GLOSSARY

allegory a literary device in which objects, persons, or actions are equated with secondary, figurative meanings that underlie their literal meaning

antagonist the character that directly opposes the protagonist in drama or fiction

catalog a list of people, things, or attributes, characteristic of biblical and Homeric literature

democracy a government in which supreme power is vested in the people

dialectical method a question-and-answer style of inquiry made famous by Socrates

empirical method a method of inquiry dependent on direct experience or observation

epithet a characterizing word or phrase; in Homeric verse, a compound adjective

used to identify a person or thing

ethics that branch of philosophy that sets forth the principles of human conduct

idealism (Platonic) the theory that holds that things in the material world are manifestations of an independent realm of unchanging, immaterial ideas of forms (see also Kantian idealism, chapter 25)

oligarchy a government in which power lies in the hands of an elite minority

protagonist the leading character in a play or story

simile a figure of speech comparing two essentially unlike things, often introduced by "like" or "as"

syllogism a deductive scheme of formal argument, consisting of two premises from which a conclusion may be drawn

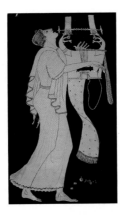

CHAPTER FIVE

The classical style

"Men are day-bound. What is a man? What is he not? Man is a shadow's dream. But when divine advantage comes, men gain a radiance and a richer life."
Pindar

The words "classic" or "classical" are commonly used to mean "first-rate" and "enduring"; but they also describe the unique style that dominated the arts during the Greek Golden Age, that is, the period that followed the Persian Wars. The classical style embraced principles of clarity, harmony, and proportioned order in the visual arts, as well as in literature and music. At its height (ca. 480–400 B.C.E.) the so-called High Classical style provided a standard of beauty and excellence that was imitated for centuries, but most immediately by the civilizations that came to prominence after the collapse of Hellenic power. During the fourth century B.C.E., Alexander the Great carried Greek language and culture into North Africa and Central Asia, thus "Hellenizing" a vast part of the civilized world. Thereafter, the Romans absorbed Greek culture and, by imitation and adaptation, ensured the survival of classicism. In music and literature, as in the visual arts, the Greeks provided models that the Romans ultimately transmitted to the West.* Most of the freestanding sculptures of the Greek masters survive only in Roman replicas, and what remains is a fraction of what once existed. The balance fell to the ravages of time and barbarian peoples, who pulverized marble statues to make mortar and melted down bronze pieces to mint coins and cast cannons.

Despite these losses, the classical conception of beauty has had a profound influence on Western cultural expression. Its mark is most visible in the numerous neoclassical ("new classical") revivals that have flourished over the centuries, beginning with the Renaissance in Italy (see chapters 16–17). Some analysis of the defining features of the classical style is essential to an appreciation (and an understanding) of how and why that style became the touchstone by which creative expression was to be judged for centuries.

*The Roman contribution to the classical style is discussed in chapter 6.

Key Features of the Classical Style

Order and Proportion

The search for a natural order was the driving force behind the evolution of the classical style, even as it was the impetus for the rise of Greek philosophy. In chapter 4, it became clear that the quest to identify the natural order—the fundamental order underlying the chaos of human perception—preoccupied the early Greek philosophers. Pythagoras, for example, tried to show that the order of the universe could be understood by observing proportion (both geometric and numerical) in nature: He produced a taut string that, when plucked, sounded a specific pitch; by pinching that string in the middle and plucking either half he generated a sound exactly consonant with (and one **octave** higher than) the first pitch. Pythagoras claimed that relationships between musical sounds obeyed a natural symmetry that might be expressed numerically and geometrically. If music was governed by proportion, was not the universe as a whole subject to similar laws? And, if indeed nature itself obeyed laws of harmony and proportion, then should not artists work to imitate them?

Among Greek artists and architects, such ideas generated the search for a canon, or set of rules for determining physical proportion. To arrive at a canon, the artist fixed on a module, or standard of measurement, that governed the relationships beween all parts of the work of art and the whole. The size of the module was not absolute, but varied according to the subject matter. In the human body, for instance, the distance between the chin to the top of the forehead, representing one-tenth of the whole body height, constituted a module by which body measurements might be calculated. Unlike the Egyptian canon (see Figure 1.21), the Greek canon was flexible: It did not employ a grid on which the human form was mapped, with fixed positions for parts of the body. Nevertheless, the

Greek canon made active use of that principle of proportion known as *symmetry*, that is, correspondence of opposite parts in size, shape, or position, as is evident in the human body.

Although little survives in the way of Greek literary evidence, Roman sources preserve information that helps us to understand the canon which, after three centuries of experimentation, artists of the Greek Golden Age put into practice. Among these sources, the best is the *Ten Books on Architecture* written by the Roman architect and engineer, Vitruvius Pollio (?–26 B.C.E.). Vitruvius recorded many of the aesthetic principles and structural techniques used by the ancient Greeks. In defining the classical canon, Vitruvius advised that the construction of a building and the relationship between its parts must imitate the proportions of the human body. Without proportion, that is, the correspondence between the various parts of the whole, there can be no design, argued Vitruvius. And without design, there can be no art. The eminent Golden Age Greek sculptor Polycleitus, himself the author of a manual on proportion (no longer in existence), is believed to have employed the canon Vitruvius describes (Figure **5.1**). But it was the Vitruvian model itself that, thanks to the efforts of the Renaissance artist/scientist Leonardo da Vinci (see chapter 17), became a symbol for the centrality of the ideally proportioned human being in an ideally proportioned universe (Figure **5.2**).

Figure 5.2 Leonardo da Vinci, *Proportional Study of a Man in the Manner of Vitruvius*, ca. 1487. Pen and ink, 13½ × 9⅝ in. Galleria dell'Accademia, Venice.

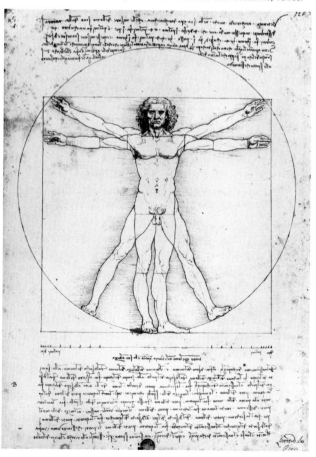

Figure 5.1 Polycleitus, *Doryphorus (Spear-Bearer)*, Roman marble copy after a bronze Greek original of ca. 450–440 B.C.E. Height 6 ft. 11 in. National Museum, Naples. Photo: Fotografica Foglia, Naples.

READING 1.18 From Vitruvius' Principles of Symmetry (ca. 46–30 B.C.E.)

On Symmetry: In Temples and in the Human Body

1 The Design of a temple depends on symmetry, the principles of which must be most carefully observed by the architect. They are due to proportion. . . . Proportion is a correspondence among the measures of the members of an entire work, and of the whole to a certain part selected as standard. From this result the principles of symmetry. Without symmetry and proportion there can be no principles in the design of any temple; that is, if there is no precise relation between its members, as in the case of those of a well shaped man.

2 For the human body is so designed by nature that the face, from the chin to the top of the forehead and lowest roots of the hair, is a tenth part of the whole height; the open hand from the wrist to the tip of the middle finger is just the same; the head from the chin to the crown is an eighth, and with the neck and shoulder from the top of the breast to the lowest roots of the hair is a sixth; from the middle of the breast to the summit of the crown is a fourth. If we take the height of the face itself, the distance from the bottom of the chin to the under side of the nostrils is one third of it; the nose from the underside of the nostrils to a line between the eyebrows is the same; from there to the lowest roots of the hair is also a third, comprising the forehead. The length of the foot is one sixth of the height of the body; of the forearm, one fourth; and the breadth of the breast is also one fourth. The other members, too, have their own symmetrical proportions, and it was by employing them that famous painters and sculptors of antiquity attained to great and endless renown.

3 Similarly, in the members of a temple there ought to be the greatest harmony in the symmetrical relations of the different parts to the general magnitude of the whole. Then again, in the human body the central point is naturally the navel. For if a man be placed flat on his back, with hands and feet extended, and a pair of compasses centered at his navel, the fingers and toes of his two hands and feet will touch the circumference of a circle described therefrom. And just as the human body yields a circular outline, so too a square figure may be found from it [see Figure 5.2]. For if we measure the distance from the soles of the feet to the top of the head, and then apply that measure to the outstretched arms, the breadth will be found to be the same as the height, as in the case of plane surfaces which are perfectly square.

4 Therefore, since nature has designed the human body so that its members are duly proportioned to the frame as a whole, it appears that the ancients had good reason for their rule, that in perfect buildings the different members must be in exact symmetrical relations to the whole general scheme. Hence, while transmitting to us the proper arrangements for buildings of all kinds, they are particularly careful to do so in the case of temples of the gods, buildings in which merits and faults usually last forever. . . .

Humanism, Realism, and Idealism

While proportion and order are two guiding principles of the classical style, other features informed Greek art from earliest times: One of these is *humanism*. Greek art is said to be humanistic not only because it observes fundamental laws derived from the human physique, but because it focuses so consistently on the actions of human beings. Greek art is fundamentally *realistic*, that is, faithful to nature; but it refines nature in a process of *idealization*, that is, the effort to achieve a perfection that surpasses nature. Humanism, realism, and idealism are hallmarks of Greek art.

Because almost all evidence of Greek wall-painting has disappeared, decorated vases are our main source of information about Greek painting. During the first three hundred years of Greek art—the *Geometric Period* (ca. 1200–700 B.C.E)—artists painted their ceramic wares with angular figures and complex geometric patterns organized according to the shape of the vessel (Figure **5.3**). By the *Archaic Period* (ca. 700–480 B.C.E.), figures painted in black or brown, and scenes from mythology, literature, and everyday life, came to dominate the central zone of the vase (Figure **5.4**; see also Figures 4.7 and 4.10). Water jars, wine jugs, storage vessels, drinking cups, and bowls all reflect the keen enjoyment of everyday activities among the Greeks: working, dancing, feasting, fighting, and gaming. In these compositions, little if any physical setting is

Figure 5.3 Krater with "Geometric" decoration, ca. 750 B.C.E. Terra-cotta, height 3 ft. 4½ in. The Metropolitan Museum of Art, New York..

5.5). They continued to position figures and objects so that they would complement the shape of the vessel (see also Figures 4.13 and 5.4). However, the red-figured style allowed artists to delineate physical details on the buff-colored surface, thereby making the human form appear more lifelike. Although still flattened and aligned side by side, figures are posed naturally. *Realism*, that is, fidelity to nature, has overtaken the decorative aspect of the geometric and archaic styles. At the same time, artists of the Classical Period moved toward aesthetic *idealism*. Socrates is noted for having described the idealizing process: He advised the painter Parrhasius that he must reach beyond the flawed world of appearances by selecting and combining the most beautiful details of many different models. To achieve ideal form, the artist must simplify the subject matter, free it of incidental detail, and impose the accepted canon of proportion. Accordingly, the art object will surpass the imperfect and transient objects of sensory experience. Like Plato's Ideal Forms, the artist's imitations of reality are lifelike in appearance, but they improve upon sensory reality in their absolute perfection. Among the Greeks, as among the Egyptians, conception played a large part in the art-making process; with the Greeks, however, the created object was no longer a static sacred sign, but a dynamic, rationalized version of the physical world.

Figure 5.4 Exekias, Black amphora with Achilles and Ajax Playing Dice, ca. 530 B.C.E. Height 24 in. Vatican Museums, Rome.

provided for the action. Indeed, in their decorative simplicity, the figures often resemble the abstract shapes that ornament the rim, handle, and foot of the vessel (see Figure 5.4). The principles of clarity and order so apparent in the Geometric style (see Figure 5.3) remain evident in the decoration of later vases, where a startling clarity of design is produced by the interplay of light and dark areas of figure and ground.

By the *Classical Period* (480–323 B.C.E.), artists had replaced the black-figured style with one in which the human body was left the color of the clay and the ground was painted black (Figure

Figure 5.5 Epictetus, Cup (detail), ca. 510 B.C.E. Terra-cotta, diameter 13 in. Reproduced by courtesy of the Trustees of the British Museum, London.

The Evolution of the Classical Style

Greek Sculpture: The Archaic Period (ca. 700–480 B.C.E.)

Nowhere is the Greek affection for the natural beauty of the human body so evident as in Hellenic sculpture, where the male nude form assumed major importance as a subject. Freestanding Greek sculptures fulfilled the same purpose as Egyptian and Mesopotamian votive statues: They paid perpetual homage to the gods. They also served as cult statues, funerary monuments, and memorials

Figure 5.7 *Calf-Bearer*, ca. 575–550 B.C.E. Marble, height 5 ft. 6 in. Acropolis Museum, Athens. © Hirmer Fotoarchiv.

designed to honor the victors of the athletic games. Since athletes both trained and competed in the nude, representation of the unclothed body was completely appropriate. Ultimately, however, the centrality of the nude in Greek art reflects the Hellenic regard for the human body as nature's perfect creation. (The fig leaves that cover the genitals of some Greek sculptures are additions dating from the Christian era.)

As in painting, so in sculpture, the quest for realism was offset by the will to idealize form. Achieving the delicate balance between real and ideal was a slow process, one that had its beginnings early in Greek history. During the Archaic phase of Greek sculpture, freestanding representations of the male youth (**kouros**) still resembled the blocklike statuary of ancient Egypt (see Figure 1.5). The kouros from Sounion (ca. 600 B.C.E) is rigidly posed, with arms close to its sides and its body weight distributed equally on both feet (Figure **5.6**). Like most Archaic stat-

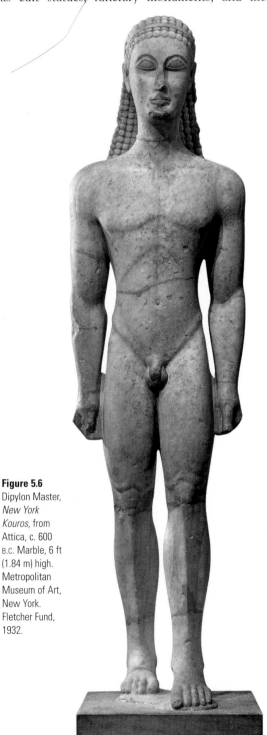

Figure 5.6
Dipylon Master, *New York Kouros*, from Attica, c. 600 B.C. Marble, 6 ft (1.84 m) high. Metropolitan Museum of Art, New York. Fletcher Fund, 1932.

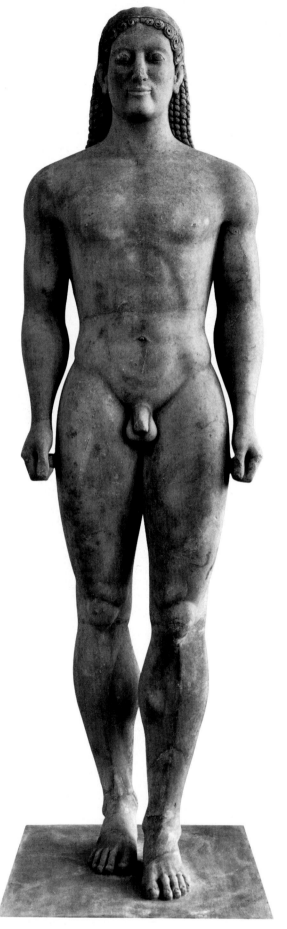

ues, the figure retains the rigid verticality of tree trunks from which early Greek sculptures were carved.

Produced some fifty years after the Sounion *kouros*, the *Calf-Bearer* (ca. 575–550 B.C.E) is more gently and more realistically modeled—note especially the abdominal muscles and the sensitively carved bull calf (Figure **5.7**). The hollow eyes of the shepherd once held inlays of semiprecious stones (mother-of-pearl, gray agate, and lapis lazuli) that would have given the face a strikingly realistic appearance. Such lifelike effects were enhanced by the brightly colored paint that (now almost gone) enlivened the lips, hair, and other parts of the figure. A quarter of a century later, the robust likeness of a warrior named Kroisos (found marking his grave) shows close anatomical attention to knee and calf muscles. Like his carved predecessors, he strides aggressively forward, but his forearms now turn in toward his body, and his chest, arms, and legs swell with powerful energy (Figure **5.8**). He also bears a blissful smile that, in contrast with the awestruck countenances of Mesopotamian votive statues (see Figure 2.9), reflects the buoyant optimism of the early Greeks.

Greek Sculpture: The Classical Period (480–323 B.C.E.)

By the early fifth century B.C.E., a major transformation occurred in Hellenic art. With the Kritios Boy, the Greek sculptor had arrived at the natural positioning of the human body that would characterize the classical style: The sensuous torso turns on the axis of the spine, and the weight of the body shifts from equal distribution on both legs to greater weight on the left leg—a kind of balanced opposition that is at once natural and graceful (Figure **5.9**). (This counterpositioning would be called **contrapposto** by Italian Renaissance artists.) The muscles of the Kritios Boy are no longer geometrically schematized, but protrude subtly at anatomical junctures. And the figure is no longer smiling, but instead, solemn and contemplative. The new poised stance, along with a complete mastery of human anatomy and proportion, are features of the High Classical style that flourished between ca. 480–400 B.C.E. At mid-century, Polycleitus brought that style to perfection with the *Doryphorus* (*Spear-Bearer*; see Figure 5.1). Known today only by way of Roman copies, the *Doryphorus* is held by some as the embodiment of the canon of ideal human proportions (see Reading 1.18). The figure, who once held a spear in his left hand, strides forward in a manner that unites motion and repose, energy and poise, confidence and grace—the qualities of the ideal warrior-athlete.

There is little to distinguish man from god in the bronze statue of Zeus (or Poseidon) hurling a weapon, the work of an unknown sculptor (Figure **5.11**). This nude, which conveys the majesty and physical vitality of a mighty Greek deity, might just as well represent a victor of the Olympic games. The Greeks were the first to employ the lost-wax method of bronze casting (see Figure 0.18) for large-sized artworks, such as the monumental Zeus (or Poseidon) itself. This sophisticated technique allowed artists to depict more vigorous action and to include

Figure 5.8 Kroisos from Anavyssos, ca. 525 B.C.E. Marble with traces of paint, height 6 ft. 4½ in. National Archeological Museum, Athens. Photo: Alison Frantz.

greater detail than was possible in the more restrictive medium of marble. Dynamically posed—the artist has deliberately exaggerated the length of the arms—the god fixes the decisive moment just before the action, when every muscle in the body is tensed, ready to achieve the mark. The sculptor has also idealized the physique in the direction of geometric clarity. Hence the muscles of the stomach are indicated as symmetrical trapezoids, and the strands of his hair and beard assume a distinctive pattern of parallel wavy lines.

Greek and Roman sculptors often made marble copies of popular bronze-cast figures. The *Discobolus (Discus Thrower)*, originally executed in bronze by Myron around 450 B.C.E, but surviving only in various Roman marble copies, is one such example (Figure **5.10**). Like the statue

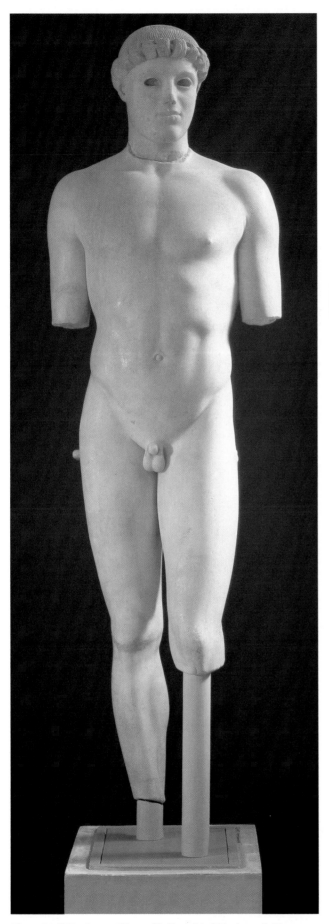

Figure 5.9 Kritios Boy, ca. 480 B.C.E. Marble, height 34 in. Acropolis Museum, Athens. Photo: Craigo Marie Mauzy, Athens.

Figure 5.10 Myron, *Discobolus (Discus Thrower)*, reconstructed Roman marble copy of a bronze Greek original of ca. 450 B.C.E. Height 5 ft. 1 in. Museo Nazionale delle Terme, Rome. Photo: SCALA.

in Figure 5.11, it captures the moment before the action, the ideal moment when intellect guides the physical effort to follow. The male nudes of the High Classical Age seem to fulfill Aristotle's idea of excellence as the exercise of human will dominated by reason.

The evolution of the female figure (kore) underwent a somewhat different course from that of the male. Early korai were fully clothed and did not appear in the nude until the fourth century B.C.E. Female statues of the Archaic period were ornamental, columnar, and (like their male counterparts) smiling (Figure 5.12). Not until the Late Classical Age (430–323 B.C.E.) did Greek sculptors arrive at the sensuous female nudes that so inspired Hellenistic, Roman, and (centuries later) Renaissance artists. The *Aphrodite of Knidos* (Figure 5.13) by Praxiteles established a model for the ideal female form: tall and poised, with small breasts and broad hips. Regarded by the Romans as the finest statue in the world, Praxiteles' goddess of love exhibits a subtle counterposition of shoulders and hips, smooth body curves, and a face that bears a dreamy, melting gaze. She is distinguished by the famous Praxitelean technique of carving that coaxed a translucent

Figure 5.11 Zeus (or Poseidon), ca. 460 B.C.E. Bronze, height 6 ft. 10 in. National Archeological Museum, Athens. Photo: Craig & Marie Mauzy, Athens.

shimmer from the fine white marble. This celebrated nude is a Roman copy of a Greek original, and the bar bracing the hip suggests that the original may have been executed in bronze.

A careful study of Greek statuary from the Archaic through the Late Classical Age (400–323 B.C.E.) reflects increasing refinements in realism and idealism: All imperfections (wrinkles, warts, blemishes) have been purged in favor of a radiant flawlessness. The classical nude is neither very old nor very young, neither very thin nor very fat. He or she is eternally youthful, healthy, and virile—

Figure 5.13 Praxiteles, *Aphrodite of Knidos*, Roman marble copy of marble Greek original of ca. 350 B.C.E. Height 6 ft. 8 in. Vatican Museums, Rome.

serene and dignified, and liberated from all accidents of nature. This synthesis of humanism, realism, and idealism in the representation of the freestanding nude was one of the great achievements of Greek art. Indeed, the Hellenic conception of the nude defined the standard of beauty in Western art for centuries.

Figure 5.12 *Kore* from Chios (?), ca. 520 B.C.E. Marble with traces of paint, height approx. 22 in. (lower part missing). Acropolis Museum, Athens. Photo: Studio Kontos Nikos, Athens.

Figure 5.14 Ictinus and Kallicrates, West end of the Parthenon, Athens, 448–432 B.C.E. Pentelic marble, height of columns 34 ft. Photo: Sonia Halliday, Weston Turville.

Greek Architecture: The Parthenon

The great monuments of classical architecture were designed to serve the living, not—as in Egypt—the dead. In contrast with the superhuman scale of the Egyptian pyramid, the Greek temple, as Vitruvius observed, was proportioned according to the human body. Greek theaters (see Figure 4.11) celebrated life here on earth rather than the life in the hereafter, while Greek temples served as shrines for the gods and depositories for civic and religious treasures. Both theaters and temples functioned as public meeting places. Much like the Mesopotamian ziggurat, the Greek temple was a communal symbol of reverence for the gods, but, whereas the ziggurat enforced the separation of priesthood and populace, the Greek temple united religious and secular domains.

The outstanding architectural achievement of Golden Age Athens is the Parthenon (Figures **5.14** and **5.15**), a temple dedicated to Athena, the goddess

of war, the patron of the arts and crafts, and the personification of wisdom. The name Parthenon derives from the Greek word *parthenos* ("maiden"), a popular epithet for Athena. Built in glittering Pentelic marble upon the ruins of an earlier temple burned during the Persian Wars, the Parthenon overlooks Athens from the highest point on the Acropolis (Figure **5.16**). Athens' preeminent temple

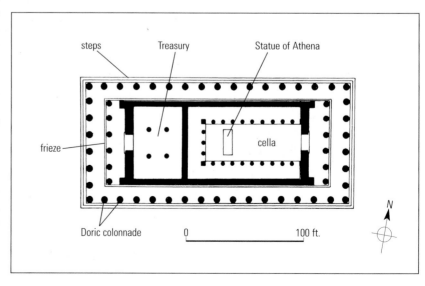

Figure 5.15 Plan of the Parthenon, Athens.

was commissioned by Pericles, designed by the architects Ictinus and Kallicrates, and embellished by the sculptor Phidias (fl. ca. 490–430 B.C.E.). Phidias directed and supervised the construction of the temple over a period of more than ten years, from 448 to 432 B.C.E. In the tradition of Egyptian builders, Greek architects used no mortar. Rather, they employed bronze clamps and dowels to fasten the individually cut marble segments.

The Parthenon represents the apex of a long history of post-and-lintel temple building among the Greeks. That history, like the history of Greek painting and sculpture, entailed a search for harmonic proportion, which came to fruition in the Parthenon. The plan of the temple, a rectangle delimited on all four sides by a colonnaded walkway, reflects the typically classical reverence for clarity and symmetry (see Figure 5.15). Freestanding columns (each 34 feet tall) make up the exterior, while two further rows of columns on the east and west ends of the temple provide inner **porticos** (see Figure 5.19). The interior of the Parthenon is divided into two rooms, a central hall (or *cella*), which held the colossal cult statue of Athena, and a smaller room used as a treasury. It was here that the much-disputed Delian League funds were stored. Entirely elevated on a raised platform, the Parthenon invited the individual to move around it, as if it were a piece of monumental sculpture. Indeed, scholars have suggested that the Parthenon was both a shrine to Athena and a victory monument.

The Parthenon makes use of the Doric **order**, one of three programs of architectural design developed by the ancient Greeks (Figure 5.17). Each of the orders—Doric, Ionic, and (in Hellenistic times) Corinthian—prescribes a fundamental set of structural and decorative parts that stand in fixed relation to each other. Each order differs in details and in the relative proportions of the parts. The Doric order, which originated on the Greek mainland, is simple and severe. In the Parthenon it reached its most refined expression. The Ionic order, originating in Asia Minor and the Aegean Islands, is more delicate and ornamental. Its slender columns terminate in capitals with paired volutes or scrolls. The Ionic order is employed in some of the small temples on the Acropolis (Figure 5.18). The Corinthian, the most ornate of the orders, is characterized by capitals consisting of acanthus leaves. It is often found on victory monuments, in **tholos** (circular) sanctuaries and shrines, as well as in various Hellenistic and Roman structures (see Figures 6.12 and 6.14).

If an ideal system governed the parts of the Greek building, a similar set of laws determined its proportions. The precise canon of proportion adopted by Phidias for the construction of the Parthenon is still, however, the subject of debate. Most architectural historians agree that a module was used, but whether the module was geometric or numerical, and whether it followed a specific ratio—such as the famous "Golden Section"—has not been resolved. The system of proportions known as the "Golden Section" or "Golden Ratio" is expressed numerically by the ratio of 1.618:1, or approximately 8:5. This ratio, which governs the proportions of the ground plan of the Parthenon and the Vitruvian canon, represents an

Figure 5.16 Model of the classical Acropolis at Athens. American School of Classical Studies at Athens: Agora Excavations.

1 Erechtheion
2 picture gallery
3 Propylaia (entrance gate)
4 Sacred Way
5 Temple of Athena Nike
6 Chalkotheke (armory)
7 Parthenon (Temple of Athena Parthenos)

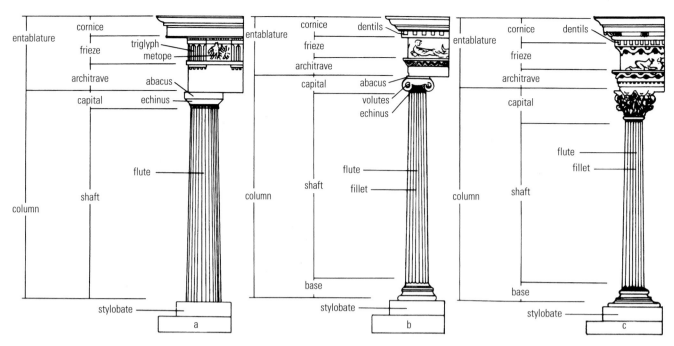

Figure 5.17 The Greek orders: (a) Doric; (b) Ionic; and (c) Corinthian.

Figure 5.18 Kallicrates, Temple of Athena Nike, Acropolis, Athens, ca. 427–424 B.C.E. Pentelic marble, 17 ft. 9 in. × 26 ft. 10 in. Photo: Alison Frantz.

aesthetic ideal found in nature and in the human anatomy. The question of the Parthenon's construction is further complicated by the fact that there are virtually no straight lines in the entire building. Its Doric columns, for instance, swell out near the center to counter the optical effect of thinning that occurs when the normal eye views an uninterrupted set of parallel lines. All columns tilt slightly inward. Corner columns are thicker than the others to compensate for the attenuating effect produced by the bright light of the sky against which the columns are viewed, and also to ensure their ability to bear the weight of the terminal segments of the superstructure. The top step of the platform on which the columns rest is not parallel to the ground, but rises four and a quarter inches at the center, allowing for rainwater to run off the convex surface even as it corrects the optical impression of sagging along the extended length of the platform. Consistently, the architects of the Parthenon corrected negative optical illusions produced by strict conformity to geometric regularity. Avoiding rigid systems of proportion, they took as their primary consideration the aesthetic and functional integrity of the building. Today the Parthenon stands as a noble ruin, the victim of an accidental gunpowder explosion in the seventeenth century, followed by centuries of vandalism, air pollution, and unrelenting tourist traffic.

The Sculpture of the Parthenon

Between 438 and 432 B.C.E. Phidias and the members of his workshop executed the sculptures that would appear in three main locations on the Parthenon: in the **pediments** of the roof **gables**, on the **metopes** or square panels between the beam ends under the roof, and in the area along the outer wall of the *cella* (Figure **5.19**). Brightly painted, as were some of the decorative portions of the building, the Parthenon sculptures relieved the stark angularity of the post-and-lintel structure. In subject matter, the temple sculptures paid homage to the patron deity of Athens: The east pediment narrates the birth of Athena with gods and goddesses in attendance (Figures **5.20** and **5.21**). The west pediment shows the contest between Poseidon and Athena for domination of Athens. The ninety-two metopes that occupy the **frieze** (see Figure **5.20**) illustrate scenes of combat between the Greeks (the bearers of civilization) and Giants, Amazons, and Centaurs (the forces of barbarism; Figure **5.22**). Carved in high relief, each metope is a masterful depic-

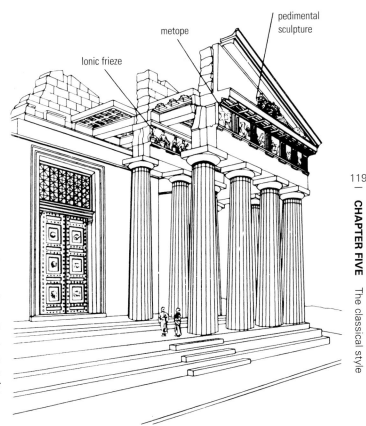

Figure 5.19 Sculptural and architectural detail of the Parthenon. **Frieze**, a decorative band along the top of a wall; **metopes**, segmented spaces on a frieze; **pediment**, a gable.

tion of two contestants, one human and the other bestial. Appropriate to a temple honoring the Goddess of Wisdom, the sculptural program of the Parthenon celebrates the victory of intellect over barbarism.

Completing Phidias' program of architectural decoration for the Parthenon is the continuous frieze that winds around the outer wall of the *cella* where that wall meets the roofline. The 524-foot-long sculptured band is thought to depict the Panathenaic Festival, a celebration held every four years in honor of the goddess Athena. Hundreds of figures—a cavalcade of horsemen (Figure **5.23**), water bearers, musicians, and votaries—are shown filing in calm procession toward an assembled group of gods and goddesses (Figure **5.24**). The figures move with graceful rhythms, in tempos that could well be translated into music. Once brightly painted and ornamented with

Figure 5.20 Drawing of a reconstruction of the east pediment of the Parthenon, central section. Acropolis Museum, Athens.

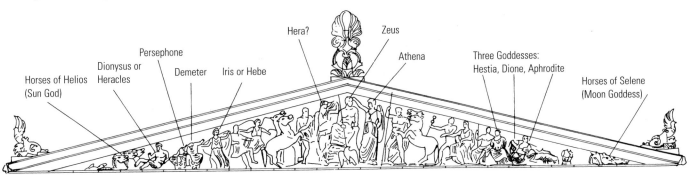

Figure 5.21 Three Goddesses: Hestia, Dione, Aphrodite, from east pediment of the Parthenon, Athens, ca. 437–432 B.C.E. Marble, over life-size. Reproduced by courtesy of the Trustees of the British Museum, London.

Figure 5.22 Lapith Overcoming a Centaur, south metope 27, Parthenon, Athens, 447–438 B.C.E. Marble relief, height 4 ft. 5 in. Reproduced by courtesy of the Trustees of the British Museum, London.

Figure 5.23 A Group of Young Horsemen, from the north frieze of the Parthenon, Athens, 447–438 B.C.E. Marble, height 3 ft. 7 in. Reproduced by courtesy of the Trustees of the British Museum, London.

Figure 5.24 East frieze of the Parthenon, Athens, ca. 437–432 B.C.E. Marble. © TAP Services, Greece.

metal details, the final effect must have been impressively lifelike. To increase this effect and satisfy a viewpoint from below, Phidias graded the relief, cutting the marble more deeply at the top than at the bottom. Housed today in the British Museum in London, where it is hung at approximately eye level, the Parthenon frieze loses much of its illusionistic subtlety. Nevertheless, this masterpiece of the Greek Golden Age reveals the harmonious reconciliation of humanism, realism, and idealism that is the hallmark of the classical style.

The Gold of Greece

The famous statue of Athena that stood in the *cella* of the Parthenon disappeared many centuries ago. However, images of the goddess abound in Hellenic art. One of the most spectacular appears in the form of a gold pendant disk that shows the head of Athena wearing a helmet bearing a sphinx, deer and griffin heads, and an elaborate triple crest (Figure 5.25). From Athena's shoulders snakes spring forth, and by her head stands an owl (the symbol of wisdom)—both motifs recalling the powers of the Minoan priestess (see Figure 4.4). Rosettes of gold filigree and enamel-colored buds ornament the complex of looped chains that hang from the disk.

The Greeks gained international acclaim for their goldworking techniques, many of which had been inher-

Figure 5.25 Gold pendant disk with the head of Athena (one of a pair), from Kul Oba, ca. 400–350 B.C.E. Height 3.95 in., diameter of disk 1.53 in. Photo: Hermitage KO 5. NOVOSTI, London.

ited from Persia and from the nomadic Scythians of northern Asia. Gold-rich mining areas of northern Greece provided craftspeople with materials for the manufacture of jewelry. Particularly popular were pendants, earrings, and headpieces in the form of miniature sculptures, some of which (like the pendant of Athena) reproduced familiar images of the gods. Much like today, gold jewelry was a mark of wealth that also bore sentimental and religious value. In Greece and especially in the cities of Asia Minor, men as well as women adorned themselves with stylish earrings and bracelets.

The Classical Style in Poetry

In classical Greece, as in other parts of the ancient world, distinctions between various forms of artistic expression were neither clear-cut nor definitive. A combination of the arts prevailed in most forms of religious ritual and in public and private entertainment. In *Antigone*, for instance, choric pantomime and dance complemented dramatic poetry. And in processions and festivals, music, poetry, and the visual arts all served a common purpose. The intimate relationship between music and poetry is revealed in the fact that many of the words we use to describe lyric forms, such as the **ode** and the **hymn**, are also musical terms. The word lyric, meaning "accompanied by the lyre," describes verse that was meant to be sung, not read silently. Lyric poetry was designed to give voice to deep emotions.

Hellenic culture produced an impressive group of lyric poets, the greatest of whom was Sappho (ca. 610–ca. 580 B.C.E.). Her personal life remains a mystery. Born into an aristocratic family, she seems to have married, mothered a daughter, and produced some nine books of poetry, of which only fragments remain. She settled on the island of Lesbos, where she led a group of young women dedicated to the cult of Aphrodite. At Lesbos, Sappho trained women in the production of love poetry and music. Her own highly self-conscious poems, many of which come to us only as fragments, are filled with passion and tenderness. They offer a glimpse of a body of poetry that inspired Sappho's contemporaries to regard her as "the female Homer." Ancient and modern poets alike admired Sappho for her powerful economy of expression and her inventive combinations of sense and sound—features that are extremely difficult to convey in translation. The first of the five poems reproduced below gives lyric voice to Sappho's homoerotic attachment to the women of the Lesbian cult. That bisexual and homosexual relationships were common among the ancient Greeks is given ample evidence in Hellenic literature and art. The scene on the elegant drinking cup by Douris (see Figure 4.14), for instance, is generally interpreted as depicting an older man propositioning a younger one. The last of the selections, a terse and pensive poem, reflects the intense spirit of this-worldliness and the generally negative view of death that typified Sappho's verse and ancient Greek expression in general.

READING 1.19 Sappho's Poems (ca. 590 B.C.E.)

He is more than a hero   1
He is a god in my eyes
the man who is allowed
to sit beside you—he

who listens intimately   5
to the sweet murmur of
your voice, the enticing

laughter that makes my own
heart beat fast. If I meet
you suddenly, I can't   10

speak—my tongue is broken;
a thin flame runs under
my skin; seeing nothing,

hearing only my own ears
drumming, I drip with sweat;   15
trembling shakes my body

and I turn paler than
dry grass. At such times
death isn't far from me

——◆——

With his venom   1
Irresistible
and bittersweet
that loosener
of limbs, Love   5
reptile-like
strikes me down

——◆——

I took my lyre and said: 1
Come now, my heavenly
tortoise shell; become
a speaking instrument

——◆——

Although they are   1
Only breath, words
which I command
are immortal

——◆——

We know this much   1
Death is an evil;
we have the gods'
word for it; they too
would die if death   5
were a good thing

While lyric poetry often conveyed deeply personal feelings, certain types of lyrics, namely odes, served as public eulogies or songs of praise. Odes honoring Greek athletes bear strong similarities to songs of divine praise, such as the Egyptian "Hymn to the Aten" (see chapter 1), the Hebrew Psalms, and Greek invocations. But the sentiments conveyed in the odes of the noted Greek poet Pindar (ca. 522–438 B.C.E.) are firmly planted in the secular world. They celebrate the achievements of the athletes who competed at the games held at the great sanctuaries of Olympia, Delphi, Nemea, and elsewhere (see Figure 4.10). Perpetuating the heroic idealism of the *Iliad*, Pindar's odes make the claim that prowess, not chance, leads to victory, which in turn renders the victor immortal. The first lines of his *Nemean Ode VI* honoring Alcimidas of Aegina (winner in the boys' division of wrestling) assert that gods and men share a common origin. The closest human beings can come to achieving godlike immortality, however, lies in the exercise of "greatness of mind/Or of body." The ode thus narrows the gap between hero-athletes and their divine prototypes. In his *Pythian Ode VIII* (dedicated to yet another victorious wrestler), Pindar develops a more modest balance of opposites: He sets the glories of youth against the adversities of aging and mortality itself. Although mortal limitations separate human beings from the ageless and undying gods, "manly action" secures the "richer life."

READING 1.20 From Pindar's Odes (ca. 420 B.C.E.)

From *Nemean Ode VI*

Single is the race, single   1
Of men and of gods;
From a single mother we both draw breath.
But a difference of power in everything
Keeps us apart;   5
For the one is as nothing, but the brazen sky
Stays a fixed habitation for ever.
Yet we can in greatness of mind
Or of body be like the Immortals,
Though we know not to what goal   10
By day or in the nights
Fate has written that we shall run.

. . . .

From *Pythian Ode VIII*

. . . .

In the Pythian games   1
you pinned four wrestlers
unrelentingly, and sent
them home in losers' gloom;
no pleasant laughter cheered them as they reached   5
their mothers' sides; shunning ridicule,
they took to alleys, licking losers' wounds.

And he, who in his youth
secures a fine advantage
gathers hope and flies   10
on wings of manly action,
disdaining cost. Men's happiness is early-
ripened fruit that falls to earth

from shakings of adversity.
Men are day-bound. What *is* a man? What is
he *not*? Man is a shadow's dream. But when divine
advantage comes, men gain a radiance and a richer life...

The Classical Style in Music and Dance

The English word *music* derives from *muse*, the Greek word describing any of the nine mythological daughters of Zeus and the Goddess of Memory. According to Greek mythology, the muses presided over the arts and the sciences. Pythagoras observed that music was governed by mathematical ratios and therefore constituted both a science and an art. As was true of the other arts, music played a major role in Greek life. However, we know almost as little about how Greek music sounded as we do in the cases of Egyptian or Sumerian music. The ancient Greeks did not invent a system of notation with which to record instrumental or vocal sounds. Apart from written and visual descriptions of musical performances, there exist only a few fourth-century-B.C.E. treatises on music theory and some primitively notated musical works. The only complete piece of ancient Greek music that has survived

Figure 5.26 The Berlin painter, ca. 490 B.C.E. Terra-cotta, height of vase 16⅜ in. The Metropolitan Museum of Art, New York. Fletcher Fund, 1956.

is an ancient song found chiselled on a first-century B.C.E. gravestone. ♪ It reads: "So long as you live, be radiant, and do not grieve at all. Life's span is short and time exacts the final reckoning." Both vocal and instrumental music were commonplace, and contests between musicians, like those between playwrights, were a regular part of public life. Vase paintings reveal that the principal musical instruments of ancient Greece were the **lyre**, the **cithara**—both belonging to the harp family and differing only in shape, size, and number of strings (Figure **5.26**)—and the **aulos**, a flute or reed pipe (see Figure 5.5). Along with percussion devices often used to accompany dancing, these string and wind instruments were probably inherited from Egypt.

The Greeks devised a system of **modes**, or types of **scales** characterized by fixed patterns of pitch and tempo within the octave. (The sound of the ancient Greek Dorian mode is approximated by playing the eight white keys of the piano beginning with the white key two notes above middle C.) Modified variously in Christian times, the modes were preserved in Gregorian Chant and Byzantine church hymnology (see chapter 9). Although the modes themselves may have been inspired by the music of ancient India, the diatonic scale (familiar to Westerners as the series of notes C, D, E, F, G, A, B, C) originated in Greece. Greek music lacked harmony as we know it. It was thus **monophonic**, that is, confined to a single, unaccompanied line of melody. The strong association between poetry and music suggests that the human voice had a significant influence in both melody and rhythm.

From earliest times, music was believed to hold magical powers and therefore exercise great spiritual influence. Greek and Roman mythology describes gods and heroes who used music to heal or destroy. Following Pythagoras, who equated musical ratios with the unchanging cosmic order, many believed that music might put one "in tune with" the universe. The planets, which Pythagoras described as a series of spheres moving at varying speeds in concentric orbits around the earth, were said to produce a special harmony, the so-called *music of the spheres*. The Greeks believed, moreover, that music had a moral influence. This argument, often referred to as the "Doctrine of Ethos," held that some modes strengthened the will, whereas others undermined it and thus damaged the development of moral character. In the *Republic*, Plato encouraged the use of the Dorian mode, which settled the temper and inspired courage, but he condemned the Lydian mode, which aroused sensuality. Because of music's potential for affecting character and mood, both Plato and Aristotle recommended that the types of music used in the education of young children be regulated by law. As with other forms of classical expression, music was deemed inseparable from its role in the advancement of the individual and the well-being of the community.

Dance was also prized for its moral value, as well as for its ability to give pleasure and induce good health (see Figure 5.5). For Plato the uneducated man was a "dance-less" man. Both Plato and Aristotle advised that children be instructed at an early age in music and dancing. However, both men distinguished noble dances from ignoble ones—Dionysian and comic dances, for instance. These they considered unfit for Athenian citizens and therefore inappropriate to the educational curriculum. Nevertheless, the dancing *maenad*, a cult follower of Dionysus, was a favorite image of revelry and intoxication in ancient Greece (Figure **5.27**).

Figure 5.27 A *maenad* leaning on a thyrsos, Roman copy of Greek original, ca. 420–410 B.C.E. Marble relief. The Metropolitan Museum of Art, New York. Fletcher Fund, 1935.

The Diffusion of the Classical Style: The Hellenistic Age (323–30 B.C.E.)

The fourth century B.C.E. was a turbulent era marked by rivalry and warfare among the Greek city-states. Ironically, however, the failure of the Greek city-states to live in peace would lead to the spread of Hellenic culture throughout the civilized world. Manipulating the shifting confederacies and internecine strife to his advantage, Philip of Macedonia eventually defeated the Greeks in 338 B.C.E. When he was assassinated two years later, his twenty-year-old son Alexander (356–323 B.C.E.) assumed the Macedonian throne (Figure **5.28**). A student of Aristotle, Alexander brought to his role as ruler the same kind of far-reaching ambition and imagination that his teacher had exercised in the intellectual realm. Alexander was a military genius: Within twelve years, he created an empire that stretched from Greece to the borders of modern India (Map **5.1**). To all parts of his empire, but especially to the cities he founded—many of which he named after himself—Alexander carried Greek language and culture. Greek art and literature made a major impact on civilizations as far east as India, where it influenced Buddhist art and Sanskrit literature (see chapter 9).

Alexander carved out his empire with the help of an army of 35,000 Greeks and Macedonians equipped with weapons that were superior to any in the ancient world. Siege machines such as catapults and battering rams were used to destroy the walls of the best-defended cities of Asia Minor, Egypt, Syria, and Persia. Finally, in northwest India, facing the prospect of confronting the formidable army of the King of Ganges and his force of five thousand elephants, Alexander's troops refused to go any further. Shortly thereafter, the thirty-two-year-old general died (probably of malaria), and his empire split into three segments: Egypt governed by the Ptolemy dynasty, Persia under the leadership of the Seleucid rulers, and Macedonia-Greece governed by the family of Antigonus the One-Eyed (see Map 5.1).

The era that followed, called Hellenistic ("Greek-like"), lasted from 323 to 30 B.C.E. The defining features of the Hellenistic Age were cosmopolitanism, urbanism, and the blending of Greek, African, and Asian cultures. Trade routes linked Arabia, east Africa, and central Asia, bringing great wealth to the cities of Alexandria, Antioch, Pergamon, and Rhodes. Alexandria, which replaced Athens as a

Figure 5.28 Head of Alexander, from Pergamum, Hellenistic portrait, ca. 200 B.C.E. Marble, height 16 in. Archeological Museum, Istanbul.

cultural center, boasted a population of more than one million people and a library of half a million books (the collection was destroyed by fire when Julius Caesar besieged the city in 47 B.C.E.). The Great Library, part of the cultural complex known as the Temple of the Muses (or "Museum"), was an ancient "think tank" that housed both scholars and books. At the rival library of Pergamon (with some 200,000 books), scribes prepared sheepskin to produce "pergamene paper," that is, parchment, the medium that would be used for centuries of manuscript production prior to the widespread dissemination of paper. The Hellenistic Age made important advances in geography, astronomy, and mathematics. Euclid, who lived in Alexandria during the late fourth century B.C.E., produced a textbook of existing geometric learning that systematized the theorems of plane and solid geometry. Archimedes of Syracuse, who flourished a century later,

calculated the value of *pi* (the ratio of the circumference of a circle to its diameter). An engineer as well as a mathematician, he invented the compound pulley, a windlass for moving heavy weights, and many other mechanical devices. "Give me a place to stand," he is said to have boasted, "and I shall move the earth." Legend describes Archimedes as the typical absent-minded scientist, who often forgot to eat; upon realizing that the water he displaced in his bathtub explained the law of specific gravity, he is said to have jumped out of the bathtub and run naked through the streets of Syracuse, shouting "*Eureka*" ("I have found it!").

Hellenistic Philosophic Thought

The Hellenistic world was considerably different from the world of the Greek city-states. In the latter, citizens identified with their community, which was itself the state; but in Alexander's vast empire, communal loyalties were unsteady and—especially in sprawling urban centers—impersonal. The intellectuals of the Hellenistic Age did not formulate rational methods of investigation in the style of Plato and Aristotle; rather they espoused

Map 5.1 The Hellenistic World.

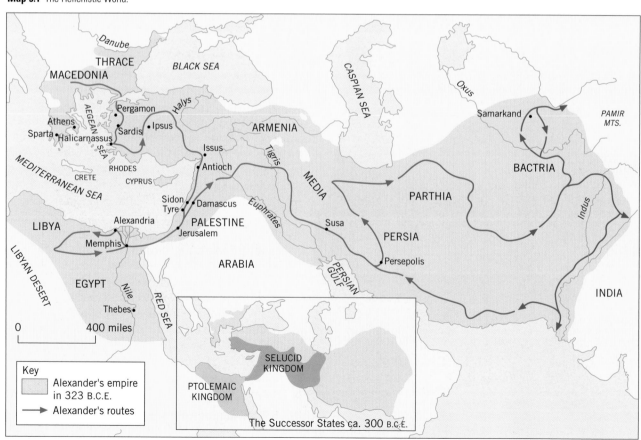

philosophic schools of thought that guided everyday existence: Skepticism, Cynicism, Epicureanism, and Stoicism. The Skeptics—much like the Sophists of Socrates' time—denied the possibility of knowing anything with certainty: They argued for the suspension of all intellectual judgment. The Cynics held that spiritual satisfaction was only possible if one renounced societal values, conventions, and material wealth. The Epicureans, followers of the Greek thinker Epicurus (341–270 B.C.E.), taught that happiness depended on avoiding all forms of physical excess; they valued plain living and the perfect union of body and mind. Epicurus held that the gods played no part in human life, and that death was nothing more than the rearrangement of atoms of which the body and all of nature consisted. Finally, the Stoics found tranquility of mind in a doctrine of detachment that allowed them to accept even the worst of life's circumstances. The aim of the Stoic was to bring the individual will into complete harmony with the will of nature, which they believed was governed by an impersonal intelligence. The Stoics also advanced the notion of universal equality. All four of these schools of thought placed the personal needs and emotions of the individual over and above the good of the community at large; in this, they constituted a practical and radical departure from the Hellenic quest for universal truth.

Hellenistic Art

The shift from city-state to empire that accompanied the advent of the Hellenistic Era was reflected in larger, more monumental forms of architecture and in the construction of utilitarian structures, such as lighthouses, theaters, and libraries. Circular sanctuaries and colossal Corinthian temples with triumphant decorative friezes were particu-

- **−280** the lighthouse at Pharos, north of Alexandria, is the tallest tower in existence
- **−260** Archimedes establishes the law of specific gravity, invents the compound pulley, studies the mechanical properties of the lever, and lays the foundations for calculus.
- **−240** Aristarchus of Samos proposes that the earth and all the planets rotate on their axes and revolve around the sun (the heliocentric theory)
- **−230** Eratosthenes of Cyrene calculates the circumference of the earth with near accuracy
- **−220** Herophilus of Alexandria discovers the human nervous system; he proposes that the arteries carry blood (not air, as previously believed) from the heart
- **−150** Hipparchus of Nicea invents trigonometry; he catalogs 805 fixed stars

larly popular in the fourth century B.C.E. and thereafter. At Pergamon (see Map 5.1) stood the largest sculptural complex in the ancient world: the Altar of Zeus (see Figure 5.29). Erected around 180 B.C.E. to celebrate the victory of the minor kingdom of Pergamon over the invading tribal Gauls achieved some fifty years earlier, the altar stands atop a 20-foot high platform enclosed by an Ionic colonnade. A massive stairway reaches upward to the shrine. Around the base of the platform runs a 300-foot long sculptured frieze depicting the mythological battle between the Olympic gods and the race of giants known as Titans. The subject matter, symbolizing the victory of

Figure 5.29 The Altar of Zeus (reconstructed), Pergamon, ca. 175 B.C.E. Marble. Pergamonmuseum, Berlin.

intellect over barbarism, recalls the metopes of the Parthenon, but both the altar and the frieze are far more theatrical in style than anything created in the Hellenic *polis*. The drama of the structure itself, which more resembles a stage than a temple, is made emphatic in the frieze: Here, high-relief figures writhe in rhythmic patterns, engaging each other in fierce combat. The goddess Athena, some 7 feet tall, grasps by the hair a serpent-tailed male, the son of the earth mother who rises from the ground on the lower right (see Figure 5.30). The deeply cut figures create strong light and dark contrasts; indeed, some seem to break free of their architectural frame. In the Altar of Zeus, classical restraint has given way to violent passion.

In free-standing Hellenistic sculpture, the new emphasis on private emotion and discrete personality gave rise to portraits that were more lifelike and less idealized than those of the Hellenic Era. The marble portrait of the ruler Alexander (Figure 5.28) manifests the new effort to capture fleeting mood and momentary expression. Hellenistic art is also notable for its sensuous female nude sculptures: The fondness for erotic expression is especially evident in works carved in the tradition of Praxiteles (see Figure 5.13). Perhaps the most notable example of the new sensuousness, however, is the male nude statue known as the *Apollo Belvedere* (see Part Opener). This Roman copy of a Hellenistic statue was destined to exercise a major influence in Western art from the moment it was recovered in

Rome in 1503. A comparison of the *Apollo* with its Hellenic counterpart, the *Spear-Bearer* (see Figure 5.1), reveals the subtle move of Hellenistic sculpture away from the High Classical to a more animated, feminized, and self-conscious style. Hellenistic artists departed from classical idealism by broadening the range of subjects to include young children and old, even deformed, people. Hellenistic sculptors continue to demonstrate a high degree of technical virtuosity, but their carving techniques are used increasingly to emphasize dynamic contrasts of light and dark and the subtleties of semi-transparent robes. These features, plus a bold display of vigorous movement, are evident in the larger-than-life **Nike** (the Greek personification of Victory) erected at Rhodes to celebrate a naval triumph over Syria (Figure 5.31). The deeply cut drapery of the *Nike of Samothrace* clings sensuously to her body as the winged figure strides into the wind, like some gigantic ship's prow.

The work that best sums up the Hellenistic aesthetic is the remarkable *Laocoön and His Sons* (Figure 5.32). This monumental marble sculpture recreates the dramatic moment when Laocoön, priest of Apollo, and his two sons are attacked by sea serpents. Legend had it that the gods had sent these creatures as punishment for Laocoön's effort to warn the Trojans against the Greek ruse—a wooden horse filled with armed soldiers—that would bring an end to the Trojan War. The tortuous pose, strained

Figure 5.30 *Athena Battling with Acyoneus,* from the frieze of the Altar of Zeus, Pergamon, ca. 180 B.C.E. Marble, Height 7 ft. 6 in. Pergamonmuseum, Berlin.

Figure 5.31 Pythocritos of Rhodes, *Nike of Samothrace*, ca. 190 B.C.E. Marble, height 8 ft. Louvre, Paris, Photo: R.M.N, Paris.

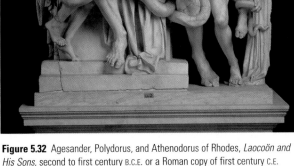

Figure 5.32 Agesander, Polydorus, and Athenodorus of Rhodes, *Laocoön and His Sons*, second to first century B.C.E. or a Roman copy of first century C.E. Marble, height 7 ft. 10½ in. Vatican Museums. Photo: Araldo de Luca.

muscles, and anguished face of the doomed priest create a sense of turbulence and agitation that contrasts sharply with the mild tranquility and dignified restraint of Hellenic art. Indeed, the *Laocoön* is a memorable symbol of an age in which classical idealism had already become part of history.

SUMMARY

No style in the history of the arts has been more influential than that which emerged during the Greek Golden Age. The classical style reflects the Hellenic devotion to rational laws of proportion, order, clarity, and balance. It is also characterized by humanism, a this-worldly belief in the dignity and inherent worth of human beings, by realism, or fidelity to nature, and by idealism, that is, the commitment to an underlying standard of perfection. The human body and human experience are central to all the arts of classical Greece. In the paintings found on Greek vases, as in the evolution of the freestanding nude figure, Hellenic artists achieved a sublime balance between realistic representation and idealized form.

The monument that best mirrors the classical style is the Parthenon, the Greek temple built atop the Acropolis to honor Athens' patron goddess of wisdom and war. In its application of the Doric order, the integration of technical refinements, and the intelligent application of architectural decoration, the Parthenon stands as one of the most noble buildings in the history of architecture.

The Hellenic synthesis of humanism and idealism, harnessed to an impassioned quest for order and proportion, also characterized literature and music. The lyric poetry of Sappho and Pindar makes the human being the measure of earthly experience. In Greek music, where the clarity of the single line of melody prevails, modal patterns of pitch and tempo were held to influence the moral condition of the listener.

During the fourth century B.C.E. Alexander the Great spread Greek language and culture throughout a vast, though short-lived, empire that extended from Macedonia to India. During the Hellenistic Age, metaphysics gave way to science and practical philosophy, and the classical style moved further toward realism and melodramatic expressiveness. Nevertheless, the Hellenistic (and thereafter, the Roman) era perpetuated the fundamental features of classicism. Indeed, for centuries to come, Western artists—like newly liberated prisoners from Plato's mythical cave—would try to throw off the chains that bound them to the imperfect world of the senses in pursuit of the classical ideal.

SUGGESTIONS FOR READING

Boardman, John. *The Diffusion of Classical Art in Antiquity*. Princeton: Princeton University Press, 1994.

—— and David Finn. *The Parthenon and its Sculptures*. Austin, Tex.: University of Texas Press, 1985.

Cook, R. M. *Greek Art*. Baltimore, Md.: Penguin, 1976.

Carpenter, Rhys. *The Architecture of the Parthenon*. Baltimore: Penguin, 1972.

Francis, E. D. *Image and Idea in Fifth Century Greece: Art and Literature after the Persian Wars*. New York: Routledge, 1990.

Fullerton, Mark D. *Greek Art*. New York: Cambridge University Press, 2000.

Havelock, Christine M. *Hellenistic Art: The Art of the Classical World from the Death of Alexander the Great to the Battle of Actium*, 2nd ed. New York: Norton, 1981.

Pedley, John G. *Greek Art and Archeology*. Englewood Cliffs, N.J.: Prentice-Hall, 1993.

Pollit, J. J. *Art and Experience in Classical Greece*. Cambridge: Cambridge University Press, 1971.

Spivey, Nigel. *Understanding Greek Sculpture: Ancient Meanings, Modern Readings*. London: Thames and Hudson, 1996.

Stewart, Andrew. *Greek Sculpture: An Exploration*. 2 vols. New Haven: Yale University Press, 1990.

Walbank, F. W. *The Hellenistic World*, rev. ed. Cambridge, Mass.: Harvard University Press, 1993.

MUSIC LISTENING SELECTION

CD One Selection 1 Anonymous, "Seikolos Song." Greek, ca. 50 C.E.

GLOSSARY

aulos a wind instrument used in ancient Greece; it had a double reed (held inside the mouth) and a number of finger holes and was always played in pairs, that is, with the performer holding one in each hand; a leather band was often tied around the head to support the cheeks, thus enabling the player to blow harder (see Figure 6.5)

cithara a large version of the lyre (having seven to eleven strings) and the principal instrument of ancient Greek music

contrapposto (Italian, "counterpoised") a position assumed by the human body in which one part is turned in opposition to another part

frieze in architecture, a sculptured or ornamented band

gable the triangular section of a wall at the end of a pitched roof

hymn a lyric poem offering divine praise or glorification

kouros (Greek, "youth"; pl. *kouroi*) a youthful male figure, usually depicted nude in ancient Greek sculpture; the female counterpart is the *kore* (Greek, "maiden"; pl. *korai*)

lyre any one of a group of plucked stringed instruments; in ancient Greece usually made of tortoise shell or horn and therefore light in weight

metope the square panel between the beam ends under the roof of a structure (see Figure 5.19)

mode a type of musical scale characterized by a fixed pattern of pitch and tempo within the octave; because the Greeks associated each of the modes with a different emotional state, it is likely that the mode involved something more than a particular musical scale, perhaps a set of rhythms and melodic turns associated with each scale pattern

monophony (Greek, "one voice") a musical texture consisting of a single, unaccompanied line of melody

Nike the Greek goddess of victory

octave the series of eight tones forming any major or minor scale

ode a lyric poem expressing exalted emotion in honor of a person or special occasion

order in classical architecture, the parts of a building that stand in fixed and constant relation to each other; the three classical orders are the Doric, the Ionic, and the Corinthian (see Figure 5.17)

pediment the triangular space forming the gable of a two-pitched roof in classical architecture; any similar triangular form found over a portico, door, or window

portico a porch with a roof supported by columns

scale (Latin, *scala*, "ladder") a series of tones arranged in ascending or descending consecutive order; the *diatonic* scale, characteristic of Western music, consists of the eight tones (or series of notes C, D, E, F, G, A, B, C) of the twelve-tone octave; the *chromatic* scale consists of all twelve tones (represented by the twelve piano keys, seven white and five black) of the octave, each a semitone apart

tholos a circular structure, generally in classical Greek style and probably derived from early tombs

CHAPTER SIX

Rome: the rise to empire

". . . remember, Roman,
To rule the people under law, to establish
The way of peace, to battle down the haughty,
To spare the meek. Our fine arts, these forever."
Virgil

At either end of the Eurasian landmass, two great empires—Rome and China—rose to power after the fourth century B.C.E. While imperial Rome and Han China traded through Asian intermediaries across a vast overland route, neither reflects the direct influence of the other. Nevertheless, the two have much in common: Both brought political stability and cultural unity to vast stretches of territory, by virtue of which achievement each created a flourishing empire. Both were profoundly secular in their approach to the world and to the conduct of human beings. Han China and imperial Rome each inherited age-old forms and practices in religion, law, literature, and the arts, which they self-consciously preserved and transmitted to future generations. The classical legacies of China and Rome would come to shape the respective histories of the East and the West.

The Roman Rise to Empire

Rome's Early History

Rome's origins are to be found among tribes of Iron Age folk called Latins, who invaded the Italian peninsula just after the beginning of the first millennium B.C.E. By the mid-eighth century B.C.E., these people had founded the city of Rome in the lower valley of the Tiber River, a spot strategically located for control of the Italian peninsula and for convenient access to the Mediterranean Sea (Map 6.1). While central Italy became the domain of the Latins, the rest of the peninsula received a continuous infusion of eastern Mediterranean people: Etruscans, Greeks, and Phoenicians, who brought with them cultures richer and more complex than that of the Latins. The Etruscans, whose origins are unknown (and whose language remains undeciphered), established themselves in northwest Italy. A sophisticated, Hellenized people with commercial contacts throughout the Mediterranean, they were experts in the arts of metallurgy, town building, and city planning. The Greeks, who colonized the tip of the Italian peninsula and Sicily, were masters of philosophy and the arts. And the Phoenicians, who settled on the northern coast of Africa, brought westward their alphabet and their commercial and maritime skills. From all of these people, but especially from the first two groups, the Latins borrowed elements that would enhance their own history. From the Etruscans, the Romans absorbed the fundamentals of urban planning, chariot racing, the toga, bronze and gold crafting, and the most ingenious structural principle of Mesopotamian architecture—the arch. The Etruscans provided their dead with tombs designed to resemble the lavish dwelling places of the deceased. On the lids of the **sarcophagi** (stone coffins) that held their cremated remains, Etruscan artists carved portraits of the dead, depicting husbands and wives relaxing and socializing on their dining couch, as if still enjoying a family banquet (Figure 6.1).

From the Greeks, the Romans borrowed a pantheon of gods and goddesses, linguistic and literary principles, and the aesthetics of the classical style. As the Latins absorbed Etruscan and Greek culture, so they drew these and other peoples into what would become the most powerful world-state in ancient history.

The Roman Republic (509–133 B.C.E.)

For three centuries, Etruscan kings ruled the Latin population, but in 509 B.C.E. the Latins overthrew the Etruscans. Over the next two hundred years, monarchy slowly gave way to a government "of the people" (*res publica*). The agricultural population of ancient Rome consisted of a powerful class of large landowners, the *patricians*, and a more populous class of small farmers called *plebeians*. The plebeians constituted the membership of a Popular Assembly. Although this body conferred civil and military authority (the **imperium**) upon two elected magistrates (called *consuls*), its lower-class members had little voice in government. The wealthy patricians—life members of the Roman Senate—controlled the lawmaking process. But step by step, the plebeians gained increasing political influence. Using as leverage their service as soldiers in the Roman army and their power to veto laws initiated by the

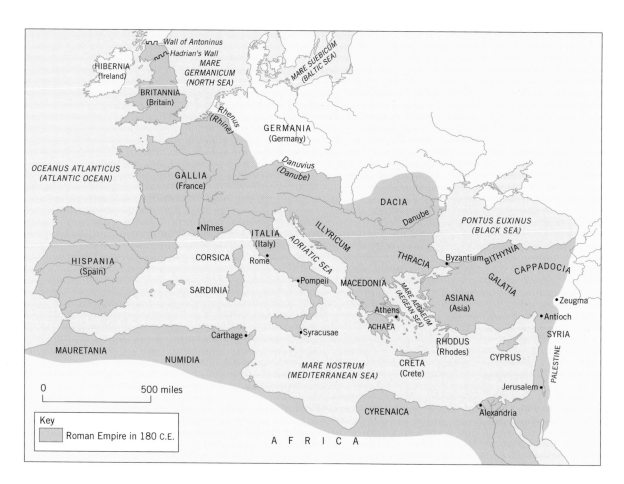

Map 6.1
The Roman
Empire in
180 C.E.

Senate, the plebeians—through their leaders, the *tribunes*—made themselves heard. Eventually, they won the freedom to intermarry with the patricians, the right to hold executive office, and, finally, in 287 B.C.E., the privilege of making laws. The stern and independent population of Roman farmers had arrived at a *res publica* by peaceful means. But no sooner had Rome become a Republic than it adopted an expansionist course that would erode these democratic achievements.

Obedience to the Roman state and service in its powerful army were essential to the life of the early Republic. Both contributed to the rise of Roman imperialism, which proceeded by means of long wars of conquest similar to those that had marked the history of earlier empires. After expelling the last of the Etruscan kings, Rome extended its power over all parts of the Italian peninsula. By the middle of the third century B.C.E., having united all of Italy by force or negotiation, Rome stood poised to rule the Mediterranean. A long-standing distrust of the

Phoenicians, and rivalry with the city of Carthage, Phoenicia's commercial stronghold in northeastern Africa, led Rome into the Punic (Latin for "Phoenician") Wars—a 150-year-period of intermittent violence that ended with the destruction of Carthage in 147 B.C.E.

Figure 6.1 Sarcophagus from Cerveteri, ca. 520 B.C.E. Painted terra-cotta, length 6 ft. 7 in. Museo Nazionale di Villa Giulia, Rome

With the defeat of Carthage, Rome assumed naval and commercial leadership in the western Mediterranean, the sea they would come to call *mare nostrum* ("our sea"). But the ambitions of army generals and the impetus of a century of warfare fueled the fire of Roman imperialism. Rome seized every opportunity for conquest, and by the end of the first century B.C.E., the Empire included most of North Africa, the Iberian peninsula, Greece, Egypt, much of Southwest Asia, and the territories constituting present-day Europe as far as the Rhine River (see Map 6.1).

Despite the difficulties presented by the task of governing such far-flung territories, the Romans proved to be efficient administrators. They demanded from their foreign provinces taxes, soldiers to serve in the Roman army, tribute, and slaves. Roman governors, appointed by the Senate from among the higher ranks of the military, ruled within the conquered provinces. Usually, local customs and even local governments were permitted to continue unmodified, for the Romans considered tolerance of provincial customs politically practical. The Romans introduced the Latin language and Roman law in the provinces. They built paved roads, freshwater aqueducts, bridges, and eventually granted the people of their conquered territories Roman citizenship.

Rome's highly disciplined army was the backbone of the Empire. During the Republic, the army consisted of citizens who served two-year terms, but by the first century C.E., the military had become a profession to which all free men might devote twenty-five years (or more) of their lives. Since serving for this length of time allowed a non-Roman to gain Roman citizenship for himself and his children, military service acted as a means of Romanizing foreigners. The Roman army was the object of fear and admiration among those familiar with Rome's rise to power. Josephus (ca. 37–100 C.E.), a Jewish historian who witnessed the Roman destruction of Jerusalem in 70 C.E., described the superiority of the Roman military machine, which he estimated to include more than three hundred thousand armed men. According to Josephus, Roman soldiers performed as though they "had been born with weapons in their hands." The efficiency of the army, reported Josephus, was the consequence of superior organization and discipline. The following description of a Roman military camp reflects the admiration and awe with which non-Romans viewed Roman might. It also describes the nature of that "perfect discipline" and dedication to duty that characterized the Roman ethos and Roman culture in general.

READING 1.21 Josephus' *Description of the Roman Army* (ca. 70 C.E.)

. . . one cannot but admire the forethought shown in this 1
particular by the Romans, in making their servant class useful
to them not only for the ministrations of ordinary life but also
for war. If one goes on to study the organization of their army
as a whole, it will be seen that this vast empire of theirs has
come to them as the prize of valor, and not as a gift of fortune.

For their nation does not wait for the outbreak of war to
give men their first lesson on arms; they do not sit with folded
hands in peace time only to put them in motion in the hour of
need. On the contrary, as though they had been born with 10
weapons in hand, they never have a truce from training, never
wait for emergencies to arise. Moreover, their peace
maneuvers are no less strenuous than veritable warfare; each
soldier daily throws all his energy into his drill, as though he
were in action. Hence that perfect ease with which they
sustain the shock of battle: no confusion breaks their
customary formation, no panic paralyzes, no fatigue exhausts
them; and as their opponents cannot match these qualities,
victory is the invariable and certain consequence. Indeed, it
would not be wrong to describe their maneuvers as bloodless 20
combats and combats as sanguinary maneuvers.

The Romans never lay themselves open to a surprise attack;
for, whatever hostile territory they may invade, they engage in
no battle until they have fortified their camp. This camp is not
erected at random or unevenly; they do not all work at once or
in disorderly parties; if the ground is uneven, it is first leveled;
a site for the camp is then measured out in the form of a
square. For this purpose the army is accompanied by a
multitude of workmen and of tools for building.

The interior of the camp is divided into rows of tents. The 30
exterior circuit presents the appearance of a wall and is
furnished with towers at regular intervals; and on the spaces
between the towers are placed "quick-firers," catapults,
"stone-throwers," and every variety of artillery engines, all
ready for use. In this surrounding wall are set four gates, one
on each side, spacious enough for beasts of burden to enter
without difficulty and wide enough for sallies of troops in
emergencies. The camp is intersected by streets symmetrically
laid out; in the middle are the tents of the officers, and
precisely in the center the headquarters of the commander-in- 40
chief, resembling a small temple. Thus, as it were, an
improvised city springs up, with its market-place, its artisan
quarter, its seats of judgment, where captains and colonels
adjudicate upon any differences which may arise. . . .

Once entrenched, the soldiers take up their quarters in their
tents by companies, quietly and in good order. All their fatigue
duties are performed with the same discipline, the same
regard for security; the procuring of wood, food-supplies, and
water, as required—each party has its allotted task. . . . The
same precision is maintained on the battle-field: the troops 50
wheel smartly round in the requisite direction, and, whether
advancing to the attack or retreating, all move as a unit at the
word of command.

When the camp is to be broken up, the trumpet sounds a
first call; at that none remain idle: instantly, at this signal, they
strike the tents and make all ready for departure. The trumpets
sound a second call to prepare for the march: at once they pile
their baggage on the mules and other beasts of burden and
stand ready to start, like runners breasting the cord on the
race-course. They then set fire to the encampment, both 60
because they can easily construct another [on the spot], and to
prevent the enemy from ever making use of it. . . .

Then they advance, all marching in silence and in good
order, each man keeping his place in the ranks, as if in face of
the enemy. . . . By their military exercises the Romans instil

into their soldiers fortitude not only of body but also of soul; fear, too, plays its part in their training. For they have laws which punish with death not merely desertion of the ranks, but even a slight neglect of duty; and their generals are held in even greater awe than the laws. For the high honors with which they reward the brave prevent the offenders whom they punish from regarding themselves as treated cruelly.

This perfect discipline makes the army an ornament of peace-time and in war welds the whole into a single body; so compact are their ranks, so alert their movements in wheeling to right or left, so quick their ears for orders, their eyes for signals, their hands to act upon them. Prompt as they consequently ever are in action, none are slower than they in succumbing to suffering, and never have they been known in any predicament to be beaten by numbers, by ruse, by difficulties of ground, or even by fortune; for they have more assurance of victory than of fortune. Where counsel thus precedes active operations, where the leaders' plan of campaign is followed up by so efficient an army, no wonder that the Empire has extended its boundaries on the east to the Euphrates, on the west to the ocean,[1] on the south to the most fertile tracts of Libya, on the north to the Ister[2] and the Rhine. One might say without exaggeration that, great as are their possessions, the people that won them are greater still. . . .

The Collapse of the Republic (133–30 B.C.E.)

By the beginning of the first millennium C.E., Rome had become the watchdog of the ancient world. Roman imperialism, however, worked to effect changes within the Republic itself. By its authority to handle all military matters, the Senate became increasingly powerful, as did a new class of men, wealthy Roman entrepreneurs (known as *equestrians*), who filled the jobs of provincial administration. The army, by its domination of Rome's overseas provinces, also became more powerful. Precious metals, booty, and slaves from foreign conquests brought enormous wealth to army generals and influential patricians; corruption became widespread. Captives of war were shipped back to Rome and auctioned off to the highest bidders, usually patrician landowners, whose farms soon became large-scale plantations (*latifundia*) worked by slaves. The increased agricultural productivity of the *latifundia* gave economic advantage to large landowners who easily undersold the lesser landowners and drove them out of business. Increasingly, the small farmers were forced to sell their farms to neighboring

patricians in return for the right to remain on the land. Or, they simply moved to the city to join, by the end of the first century B.C.E., a growing unemployed population. The disappearance of the small farmer signaled the decline of the Republic.

As Rome's rich citizens grew richer and its poor citizens poorer, the patricians fiercely resisted efforts to redistribute wealth more equally. But reform measures failed and political rivalries increased. Ultimately, Rome fell victim to the ambitions of army generals, who, having conquered in the name of Rome, now turned to conquering Rome itself. The first century B.C.E. was an age of military dictators, whose competing claims to power fueled a spate of civil wars. As bloody confrontations replaced reasoned compromises, the Republic crumbled.

In 46 B.C.E., an extraordinary army commander named Gaius Julius Caesar (Figure **6.2**) triumphantly entered the city of Rome and established a dictatorship. Caesar, who had spent nine years conquering Gaul (present-day France and Belgium), was as shrewd in politics as he was brilliant in war. These campaigns are described in his prose *Commentaries on the Gallic War*. His brief but successful campaigns in Syria, Asia Minor, and Egypt— where his union with the Egyptian Queen Cleopatra (69–30 B.C.E.) produced a son–inspired his famous boast: *Veni, vidi, vici* ("I came, I saw, I conquered"). A superb organizer, Caesar took strong measures to restabilize Rome: He codified the laws, regulated taxation, reduced debts, sent large numbers of the unemployed proletariat to overseas colonies, and inaugurated public works projects. He also granted citizenship to non-Italians and reformed the Western calendar to comprise 365 days and twelve months (one of which—July—he named after himself). Threatened by Caesar's populist reforms and his contempt for republican institutions, a group of his senatorial opponents, led by Marcus Junius Brutus, assassinated him in 44 B.C.E. Despite Caesar's inglorious death, the name *Caesar* would be used as an honorific title by all his imperial successors well into the second century C.E., as well as by many modern-day dictators.

The Roman Empire (30 B.C.E.–180 C.E.)

Following the assassination of Julius Caesar, a struggle for power ensued between Caesar's first lieutenant, Mark Anthony

Figure 6.2 Bust of Julius Caesar, first century B.C.E. Marble, height 1 ft. 4⅛ in. Photo: The Staatliche Museum, Berlin.

[1] The Atlantic.
[2] The Roman name for the Danube River.

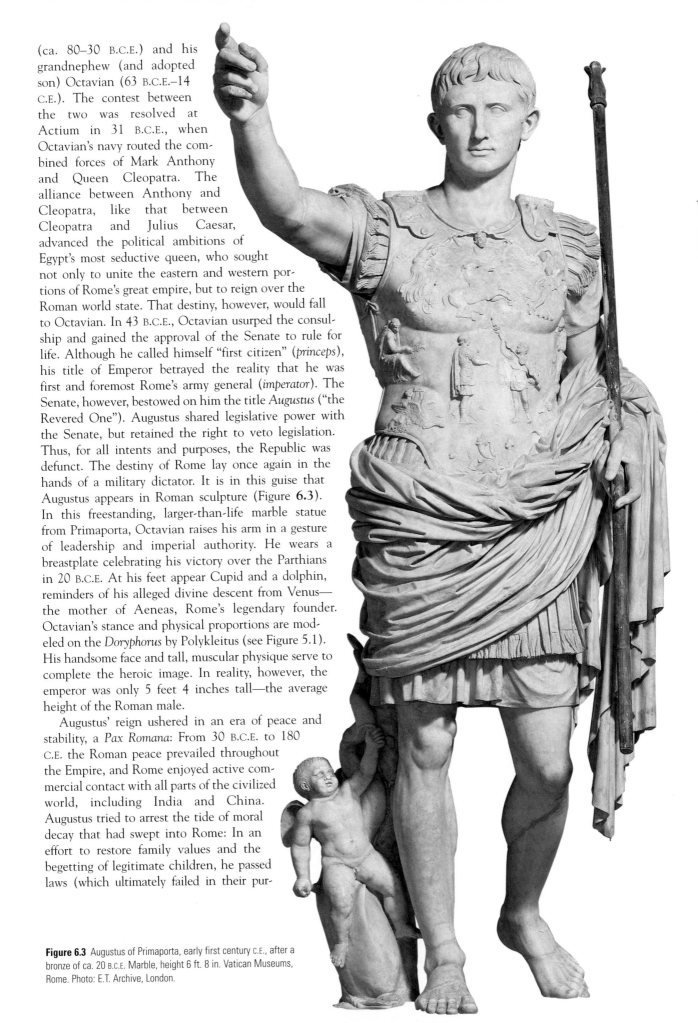

(ca. 80–30 B.C.E.) and his grandnephew (and adopted son) Octavian (63 B.C.E.–14 C.E.). The contest between the two was resolved at Actium in 31 B.C.E., when Octavian's navy routed the combined forces of Mark Anthony and Queen Cleopatra. The alliance between Anthony and Cleopatra, like that between Cleopatra and Julius Caesar, advanced the political ambitions of Egypt's most seductive queen, who sought not only to unite the eastern and western portions of Rome's great empire, but to reign over the Roman world state. That destiny, however, would fall to Octavian. In 43 B.C.E., Octavian usurped the consulship and gained the approval of the Senate to rule for life. Although he called himself "first citizen" (*princeps*), his title of Emperor betrayed the reality that he was first and foremost Rome's army general (*imperator*). The Senate, however, bestowed on him the title *Augustus* ("the Revered One"). Augustus shared legislative power with the Senate, but retained the right to veto legislation. Thus, for all intents and purposes, the Republic was defunct. The destiny of Rome lay once again in the hands of a military dictator. It is in this guise that Augustus appears in Roman sculpture (Figure **6.3**). In this freestanding, larger-than-life marble statue from Primaporta, Octavian raises his arm in a gesture of leadership and imperial authority. He wears a breastplate celebrating his victory over the Parthians in 20 B.C.E. At his feet appear Cupid and a dolphin, reminders of his alleged divine descent from Venus— the mother of Aeneas, Rome's legendary founder. Octavian's stance and physical proportions are modeled on the *Doryphorus* by Polykleitus (see Figure 5.1). His handsome face and tall, muscular physique serve to complete the heroic image. In reality, however, the emperor was only 5 feet 4 inches tall—the average height of the Roman male.

Augustus' reign ushered in an era of peace and stability, a *Pax Romana*: From 30 B.C.E. to 180 C.E. the Roman peace prevailed throughout the Empire, and Rome enjoyed active commercial contact with all parts of the civilized world, including India and China. Augustus tried to arrest the tide of moral decay that had swept into Rome: In an effort to restore family values and the begetting of legitimate children, he passed laws (which ultimately failed in their pur-

Figure 6.3 Augustus of Primaporta, early first century C.E., after a bronze of ca. 20 B.C.E. Marble, height 6 ft. 8 in. Vatican Museums, Rome. Photo: E.T. Archive, London.

The Julio-Claudian Dynasty	
27 B.C.E.–14 C.E.	Augustus
14–37	Tiberius
37–41	Gaius Caligula
41–54	Claudius
54–68	Nero

The Flavian Dynasty	
68–79	Vespasian
79–81	Titus
81–96	Domitian

The "Good Emperors"	
96–98	Nerva
97–117	Trajan
117–138	Hadrian
138–161	Antoninus Pius
161–180	Marcus Aurelius

Beginning of Decline	
180–192	Commodus

The Severan Dynasty	
193–211	Septimius Severus
211–217	Caracalla
222–235	Alexander Severus
235–284	Anarchy
284–305	Diocletian
306–337	Constantine I

Figure 6.4 Principal Roman Emperors.

pose) to curb adultery and to prevent bachelors from receiving inheritances. The *Pax Romana* was also a time of artistic and literary productivity. An enthusiastic patron of the arts, Augustus commissioned literature, sculpture, and architecture. He boasted that he had come to power when Rome was a city of brick and would leave it a city of marble. In most cases, this meant a veneer of marble that was, by standard Roman building practices, laid over the brick surface. In a city blighted by crime, noise, poor hygiene, and a frequent scarcity of food and water, Augustus initiated many new public works (including three new aqueducts and some 500 fountains) and such civic services as a police force and a fire department. The reign of Octavian also witnessed the rise of a new religion, Christianity, which, in later centuries, would spread throughout the Empire (see chapters 8 and 9).

Augustus put an end to the civil wars of the preceding century, but he revived neither the political nor the social equilibrium of the early Republic. Following his death, Rome continued to be .ruled by military officials. Since there was no machinery for succession to the imperial throne, Rome's rulers held office until they either died or

were assassinated (figure **6.4**). Of the twenty-six emperors who governed Rome during the fifty-year period between 335 and 385 C.E., only one died a natural death. Government by and for the people had been the hallmark of Rome's early history, but the enterprise of imperialism ultimately overtook these lofty republican ideals.

Roman Law

Against this backdrop of conquest and dominion, it is no surprise that Rome's contributions to the humanistic tradition were practical rather than theoretical. The sheer size of the Roman Empire inspired engineering programs, such as bridge and road building, that united all regions under Roman rule. Law—a less tangible means of unification—was equally important in this regard. The development of a system of law was one of Rome's most original and influential achievements.

Roman law (the Latin *jus* means both "law" and "justice") evolved out of the practical need to rule a world-state, rather than—as with the ancient Greeks—as a dialectic on the role of the citizen within the *polis*. Inspired by the laws of Solon, the Romans published their first civil code, the Twelve Tables of Law, in 450 B.C.E. They placed these laws on view in the Forum, the public meeting area for the civic, religious, and commercial activities of Rome. The Twelve Tables of Law provided Rome's basic legal code for almost a thousand years. To this body of law were added the acts of the Assembly and the Senate, and public decrees of the emperors. For some five hundred years, *praetors* (magistrates who administered justice) and *jurisconsults* (experts in the law) interpreted the laws, bringing commonsense resolutions to private disputes. Their interpretations constituted a body of "case law." In giving consideration to individual needs, these magistrates cultivated the concept of equity, which puts the spirit of the law above the letter of the law. The decisions of Roman jurists became precedents that established comprehensive guidelines for future judgments. Thus, Roman law was not fixed, but was an evolving body of opinions on the nature and dispensation of justice.

Early in Roman history, the law of the land (*jus civile*) applied only to Roman citizens, but as Roman citizenship was extended to the provinces, so too was the law. Law that embraced a wider range of peoples and customs, the law of the people (*jus gentium*), assumed an international quality that acknowledged compromises between conflicting customs and traditions. The law of the people was, in effect, a law based on universal principles, that is, the law of nature (*jus naturale*). The full body of Roman law came to incorporate the decisions of the jurists, the acts passed by Roman legislative assemblies, and the edicts of Roman emperors. In the sixth century C.E., two hundred years after the division of the Empire into eastern and western portions and a hundred years after the collapse of Rome, the Byzantine (East Roman) Emperor Justinian would codify this huge body of law, thereafter known as the *Corpus Juris Civilis*. The Roman system of law influenced the development of codified law in all European countries with the exception of England.

The Roman Contribution to Literature

Roman Philosophic Thought

Roman contributions to law were numerous, but such was not the case with philosophy. More a practical than a speculative people, they produced no systems of philosophic thought comparable to those of Plato and Aristotle. Yet they respected and preserved the writings of Hellenic and Hellenistic thinkers. Educated Romans admired Aristotle and absorbed the works of the Epicureans and the Stoics. The Latin poet Lucretius (ca. 95–ca. 55 B.C.E.) popularized the materialist theories of Democritus and Leucippus, which described the world in purely physical terms and denied the existence of the gods and other supernatural beings. Since all of reality, including the human soul, consists of atoms, he argued in his only work, *On the Nature of Things*, there is no reason to fear death: "We shall not feel because we shall not be."

In the vast, impersonal world of the Empire, many Romans cultivated the attitude of rational detachment popular among the Stoics. Like their third-century-B.C.E. forebears, Roman Stoics believed that an impersonal force (Providence or Divine Reason) governed the world, and that happiness lay in one's ability to accept one's fate (see chapter 5). Stoics rejected any emotional attachments that might enslave them. The ideal spiritual condition and the one most conducive to contentment, according to the Stoic point of view, depended on the subjugation of the emotions to reason.

The commonsense tenets of Stoicism encouraged the Roman sense of duty. At the same time, the Stoic belief in the equality of all people had a humanizing effect on Roman jurisprudence and anticipated the all-embracing outlook of early Christian thought (see chapter 8). Stoicism was especially popular among such intellectuals as the noted playwright and essayist Lucius Annaeus Seneca (ca. 4 B.C.E.–65 C.E.) and the Emperor Marcus Aurelius (121–180 C.E.), both of whom wrote stimulating treatises on the subject. Seneca's *On Tranquility of Mind*, an excerpt from which follows, argues that one may achieve peace of mind by avoiding burdensome respon-sibilities, gloomy companions, and excessive wealth. Stoicism offered a reasoned retreat from psychic pain and moral despair, as well as a practical set of solutions to the daily strife between the self and society.

READING 1.22 From Seneca's *On Tranquility of Mind* (ca. 40 C.E.)

. . . our question, then, is how the mind can maintain a consistent and advantageous course, be kind to itself and take pleasure in its attributes, never interrupt this satisfaction but abide in its serenity, without excitement or depression. This amounts to tranquility. We shall inquire how it may be attained. . . . **1**

A correct estimate of self is prerequisite, for we are generally inclined to overrate our capacities. One man is tripped by confidence in his eloquence, another makes greater demands upon his estate than it can stand, another burdens a frail body with an exhausting office. Some are too bashful for politics, which require aggressiveness; some are too headstrong for court; some do not control their temper and break into unguarded language at the slightest provocation; some cannot restrain their wit or resist making risky jokes. For all such people retirement is better than a career; an assertive and intolerant temperament should avoid incitements to outspokenness that will prove harmful. **10**

Next we must appraise the career and compare our strength with the task we shall attempt. The worker must be stronger than his project; loads larger than the bearer must necessarily crush him. Certain careers, moreover, are not so demanding in themselves as they are prolific in begetting a mass of other activities. Enterprises which give rise to new and multifarious activities should be avoided; you must not commit yourself to a task from which there is no free egress. Put your hand to one you can finish or at least hope to finish; leave alone those that expand as you work at them and do not stop where you intend they should. **20**

In our choice of men we should be particularly careful to see whether they are worth spending part of our life on and whether they will appreciate our loss of time; some people think we are in their debt if we do them a service. Athenadorus said he would not even go to dine with a man who would not feel indebted for his coming. Much less would he dine with people, as I suppose you understand, who discharge indebtedness for services rendered by giving a dinner and count the courses as favors, as if their lavishness was a mark of honor to others. Take away witnesses and spectators and they will take no pleasure in secret gormandizing. **30**

But nothing can equal the pleasures of faithful and congenial friendship. How good it is to have willing hearts as safe repositories for your every secret, whose privity you fear less than your own, whose conversation allays your anxiety, whose counsel promotes your plans, whose cheerfulness dissipates your gloom, whose very appearance gives you joy! But we must choose friends who are, so far as possible, free from passions. Vices are contagious; they light upon whoever is nearest and infect by contact. During a plague we must be **50**

−312	Consul Appius Claudius orders construction of the "Appian Way," the first in a strategic network of Roman roads[†]
−101	the Romans use water power for milling grain
246	Caesar inaugurates the "Julian Calendar" on which the modern calendar is based
77	Pliny the Elder completes a 37-volume encyclopedia called *Natural History*, which summarized information about astronomy, geography, and zoology
79	Pliny the Younger writes a detailed account of the eruption of Mount Vesuvius

[†]Minus (−) signifies B.C.E.

careful not to sit near people caught in the throes and burning with fever, because we would be courting danger and drawing poison in with our breath; just so in choosing friends we must pay attention to character and take those least tainted. To mingle the healthy with the sick is the beginning of disease. But I would not prescribe that you become attached to or attract no one who is not a sage. Where would you find him? We have been searching for him for centuries. Call the least bad man the best. You could not have a more opulent choice, if you were looking for good men, than among the Platos and Xenophons[1] and the famous Socratic brood, or if you had at your disposal the age of Cato,[2] which produced many characters worthy to be his contemporaries (just as it produced many unprecedentedly bad, who engineered monstrous crimes. Both kinds were necessary to make Cato's quality understood: he needed bad men against whom he could make his strength effective and good men to appreciate his effectiveness). But now there is a great dearth of good men, and your choice cannot be fastidious. But gloomy people who deplore everything and find reason to complain you must take pains to avoid. With all his loyalty and good will, a grumbling and touchy companion militates against tranquility. 70

We pass now to property, the greatest source of affliction to humanity. If you balance all our other troubles—deaths, diseases, fears, longings, subjection to labor and pain—with the miseries in which our money involves us, the latter will far outweigh the former. Reflect, then, how much less a grief it is not to have money than to lose it, and then you will realize that poverty has less to torment us with in the degree that it has less to lose. If you suppose that rich men take their losses with greater equanimity you are mistaken; a wound hurts a big man as much as it does a little. Bion[3] put it smartly: a bald man is as bothered when his hair is plucked as a man with a full head. The same applies to rich and poor, you may be sure; in either case the money is glued on and cannot be torn away without a twinge, so that both suffer alike. It is less distressing, as I have said, and easier not to acquire money than to lose it, and you will therefore notice that people upon whom Fortune never has smiled are more cheerful than those she has deserted. . . . 90

All life is bondage. Man must therefore habituate himself to his condition, complain of it as little as possible, and grasp whatever good lies within his reach. No situation is so harsh that a dispassionate mind cannot find some consolation in it. If a man lays even a very small area out skillfully it will provide ample space for many uses, and even a foothold can be made livable by deft arrangement. Apply good sense to your problems; the hard can be softened, the narrow widened, and the heavy made lighter by the skillful bearer. . . .

Latin Prose Literature

Roman literature reveals a masterful use of Latin prose for the purposes of entertainment, instruction, and record-keeping. Ever applying their resources to practical ends,

the Romans found prose the ideal vehicle for compiling and transmitting information. Rome gave the West its first geographies and encyclopedias, as well as some of its finest biographies, histories, and manuals of instruction. In the writing of history, in particular, the Romans demonstrated their talent for the collection and analysis of factual evidence. Although Roman historians tended to glorify Rome and its leadership, their attention to detail often surpassed that of the Greek historians. One of Rome's greatest historians, Titus Livius ("Livy," ca. 59 B.C.E.–17 C.E.), wrote a history of Rome from the eighth century B.C.E. to his own day. Although only a small portion of Livy's original 142 books survive, this monumental work—commissioned by Octavian himself—constitutes our most reliable account of political and social life in the days of the Roman Republic.

The Romans were masters, as well, in **oratory**, that is, the art of public speaking, and in the writing of **epistles** (letters). In both of these genres, the statesman Marcus Tullius Cicero (106–43 B.C.E.) excelled. A contemporary of Julius Caesar, Cicero produced more than 900 letters—sometimes writing three a day to the same person—and more than one hundred speeches and essays. Clarity and eloquence are the hallmarks of Cicero's prose style, which Renaissance humanists hailed as the model for literary excellence (see chapter 16). While Cicero was familiar with the theoretical works of Aristotle and the Stoics, his letters reflect a profound concern for the political realities of his own day. In his lifetime, Cicero served Rome as consul, statesman, and orator; his carefully reasoned speeches helped to shape public opinion. While he praised Julius Caesar's literary style, he openly opposed his patron's dictatorship. (Caesar congenially confessed to Cicero, "It is nobler to enlarge the boundaries of human intelligence than those of the Roman Empire.") As we see in the following excerpt from his essay *On Duty*, Cicero considered public service the noblest of human activities—one that demanded the exercise of personal courage equal to that required in military combat.

READING 1.23 From Cicero's *On Duty* (44 B.C.E.)

. . . that moral goodness which we look for in a lofty, high-minded spirit is secured, of course, by moral, not by physical, strength. And yet the body must be trained and so disciplined that it can obey the dictates of judgment and reason in attending to business and in enduring toil. But that moral goodness which is our theme depends wholly upon the thought and attention given to it by the mind. And, in this way, the men who in a civil capacity direct the affairs of the nation render no less important service than they who conduct its wars: by their statesmanship oftentimes wars are either averted or terminated; sometimes also they are declared. Upon Marcus Cato's[1] counsel, for example, the Third Punic War was undertaken, and in its conduct his influence was

---

[1] A Greek historian and biographer who lived ca. 428–354 B.C.E.
[2] Marcus Porcius Cato (234–149 B.C.E.), known as "the Censor," a Roman champion of austerity and simplicity.
[3] A Greek poet who lived around 100 B.C.E.

---

[1] Known as "the Censor," the Roman senator Cato (234–149 B.C.E.) repeatedly demanded the total destruction of Carthage.

dominant, even after he was dead. And so diplomacy in the friendly settlement of controversies is more desirable than courage in settling them on the battlefield; but we must be careful not to take that course merely for the sake of avoiding war rather than for the sake of public expediency. War, however, should be undertaken in such a way as to make it evident that it has no other object than to secure peace. 20

But it takes a brave and resolute spirit not to be disconcerted in times of difficulty or ruffled and thrown off one's feet, as the saying is, but to keep one's presence of mind and one's self-possession and not to swerve from the path of reason.

Now all this requires great personal courage; but it calls also for great intellectual ability by reflection to anticipate the future, to discover some time in advance what may happen whether for good or for ill, and what must be done in any possible event, and never to be reduced to having to say 30 "I had not thought of that."

These are the activities that mark a spirit strong, high, and self-reliant in its prudence and wisdom. But to mix rashly in the fray and to fight hand to hand with the enemy is but a barbarous and brutish kind of business. Yet when the stress of circumstances demands it, we must gird on the sword and prefer death to slavery and disgrace.

As to destroying and plundering cities, let me say that great care should be taken that nothing be done in reckless cruelty or wantonness. And it is a great man's duty in troublous times 40 to single out the guilty for punishment, to spare the many, and in every turn of fortune to hold to a true and honorable course. For whereas there are many, as I have said before, who place the achievements of war above those of peace, so one may find many to whom adventurous, hot-headed counsels seem more brilliant and more impressive than calm and well-considered measures.

We must, of course, never be guilty of seeming cowardly and craven in our avoidance of danger; but we must also beware of exposing ourselves to danger needlessly. Nothing 50 can be more foolhardy than that. Accordingly, in encountering danger we should do as doctors do in their practice: in light cases of illness they give mild treatment; in cases of dangerous sickness they are compelled to apply hazardous and even desperate remedies. It is, therefore, only a madman who, in a calm, would pray for a storm; a wise man's way is, when the storm does come, to withstand it with all the means at his command, and especially when the advantages to be expected in case of a successful issue are greater than the hazards of the struggle. 60

The dangers attending great affairs of state fall sometimes upon those who undertake them, sometimes upon the state. In carrying out such enterprises, some run the risk of losing their lives, others their reputation and the good-will of their fellow-citizens. It is our duty, then, to be more ready to endanger our own than the public welfare and to hazard honor and glory more readily than other advantages. . . .

As Cicero indicates, Roman education emphasized civic duty. It aimed at training the young for active roles in civic life. For careers in law and political administration, the art of public speaking was essential. Indeed, in the provinces, where people of many languages mingled, oratory was the ultimate form of political influence. Since the art of public speaking was the distinctive mark of the educated Roman, the practical skills of grammar and rhetoric held an important place in Roman education. One of the greatest spokesmen for the significance of oratory in public affairs was the Roman historian and politician, P. Cornelius Tacitus (ca. 56–120 C.E.). Tacitus' *Dialogue on Oratory* describes the role of public speaking in ancient Roman life. It bemoans the passing of a time when "eloquence led not only to great rewards, but was also a sheer necessity."

READING 1.24 From Tacitus' *Dialogue on Oratory* (ca. 100–105 C.E.)

. . . great oratory is like a flame: it needs fuel to feed it, 1 movement to fan it, and it brightens as it burns.

At Rome too the eloquence of our forefathers owed its development to [special] conditions. For although the orators of today have also succeeded in obtaining all the influence that it would be proper to allow them under settled, peaceable, and prosperous political conditions, yet their predecessors in those days of unrest and unrestraint thought they could accomplish more when, in the general ferment and without the strong hand of a single ruler, a speaker's political 10 wisdom was measured by his power of carrying conviction to the unstable populace. This was the source of the constant succession of measures put forward by champions of the people's rights, of the harangues of state officials who almost spent the night on the hustings,[1] of the impeachments of powerful criminals and hereditary feuds between whole families, of schisms among the aristocracy and never-ending struggles between the senate and the commons.[2] All this tore the commonwealth in pieces, but it provided a sphere for the oratory of those days and heaped on it what one saw were 20 vast rewards. The more influence a man could wield by his powers of speech, the more readily did he attain to high office, the further did he, when in office, outstrip his colleagues in the race for precedence, the more did he gain favor with the great, authority with the senate, and name and fame with the common people. These were the men who had whole nations of foreigners under their protection, several at a time; the men to whom state officials presented their humble duty on the eve of their departure to take up the government of a province, and to whom they paid their respects on their 30 return; the men who, without any effort on their own part, seemed to have praetorships and consulates at their beck and call; the men who even when out of office were in power, seeing that by their advice and authority they could bend both the senate and the people to their will. With them, moreover, it was a conviction that without eloquence it was impossible for anyone either to attain to a position of distinction and prominence in the community, or to maintain it; and no wonder

---

[1]The speaker's platform.
[2]The Popular Assembly.

they cherished this conviction, when they were called on to appear in public even when they would rather not, when it was not enough to move a brief resolution in the senate, unless one made good one's opinion in an able speech, when persons who had in some way or other incurred odium, or else were definitely charged with some offence, had to put in an appearance in person, when, moreover, evidence in criminal trials had to be given not indirectly or by affidavit, but personally and by word of mouth. So it was that eloquence not only led to great rewards, but was also a sheer necessity; and just as it was considered great and glorious to have the reputation of being a good speaker, so, on the other hand, it was accounted discreditable to be inarticulate and incapable of utterance. . . .

Roman Epic Poetry

While the Romans excelled in didactic prose, they also produced some of the world's finest verse. Under the patronage of Octavian, Rome enjoyed a Golden Age of Latin literature whose most notable representative was Virgil (Publius Vergilius Maro, 70–19 B.C.E.). Rome's foremost poet-publicist, Virgil wrote the semilegendary epic that immortalized Rome's destiny as world ruler. The *Aeneid* was not the product of an oral tradition, as were the Homeric epics; rather, it was a literary epic, undertaken as a work that might rival the epics of Homer. The hero of Virgil's poem is Rome's mythical founder, the Trojan-born Aeneas. As the typical epic hero, Aeneas undertakes a long journey and undergoes a series of adventures that test his prowess. The first six books of the *Aeneid* recount the hero's journey from Troy to Italy and his love affair with the beautiful Carthaginian princess, Dido. The second six books describe the Trojan conquest of Latium and the establishment of the Roman state. No summary of the *Aeneid* can represent adequately the monumental impact of a work that was to become the foundation for education in the Latin language. Yet, the following two excerpts capture the spirit of Virgil's vision. In the first, Aeneas, pressed to fulfill his divine mission, prepares to take leave of the passionate Dido. Here, his Stoic sense of duty overcomes his desire for personal fulfillment. The second passage, selected from the lengthy monologue spoken by the ghost of Aeneas' father, Anchises, eloquently sums up the meaning and purpose of Rome's historic mission.

READING 1.25 From Virgil's *Aeneid* (Books Four and Six) (ca. 20 B.C.E.)

[Mercury, the divine herald, urges Aeneas to leave Carthage and proceed to Italy.]

Mercury wastes no time:—"What are you doing,   1
Forgetful of your kingdom and your fortunes,
Building for Carthage? Woman-crazy fellow,
The ruler of the Gods, the great compeller
Of heaven and earth, has sent me from Olympus   5
With no more word than this: what are you doing,
With what ambition wasting time in Libya?
If your own fame and fortune count as nothing,
Think of Ascanius[1] at least, whose kingdom
In Italy, whose Roman land, are waiting   10
As promise justly due." He spoke, and vanished
Into thin air. Apalled, amazed, Aeneas
Is stricken dumb; his hair stands up in terror,
His voice sticks in his throat. He is more than eager
To flee that pleasant land, awed by the warning   15
Of the divine command. But how to do it?
How get around that passionate queen?[2] What opening
Try first? His mind runs out in all directions,
Shifting and veering. Finally, he has it,
Or thinks he has: he calls his comrades to him,   20
The leaders, bids them quietly prepare
The fleet for voyage, meanwhile saying nothing
About the new activity; since Dido
Is unaware, has no idea that passion
As strong as theirs is on the verge of breaking,   25
He will see what he can do, find the right moment
To let her know, all in good time. Rejoicing,
The captains move to carry out the orders.

     Who can deceive a woman in love? The queen
Anticipates each move, is fearful even   30
While everything is safe, foresees this cunning,
And the same trouble-making goddess, Rumor,
Tells her the fleet is being armed, made ready
For voyaging. She rages through the city
Like a woman mad, or drunk, the way the Maenads[3]   35
Go howling through the night-time on Cithaeron[4]
When Bacchus' cymbals summon with their clashing.
She waits no explanation from Aeneas;
She is the first to speak: "And so, betrayer,
You hoped to hide your wickedness, go sneaking   40
Out of my land without a word? Our love
Means nothing to you, our exchange of vows,
And even the death of Dido could not hold you.
The season is dead of winter, and you labor
Over the fleet; the northern gales are nothing—   45
You must be cruel, must you not? Why, even,
If ancient Troy remained, and you were seeking
Not unknown homes and lands, but Troy again,
Would you be venturing Troyward in this weather?
I am the one you flee from: true? I beg you   50
By my own tears, and your right hand—(I have nothing
Else left my wretchedness)—by the beginnings
Of marriage, wedlock, what we had, if ever
I served you well, if anything of mine
Was ever sweet to you, I beg you, pity   55
A falling house; if there is room for pleading
As late as this, I plead, put off that purpose.
You are the reason I am hated; Libyans,
Numidians, Tyrians, hate me; and my honor
Is lost, and the fame I had, that almost brought me   60

---

[1]Aeneas' son.
[2]Dido, Queen of Carthage.
[3]"Mad women," the votaries of Bacchus (Dionysus).
[4]A mountain range between Attica and Boetia.

High as the stars, is gone. To whom, O guest—
I must not call you husband any longer—
To whom do you leave me? I am a dying woman;
Why do I linger on? Until Pygmalion,
My brother, brings destruction to this city?   65
Until the prince Iarbas leads me captive?
At least if there had been some hope of children
Before your flight, a little Aeneas playing
Around my courts, to bring you back, in feature
At least, I would seem less taken and deserted."   70
    There was nothing he could say. Jove bade him keep
Affection from his eyes, and grief in his heart
With never a sign. At last, he managed something:—
"Never, O Queen, will I deny you merit
Whatever you have strength to claim; I will not   75
Regret remembering Dido, while I have
Breath in my body, or consciousness of spirit.
I have a point or two to make. I did not,
Believe me, hope to hide my flight by cunning;
I did not, ever, claim to be a husband,   80
Made no such vows. If I had fate's permission
To live my life my way, to settle my troubles
At my own will, I would be watching over
The city of Troy, and caring for my people,
Those whom the Greeks had spared, and Priam's palace   85
Would still be standing; for the vanquished people
I would have built the town again. But now
It is Italy I must seek, great Italy,
Apollo orders, and his oracles
Call me to Italy. There is my love,   90
There is my country. If the towers of Carthage,
The Libyan citadels, can please a woman
Who came from Tyre,[5] why must you grudge the Trojans
Ausonian land?[6] It is proper for us also
To seek a foreign kingdom. I am warned   95
Of this in dreams: when the earth is veiled in shadow
And the fiery stars are burning, I see my father,
Anchises, or his ghost, and I am frightened;
I am troubled for the wrong I do my son,
Cheating him out of his kingdom in the west,   100
And lands that fate assigns him. And a herald,
Jove's[7] messenger—I call them both to witness—
Has brought me, through the rush of air, his orders;
I saw the god myself, in the full daylight,
Enter these walls, I heard the words he brought me.   105
Cease to inflame us both with your complainings;
I follow Italy not because I want to."

[In the Underworld described in Book 6, Aeneas
encounters the soul of his father, Anchises, who foretells
the destiny of Rome.]

"Others, no doubt, will better mould the bronze
To the semblance of soft breathing, draw from marble,
The living countenance; and others please   110

With greater eloquence, or learn to measure
Better than we, the pathways of the heavens,
The risings of the stars: remember, Roman,
To rule the people under law, to establish
The way of peace, to battle down the haughty,   115
To spare the meek. Our fine arts, these forever."

Roman Lyric Poetry and Satire

While Virgil is best known for the *Aeneid*, he also wrote pastoral poems, or **eclogues**, that glorify the natural landscape and its rustic inhabitants. Virgil's *Eclogues* found inspiration in the pastoral sketches of Theocritus, a third-century-B.C.E. Sicilian poet. Many classicists besides Virgil looked to Hellenic prototypes. The poetry of Catullus (ca. 84–54 B.C.E.), for instance, reflects familiarity with the art of Sappho, whose lyrics he admired. The greatest of the Latin lyric poets, Catullus came to Rome from Verona. A young man of some wealth and charm, he wrote primarily on the subjects that consumed his short but intense life: friendship, love, and sex. His passionate affair with Clodias, the adulterous wife of a Roman consul, inspired some of his finest poems, three of which appear below. These trace the trajectory from the poet's first fevered amorous passions to his despair and bitterness at the collapse of the affair. The fourth poem betrays the raw invective and caustic wit that Catullus brought to many of his verses, including those with themes of jealousy and possession related to his bisexual liaisons. Candid and deeply personal, these poems strike us with the immediacy of a modern, secular voice.

READING 1.26 The Poems of Catullus

(ca. 60 B.C.E.)

Come, Lesbia,[1] let us live and love,   1
nor give a damn what sour old men say.
The sun that sets may rise again
but when our light has sunk into the earth,
it is gone forever.   5
    Give me a thousand kisses,
then a hundred, another thousand,
another hundred
    and in one breath
still kiss another thousand,   10
another hundred.
    O then with lips and bodies joined
many deep thousands;
    confuse
their number,   15
    so that poor fools and cuckolds (envious
even now) shall never
learn our wealth and curse us
with their
evil eyes.   20

—◆—

---

[5]A maritime city of ancient Phoenicia, ruled by Dido's father.
[6]From *Ausones*, the ancient name for the inhabitants of middle and southern Italy.
[7]Jupiter, the sky god.

[1]The name Catullus gave to Clodias, a reference to Sappho of Lesbos.

He is changed to a god he who looks on her,   1
godlike he shines when he's seated beside her,
immortal joy to gaze and hear the fall of
　　her sweet laughter.

All of my senses are lost and confounded;   5
Lesbia rises before me and trembling
I sink into earth and swift dissolution
　　seizes my body.

Limbs are pierced with fire and the heavy tongue fails,
ears resound with noise of distant storms shaking   10
this earth, eyes gaze on stars that fall forever
　　into deep midnight.

This languid madness destroys you Catullus,
long day and night shall be desolate, broken,
as long ago ancient kings and rich cities   15
　　fell into ruin.

— ◆ —

Lesbia, forever spitting fire at me, is never silent, And now   1
if Lesbia fails to love me, I shall die. Why
do I know in truth her passion burns for me? Because I am
　　like her,
because I curse her endlessly. And still, O hear me gods,   5
I love her.

— ◆ —

Furius, Aurelius, I'll work your own perversions   1
upon you and your persons, since you say my poems
prove that I'm effeminate, deep in homosexual
　　vice.
A genuine poet must be chaste, industrious,
though his verse may give us   5
rich, voluptuous passion to please the
taste of those who read him and not only
delicate boys, but bearded men whose limbs are
stiff and out of practice. And you because my verses
contain many (thousands of) kisses, look at me   10
as though I were a girl. Come at me, and I'll be ready
to defile you and seduce you.

The poetry of Catullus notwithstanding, passion and
personal feeling were not typical of Latin literature, which
inclined more usually toward instruction and satire. One
of Rome's most notable poets, Publius Ovidius Naso, or
Ovid (43 B.C.E.–17 C.E.), earned centuries of fame for
his narrative poem, the *Metamorphoses*; this vast collection
of stories about Greek and Roman gods develops the
theme of supernatural transformation. Ovid himself pursued
a career of poetry and love. Married three times,
he seems to have been a master in the art of seduction.
His witty guide on the subject, *The Art of Love*, brought
him into disfavor with Augustus, who (finding the work
morally threatening) sent Ovid into exile. Though written
with tongue-in-cheek, *The Art of Love* swelled an already
large canon of misogynic, or antifemale, classical literature.
In his satiric "handbook," Ovid offers vivid glimpses
into everyday life in Rome, but he clearly holds that
the greatest human crimes issue from women's lust,
which, according to the poet, is "keener, fiercer, and more
wanton" than men's.

Roman poets were at their most typical when they were
moralizing. Octavian's poet laureate, Quintus Haeredes
Flaccus, better known as Horace (65–8 B.C.E.), took a critical
view of life. Though lacking the grandeur of Virgil and
the virtuosity of Ovid, Horace composed verse that pointed
up the contradictions between practical realities and
philosophic ideals. Having lived through the devastating
civil wars of the first century B.C.E., Horace brought a commonsense
insight to the subject of war, as we see in the
first of the following poems. The second poem exemplifies
the Roman taste for **satire**, a literary genre that uses humor
to denounce human vice and folly. Satire—Rome's unique
contribution to world literature—is a kind of moralizing in
which human imperfection is not simply criticized, but
rather, mocked through biting wit and comic exaggeration.
To Be Quite Frank is a caustic description of a middle-aged
lady with teenage pretensions, a characterization as unvarnished
and true-to-life as most Roman portraits. Finally, in
the third poem below, Horace discloses his Stoic disbelief
in human perfection: He advises us to "Seize the day"
(*carpe diem*) and "Learn to accept whatever is to be."

READING 1.27 The Poems of Horace

(ca. 30–15 B.C.E.)

Civil War

Why do ye rush, oh wicked folk,   1
　　To a fresh war?
Again the cries, the sword, the smoke—
　　What for?

Has not sufficient precious blood   5
　　Been fiercely shed?
Must ye spill more until ye flood
　　The dead?

Not even armed in rivalry
　　Your hate's employed;   10
But 'gainst yourselves until ye be
　　Destroyed!

Even when beasts slay beasts, they kill
　　Some other kind.
Can it be madness makes ye still   15
　　So blind?

Make answer! Is your conscience numb?
　　Each ashy face
Admits, with silent lips, the dumb
　　Disgrace.   20

Murder of brothers! Of all crime,
　　Vilest and worst!

Pause—lest ye be, through all of time,
    Accursed.

To Be Quite Frank

Your conduct, naughty Chloris, is   1
    Not just exactly Horace's
Ideal of a lady
    At the shady
Time of life;   5
You mustn't throw your soul away
On foolishness, like Pholoë—
    Her days are folly-laden—
    She's a maiden,
        You're a wife.   10

Your daughter, with propriety,
May look for male society,
    Do one thing and another
    In which mother
        Shouldn't mix;   15
But revels Bacchanalian
Are—or should be—quite alien
    To you a married person,
    Something worse'n
        Forty-six!   20

Yes, Chloris, you cut up too much,
You love the dance and cup too much,
    Your years are quickly flitting—
    To your knitting
        Right about!   25
Forget the incidental things
That keep you from parental things—
    The World, the Flesh, the Devil,
    On the level,
        Cut 'em out!   30

Carpe Diem

Pry not in forbidden lore,   1
    Ask no more, Leuconoë,
How many years—to you?—to me?—
The gods will send us
Before they end us;   5
Nor, questing, fix your hopes
On Babylonian horoscopes.
Learn to accept whatever is to be:
Whether Jove grant us many winters,
Or make of this the last, which splinters   10
Now on opposing cliffs the Tuscan sea.

Be wise; decant your wine; condense
Large aims to fit life's cramped circumference.
We talk, time flies—you've said it!
Make hay today,   15
Tomorrow rates no credit.

While Horace's satirical lyrics are, for the most part, genial, those of Rome's most famous satirist, Juvenal (Decimus Junius Juvenalis, ca. 60–130 C.E.), are among the most devastating ever written. Juvenal came to Rome from the provinces. His subsequent career as a magistrate and his experience of poverty and financial failure contributed to his negative perception of Roman society, which he describes in his sixteen bitter *Satires* as swollen with greed and corruption. Juvenal's attack on the city of Rome paints a picture of a noisy, dirty, and crowded urban community inhabited by selfish, violent, and self-indulgent people.

READING 1.28a From Juvenal's "Against the City of Rome" (ca. 110–127)

"Rome, good-bye! Let the rest stay in the town if they
    want to,   1
Fellows like A, B, and C, who make black white at their
    pleasure,
Finding it easy to grab contracts for rivers and harbors,
Putting up temples, or cleaning out sewers, or hauling
    off corpses,
Or, if it comes to that, auctioning slaves in the market. 5
Once they used to be hornblowers, working the carneys;
Every wide place in the road knew their puffed-out
    cheeks and their squealing.
Now they give shows of their own. Thumbs up! Thumbs
    down![1] And the killers
Spare or slay, and then go back to concessions for
    private privies.
Nothing they won't take on. Why not?—since the
    kindness of Fortune   10
(Fortune is out for laughs) has exalted them out of the
    gutter.

. . . .

"If you're poor, you're a joke, on each and every occasion.
What a laugh, if your cloak is dirty or torn, if your toga
Seems a little bit soiled, if your shoe has a crack in the
    leather,
Or if more than one patch attests to more than one
    mending!   15
Poverty's greatest curse, much worse than the fact of it,
    is that
It makes men objects of mirth, ridiculed, humbled,
    embarrassed.
'Out of the front-row seats!' they cry when you're out of
    money,
Yield your place to the sons of some pimp, the spawn of
    some cathouse,
Some slick auctioneer's brat, or the louts some trainer
    has fathered   20
Or the well-groomed boys whose sire is a gladiator.

. . . .

———
[1]To turn the thumb down was the signal to kill a wounded gladiator;
to turn it up signaled that he should be spared.

"Here in town the sick die from insomnia mostly.
Undigested food, on a stomach burning with ulcers,
Brings on listlessness, but who can sleep in a flophouse?
Who but the rich can afford sleep and a garden
    apartment?   25
That's the source of infection. The wheels creak by on
    the narrow
Streets of the wards, the drivers squabble and brawl
    when they're stopped,
More than enough to frustrate the drowsiest son of a sea
    cow.
When his business calls, the crowd makes way, as the
    rich man,
Carried high in his car, rides over them, reading or
    writing,   30
Even taking a snooze, perhaps, for the motion's composing.
Still, he gets where he wants before we do; for all of our
    hurry
Traffic gets in our way, in front, around and behind us.
Somebody gives me a shove with an elbow, or two-by-
    four scantling.²
One clunks my head with a beam, another cracks down
    with a beer keg.   35
Mud is thick on my shins, I am trampled by somebody's
    big feet.
Now what?—a soldier grinds his hobnails into my toes."

If Juvenal found much to criticize among his peers, he was equally hostile toward foreigners and women. His sixth *Satire*, "Against Women," is one of the most bitter antifemale diatribes in the history of Western literature. Here, the poet laments the disappearance of the chaste Latin woman whose virtues, he submits, have been corrupted by luxury. Though Juvenal's bias against womankind strikes a personal note, it is likely that he was reflecting the public outcry against the licentiousness that was widespread in his own day. Increasingly during the second century, men openly enjoyed concubines, mistresses, and prostitutes. Infidelity among married women was on the rise, and divorce was common, as were second and third marriages for both sexes.

The women of imperial Rome did not have many more civil rights than did their Golden Age Athenian sisters. They could neither vote nor hold public office. However, they did not occupy separate household quarters from males, they could own property, and they were free to manage their own legal affairs. Roman girls were educated along with boys, and most middle-class women could read and write. Some female aristocrats were active in public life, and the consorts of Rome's rulers often shaped matters of succession and politics by way of their influence on their husbands and sons. Roman records confirm that in addition to the traditional occupations of women in food and textile production and in prostitution, they also held positions as musicians, painters, priestesses, midwives, and gladiators.

---
²A piece of lumber.

READING 1.28b From Juvenal's "Against Women" (ca. 110–127)

Where, you ask, do they come from, such monsters as
    these? In the old days   1
Latin women were chaste by dint of their lowly fortunes.
Toil and short hours for sleep kept cottages free from
    contagion,
Hands were hard from working the wood, and husbands
    were watching,
Standing to arms at the Colline Gate, and the shadow of
    Hannibal's looming.¹   5
Now we suffer the evils of long peace. Luxury hatches
Terrors worse than the wars, avenging a world beaten
    down.
Every crime is here, and every lust, as they have been
Since the day, long since, when Roman poverty perished.
Over our seven hills,² from that day on, they came
    pouring.   10
The rabble and rout of the East, Sybaris, Rhodes, Miletus,
Yes, and Tarentum³ too, garlanded, drunken, shameless.
Dirty money it was that first imported among us
Foreign vice and our times broke down with
    overindulgence.
Riches are flabby, soft. And what does Venus care for   15
When she is drunk? She can't tell one end of a thing
    from another,
Gulping big oysters down at midnight, making the
    unguents
Foam in the unmixed wine, and drinking out of a
    conchhorn
While the walls spin round, and the table starts in
    dancing,
And the glow of the lamps is blurred by double their
    number.   20

. . . .

There's nothing a woman won't do, nothing she thinks is
    disgraceful
With the green gems at her neck, or pearls distending
    her ear lobes.
Nothing is worse to endure than your Mrs. Richbitch,
    whose visage
Is padded and plastered with dough, in the most
    ridiculous manner.
Furthermore, she reeks of unguents, so God help her
    husband   25
With his wretched face stunk up with these, smeared by
    her lipstick.
To her lovers she comes with her skin washed clean. But
    at home

---
¹In 213 B.C.E. the Carthaginian general, Hannibal, Rome's most formidable enemy, was camped only a few miles outside Rome, poised to attack (see Livy, xxvi:10).
²The hills surrounding the city of Rome.
³Greek cities associated with luxury and vice.

Why does she need to look pretty? Nard[4] is assumed for
   the lover,
For the lover she buys all the Arabian perfumes.
It takes her some time to strip down to her face,
   removing the layers   **30**
One by one, till at last she is recognizable, almost,
Then she uses a lotion, she-asses' milk; she'd need
   herds
Of these creatures to keep her supplied on her
   northernmost journeys.
But when she's given herself the treatment in full, from
   the ground base
Through the last layer of mud pack, from the first wash
   to a poultice,   **35**
What lies under all this—a human face, or an ulcer?

· · · · · · · · · ·

Roman Drama

Roman tragedies were roughly modeled on those of
Greece. They were moral and didactic in intent, and their
themes were drawn from Greek and Roman history.
Theatrical performances in Rome were not, however, of
religious solemnity as they were in Greece. Rather, they
were a form of entertainment offered along with the public games that marked the major civic festivals known
as *ludi*. Unlike the rituals and athletic contests of the
Greeks, the *ludi* featured displays of gladiatorial combat,
chariot races, animal contests, and a variety of other
violent amusements. The nature of these public spectacles
may explain why many of the tragedies written to compete
with them were bloody and ghoulish in character. The
lurid plays of the Stoic writer Seneca drew crowds in
Roman times and were to inspire—some 1500 years
later—such playwrights as William Shakespeare.

The Romans seem to have enjoyed comedies over
tragedies, for most surviving Roman plays are in the comic
genre. Comic writers employed simple plots and broad
(often obscene) humor. The plays of Plautus (ca. 250–184
B.C.E.) are filled with stock characters, such as the good-
hearted prostitute, the shrewish wife, and the clever servant. The characters engage in farcical schemes of the
kind common to today's television situation comedies. In
the comic theater of the Romans, as in Roman culture in
general, everyday life took precedence over fantasy, and
the real, if imperfect, world was the natural setting for
down-to-earth human beings.

The Arts of the Roman Empire

Roman Architecture

Rome's architecture reflected the practical needs of a
sprawling empire whose urban centers suffered from the
congestion, noise, and filth described by Juvenal. To link
the provinces that ranged from the Atlantic Ocean to the
Euphrates River, Roman engineers built fifty thousand
miles of paved roads, many of which are still in use today.
Roman bridges and tunnels defied natural barriers, while
some eighteen aqueducts brought fresh water to Rome's
major cities. The aqueducts, some of which delivered
well over forty million gallons of water per day to a single
site, were the public works that the Romans considered
their most significant technological achievement. The
need to house, govern, and entertain large numbers of
citizens inspired the construction of tenements, meeting
halls, baths, and amphitheaters. Eight- and nine-story
tenements provided thousands with cheap (if often
rat-infested) housing.

Superb engineers, the Romans employed the structural
advantages of the arch (the knowledge of which they
inherited from the Etruscans) to enclose great volumes of
uninterrupted space (Figure **6.5**). The arch constituted a
clear technical advance over the post-and-lintel construction used by the Greeks in buildings like the Parthenon
(see Figure 5.15). The Romans adapted this structural
principle inventively: They placed arches back to back to
form a barrel **vault**, at right angles to each other to form a
cross or groined vault, and around a central point to form
a dome. These innovations allowed the Romans to contain areas of space that were larger than any previously
known. Roman building techniques reveal a combination
of practicality and innovation: The Romans were the first
to use concrete (an aggregate of sand, lime, brick-and-
stone rubble, and water), a medium that made possible
cheap, large-scale construction. They laid their foundations with concrete, raised structures with brick, rubble,
and stone, and finished exterior surfaces with veneers of
marble, tile, bronze, or plaster.

Roman architecture and engineering were considered
one and the same discipline. Vitruvius' *Ten Books on
Architecture* (see chapter 5), the oldest and most influential work of its kind, includes instructions for hydraulic
systems, city planning, and mechanical devices. For the
Roman architect, the function of a building determined

---

[4]Spikenard, a fragrant ointment.

Figure 6.5 Arch principle and arch construction. (A) Arch consisting of voussoirs, wedge-shaped blocks (a,b,c,); (B) Post-and-lintel; (C) Barrel or tunnel vault; (D and E) Groined vault; (F) Dome.

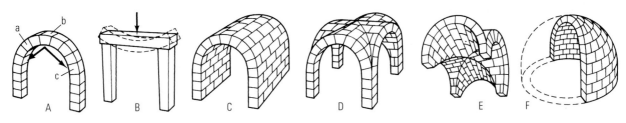

Figure 6.6 Pont du Gard, near Nîmes, France, ca. 20–10 B.C.E. Stone, height 180 ft., length ca. 900 ft. Photo: Paul M.R. Maeyaert, Belgium.

its formal design. The design of villas, theaters, and temples received the same close attention as that given to hospitals, fortresses, and—as Josephus reveals—military camps. One of Rome's most spectacular large-scale engineering projects is the 900-foot-long Pont du Gard, part of a 25-mile-long aqueduct that brought fresh water to the city of Nîmes in southern France (Figure 6.6). Built of six-ton stones and assembled without mortar, the structure reflects the practical function of arches at three levels, the bottom row supporting a bridge and the second row undergirding the top channel through which water ran by gravity to its destination.

Figure 6.7 Reconstruction of fourth-century C.E. Rome by I. Gismondi. Museum of Roman Civilization, Rome.

Figure 6.8 Colosseum, Rome (aerial view), 70–82 C.E. Photo: Fototeca Unione.

crowd. To provide shade from the sun, an awning at the roof level could be extended by means of a system of pulleys. On each level of the exterior, arches were framed by a series of decorative, or engaged, columns displaying the three Greek orders: Doric (at ground level), Ionic, and Corinthian (Figure **6.9**). The ingenious combination of arch and post-and-lintel structural elements in the design of the Colosseum would be widely imitated for centuries, and especially during the Italian Renaissance. More generally, the influence of this Roman amphitheater is apparent in the design of the modern sports arena.

Roman architectural genius may be best illustrated by the Pantheon, a temple whose structural majesty depends on the combination of Roman technical ingenuity and dramatic spatial design. Dedicated to the seven planetary deities, the Pantheon was built in the early second century C.E. Its monumental exterior—once covered with a veneer of white marble and bronze—features a portico with eight Corinthian columns originally elevated by a flight of stairs that now lie

---

90	a system of aqueducts provide water for the city of Rome
122	in Roman Britain, the emperor Hadrian begins construction of a wall to protect against invasion from the North
140	the Alexandrian astronomer Ptolemy produces the *Almagest*, which posits a geocentric (earth-centered) universe (and becomes the basis for Western astronomy for centuries)
160	Claudius Galen writes over 100 medical treatises (despite errors, they became the basis for Western medical practice for centuries)

The sheer magnitude of such Roman amphitheaters as the Circus Maximus, which seated 200,000 spectators (Figure **6.7**, foreground) and the Colosseum, which covered six acres and accommodated fifty thousand (Figure **6.8**), is a reminder that during the first century C.E., Rome's population exceeded one million people, many of whom were the impoverished recipients of relief in the form of wheat and free entertainment, hence "bread and circuses." The Roman amphitheaters testify to the popular taste for entertainments that included chariot races, mock sea battles, gladiatorial contests, and a variety of violent and brutal blood sports. At the Colosseum, three levels of seating rose above the arena floor. Beneath the floor was a complex of rooms and tunnels from which athletes, gladiators, and wild animals emerged to entertain the cheering

Figure 6.9 Outer wall of the Colosseum, Rome, 70–82 C.E. Photo: A F Kersting, London.

Figure 6.10 Giovanni Paolo Panini, *The Interior of the Pantheon*, ca. 1734–1735. Oil on canvas, 4 ft. 2½ in. × 3 ft. 3 in. National Gallery of Art, Washington, D.C. Samuel H. Kress Collection.

Figure 6.11 The Pantheon, Rome, ca. 118–125 C.E. Photo: R. Liebermann.

buried beneath the city street (Figure **6.11**). One of the few buildings from Classical Antiquity to have remained almost intact, the Pantheon boasts a nineteen-foot-thick rotunda that is capped by a solid dome consisting of five thousand tons of concrete (Figure **6.12**). The interior of the dome, once painted blue and gold to resemble the vault of heaven, is pierced by a 30-foot-wide *oculus*, or "eye," that invites light and air (Figure **6.10**). The proportions of the Pantheon observe the classical principles of symmetry and harmony as described by Vitruvius (see Reading 1.18): The height from the floor to the apex of the dome (143 feet) equals the diameter of the rotunda. The Pantheon has inspired more works of architecture than any other monument in Greco-Roman history. It

Figure 6.12 Plan and section of the Pantheon (after Sir Banister Fletcher). From Horst de la Croix and Richard Tansey, *Art Through the Ages*, sixth edition, © 1975 by Harcourt Brace Jovanovich, Inc., reprinted by permission of the publisher.

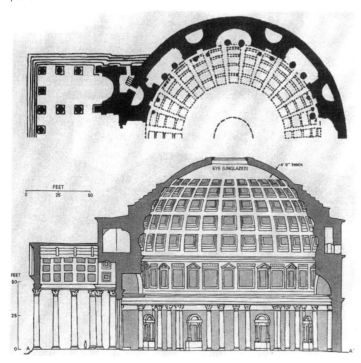

Figure 6.13 Thomas Jefferson, The Rotunda, University of Virginia, Charlottesville, Virginia, 1822–1826. Photo: Virginia State Library, Richmond.

awed and delighted such eminent late eighteenth-century neoclassicists as Thomas Jefferson, who used it as the model for many architectural designs, including that of the Rotunda of the University of Virginia (Figure **6.13**).

The Pantheon is distinctly Roman in spirit; however, other Roman buildings imitated Greek models. The temple in Nîmes, France, for instance, known as the Maison Carrée, stands like a miniature Greek shrine atop a high podium (Figure **6.14**). A stairway and a colonnaded portico accentuate the single entranceway and give the building a frontal "focus" usually lacking in Greek temples. The Corinthian order (see Figure 5.17) appears in the portico, and engaged columns adorn the exterior wall.

The epitome of classical refinement, the Maison Carrée inspired numerous European and American copies. Indeed, the Virginia State Capitol, designed by Thomas Jefferson, offers clear evidence of the use of classical models to convey the dignity, stability, and authority that neoclassicists associated with the world of Greece and Rome.

If temples such as the Pantheon and the Maison Carrée answered the spiritual needs of the Romans, the baths, such as those named for the Emperor Caracalla, satisfied some of their temporal requirements (Figure **6.15**). Elaborate structures fed by natural hot springs (Figure **6.16**), the baths provided a welcome refuge from the noise and grime of the city streets. In addition to rooms in which pools of water were heated to varying degrees, such spas often included steam rooms, exercise rooms, art galleries, shops, cafés, reading rooms, and chambers for physical intimacy. Though most baths had separate women's quarters, many permitted mixed bathing. The popularity of the baths is reflected in the fact that by the third century C.E., there were more than 900 of them in the city of Rome.

Figure 6.14 (above) Maison Carrée, Nîmes, France, ca. 19 B.C.E. Photo: Paul M. R. Maeyaert, Belgium.

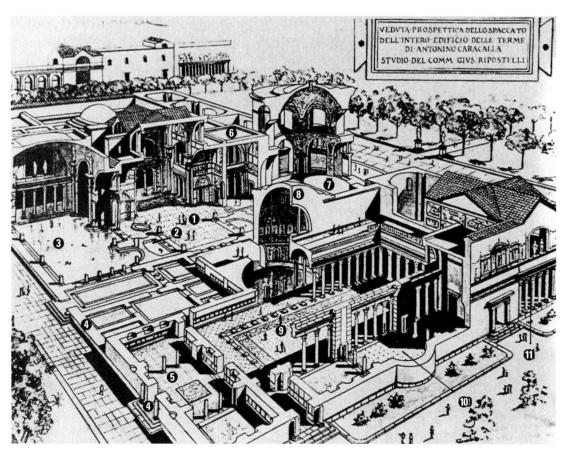

Figure 6.15
Restoration of the Baths of Caracalla in Rome, 211–217 C.E.

 1 Great Hall
 2 Oval pools (cool baths)
 3 Swimming pool
 4 Entrance
 5 Vestibule
 6 Heated rooms
 7 Hot baths
 8 Steam baths
 9 Colonnaded court
10 Lecture halls
11 Lounges.

Engraving. The Bettmann Archive.

Figure 6.16 Great Bath, Roman bath complex, Bath, England, 54 C.E. Part of the finest group of Roman remains in England, this sumptuous pool is still fed by natural hot springs. Photo: Spectrum Picture Library, London.

The Roman baths centered on a **basilica**, a rectangular colonnaded hall commonly used for public assemblies. The basilica was the ideal structure for courts of law, meeting halls, and marketplaces. The huge meeting hall known as the Basilica of Maxentius consisted of a three-hundred-foot-long central nave, four side aisles, and a semicircular recess called an **apse** (Figure **6.17**). The Roman basilica might be roofed by wooden beams or—as in the case of the Basilica of Maxentius (Figure **6.18**)—by gigantic stone vaults. Completed by the Emperor Constantine in the fourth century C.E., these enormous vaults rested on brick-faced concrete walls some twenty feet thick. In floor plan and construction features, the Roman basilica became the model for the early Christian Church in the West.

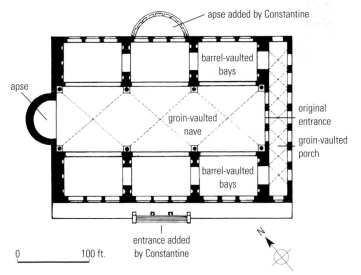

Figure 6.17 (right) Plan of the Basilica of Maxentius and Constantine.

Figure 6.18 Basilica of Maxentius, Rome, begun 306–310 C.E., completed by Constantine after 313 C.E. Scala/Art Resource, New York.

Roman Sculpture

Like its imperialistic predecessors, Rome advertised its military achievements in monumental, public works of art. These consisted mainly of triumphal arches and victory columns, which, like the obelisks of Egyptian pharaohs, commemorated the conquests of strong rulers. The 100-foot-tall marble column erected in 113 C.E. by Emperor Trajan to document his victory over the Dacians includes 2500 figures—a huge picture scroll carved in brilliant low relief (Figures **6.19** and **6.21**). Some sixty triumphal arches in Rome—and many more throughout the Empire—bear further witness to the grandeur of the Roman world-state. A typical example is the Arch of Titus in Rome, erected to immortalize that emperor's conquest of Jerusalem in 70 C.E. (Figure **6.20**). The marble-faced concrete vault of the arch is elevated between two massive piers that bear engaged Corinthian columns and an **attic** or superstructure carrying a commemorative inscription.

Figure 6.20 Arch of Titus, Rome, ca. 81 C.E. Marble, height approx. 50 ft., width approx. 40 ft. Photo: Scala.

Figure 6.19 Trajan's Victory Column, Rome, C.E. 113. Marble, height (with base) 125 ft. Photo: Scala/Florence.

Narrative relief panels on the interior sides of the vault depict a typical Roman triumphal procession: It celebrates the destruction of Jerusalem and the pillage of the Temple of Solomon (Figure **6.22**). Crowned with laurel wreaths of victory, Roman soldiers march through a city gate carrying the menorah and other spoils of victory. Subtly carved in various depths from low to high relief, the scene evokes the illusion of deep space. Even in its damaged state, *The Spoils of Jerusalem* remains a vivid record of conquest and triumph. It is the product of an age that depended on realistic narrative relief—as we today depend on photography and film—to document (and immortalize) key historical events.

While triumphal arches served as visual propaganda for Rome's military exploits, monumental sculpture glorified Roman rulers. The statue of Augustus from Primaporta (see Figure 6.3), is one of the best examples of Roman heroic portraiture. It exemplifies the classical synthesis of realistic detail (most evident in the treatment of the breastplate and toga) and the idealized form (obviously in the handsome face and canonic proportions) that dominated official Roman art, including that found on Rome's mass-produced coins.

During the second century C.E., the tradition of heroic portraiture assumed an even more magisterial stamp in the image of the ruler on horseback: the **equestrian** statue

Figure 6.21 Detail from Trajan's Victory Column, Rome 113 C.E. Marble. Photo: Scala/Florence.

Figure 6.22 Spoils from the Temple in Jerusalem. Relief from the Arch of Titus, Rome, ca. 81 C.E. Marble, height approx. 7 ft. Alinari/Art Resource, New York.

(Figure **6.23**). The equestrian portrait of the Roman Emperor Marcus Aurelius depicts the general addressing his troops with the traditional gesture of imperial authority. The body of a conquered warrior once lay under the raised right hoof of the spirited charger, whose veins and muscles seem to burst from beneath his bronze skin.

While the public portrayal of the ruler usually demanded a degree of flattering idealization, images intended for private use invited realistic detail. The Roman taste for realism is perhaps best illustrated in the three-dimensional portraits of Roman men and women, often members of the ruling class or wealthy patricians. In contrast to the idealized portraits of Golden Age Greece (see Figure 4.9), many Roman likenesses reflect obsessive fidelity to nature. So true to life seem some Roman portrait heads that scholars suspect they may have been executed from wax death masks. Roman portrait sculpture tends to reflect the personality and character of the sitter, a fact perhaps related to the ancient custom of honoring the "genius" or in-dwelling spirit of the dead ancestor. The lifelike portrait bust of Julius Caesar, carved in green slate with inset crystal eyes, captures the spirit of resolute determination (see Figure 6.2). It is the record of a particular person at a particular time in his life; as such it conveys a degree of psychological realism absent from most classical Greek portraits. In that portrait sculpture served much as our photographs do today—as physical reminders of favorite relatives and friends—the emphasis on realism is understandable. The balding patrician who carries two portrait busts of his ancestors (Figure **6.24**) reminds us that the Roman family placed extraordinary emphasis on its lineage and honored the father of the family (*paterfamilias*) no

Figure 6.23 Equestrian statue of Marcus Aurelius, ca. 173 C.E. Bronze, height 16 ft. 8 in. Piazza del Campidoglio, Rome. Photo: The Ancient Art and Architecture Collection, London.

less devotedly than did the ancient Chinese. Such intimate sculptured likenesses of the deceased would have been displayed and venerated at special altars and shrines within the Roman home. Finally, the portrait of the square-jawed aristocratic woman, whose wig or hairdo surely required the fastidious application of the curling

Figure 6.24 Roman aristocrat holding portrait busts of his ancestors, late first century B.C.E. Marble, Museo Capitolino, Rome. Photo: Araldo de Luca.

Figure 6.25 Flavian Woman, ca. 89 C.E. Marble, life-size. Museo Capitolino, Rome.

iron, discloses the proud confidence of a Roman matron (Figure **6.25**). Whether cast in bronze, or carved in marble, slate, or terra-cotta, these psychologically penetrating studies are often as unflattering as they are honest. In their lack of idealization and their affection for literal detail, they are representative of Roman sculpture as a record of commonplace reality.

Roman Painting

A similar taste for realism appears in the frescoes with which the Romans decorated their meeting halls, baths, and country villas. Possibly inspired by Greek murals, of which only a few examples survive, Roman artists painted scenes drawn from literature, mythology, and everyday life. Among the finest examples of Roman frescoes are those found in and around Pompeii and Herculaneum, two southern Italian cities that attracted a population of wealthy Romans. But even in the outer reaches of the empire, such as at Zeugma in modern Turkey (uncovered as recently as 1992), the Roman taste for visual representation is evident in magnificently decorated palatial villas, a legacy soon to be submerged in the waters of an urgently needed hydroelectric dam. Pompeii and Herculaneum remain the showcases of Roman suburban life: Both cities were engulfed and destroyed by a mountain of ash from the volcanic eruption of Mount Vesuvius of 79 C.E., but the lava from the disaster preserved many of the area's suburban homes. These residential villas, constructed around an **atrium** (a large central hall open to the sky), are valuable sources of information concerning the lifestyles of upper-class Romans (Figure **6.27**).

At a villa in Boscoreale, about a mile north of Pompeii, floor surfaces display fine, ornamental motifs and scenes illustrated in **mosaic**, a technique by which small pieces of stone or glass are embedded into wet cement surfaces. The walls of many rooms are painted with frescoes designed to give viewers the impression that they are looking out upon gardens and distant buildings (Figure **6.26**). Such illusionism is a kind of visual artifice known by the French phrase *trompe l'oeil* ("fool the eye"). Designed to deceive the eye, they reveal the artist's competence in mastering *empirical perspective*, the technique of achieving a sense of three-dimensional space on a two-dimensional

surface. Other devices, such as light and shade, are also employed to seduce the eye into believing it perceives real objects in deep space: In the extraordinary *Still Life With Eggs and Thrushes*, for instance, one of a series of frescoes celebrating food and found in a villa at Pompeii, light seems to bounce off the metal pitcher, whose shiny surface contrasts with the densely textured towel and the ceramic plate holding ten lifelike eggs (Figure **6.28**). Roman artists integrated illusionistic devices in ways that would not be seen again in Western art for a thousand years (see chapter 23).

The invention of still life as an independent genre (or type) of art confirmed the Roman fondness for the tangible things of the material world. Similarly, their affection for nature led them to pioneer the genre of landscape painting. First-century-B.C.E. frescoes illustrating the adventures of the Greek hero Odysseus feature spacious

Figure 6.26 Bedroom from the Villa of P. Fannius Synistor, Boscoreale, first century B.C.E. Mosaic floor, couch, and footstool come from other Roman villas of later date. Fresco on lime plaster, 8 ft. 8½ in. × 19 ft. 1⅛ in. × 10 ft. 11½ in. The Metropolitan Museum of Art, New York, Rogers Fund, 1903 (03.14.13). Photo: Schecter Lee.

landscapes filled with rocky plains, feathery trees, animals, and people (Figure 6.29). Bathed in light and shade, the naturalistically modeled figures cast shadows to indicate their physical presence in atmospheric space. Evident in these Roman landscapes is a deep affection for the countryside and for the pleasures of nature. Arcadia, the mountainous region in the central Peloponnesus inhabited by the peaceloving shepherds and nymphs of ancient Greek legend, provided the model for the classical landscape, which celebrated (as did Greek and Latin **pastoral** poetry) a life of innocence and simplicity. The glorification of bucolic freedom—the "Arcadian Myth"—reflected the Roman disenchantment with city life. The theme was to reappear frequently in the arts of the West, especially during periods of rising urbanization.

Figure 6.28 *Still Life with Eggs and Thrushes*, from the House (or Villa) of Julia Felix, Pompeii, before 79 C.E. Fresco, 35 in. × 48 in. Photo: Fotografic Foglia, Naples.

Figure 6.29 Ulysses in the Land of the Lestrygonians, part of the Odyssey Landscapes, second-style ("architectural") wall-painting from a house in Rome, late first century B.C.E. Height approx. 5 ft. Vatican Library, Rome.

Roman Music

While Roman civilization left abundant visual and literary resources, the absence of surviving examples in music make it almost impossible to evaluate the Roman contribution in this domain. Passages from the writings of Roman historians suggest that Roman music theory was adopted from the Greeks, as were most Roman instruments. In drama, musical interludes replaced the Greek choral odes, a change that suggests the growing distance between drama and its ancient ritual function. Music was, however, essential to most forms of public entertainment and also played an important role in military life; for the latter, the Romans developed brass instruments, such as trumpets and horns, and drums for military processions.

SUMMARY

A genius for practical organization marked all aspects of Roman history. From its Latin beginnings, Rome showed an extraordinary talent for adopting and adapting the best of other cultures: Etruscan and Greek. Although the Roman Republic engaged all citizens in government, power rested largely with the wealthy and influential patri-

cian class. As Rome built an empire and assumed mastery of the civilized world, the Republic fell increasingly into the hands of military dictators, the greatest of whom was Julius Caesar. Caesar's heir, the emperor Octavian, ushered in the *Pax Romana*, a time of peace and high cultural productivity.

The Romans produced no original philosophy but cultivated Hellenistic schools of thought such as Stoicism. Roman literature manifests a practical bias for factual information. The Romans gave the world its first encyclopedias, as well as memorable biographies, essays, speeches, histories, and letters. The high moral tone and lucid prose of Cicero and Tacitus characterize Roman writing at its best. In poetry, Virgil paid homage to the Roman state in the *Aeneid*, Catullus sang of love and loss, while Horace and Juvenal offered a critical view of Roman life in satiric verse, the genre that constitutes Rome's most original contribution to literature.

Rome's most enduring accomplishments lay in the practical areas of law, language, and political life. However, Rome's architectural and engineering projects, which engaged the inventive use of the arch and the techniques of concrete and brick construction, exercised an equally important influence on subsequent civilizations in the West. To the classical style in architecture, the Romans contributed domed and stone-vaulted types of construction that enclosed vast areas of space. Rome borrowed Hellenic models in all of the arts, but the Roman taste for realism dominated narrative relief sculpture, portrait busts, and fresco painting. These genres disclose a love for literal truth that contrasts sharply with the Hellenic effort to generalize and idealize form.

For almost a thousand years, the Romans held together a geographically and ethnically diverse realm, providing a large population with such a high quality of life as to move future generations to envy and praise. The Roman contribution is imprinted on the language, laws, and architecture of the West. By its preservation and transmission of the classical legacy, Rome's influence on the humanistic tradition was felt long after Roman glory and might had faded.

Suggestions for Reading

Bradley, K. R. *Slaves and Masters in the Roman Empire*. Berkeley, Calif.: University of California Press, 1987.

Christ, Karl. *The Romans: An Introduction to Their History and Civilization*. Berkeley, Calif.: University of California Press, 1984.

D'Ambra, Eve. *Roman Painting*. New York: Cambridge University Press, 1999.

Fantham, Elaine. *Roman Literary Culture: From Cicero to Apuleius*. Baltimore, Md.: Johns Hopkins University Press, 1999.

Galinsky, Karl. *Augustan Culture: An Interpretive Introduction*. Princeton: Princeton University Press, 1996.

Hooper, Finley. *Roman Realities*. Detroit: Wayne State University Press, 1980.

Jones, P. V. and K. Sidwell, eds. *The World of Rome: An Introduction to Roman Culture*. New York: Cambridge University Press, 1997.

Kebric, Robert B. *Roman People*. Mountain View, Calif.: Mayfield, 1997.

Kleiner, Diana E. E. *Roman Sculpture*. New Haven, Conn.: Yale University Press, 1992.

Klingaman, William K. *The First Century: Emperors, Gods, and Everyman*. New York: Harper, 1986.

L'Orange, H. P. *The Roman Empire: Art Forms and Civic Life*. New York: Rizzoli, 1985.

Strong, Donald. *Roman Art: The Yale University Press Pelican History of Art*, 3rd edition. New Haven, Conn.: Yale University Press, 1992.

Zanker, Paul. *The Power of Images in the Age of Augustus*. Ann Arbor: University of Michigan Press, 1988.

GLOSSARY

apse a vaulted semicircular recess at one or both ends of a basilica

atrium the inner courtyard of a Roman house, usually colonnaded and open to the sky

attic the superstructure or low upper story above the main order of a facade

basilica a large, colonnaded hall commonly used for public assemblies, law courts, baths, and marketplaces

eclogue a pastoral poem, usually involving shepherds in an idyllic rural setting

epistle a formal letter

equestrian mounted on horseback

imperium (Latin, "command," "empire") the civil and military authority exercised by the rulers of ancient Rome (and the root of the English words "imperialism" and "empire"); symbolized in ancient Rome by an eagle-headed scepter and the *fasces*, an ax bound in a bundle of rods

mosaic a medium by which small pieces of glass or stone are embedded in wet cement on wall and floor surfaces; any picture or pattern made in this manner

oratory the art of public speaking

pastoral pertaining to the country, to shepherds, and the simple rural life; also, any work of art presenting an idealized picture of country life

res publica (Latin, "of the people") a government in which power resides in citizens entitled to vote and is exercised by representatives responsible to them and to a body of law

sarcophagus (plural, **sarcophagi**) a stone coffin

satire a literary genre that ridicules or pokes fun at human vices and follies

trompe l'oeil (French, "fool the eye") a form of illusionistic painting that tries to convince the viewer that the image is real and not painted

vault a roof or ceiling constructed on the arch principle (see Figure 6.5)

CHAPTER SEVEN

China: the rise to empire

"He who learns but does not think is lost.
He who thinks but does not learn is in great danger."
Confucius

In the thousand year period during which Greco-Roman civilization established itself throughout the Mediterranean—roughly 500 B.C.E. to 500 C.E.—the civilizations of China and India produced cultures that were both definitive and enduring, hence "classical." China and India each generated a body of learning and an artistic heritage that have served for centuries as models for other East Asian cultures. As with the civilizations of ancient Greece and Rome, those of China and India have left legacies that reach beyond the East to embellish the larger humanistic tradition. In this chapter, however, Classical China receives our exclusive attention, primarily because the culture of classical China, as well as China's rise to empire, offer intriguing parallels with the histories of ancient Greece and Rome. The central features of India's classical history—the birth of Buddhism and the revival of Hindu culture—are surveyed elsewhere in this series (see chapters 8, 9, and 14).

Confucius and the Classics

After 771 B.C.E., as warring rebels competed for political power, the Zhou dynasty, which had ruled since 1027 B.C.E., slowly disintegrated. But in the waning years of the Zhou, trade and urban life continued to flourish, and China developed some of her most significant and lasting material and philosophic traditions. Chopsticks, cast iron, square-holed coins, and finely lacquered objects were all developed during the sixth century B.C.E. At the same time, and parallel with (but totally independent of) the rise of philosophic thought in Greece, China experienced a burst of intellectual creativity: China's classical texts date from this period, and with them came the formulation of some of China's oldest moral and religious precepts. As we saw in chapter 3, the ancient Chinese regarded the natural order as the basis for spiritual life, political stability (witness the Mandate of Heaven), and the social order. To know one's place within the order and to act

accordingly were essential to the well-being of both the individual and the community. The Chinese describe this ethical imperative with the word *li*, which translates variously as "propriety," "ritual," and "arrangement." The original meaning of the word *li* is found in the act of ritual sacrifice, that is, the proper performance of traditional Chinese rites. But by the middle of the Zhou era, *li* had come to refer to the pattern or principles governing appropriate behavior, or action in conformity with the rules of decorum and propriety. Formative in the evolution of this concept were the teachings of the philosopher Kong-fuzi (551–479 B.C.E.), better known as Confucius, a Latinization of his Chinese name. Confucius was China's most notable thinker. According to tradition, he was as well the compiler and editor of the five Chinese classics (Figure 7.1). A self-educated man, who served as a local administrator, Confucius pursued the career of a teacher and social reformer. Like his Greek contemporary, Socrates, he himself wrote nothing. He earned renown through the force of his teachings, which his disciples

---

The Five Chinese Classics*

1 *The Book of Changes* (*I jing*)—a text for divination
2 *The Book of History* (*Shu jing*)—government records: speeches, reports, and announcements by rulers and ministers of ancient China
3 *The Book of Songs* (*Shi jing*)—an anthology of some 300 poems: folk songs, ceremonial and secular poems
4 *The Book of Rites* (*Li chi*)—a collection of texts centering on rules of conduct for everyday life
5 *The Spring and Autumn Annals* (*Chun-chiu*)—commentaries that chronicle events up to the fifth century B.C.E.

*A sixth classic, on music, is no longer in existence

Figure 7.1 The Five Chinese Classics.

transcribed after his death. This collection of writings came to be known as the *Analects*. As eclectic in their origins and dating as the Hebrew Bible, the *Analects* embody the words of Confucius on matters as diverse as music, marriage, and death. But they center on questions of conduct: the proper behavior of the individual in the society at large. They articulate the ancient Chinese conviction that human beings must heed a moral order that is fixed in nature, not in divine pronouncement (see chapter 3). Confucius confidently maintained that human character, not birth, determined the worth and status of the individual. He had little to say about gods and spirits; nor did he pursue ultimate truth (in the manner of the Greek philosophers). Rather, he taught the importance of tradition, filial piety (respect for one's elders), and the exercise of *li*. In doing so, he formulated the first expression of the so-called "Golden Rule:" "What you do not wish for yourself, do not do to others."

The teachings of Confucius preserved social and political ideas as old as the Shang and Zhou dynasties. In that Confucius lived during the turbulent years just prior to the collapse of the Zhou and the era of the Warring States (403–221 B.C.E.), he may have sought to insure the survival of traditional values and ideals. Basic to these was the notion that the ruler was the parent of the people. The cultivation of character and the successful regulation of the family preceded the ruler's ability to govern. The good influence and high moral status of the ruler—a figure much like Plato's philosopher-king—was of greater political value than physical force or the threat of punishment. If a ruler was not himself virtuous, he could not expect to inspire virtue among his subjects. For Confucius, as for Plato, moral and political life were one. Moral harmony was the root of political harmony, and moral rectitude made government all but unnecessary. Such precepts were basic to humanist thought in China for well over 2000 years.

READING 1.29 From the *Analects* of Confucius

2.1 The Master said: "He who rules by virtue is like the polestar, which remains unmoving in its mansion while all the other stars revolve respectfully around it."

2.2 The Master said: "The three hundred *Poems* are summed up in one single phrase: 'Think no evil.' "

2.3 The Master said: "Lead them by political maneuvers, restrain them with punishments: the people will become cunning and shameless. Lead them by virtue, restrain them with ritual: they will develop a sense of shame and a sense of participation."

2.13 Zigong asked about the true gentleman. The Master said: "He preaches only what he practices."

2.14 The Master said: "The gentleman considers the whole rather than the parts. The small man considers the parts rather than the whole."

2.15 The Master said: "To study without thinking is futile. To think without studying is dangerous."

2.17 The Master said: "Zilu, I am going to teach you what knowledge is. To take what you know for what you know, and what you do not know for what you do not know, that is knowledge indeed."

2.20 Lord Ji Kang asked: "What should I do in order to make the people respectful, loyal, and zealous?" The Master said: "Approach them with dignity and they will be respectful. Be yourself a good son and a kind father, and they will be loyal. Raise the good and train the incompetent, and they will be zealous."

2.24 The Master said: "To worship gods that are not yours, that is toadyism. Not to act when justice commands, that is cowardice."

4.7 The Master said: "Your faults define you. From your very faults one can know your quality."

4.11 The Master said: "A gentleman seeks virtue; a small man seeks land. A gentleman seeks justice; a small man seeks favors."

4.14 The Master said: "Do not worry if you are without a position; worry lest you do not deserve a position. Do not worry if you are not famous; worry lest you do not deserve to be famous."

4.16 The Master said: "A gentleman considers what is just; a small man considers what is expedient."

4.17 The Master said: "When you see a worthy man, seek to emulate him. When you see an unworthy man, examine yourself."

4.19 The Master said: "While your parents are alive, do not travel afar. If you have to travel, you must leave an address."

4.21 The Master said: "Always keep in mind the age of your parents. Let this thought be both your joy and your worry."

4.24 The Master said: "A gentleman should be slow to speak and prompt to act."

12.16 The Master said: "A gentleman brings out the good that is in people, he does not bring out the bad. A vulgar man does the opposite."

12.21 Fan Chi was taking a walk with Confucius under the Rain Dance Terrace. He said: "May I ask how one can accumulate moral power, neutralize hostility, and recognize emotional incoherence?" The Master said: "Excellent question! Always put the effort before the reward: is this not the way to accumulate moral power? To attack evil in itself and not the evil that is in people: is this not the way to neutralize hostility? To endanger oneself and one's kin in a sudden fit of anger: is this not an instance of incoherence?"

15.6 Zizhang asked about conduct. The Master said: "Speak with loyalty and good faith, act with dedication and deference, and even among the barbarians your conduct will be irreproachable. If you speak without loyalty and good faith, if you act without dedication or deference, your conduct will be unacceptable, even in your own village. Wherever you stand, you should have this precept always in front of your eyes; have it carved upon the yoke of your chariot, and only then will you be able to move ahead." Zizhang wrote it on his sash.

15.8 The Master said: "When dealing with a man who is capable of understanding your teaching, if you do not teach him, you waste the man. When dealing with a man who is incapable of understanding your teaching, if you do teach him, you waste your teaching. A wise teacher wastes no man and wastes no teaching."

15.9 The Master said: "A righteous man, a man attached to humanity, does not seek life at the expense of his humanity; there are instances where he will give his life in order to fulfill his humanity."

15.12 The Master said: "A man with no concern for the future is bound to worry about the present."

15.13 The Master said: "The fact remains that I have never seen a man who loved virtue as much as sex."

15.15 The Master said: "Demand much from yourself, little from others, and you will prevent discontent."

15.18 The Master said: "A gentleman takes justice as his basis, enacts it in conformity with the ritual, expounds it with modesty, and through good faith, brings it to fruition. This is how a gentleman proceeds."

15.19 The Master said: "A gentleman resents his incompetence; he does not resent his obscurity."

15.20 The Master said: "A gentleman worries lest he might disappear from this world without having made a name for himself."

15.21 The Master said: "A gentleman makes demands on himself; a vulgar man makes demands on others."

15.24 Zigong asked: "Is there any single word that could guide one's entire life?" The Master said: "Should it not be *reciprocity*? What you do not wish for yourself, do not do to others."

Confucianism and Legalism

The two centuries following the death of Confucius marked an era of turbulence and social upheaval inflicted by the armies of China's warring states. But during that time (and perhaps because of its instability) there emerged competing schools of thought on questions concerning human nature and, by extension, the ideal form of government. Such speculation took place among the class of China's scholars, who, much like the Hellenic Aristotle, took a practical approach to the investigation of morality. Mencius (372–289 B.C.E.), China's most significant voice after Confucius, expanded Confucian concepts of government as a civilizing force and the ruler as the moral model. Mencius held that human beings are born good; they fall into evil only by neglect or abuse. In defining human nature, Mencius insisted:

The tendency of human nature to do good is like that of water to flow downward. There is no man who does not tend to do good; there is not water that does not flow downward. Now you may strike water and make it splash over your forehead, or you may even force it up the hills. But is this in the nature of water? It is of course due to the force of circumstances. Similarly, man may be brought to do evil, and that is because the same is done to his nature.*

Based on this view of humankind, Mencius envisioned the state as an agent for cultivating the goodness of the individual.

An opposing body of thought challenged this point of view. In contrast to the Confucians, who generally perceived humankind as good, those who came to be called Legalists described the nature of humankind as inherently evil. From this negative premise, the Legalists concluded that the best state was one in which rulers held absolute authority to uphold (strict) laws and dole out punishment to violators. The leading Legalist, Han Fei Zi (?–233 B.C.E.), argued that the rationality of an adult was no more reliable than that of an infant. The innate selfishness of humankind justified strong central authority and harsh punishment. "Now take a young fellow who is a bad character," he writes:

His parents may get angry at him, but he never makes any change. The villagers may reprove him, but he is not moved. His teachers and elders may admonish him, but he never reforms. The love of his parents, the efforts of the villagers, and the wisdom of his teachers and elders . . . are applied to him, and yet not even a hair on his chin is altered. It is only after the district magistrate sends out his soldiers and in the name of the law searches for wicked individuals that the young man becomes afraid and changes his ways and alters his deeds. So while the love of parents is not sufficient to discipline the children, the severe penalties of the district magistrate are. This is because men become naturally spoiled by love, but are submissive to authority.**

The Legalism of Han Fei would become the fundamental philosophy of China's first empire.

Sources of Chinese Tradition, compiled by Wm. Theodore de Bary and others (New York: Columbia University Press, 1960), 103.
**Sources of Chinese Tradition*, compiled by Wm. Theodore de Bary and others (New York: Columbia University Press, 1960), 146–147.

The Chinese Rise to Empire

The Qin Dynasty (221–206 B.C.E.)

Even as the great Roman *imperium* came to dominate the Western world, a comparable empire arose on the eastern end of the vast Asian landmass. The first great period of unity in China came about under the Qin (pronounced "chin"), the dynasty from which the English word "China" is derived. Like the kings of ancient China, Qin rulers held absolute responsibility for maintaining order and harmony. As with the history of imperial Rome, the Qin rise to power followed almost two hundred years of warfare, and its founders were resolved to eliminate the possibility of further conflict. They therefore forced the nobility to give up their lands and relocated them to the capital at Xian.

They then took over their lands and organized China into a network of provinces and districts governed by non-hereditary officials. By way of these governors, the Qin enforced the laws, collected taxes, and drafted men to defend the newly annexed regions.

Having defeated all rival states, in 221 B.C.E. the Qin prince Shih Huang Ti (ca. 259–210 B.C.E.) declared himself "First Emperor". The First Emperor appointed a large, salaried bureaucracy that worked to centralize political power by various administrative devices. These included a census of China's population (the first of its kind in world history), the standardization of the written Chinese language, the creation of uniform coinage, as well as a system of weights and measures, and the division of China into provinces that exist to this day. In a practical move worthy of the Romans, the First Emperor standardized the width of all axles manufactured for Chinese wagons, so that the wagons would fit the existing ruts in Chinese roads (thus speeding travel and trade). Royal promotion of the silk industry attracted long-distance merchants and brought increasing wealth to China. While imperial policies fostered the private ownership of land by peasant farmers, the new system permitted the governors to tax those farmers, which they did mercilessly. Peasant protest was a constant threat to imperial power, but the most serious challenge to Qin safety came from the repeated invasions by the nomadic Central Asian Huns along China's northern borders. To discourage invasion, the Qin commissioned the construction (and in some stretches the reconstruction) of the 1,500-mile-long Great Wall of China (Figure 7.2). This spectacular engineering feat is often compared with the wall built by the Roman Emperor Hadrian: Hadrian's Wall, only 73 miles

Figure 7.2 The Great Wall, near Beijing, China, begun third century B.C.E. Length approx. 1500 miles, height and width approx. 25 ft. This photo shows watch towers placed strategically along the wall. Photo: Spectrum, London.

Figure 7.3 Terra-cotta army of soldiers, horses, and chariots, tomb of the First Emperor of the Qin Dynasty, 221–207 B.C.E. Spectrum Picture Library, London.

long, would be raised in the early second century in an effort to deter barbarian attacks on Roman Britain's northernmost border. Like Hadrian's Wall, the Great Wall of China would not stop an army on foot, but rather, discouraged mounted men, wagons, and the like from making raids across the borders.

The building of the Great Wall required the labor of some 700,000 people. An equal number of workers is said to have labored for over fifteen years on the Emperor's tomb. The entrance to that tomb, part of a twenty-one-square-mile burial site near the Qin capital at Xian, provides an immortal record of the Qin military machine. It contains almost 8,000 life-sized **terra-cotta** soldiers, most of which are armed with actual swords, spears, and crossbows (Figure 7.3). Standing at strict attention, the huge army of footsoldiers and cavalry guards the tomb itself, which has not yet been opened. These figures may have served to replace the living sacrifices that went to the grave with earlier Chinese kings (see chapter 3). The bodies of the ceramic warriors seem to have been mass-produced from molds, but the faces, no two of which are exactly alike, were individually carved and painted (Figure 7.4). In their lifelike intensity, these images resemble Roman portrait busts (see Figure 6.2). Yet the portraits of Rome were created for the appreciation of the living,

- **−350** Shin Shen completes a catalogue of some 800 stars
- **−300** cast iron is produced in China
- **−250** the crossbow is invented in China
- **−214** the First Emperor orders the construction of the Great Wall (which is not completed until the seventeenth century)

while those of Qin China were intended for the dead. Nevertheless, the subterranean legions of the First Emperor glorify an armed force that the Romans might have envied.

Legalist theory provided justification for the stringency of the law under the Qin, as well as for the civil and political oppressiveness of imperial authority. The Legalist First Emperor so feared public opposition and the free exercise of thought that he required all privately owned copies of the Confucian classics burned and all who opposed his government beheaded, along with their families. On the other hand, they were loyal students of the *Sun Zi* (*The Art of War*), the world's first treatise on military strategy. This anonymous military classic, dating from the era of the

Figure 7.4 Two terra-cotta soldiers, tomb of the First Emperor of the Qin Dynasty, 221–207 B.C.E. Height 75.5 in. and 48 in. Photo: Dagli Orti, Paris.

Warring States, emphasized the tactical, as well as the strategic and psychological aspects of combat.

The Han Dynasty (206 B.C.E.–220 C.E.)

The Qin dynasty lasted only fifteen years, but under the leadership of succeeding dynasties, China's empire would last more than four centuries. Just as the Roman Empire marked the culmination of classical civilization in the West, so the Han Dynasty represented the high point and the classical phase of Chinese civilization. The intellectual and cultural achievements of the Han, which would remain in place for 2,000 years, made an indelible mark on the history of neighboring Korea, Vietnam, and Japan, whose cultures adopted Chinese methods of writing and the Confucian precepts of filial piety and propriety. The Chinese have long regarded the era of the Han as their classical age, and to this day refer to themselves as the "children of the Han." Han intellectual achievements ranged from the literary and artistic to the domains of **cartography**, medicine, mathematics, and astronomy. The invention of paper, block printing, the seismograph, the

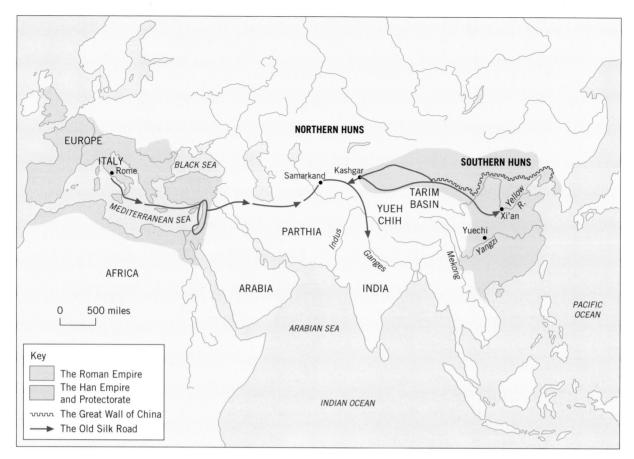

Map 7.1 Han and Roman Empires

horse collar, and the wheelbarrow are but a few of the technological advances of the late Han era.

Han rulers tripled the size of the empire they inherited from the Qin. At its height, the Han empire was roughly equivalent to that of Rome in power and prestige, but larger in actual population—a total of 57 million people, according to the census of 2 C.E. (Map **7.1**). Improvements in farming and advances in technology insured economic prosperity, which in turn stimulated vigorous long-distance trade. In exchange for Western linen, wool, glass, and metalware, the Chinese exported silk, ivory, gems, and spices. Trade proceeded by way of Asian intermediaries, who led camel caravans across the vast "Silk Road" that stretched from Asia Minor to the Pacific Ocean. China traditionally scorned its merchants (whom the Chinese perceived as profiting from the labor of others) and regarded its farmers as honorable. Nevertheless, while Chinese merchants flourished, Chinese peasants failed to reap the benefits of Han prosperity. Conscripted for repeated wars, they fought the nomadic tribes along the

bitter cold northern frontier. They also served in the armies that conquered western Korea and northern Vietnam. Heavy taxes levied on Chinese farmers to support the Han machinery of state forced many to sell their lands. Wealthy landowners purchased these lands, on which (in a manner reminiscent of the late Roman republic) bankrupt farmers became tenants or unfree peasants. By the early third century, violent peasant revolts accompanied by "barbarian" incursions, led to the overthrow of the Han dynasty. Like the Roman empire, the great Han empire fell victim to internal and external pressures it could not withstand.

The Literary Contributions of Imperial China

Just as the Romans borrowed the best of the cultural achievements that preceded them, so Han rulers preserved the enduring works of their forebears. These they passed on to future generations as a body of classical learning and thought. Han rulers restored Confucianism to China, and with it came the restoration of Confucian texts and the Confucian scholar/official.

Chinese Prose Literature

As with the Greeks and the Romans, the Chinese placed high value on record-keeping. Hence, the writing of history was one of China's greatest achievements.

−150	iron wheels are designed for shaping jade and reeling silk
−110	the Chinese devise the collar harness (for horses)
−100	the Chinese invent the crank (for turning wheels)
−1	cast iron is used in Chinese suspension bridges

According to tradition, Chinese court historians kept chronicles of events as far back as one thousand years before the Han Era. Unfortunately, many of these chronicles were lost in the wars and notorious "book-burnings" of the Qin era. Beginning with the second century B.C.E., however, palace historians kept a continuous record of rulership. Ancient China's greatest historian Sima Qian (145–90 B.C.E.), the rival of both Thucydides and Livy, produced the monumental *Shih Chi (Records of the Grand Historian)*, a narrative account of Chinese history from earliest times through the lifetime of the author. Sima Qian, himself the son of a palace historian–astronomer, served at the court of the Emperor Wudi, the vigorous ruler who brought Han China to the peak of its power. On Sima's death, China's first woman historian Ban Zhao (45–114) continued his court chronicle. Ban also won fame for her handbook, *Lessons for Women*, which outlined the obligations and duties of the wife to her husband.

The following excerpt from Sima Qian's chapter on "Wealth and Commerce" offers a detailed description of the Han economy, as well as its social and moral life. Whereas economic activity follows the natural order, morals, observes the author, "come as the effects of wealth." In Sima's view, wealth and virtue are interdependent. A flourishing economy will encourage the people to be virtuous, while poverty leads inevitably to moral decay. Stylistically, Sima Qian's *Records* display the economy and vigor of expression that characterizes the finest Han prose.

READING 1.30 From Sima Qian's *Records of the Grand Historian* (ca. 100 B.C.E.)

I do not know about prehistoric times before Shennong,[1] but 1
since [Emperor Yu and the Xia dynasty, after the] twenty-second century B.C.E. during the period discussed by the historical records, human nature has always struggled for good food, dress, amusements, and physical comfort, and has always tended to be proud of wealth and ostentation. No matter how the philosophers may teach otherwise, the people cannot be changed. Therefore, the best of men leave it alone, and next in order come those who try to guide it, then those who moralize about it, and then those who try to make 10
adjustments to it, and lastly come those who get into the scramble themselves. Briefly, Shanxi produces timber, grains, linen, ox hair, and jades. Shandong produces fish, salt, lacquer, silks, and musical instruments. Jiangnan [south of the Yangzi] produces cedar, *zi* [a hard wood for making wood blocks], ginger, cinnamon, gold and tin ores, cinnabar, rhinoceros horn, tortoise shell, pearls, and hides. Longmen produces stone for tablets. The north produces horses, cattle, sheep, furs, and horns. As for copper and iron, they are often found in mountains everywhere, spread out like pawns on a 20
chessboard. These are what the people of China like and what provide the necessities for their living and for ceremonies for

the dead. The farmers produce them, the wholesalers bring them from the country, the artisans work on them, and the merchants trade on them. All this takes place without the intervention of government or of the philosophers. Everybody exerts his best and uses his labor to get what he wants. Therefore prices seek their level, cheap goods going to where they are expensive and higher prices are brought down. People follow their respective professions and do it on their own 30
initiative. It is like flowing water which seeks the lower level day and night without stop. All things are produced by the people themselves without being asked and transported to where they are wanted. Is it not true that these operations happen naturally in accord with their own principles? *The Book of Zhou*[2] says, "Without the farmers, food will not be produced; without the artisans, industry will not develop; without the merchants, the valuable goods will disappear; and without the wholesalers, there will be no capital and the natural resources of lakes and mountains will not be opened 40
up." Our food and our dress come from these four classes, and wealth and poverty vary with the size of these sources. On a larger scale, it benefits a country, and on a smaller scale, it enriches a family. These are the inescapable laws of wealth and poverty. The clever ones have enough and to spare, while the stupid ones have not enough. . . .

Therefore, first the granaries must be full before the people can talk of culture. The people must have sufficient food and good dress before they can talk of honor. The good customs and social amenities come from wealth and disappear when 50
the country is poor. Even as fish thrive in a deep lake and the beasts gravitate toward a deep jungle, so the morals of mankind come as effects of wealth. The rich acquire power and influence, while the poor are unhappy and have no place to turn to. This is even truer of the barbarians. Therefore it is said: "A wealthy man's son does not die in the market place," and it is not an empty saying. It is said:

The world hustles
    Where money beckons.
The world jostles 60
    Where profit thickens.

Even kings and dukes and the wealthy gentry worry about poverty. Why wonder that the common people and the slaves do the same? . . .

[Here follows a long section on the economic products and conditions and the people's character and way of living of the different regions.]

Therefore you see the distinguished scholars who argue at courts and temples about policies and talk about honesty and self-sacrifice, and the mountain recluses who achieve a great 70
reputation. Where do they go? They seek after the rich. The honest officials acquire wealth as time goes on, and the honest merchants become wealthier and wealthier. For wealth is something which man seeks instinctively without being taught. You see soldiers rush in front of battle and perform great exploits in a hail of arrows and rocks and against great

---

[1]A legendary cultural hero, inventor of agriculture and commerce, ca. 2737 B.C.E.

---

[2]The book of documents devoted to the Zhou Dynasty (1111–221 B.C.E.)

dangers, because there is a great reward. You see young men steal and rob and commit violence and dig up tombs for treasures, and even risk the punishments by law, throwing all considerations of their own safety to the winds—all because of money. The courtesans of Zhao and Zheng dress up and play music and wear long sleeves and pointed dancing shoes. They flirt and wink, and do not mind being called to a great distance, irrespective of the age of the men—all are attracted by the rich. The sons of the rich dress up in caps and carry swords and go about with a fleet of carriages just to show off their wealth. The hunters and the fishermen go out at night, in snow and frost, roam in the wooded valleys haunted by wild beasts, because they want to catch game. Others gamble, have cock fights, and match dogs in order to win. Physicians and magicians practice their arts in expectation of compensation for their services. Bureaucrats play hide-and-seek with the law and even commit forgery and falsify seals at the risk of penal sentences because they have received bribes. And so all farmers, artisans, and merchants and cattle raisers try to reach the same goal. Everybody knows this, and one hardly ever hears of one who works and declines pay for it. . . . 80 90

Sima Qian's narrative describes the men and women of the Han Era as practical and this-worldly, in fact, as remarkably similar to Romans. This sensibility, which unites a typically Chinese holism with sober realism, is also visible in the large body of Confucianist essays from the Han period. Of these, only one brief example may be cited, for its similarity to the rationalism of Seneca, Lucretius, and other Roman thinkers is striking. *A Discussion of Death* by Wang Chong (17–100 C.E.), offers a skeptical view of the supernaturalism that attracted the large masses of Chinese people. Wang writes,

> Before a man is born he has no consciousness, so when he dies and returns to this original unconscious state how could he still have consciousness? The reason a man is intelligent and understanding is that he possesses the forces of the five virtues [humanity, righteousness, decorum, wisdom, and faith]. The reason he possesses these is that he has within him the five organs [heart, liver, stomach, lungs, and kidneys]. If these five organs are unimpaired, a man has understanding, but if they are diseased, then he becomes vague and confused and behaves like a fool or an idiot. When a man dies, the five organs rot away and the five virtues no

longer have any place to reside. Both the seat and the faculty of understanding are destroyed. The body must await the vital force [*qi*] before it is complete, and the vital force must await the body before it can have consciousness. Nowhere is there a fire that burns all by itself. How then could there be a spirit with consciousness existing without a body?*

Chinese Poetry

The writing of poetry has a long and rich history in China. While China's earliest poems drew on an ancient oral tradition (see chapter 3), the poems of the Han era originated as written works—a circumstance that may have been encouraged by the Chinese invention of paper. Chinese poetry is striking in its simplicity and its refinement. Humanism and common sense are fundamental to Han poetic expression, and Han verse seems to have played an indispensable part in everyday life. As with Greek and Roman lyrics, Chinese poetry took the form of hymns and ritual songs accompanied by the lute or other stringed instruments. Poems served as entertainments for various occasions, such as banquets, and as expressions of affection that were often exchanged as gifts. In contrast with the Greco-Roman world, however, the Chinese produced neither epics nor heroic poems. Their poetry does not so much glorify individual prowess or valorous achievement as it meditates on human experience. Han poetry, much of which takes the form of the "prose-poem," is personal and intimate rather than moralizing and eulogistic. Even in cases where the poem is the medium for social or political complaint, it is more a mirror of the poet's mood than a vehicle of instruction. Notable too (especially in contrast with Roman poetry) is the large number of female poets among the Chinese. The four poems that appear below (translated by Burton Watson) are drawn from the vast collection of Han poetry. They have been selected not only for their lyric beauty, but as expressions of some of the deepest concerns of Han poets, such as the practice of bestowing women upon neighboring tribes as "conciliatory" gifts and the conscription of laborers for public works projects. The perceptive reader should discover a number of interesting parallels, as well as contrasts, between these poems and those of the Greeks, Sappho and Pindar, and the Romans, Virgil, Horace, and Juvenal.

READING 1.31 A Selection of Han Poems

Song of Sorrow

My family has married me   1
  in this far corner of the world,
sent me to a strange land,
  to the king of the Wu-sun.
A yurt¹ is my chamber,   5

---

*Translated by Burton Watson in *Anthology of Chinese Literature*, edited by Cyril Birch (New York: Grove Press, Inc., 1965), pp. 89–90.
¹A circular tent of felt and skins on a framework of poles, the common habitation of the nomads of Mongolia.

70	China begins building the Grand Canal (eventually 600 miles long)
90	the Chinese invent a winnowing device that separates grain from the chaff
100	the first insecticide is produced from dried chrysanthemums in China
105	cellulose-based paper is first produced in China
132	Zhang Heng invents the first seismograph

felt is my walls,
flesh my only food,[2]
   kumiss[3] to drink.
My thoughts are all of my homeland,
   my heart aches within.   10
Oh to be the yellow crane
   winging home again!

                 Liu Xijun, ca. 107 B.C.E.

Song: I Watered My Horse at the Long Wall Caves

I watered my horse at the Long Wall caves,   1
water so cold it hurt his bones;
I went and spoke to the Long Wall boss:
"We're soldiers from Tai-yuan—will you keep us here
   forever?"
"Public works go according to schedule—   5
swing your hammer, pitch your voice in with the rest!"
A man'd be better off to die in battle
than eat his heart out building the Long Wall!
The Long Wall—how it winds and winds,
winds and winds three thousand li;[1]   10
here on the border, so many strong boys;
in the houses back home, so many widows and wives.
I sent a letter to my wife:
"Better remarry than wait any longer—
serve your new mother-in-law with care   15
and sometimes remember the husband you once had."
In answer her letter came to the border:
"What nonsense do you write me now?
Now when you're in the thick of danger,
how could I rest by another man's side?"   20
(HE) If you bear a son, don't bring him up!
   But a daughter—feed her good dried meat.
   Only *you* can't see, here by the Long Wall,
   the bones of the dead men heaped about!
(SHE) I bound up my hair and went to serve you;   25
   constant constant was the care of my heart.
   Too well I know your borderland troubles;
   and I—can I go on like this much longer?

                 Chen Lin (d. 217)

Two Selections from "Nineteen Old Poems of the Han"

I turn the carriage, yoke and set off,   1
far, far, over the never-ending roads.
In the four directions, broad plain on plain;
east wind shakes the hundred grasses.
Among all I meet, nothing of the past;   5
what can save us from sudden old age?
Fullness and decay, each has its season;
success—I hate it, so late in coming!
Man is not made of metal or stone;
how can he hope to live for long?   10
Swiftly he follows in the wake of change.

---

[2]Meat was a staple of the Mongol diet.
[3]The fermented milk of a horse, mule, or donkey.
[1]A *li* equals approximately one-third of a mile.

A shining name—let that be the prize!

         Anonymous, late second century

Man's years fall short of a hundred;   **1**
a thousand years of worry crowd his heart.
If the day is short and you hate the long night,
why not take the torch and go wandering?
Seek out happiness in season;   **5**
who can wait for the coming year?
Fools who cling too fondly to gold
earn no more than posterity's jeers.
Prince Qiao,[2] that immortal man—
small hope we have of matching him!   **10**

         Anonymous, late second century

The Visual Arts and Music in Han China

Before the introduction of Buddhism into China late in the Han era (see chapter 9), the Chinese produced no monumental architecture comparable to that of Rome. But because the Chinese built primarily in the impermanent medium of wood, nothing remains of the palaces and temple structures erected during the Han era. Yet some idea of Chinese architecture is provided by the polychromed, ceramic models of the traditional multiroofed buildings—houses and watchtowers—that are found in Chinese tombs (Figure **7.5**). Such engineering projects as

---

[2]According to Chinese legend, a prince who became an immortal spirit.

Figure 7.5 Tomb model of a house, Eastern Han Dynasty, first century C.E. Earthenware with unfired pigments, 52 × 33½ × 27 in. The Nelson-Atkins Museum of Art, Kansas City, Missouri (Purchase: Nelson Trust) 33–521.

the Great Wall testify to the high level of Qin and Han building skills. China's royal tombs were replicas of the imperial palace, which was laid out according to a cosmological model: The central building was symmetrical and bisected by a north–south axis. Its foundation was square, symbolizing the earth (*yin*), and its roof was round, symbolizing heaven (*yang*). In its geometric regularity, such designs share the Greco-Roman search for harmony and balanced proportion. However, classical design among the Chinese was less an effort to idealize nature than it was a means of representing the natural order. Cosmological diagrams are frequently inscribed on bronze mirrors found in Han graves (Figure 7.6). The square and circle, along with stylized dragons and sky symbols, belong to an elaborate diagrammatic description of the prevailing Chinese theory of the universe, which involves the

interaction of *yin/yang* forces with the five elements and the forces of nature (see Chapter 3). Similar designs are found on gaming boards on which players pit their human skills against the divine powers.

During the Han era, the visual arts flourished. Like their forebears, the Han excelled in bronze casting: Bronze chariots and weapons, mirrors, and jewellery are found in royal burial tombs. Han craftspeople also produced exquisite works in jade and gold, lacquered wood, and silk. But it is in the medium of terra-cotta—glazed for durability—that the Han left a record of daily life almost as detailed as that found in ancient Egyptian tombs. Scenes of threshing, baking, juggling, music-making, game-playing, and other everyday activities appear routinely in three-dimensional polychromed ceramic models recovered from Han funerary chambers (Figure 7.7). Han art does not consistently demonstrate the high degree of realism that is apparent in Greek and Roman representation. Yet the central place given to figural subject matter in art (as in literature) suggests a similar this-worldly bias. The carved, low reliefs on one Han stone tomb entrance depict an interesting combination of secular and spiritual subjects (Figure 7.9). The top register of the lintel depicts a lively procession of chariots and horses; beneath are scenes of hunting, while on either side human guardians and winged spirits protect the chamber from evil. On the doors themselves appear fabulous creatures—elegant phoenixes and raging unicorns.

The technical and aesthetic achievement of the Han in the visual

Figure 7.6 Bronze mirror back with cosmic motifs, Han Dynasty, first century C.E. Diameter 14 cm. Barlow Collection, University of Sussex. Photo: Jeff Teasdale.

Figure 7.7 *Musicians.* Chinese, early sixth century mold-pressed clay with traces of unfired pigments. Height 11″ each. Northern Wei Dynasty (A.D. 386–534) The Nelson-Atkins Museum of Art, Kansas City, Missouri 32-186/1-7

Figure 7.8
Bronze bells from the tomb of the Marquis Yi of Zeng.

arts seems to have been matched in music. As early as the Shang era, bronze bells were buried in royal tombs (see Chapter 3), and the tradition of burying sets of royal bells continued for centuries. A set of sixty-five bells, seven large zithers, two panpipes, three transverse flutes, three drums, and other musical instruments accompanied the fifth-century B.C.E. Marquis Yi of Zeng to his grave (Figure 7.8). The instruments (along with the bodies of eight young women and a dog) occupied a subterranean room that replicated the great hall of a palace. Each bell can produce two notes (depending on where the bell is struck) and the name of each note is inscribed in gold on the bell. A set of bells was thus able to range over several octaves, each containing up to ten notes. Whether the bells were used in ceremonial, ritual, or secular events is unclear, but other evidence of other sorts, such as the small ceramic

Figure 7.9 Reliefs of tomb entrance, Eastern Han Dynasty, 25–220 C.E.

orchestra pictured in Figure 7.7 and the bronze buckle with dancers holding cymbals (Figure **7.10**) suggests the Han enjoyed a variety of musical entertainments.

SUMMARY

In a period approximately parallel to the Greco-Roman era, the civilization of China produced many of the definitive and enduring features of its 3,000-year-old culture. During the fifth century B.C.E., Confucius, China's leading thinker, articulated the fundamental rules of proper conduct. Under this influence, the Five Classics came to provide the basis for Chinese education and culture. Confucian thought confirmed ancient Chinese notions of proper behavior and proper rule, which held that the ruler, by his virtuous conduct, exercised the will of heaven on earth.

Two centuries after the death of Confucius, the short-lived and militant Qin dynasty created China's first unified empire. Qin emperors embraced the harsh principles of Legalism, rather than the humanistic teachings of Confucius. Like the Romans, the Chinese expanded the empire by way of an aggressive military machine, a detailed record of which survives in the tombs of its emperors. Successors to the Qin, the Han rulers played a vital part in establishing classical Chinese culture. In the 400 years of Han rule, Chinese culture flourished: An educated bureaucracy revived the teachings of Confucius, while a healthy economy encouraged long-distance trade between East and West. As in the Greco-Roman world, the Han produced a body of literature and art that displays a this-worldly affection for nature and a passion for the good life. Han historians and poets assessed the secular world with critical insight and candour. The Han talent

Figure 7.10 Buckle ornament with dancers, Western Han Dynasty, 206–8 C.E. Gilt bronze 4¾ × 7¼ in. Yunnan Provincial Museum, Kumming, China.

for technological invention challenged and even surpassed that of Rome. Nevertheless, it was Han humanism that would come to hold the pivotal place in the classical legacy of East Asia.

Suggestions for Reading

Bodde, Derk. *Chinese Thought, Society, and Science: The Intellectual and Social Background of Science and Technology in Pre-Modern China.* Honolulu: University of Hawaii Press, 1991.

Chang, Kwang-chin. *Art, Myth, and Ritual: The Path to Political Authority in Ancient China.* Cambridge, Mass.: Harvard University Press, 1983.

Fingarette, Herbert. *Confucius: The Secular as Sacred.* New York: Harper & Row, 1972.

Hucker, Charles O. *China's Imperial Past: An Introduction to Chinese History and Culture.* Stanford, CA.: Stanford University Press, 1975.

Loewe, M. *Everyday Life in Early Imperial China.* New York: Dorset Press, 1988.

Miller, Barbara Stoler, ed. *Masterworks of Asian Literature in Comparative Perspective.* Armonk, N.Y.: M.E. Sharpe, 1994.

Needham, Joseph and Robert K. G. Temple. *The Genius of China: 3,000 Years of Science, Discovery, and Invention.* New York: Prion, 1986.

Rawson, Jessica, ed. *The British Museum Book of Chinese Art.* London: Thames and Hudson, 1993.

Schirokauer, Conrad. *A Brief History of Chinese Civilization.* New York: Harcourt, 1991.

Wang, Zhongshu. *Han Civilization,* trans., K. C. Chang. New Haven, Conn.: Yale University Press, 1982.

GLOSSARY

cartography the art of making maps or charts

li (Chinese, "propriety", "ritual", or "arrangement") originally, the proper performance of ritual, but eventually also the natural and moral order, thus, appropriate behavior in all aspects of life

terra-cotta (Italian, "baked earth") a clay medium that may be glazed or painted; also called "earthenware"

CREDITS

Calmann & King, the author, and the literature researcher wish to thank the publishers and individuals who have kindly allowed their copyright material to be reproduced in this book, as listed below. Every effort has been made to contact copyright holders, but should there be any errors or omissions, Calmann & King would be pleased to insert the appropriate acknowledgment in any subsequent edition of this publication.

CHAPTER 1

Reading 1.1 (p. 2): From Leo Frobenius and Douglas C. Fox, *Prehistoric Rock Pictures in Europe and Africa* (1937). Reprinted by permission of The Museum of Modern Art, New York.

Reading 1.2 (p. 15): "The Song of Creation" (translated from the *Rig Veda*) in *The Wonder That Was India* by A. L. Basham (Macmillan, 1954). Reprinted by permission of the publisher; "How Man Was Created" (Mohawk Tale) from *American Indian Legends*, edited by Allan MacFarlan (The Heritage Press, 1968).

Reading 1.3 (p. 19): From "The Hymn to the Aten" in *The Literature of Ancient Egypt*, edited by William Kelly (Yale University Press, 1973), © 1973 Yale University Press. Reprinted by permission of the publisher.

Reading 1.4 (p. 33); "I will lie down within...", "My sister has come to me" and "The Voice of the goose sounds forth..." from *Love Lyrics of Ancient Egypt*, translated by Barbara Hughes Fowler (University of North Carolina Press).

CHAPTER 2

Reading 1.5 (p. 37): From *Poems of Heaven and Hell from Ancient Mesopotamia*, translated by N. K. Sandars (Penguin Classics, 1971), © N. K. Sandars, 1971. Reprinted by permission of the publisher.

Reading 1.6 (p. 39): From *The Epic of Gilgamesh*, translated by N. K. Sandars (Penguin Classics, 1960; Second revised edition, 1972), © N. K. Sandars, 1960, 1964, 1972. Reprinted by permission of the publisher.

Reading 1.7 (p. 44): From "The Code of Hammurabi" in *The Hammurabi Code and the Sinaitic Legislation*, translated by Chilperic Edwards (Kennikat Press, 1971).

Reading 1.8a (p. 48), **1.8b** (p. 49), **1.8c** (p. 51): From *The Jerusalem Bible*, edited by Alexander Jones (Darton, Longman & Todd Ltd./Doubleday, 1966), © 1966 by Darton, Longman & Todd Ltd. and Doubleday, a division of Bantam Doubleday Dell Publishing group Inc. Reprinted by permission of Doubleday.

CHAPTER 3

Reading 1.9 (p. 60): From *The Bhagavad-Gita* in *The Song of God: The Bhagavad-Gita*, translated by Swami Prabhavanda to Christopher Isherwood (1951). Reprinted by permission of Vedanta Press, California.

Reading 1.10 (p. 65): Lao Tzu, "Thirty spokes will converge..." from *The Way of Life*, translated by Raymond B. Blakney (New American Library, 1955), © 1955 by Raymond B. Blakney, renewed (c) 1983 by Charles Philip Blakney. Reprinted by permission of Dutton Signet, a division of Penguin Putnam Inc.

CHAPTER 4

Reading 1.11 (p. 74): From *The Iliad of Homer*, translated by R. Lattimore (University of Chicago Press, 1965), © 1965 The University of Chicago Press. Reprinted by permission of the publisher.

Reading 1.12 (p. 80): Pericles' "Funeral Speech" from Thucydides, *History of the Peloponnesian War*, translated by Benjamin Jowett, in *The Greek Historian*, edited by F. R. B. Godolphin (Random House, 1942).

Reading 1.13 (p. 84): From Sophocles, *Antigone*, translated by Shaemas O'Sheel, in *Ten Greek Plays in Contemporary Translations*, edited by L. R. Lind (1957), © the Estate of Shaemas O'Sheel.

Reading 1.14 (p. 93): From Aristotle, *Poetics*, translated by Ingram Bywater, in *The Works of Aristotle*, Vol. 11, edited by W. D. Ross (Oxford University Press, 1925). Reprinted by permission of the publisher.

Reading 1.15 (p. 97): From Plato, *Crito*, in *Authyphro, Apology, Crito*, translated by F. J. Church (Macmillan Library of the Liberal Arts, 1956), © 1955. Reprinted by permission of Prentice-Hall Inc., Upper Saddle River, NJ.

Reading 1.16 (p. 99): Plato, "Allegory of the Cave" in *The Republic of Plato*, translated by F. M. Cornford (Oxford University Press, 1941). Reprinted by permission of the publisher.

Reading 1.17 (p. 103): From Aristotle, *Ethics*, in *The Nicomachean Ethics of Aristotle*, translated by J. E. C. Welldon (Macmillan, 1927). Reprinted by permission of the publisher.

CHAPTER 5

Reading 1.18 (p. 109): From Vitruvius, *Principles of Symmetry*, in *Ten Books on Architecture*, translated by Morris Hicky Morgan (Dover Publications, 1960). Reprinted by permission of the publisher.

Reading 1.19 (p. 123): From Mary Barnard, *Sappho: A New Translation* (University of California Press, 1958), © 1958 The Regents of the University of California; © renewed 1984 Mary Barnard. Reprinted by permission of the publisher.

Reading 1.20 (p. 123): From Pindar, *Nemean Ode VI*, translated by C. M. Bowra (Oxford University Press, 1964). Reprinted by permission of the publisher; from Pindar, *Pythian Ode VIII*, translated by Roy Arthur Swans, in *Pindar's Odes* (Bobbs-Merrill Company).

CHAPTER 6

Reading 1.21 (p. 133): From Josephus, *The Jewish War*, Vol. II, translated by S. St. J. Thackeray (Harvard University Press, 1927). Reprinted by permission of the publisher and the Loeb Classical Library.

Reading 1.22 (p. 137): From Seneca, *On Tranquility of Mind*, in *The Stoic Philosophy of Seneca*, translated by Moses Hadas (Doubleday, 1958), © 1958 by Moses Hadas. Reprinted by permission of Doubleday, a division of Bantam Doubleday Dell Publishing Group Inc.

Reading 1.23 (p. 138): From Cicero, *On Duty*, in *Cicero: De Officiis*, Vol. XXI, translated by Walter Miller (Harvard University Press, 1961). Reprinted by permission of the publisher and the Loeb Classical Library.

Reading 1.24 (p. 139): From Tacitus, *Dialogue on Oratory*, in *Tacitus: Dialogus*, translated by W. Peterson (Harvard University Press, 1958). Reprinted by permission of the publisher and the Loeb Classical Library.

Reading 1.25 (p. 140): From Virgil, *Aeneid*, in *The Aeneid of Virgil*, translated by Rolfe Humphries (Scribner, 1951), © 1951 by Charles Scribner's Sons. Reprinted by permission of Scribner, a division of Simon & Schuster.

Reading 1.26 (p. 141): Poems #5, 16, 51, 92 from *The Poems of Catullus*, translated by Horace Gregory (Grove Press, 1956).

Reading 1.27 (p. 142): "Civil War", "To be Quite Frank" and "Carpe Diem" from *Selected Poems of Horace*, introduction by George F. Whicher (Van Nostrand Reinhold, 1947), copyright 1947 Van Nostrand Reinhold; copyright renewed 1975 Susan W. Whicher, Stephen F. Whicher and Nancy Whicher Greene.

Reading 1.28a (p. 143), **1.28b** (p. 144): From Juvenal, "Against the City of Rome" and "Against Women" in *The Satires of Juvenal*, translated by Rolfe Humphries (Indiana University Press, 1958),

© 1958 by Indiana University Press. Reprinted by permission of the publisher.

CHAPTER 7

Reading 1.29 (p. 161): From *The Analects of Confucius*, translated by Simon Leys (W. W. Norton, 1997).

[Extracts (p. 163): From Mencius and Han Fei, in *Sources of Chinese Tradition*, compiled by William Theodore de Bary and others (Columbia University Press, 1960).

Reading 1.30 (p. 167): From Sima Qian, *Records of the Grand Historian*, in *Wisdom of China and India* by Lin Yutang (Random House, 1942), © 1942 and renewed 1970 by Random House Inc. Reprinted by permission of the publisher.

Reading 1.31 (p. 168): Han poems, in *The Columbia Book of Chinese Poetry*, translated by Burton Watson (Columbia University Press, 1984), © 1984 by Columbia University Press. Reprinted by permission of the publisher.

INDEX